ETHICAL ISSUES
IN BUSINESS

ETHICAL ISSUES IN BUSINESS
A Philosophical Approach

Edited by

Thomas Donaldson
Patricia H. Werhane
Loyola University of Chicago

PRENTICE-HALL, INC.
Englewood Cliffs, New Jersey 07632

Library of Congress Cataloging in Publication Data
Main entry under title:

Ethical issues in business.

    1. Business ethics—Addresses, essays, lectures.
2. Industry—Social aspects—Addresses, essays, lectures.
I. Donaldson, Thomas, 1945–   II. Werhane, Patricia
Hogue.
HF5387.E8   174'.4   78-23815
ISBN 0-13-290064-5

Printed in the United States of America
10 9 8 7 6 5 4

Editorial/production supervision and internal
  design by Teru Uyeyama
Cover design by R. L. Communication
Manufacturing buyer: John Hall

PRENTICE-HALL INTERNATIONAL, INC., *London*
PRENTICE-HALL OF AUSTRALIA PTY. LIMITED, *Sydney*
PRENTICE-HALL OF CANADA, LTD., *Toronto*
PRENTICE-HALL OF INDIA PRIVATE LIMITED, *New Delhi*
PRENTICE-HALL OF JAPAN, INC., *Tokyo*
PRENTICE-HALL OF SOUTHEAST ASIA PTE. LTD., *Singapore*
WHITEHALL BOOKS LIMITED, *Wellington, New Zealand*

To Chuck and Jean

CONTENTS

Part III

Part IV

PREFACE

This book grew out of our teaching experiences at Loyola University in Chicago. In attempting to develop a course which investigated ethical issues in business, we discovered the importance of analyzing business issues from the viewpoint of theoretical philosophy. When philosophy has been coupled with other disciplines the result has invariably been the enrichment of both philosophy and the discipline involved. The ideas and methods of philosophy have yielded especially fruitful consequences when applied recently to fields such as law, science, and medicine. The philosophy of law, the philosophy of science, and medical ethics are today recognized as full-fledged areas of inquiry. Yet never before has philosophy been coupled straightforwardly with business. It is, however, a natural union: ethics has traditionally served as one of the major elements in the philosopher's repertoire, and morality has always been one of the major issues in the world of business. Today, ethical issues are becoming even more important in the evaluation of business practices and organizational structures. It is thus a natural course of events for the ethical aspects of business and philosophy to be synthesized in a way which sheds light on both fields.

This anthology contains both modern and traditional philosophical material which relates to business problems. It also incorporates one of the most significant innovations in business education—the case study method. This method, which invites students to consider theoretical issues in the context of actual cases, is now successfully practiced in most major business schools. The role of the instructor in such studies is typically value-neutral; he or she guides and encourages the students without actually interfering. Even a casual reading of this book will reveal the significant debt it owes to those who contributed the many case studies it contains.

We are deeply obliged to Loyola University of Chicago for its continuing encouragement and support of our projects in business ethics, and to the Mellon Foundation for its generous grant with which we initiated work on this anthology. A number of individuals have also been of invaluable assistance. Among them are Professor Kenneth Thompson, Jr., Chairperson of the Loyola Philosophy Department, who encouraged and helped facilitate our research in this area, and Professors Stanley Clayes, Richard DeGeorge, Burton Leiser, David Ozar, David Schweickart, and Thomas McMahon, C.S.V.—all of whom offered intellectual and editorial assistance. We wish to thank also the secretaries and typists, Mary Ann Connelly, Marla Friedman, Anne Luzniak, and Gregoria Vega, who worked patiently and tirelessly on this project. Finally, a special word of thanks to Norwell Therien and Teru Uyeyama at Prentice-Hall for their cooperative and thorough editorial assistance.

THOMAS DONALDSON
PATRICIA H. WERHANE

ETHICAL ISSUES IN BUSINESS

GENERAL
INTRODUCTION

There is one and only one social responsibility of business . . . to increase its profits. . . .

Milton Friedman

Business executives and the companies they serve have a personal and vested interest in the resolution of ethical and social responsibility dilemmas.

Steven Brenner and Earl Molander

It has often been suggested—though perhaps in jest—that the idea of business ethics constitutes a contradiction in terms. "Business is business," it has been said, "and ethics is not business." Yet each day we hear of the controversies about discrimination in hiring, consumer rights, deceptive advertising, bribery and payoffs, and pollution problems of such magnitude that we cannot remain unaffected.

Ethical problems in business are as old as business itself. Just as we are acutely aware of the problems surrounding the Lockheed bribery scandal or the complaints made by consumer advocate Ralph Nader, earlier generations were aware of other ethical issues confronting business. Names such as the "Teapot dome scandal" or the "Mississippi bubble" are not familiar today, but they were once as well-known as "Lockheed" and "Nader" are now. The issues about which there has been public concern include trusts and monopolies, child labor, working hours and conditions, meat packing standards, the distribution of salaries, and the liability of producers for dangerous products. Not only complaints but attempts at reform have a long and interesting history. The Code of Hammurabi, written nearly two thousand years before Christ, records the fact that Mesopotamian rulers attempted to legislate honest prices from local merchants by instituting wage and price controls.

To explain the special relationship between business and ethics, it is necessary to see how focusing merely on problems of business efficiency and profit making may overlook important moral issues. For example, when the manufacture of a certain product can be linked eventually to human disease or a decrease in the quality of human life, then the issues surrounding it are no longer simply traditional "business" issues. No amount of expertise in marketing, accounting, or management can deal adequately with such problems, and yet they are clearly connected to the activities of the business world. Nor can situations like these be reduced simply to legal problems, understandable only to the lawyer. When Ralph Nader claimed in the late 1960s that General Motors was producing automobiles which, despite their many consumer advantages, were contributing to thousands of highway deaths each year, he was not arguing that GM's practices were against the law—because at that time they were not illegal at all. Rather, Nader was arguing that General Motors had special obligations to its consumers, which were not simply of a traditional business nature, and that the company was not living up to them. Those obligations were *ethical* or *moral* ones.

It appears, then, that confronting questions like those implied by the Nader case—as "Does business have an obligation to its consumers (or to others) which extends beyond its obligation to make a profit and satisfy its investors?"—means confronting ethical and moral issues. The words "ethical" and "moral" in this book are not simply used as they might be by a modern newspaper, e.g., "That movie is thoroughly immoral" (meaning, "That movie is pornographic"). Instead, they are used as philosophers have traditionally used them, as words which arise from the study or science of what is good or right. Although there is dispute even among philosophers over how to define the subject matter of ethics, most would agree that it includes the study of what people ought to pursue, i.e., what the *good* is for people, or alternatively, the determination of which actions are the *right* actions for people to perform. Such general definitions may leave one with the feeling that studying ethics must be a hopelessly vague task; yet interestingly, ethical philosophers have succeeded in presenting a great many detailed ethical theses and in conducting a number of successful investigations into specific ethical topics.

The word "ethics," then, refers generally to the study of whatever is right and good for humans. The study of *business* ethics seeks to understand business practices, institutions, and actions in light of some concept of human value. Traditional business ends, e.g., profit making, growth, or technical advance, could be relevant to the subject of business ethics insofar as they could be related to the achievement of some human good. In other words, business ethics would not be concerned with corporate profits per se but with respect to the achievement of some basic human good, perhaps increased investor satisfaction, higher levels of employment, or increased capacity to improve working conditions.

Because business ethics involves relating business activities to some concept of human good, it is a study which has as one of its aspects the *evaluation* of business practices. Indeed, most of the fundamental criticisms and commendations of contemporary business practices are cast in terms of how modern business either contributes or fails to contribute to the general human good. For example, when modern corporations are criticized for their failure to respond to environmental needs by limiting the amount of pollutants they discharge, they are being evaluated on ethical grounds—the charge is that they are neglecting the public good. Alternatively, when businesses are praised for achieving high levels of efficiency and satisfying consumer needs, it is implied that efficiency and consumer satisfaction contribute directly to the sum total of human good. Even traditional conservative economic theory justifies economic practices in the light of their contribution to human good: The classical economist, Adam Smith, for example, justifies the pursuit of self-interest in business by referring to the public benefits which such action secures.

Another aspect of the evaluative dimension in business ethics—or any ethical study—is seen in the contrast between evaluation and simple description. There is a special difference between answering a moral question and answering a question in the areas of, say, marketing and economics. In the latter, it is often sufficient to establish the immediate facts which pertain to the subject. For example, if one hopes to determine the best advertising strategy for the introduction of a new product, then one would only need to determine that a certain advertising strategy will have, as a matter of fact, the desired effect, i.e., that it *will* sell the product. It is usually possible in such cases to utilize indicators which more or less establish whether or not a given strategy will be effective: consumer polls, trends in sales, etc.

However, answering an ethical question may demand very different methods. Determining the immediate and specific facts may only be the first step in a long process which, in the end, may take one far beyond immediate facts. For example, if one wants to determine whether discriminatory hiring practices by corporations *ought* to be corrected by introducing quotas (to ensure the hiring of a certain number of blacks and females in the future), there may be no question at all about the immediate facts. Two people could thoroughly agree that discrimination of a certain type has taken place and that blacks and women need equal job opportunities in order to reach relevant levels of social equality, and so on. Yet, after agreeing on all these issues the two people may still disagree— and disagree vehemently—over whether quota hiring systems for racial minorities *ought* to be imposed in the wake of past discriminatory practices. Thus, solving an ethical problem may require making *evaluative* judgments about issues which seem far removed from the facts at hand.

Even though business ethics focuses primarily on evaluative issues, its scope is surprisingly large. Insofar as it is concerned with relating business practices to some concept of human good, almost any business issue which relates to human value may become part of its subject matter. Thus the scope of business ethics includes such issues as

1. advertising practices, e.g., false or misleading advertising;
2. product safety;

3. monopolistic price schemes and their effects on the consumer;
4. pursuit of profits;
5. treatment of workers, including salaries, working conditions, worker participation, access to pension plans and benefits, etc.;
6. effects of pollution, both economic and environmental;
7. payments of "sensitive" sums of money to foreign governments, foreign agents, or local politicians;
8. proper roles of shareholders, management, government, and the public in determining corporate policy;
9. discriminatory hiring policies, conditions, and policies of advancement;
10. limits of private ownership.

The analysis of such issues requires a systematic investigation of both general ethical theory and specific business practices. To accomplish this goal, the editors of this anthology have carefully selected a series of writings which includes, not only theoretical and philosophical material relevant to business practices, but also actual case descriptions of ethical problems found in the business world. The philosophical material often has already gained wide support in traditional ethical philosophy; and the case descriptions include cases which had an actual impact upon business and society. This book has not attempted, however, to provide its readers with a series of ethical codes of conduct. Such codes have often proved to be unsuccessful in achieving their presumed purpose; and more importantly, their existence can imply what is false about the field of business ethics: that the work needed to understand ethical issues can be made unnecessary, and that serious issues can be resolved by simply writing and studying lists of ethical rules.

The advantage of investigating ethical problems from a philosophical point of view should be apparent. One cannot successfully examine a case involving payments made by U.S. corporations to foreign governments, for example, until one has considered the more general issue of whether different ethical attitudes (as might exist in the United States and in foreign countries) affect the morality of such actions. This question has traditionally been treated by philosophers under the heading of "ethical relativism," and the work of philosophers on this subject can be of great help.

In Part I, four ethical issues have been selected: ethical egoism, truth telling, ethical relativism, and morality and organizations. Each of these topics is discussed in the context of actual business dilemmas. Part II focuses upon three important economic and political issues: the profit motive, the notion of private property, and the concept of justice. In Part III, three essential business relationships are examined: that between business and the employee, between the corporation and the consumer, and between business and the government. These issues are then connected to theoretical questions about human rights, obligations, and responsibility. Finally, Part IV deals with the general topic of the role of business in contemporary and future society, including its relationship to pollution and other environmental problems. Every section of this anthology contains at least one case history of an actual business problem, although sometimes fictitious names are used for corporations and individuals in order to avoid unwanted publicity.

PHILOSOPHICAL ISSUES IN BUSINESS ETHICS

Part I

At a time when the reputation of business in general is low . . . at such a time one would expect corporate executives to be especially sensitive even to appearances of conflict of interest. . . . Yet this seems not, on the whole, to be the case. . . .

Irving Kristol

Consider the following ethical situations:

If you were an employee of a large corporation producing equipment for the aircraft industry, would you protest the manufacture of defective products even if it meant the loss of your job?

Suppose you, as an employee of an advertising agency, knew that one of the advertisements for which you were responsible presented false or seriously misleading information about a product. Would you request a change in the advertisement?

If you were operating a branch of a U.S. company in a foreign country, would you follow the necessary foreign procedures for filing taxes even if (1) these conflicted with procedures in the United States, or (2) they clearly involved what you considered unethical practices?

Each of these questions is drawn from an actual business situation, and such incidents occur more frequently than one might expect. Understanding their ethical implications requires, not only an awareness of the concrete situations, but also the ability to subsume business problems under categories of more general ethical concern. The philosophical material in Part I involves three traditional ethical issues: ethical egoism, truth telling, and ethical relativism. Stated as questions, these issues are as follows:

1. *Ethical egoism:* Is it morally acceptable for one to act always in one's own self-interest?
2. *Truth telling:* What obligations exist, if any, for individuals and organizations to communicate honestly?
3. *Ethical relativism:* Are values simply relative to the people who espouse them, or is it possible to identify universal values which apply on all levels?

The last section of Part I considers an additional topic, which relates philosophical issues in ethics to the modern corporation, namely, the nature of organizational responsibility.

ETHICAL EGOISM

Ethical egoism is a theory about what constitutes the proper form of motivation for human conduct. The ethical egoist believes that all actions should be motivated by a desire to achieve one's own self interest—and nothing else. In short, he or she insists that we should act only for the sake of our own interests and satisfactions. We should consider what benefits us, and then act to maximize our own gratification. The ethical egoist defends the view of self-interested motivation as a *normative* theory of ethics; that is, it is a theory about what people *should* do.

Yet any discussion of ethical egoism would be incomplete without some understanding of a closely related theory known as *psychological* egoism. Ethical egoism is, as its name implies, an ethical theory, whereas psychological egoism is a factual theory about how people are motivated. The latter describes human motivation exclusively in terms of self-interest; it argues, simply, that we are all constituted in such a way that we are motivated exclusively by our own desires and self-interests. Therefore, all actions are directed toward the satisfaction of merely personal ends, and even actions which appear to be disinterested are motivated by one's long-term self-gain.

It is possible to defend ethical egoism without defending psychological egoism. One could deny that people *do always* act in a self-interested manner, and admit that purely benevolent actions are possible, but still assert that people *ought* to act selfishly. Perhaps such an ethical egoist views all forms of benevolent behavior as forms of human weakness, and holds that, in turn, there are simply no reasons which can show that a person should not act in his own self-interest.

The ethical egoist focuses his attention on the motivating principles of human conduct and not on the consequences of his actions for other people. Even so, an ethical egoist may argue that self-interested actions often result in benefits for others. Indeed, it seems likely that the eighteenth-century philosopher and economist, Adam Smith (whose views we shall examine in Part II), believed that self-interested actions, as a matter of fact, frequently benefit others—at least when the actions are economically motivated. Such an argument does not follow necessarily from an ethical egoist's position, because he or she is concerned primarily with justifying self-interested activity by itself rather than in relation to some possible benefits. But many people discuss ethical egoism, just as Smith does, in the light of its possible contribution to the general welfare.

The seventeenth-century philosopher, Thomas Hobbes, may be understood primarily as a psychological egoist. In the selections from Hobbes' *Leviathan* included in this section, he argues that men in their original natural state are passionate and selfish. They are motivated by three interests: self-preservation, achieving power over other men, and self-gain. Hobbes argues, however, that in addition to being passionate and self-interested, men are also rational, and he makes the reasonable assumption that obtaining even selfish ends is impossible in a state where all people are allowed to pursue their own selfish ends. Therefore, he concludes, people form political societies, which are called "commonwealths," in order to control the unlimited pursuit of self-interests. A properly constructed commonwealth should reflect the truth of psychological egoism by insuring the orderly development of the self-interests of all members of that society.

In sharp contrast to the egoism of Hobbes, Joseph Butler argues in excerpts from his *Fifteen Sermons* that people are motivated not only by self-interest but by an interest in society, or benevolence. A bishop of the Anglican Church in eighteenth-century England, Butler wanted to expose the logical flaws which he believed existed in all doctrines of egoism. He claims that both egoism and benevolence participate in human motivation and moreover, that the actions of all people are *evaluated* in terms of the benevolence of those acts, and not on how much self-gain is achieved. The heart of the ethical issue raised in this section, then, rests with the dispute between Hobbes and Butler. Is Hobbes right to conclude that people are naturally selfish and that we should structure our institutions to reflect this fact? Or is Butler right in his claims that people can and should be motivated by benevolence, and if so, what implications arise for the design of social institutions?

The general issue of egoism is well illustrated in a case study entitled "The Aircraft Brake Scandal," which is presented in this section. This case involves a large U.S. corporation, B. F. Goodrich, which became involved in serious ethical problems over the testing procedures it used in the fulfillment of a government contract for jet aircraft brakes. The case has been labeled a scandal because the pressures upon corporate employees, including those of job security and advancement, were strong enough to result in the marketing of dangerous and defective aircraft brakes. The dilemma of one employee, Vandivier, who finally blew the whistle on Goodrich, is a revealing illustration of some of the conflicts which can occur between self-interest and one's own sense of moral obligation.

TRUTH TELLING

The issue of ethical egoism constitutes a fundamental locus for discussion of *motivation*, self-interested or otherwise, in business. In the same way, truth telling represents a fundamental point of departure for discussions about *communication* in business and can be used to investigate a wide variety of issues, including honesty in advertising, the accuracy of consumer information, and the responsibilities a business has to communicate honestly with its employees and stockholders.

A philosopher who is well known for his vigorous defense of truth telling is the eighteenth-century German philosopher, Immanuel Kant. In this section, selections from a little-known work, *Lectures on Ethics,* are presented, in which Kant claims that truth telling is an essential feature of right action. He equates honesty both with frankness and reserve, and he supports the principle of never telling a lie on three grounds. First, the principle of truth telling is one which each of us would like everyone else to follow. In other words, it is a principle which Kant calls "universalizable," meaning that each of us would like to see it universally followed by all human beings. Second, truth telling is a necessary element for society because all societies depend upon mutual bonds of honesty and truthfulness to enforce their unity and orderly continuation. Finally, lying destroys the major source of human development, i.e., knowledge, since it thwarts the discovery of new truths.

One of the case studies in this part, "Italian Tax Mores," presents a situation in which truth telling is the major issue. The case concerns an American executive, working at a branch of a U.S. company in Italy, who finds that typical Italian tax practices encourage actions which he believes constitute lying and bribery. Is it morally acceptable to alter and misrepresent the company's income tax figures *if* it appears that most other companies do the same thing? Can one make adjustments in these situations? And are there limits to such adjustments?

This case is not an isolated example of problems about truth telling in business; the question of false or misleading advertising is another. Although few advertisers actually lie about products, many advertisements are considered deceptive or misleading. In this section, the contemporary philosopher, Burton Leiser, discusses what counts as "misleading" advertising and attempts to isolate the major ethical issues surrounding it.

ETHICAL RELATIVISM

The questions of self-interest and honesty are difficult issues in practice because they must be faced every day. The third issue, the relativity of value judgments, is less obviously commonplace. It asks if some moral principles apply universally or if all values and ethical judgments are relative to particular cultural contexts. The case study, "Lockheed Aircraft Corporation," raises the question of which ethical principles or value system, if any, a multinational corporation should adopt. Lockheed, trying to gain business favors, made "sensitive payments" to Japanese government officials; but the former president of Lockheed defended these payments, considered both illegal and unethical in this country, as consistent with (1) practices of other multinational corporations, and (2) accepted practice in other countries and thereby necessary for conducting business abroad. Arguments such as (1) and (2) involve ethical relativism insofar as right and wrong are assumed to depend on the particular cultural or social context being considered. Implicit in Lockheed's arguments is also a third justification, that (3) American corporations provide needed technology and economic services to foreign countries, thus raising the standards for citizens in these countries. The means through which one makes these goods and services available, e.g., sensitive payments, are thus justified by long-range economic results.

Frequently ethical relativism uses evidence provided by another, but closely related, point of view known as *cultural* relativism. The latter argues that the way in which people reason about morality varies in different cultures because of different customs, religious traditions, and methods of education. Using this argument, the ethical relativist claims that there are no ultimate, universal ethical principles and that all value judgments are relative to particular cultural contexts. Richard Brandt, in "Ethical Relativism," which is included in this section, suggests that there is little hard evidence for the claim that there are ultimate ethical principles—thus offering some support to the ethical relativists' position.

An obvious way to challenge this position is to argue that there are some values which are universal—that is, which apply without exception. For example, one might argue that skinning live babies for sport is not acceptable anywhere, despite anyone's belief. W. T. Stace, in his article, "Ethical Relativity and Ethical Absolutism," defends just such a point of view. He recognizes that there are practical difficulties in specifying particular ethical principles which apply universally, but these difficulties do not imply that ethical relativism is correct. If Stace's arguments are valid, they might be used to show that some justifications such as (1) and (2) for sensitive payments abroad are questionable and that other justifications such as (3) are inconsistent with (1) and (2). For when some corporations defend their activities by referring to the economic advantages for the foreign countries in which they operate, are they not assuming that economic growth is a universal value and should be espoused by every country?

MORALITY AND ORGANIZATIONS

We have assumed that the basic ethical issues raised so far apply both to individuals and to organizations. In this last section of Part I, however, the nature of organizational responsibility is specifically analyzed. The readings generate a number of questions about organizations, including whether economic organizations such as corporations are structured so as to permit the ascription of moral responsibility. We often assume that corporations should behave ethically, just as we also assume that individual people should behave ethically. But in an important article, "Morality and the Ideal of Rationality in Formal Organizations," the contemporary philosopher, John Ladd, challenges the claim that corporations can be held morally responsible. Ladd argues that a corporation is an autonomous, independent institution which has its own self-determined goals. Because of its very structure, it can try to achieve only its formal ends—which cannot, by definition, be moral ones. Thus Ladd regards the corporation much like a complicated machine, and like a machine, it cannot have genuine moral and social responsibilities.

In response, the philosopher Kenneth Goodpaster, in "Morality and

Organizations," analyzes the limits of Ladd's organizational model and concludes that organizational rationality and moral responsibility are not incompatible. When properly understood, Goodpaster asserts, the concept of organizational structure allows a "space" for the application of moral categories to corporate organizations. The outcome of the dispute between Ladd and Goodpaster is crucial to the question of how corporations should be regarded from an ethical perspective. If Ladd is correct, the modern corporation cannot be expected to shoulder genuine moral and social responsibilities. At most, his view implies that corporations could act morally when subjected to external regulation. On the other hand, if Goodpaster's view is correct, then corporations can and *should* be expected to exercise moral awareness and to recognize ethical limitations on their actions.

ETHICAL EGOISM

Case Study—The Aircraft Brake Scandal

KERMIT VANDIVIER

The B. F. Goodrich Company is what business magazines like to refer to as "a major American corporation." It has operations in a dozen states and as many foreign countries; and of these far-flung facilities, the Goodrich plant at Troy, Ohio, is not the most imposing. It is a small, one-story building, once used to manufacture airplanes. Set in the grassy flatlands of west-central Ohio, it employs only about six hundred people. Nevertheless, it is one of the three largest manufacturers of aircraft wheels and brakes, a leader in a most profitable industry. Goodrich wheels and brakes support such well-known planes as the F111, the C5A, the Boeing 727, the XB70, and many others.

Contracts for aircraft wheels and brakes often run into millions of dollars, and ordinarily a contract with a total value of less than $70,000, though welcome, would not create any special stir of joy in the hearts of Goodrich sales personnel. But purchase order P-237138—issued on June 18, 1967, by the LTV Aerospace Corporation, ordering 202 brake assemblies for a new Air Force plane at a total price of $69,417—was received by Goodrich with considerable glee. And there was good reason. Some ten years previously, Goodrich had built a brake for LTV that was, to say the least, considerably less than a rousing success. The brake had not lived up to Goodrich's promises, and after experiencing considerable difficulty, LTV had written off Goodrich as a source of brakes. Since that time, Goodrich salesmen had been unable to sell so much as a shot of brake fluid to LTV. So in 1967, when LTV requested bids on wheels and brakes for the new A7D light attack aircraft it proposed to build for the Air Force, Goodrich submitted a bid that was absurdly low, so low that LTV could not, in all prudence, turn it down.

Goodrich had, in industry parlance, "bought into the business." The company did not expect to make a profit on the initial deal; it was prepared, if necessary, to lose money. But aircraft brakes are not something that can be ordered off the shelf. They are designed for a particular aircraft, and once an aircraft manufacturer buys a brake, he is forced to purchase all replacement parts from the brake manufacturer. The

From *In the Name of Profit* by Robert Heilbroner *et al.* Copyright © 1972 by Kermit Vandivier. Reprinted by permission of Doubleday & Co., Inc.

$70,000 that Goodrich would get for making the brake would be a drop in the bucket when compared with the cost of the linings and other parts the Air Force would have to buy from Goodrich during the lifetime of the aircraft.

There was another factor, besides the low bid, that had undoubtedly influenced LTV. All aircraft brakes made today are of the disk type, and the bid submitted by Goodrich called for a relatively small brake, one containing four disks and weighing only 106 pounds. The weight of any aircraft is extremely important: the lighter a part is, the heavier the plane's payload can be.

The brake was designed by one of Goodrich's most capable engineers, John Warren. A tall, lanky, blond graduate of Purdue, Warren had come from the Chrysler Corporation seven years before and had become adept at aircraft brake design. The happy-go-lucky manner he usually maintained belied a temper that exploded whenever anyone ventured to offer criticism of his work, no matter how small. On these occasions, Warren would turn red in the face, often throwing or slamming something and then stalking from the scene. As his coworkers learned the consequences of criticizing him, they did so less and less readily, and when he submitted his preliminary design for the A7D brake, it was accepted without question.

Warren was named project engineer for the A7D, and he, in turn, assigned the task of producing the final production design to a newcomer to the Goodrich engineering stable, Searle Lawson. Just turned twenty-six, Lawson had been out of the Northrop Institute of Technology only one year when he came to Goodrich in January 1967. He had been assigned to various "paper projects" to break him in, and after several months spent reviewing statistics and old brake designs, he was beginning to fret at the lack of challenge. When told he was being assigned to his first "real" project, he was elated and immediately plunged into his work.

The major portion of the design had already been completed by Warren, and major subassemblies for the brake had already been ordered from Goodrich suppliers. Naturally, however, before Goodrich could start making the brakes on a production basis, much testing would have to be done. Lawson would have to determine the best materials to use for the linings and discover what minor adjustments in the design would have to be made.

Then, after the preliminary testing and after the brake was judged ready for production, one whole brake assembly would undergo a series of grueling, simulated braking stops and other severe trials called qualification tests. These tests are required by the military, which gives very detailed specifications on how they are to be conducted, the criteria for failure, and so on. They are performed in the Goodrich plant's test laboratory, where huge machines called dynamometers can simulate the weight and speed of almost any aircraft.

Searle Lawson was well aware that much work had to be done before the A7D brake could go into production, and he knew that LTV had set the last two weeks in June 1968 as the starting dates for flight tests. So he decided to begin testing immediately. Goodrich's suppliers had not yet delivered the brake housing and other parts, but the brake disks had arrived, and using the housing from a brake similar in size and weight to the A7D brake, Lawson built a prototype. The prototype was installed in a test wheel and placed on one of the big dynamometers in the plant's test laboratory. Lawson began a series of tests, "landing" the wheel and brake at the A7D's landing speed and braking it to a stop. The main purpose of these preliminary tests was to learn what temperatures would develop within the brake during the simulated stops and to evaluate lining materials tentatively selected for use.

During a normal aircraft landing the temperatures inside the brake may reach 1,000 degrees, and occasionally a bit higher. During Lawson's first simulated landings, the temperature of his prototype brake reached 1,500 degrees. The brake glowed a bright cherry-red and threw off incandescent particles of metal and lining material as the temperature reached its peak. After a few such stops, the brake was dismantled and the linings were found to be almost completely disintegrated. Lawson chalked this first failure up to chance, and ordering new lining materials, tried again.

The second attempt was a repeat of the first. The brake became extremely hot, causing the lining materials to crumble into dust.

After the third such failure, Lawson, inexperienced though he was, knew that the fault lay not in defective parts or unsuitable lining material but in the basic design of the brake itself. Ignoring Warren's original computations, Lawson made his own, and it didn't take him long to discover where the trouble lay—the brake was too small. There simply was not enough surface area on the disks to stop the aircraft without generating the excessive heat that caused the linings to fail.

The answer to the problem was obvious, but far from simple—the four-disk brake would have to be scrapped, and a new design, using five disks, would have to be developed. The implications were not lost on Lawson. Such a step would require junking the four-disk-brake sub-assemblies, many of which had now begun to arrive from the various suppliers. It would also mean several weeks of preliminary design and testing and many more weeks of waiting while the suppliers made and delivered the new subassemblies.

Yet, several weeks had already gone by since LTV's order had arrived, and the date for delivery of the first production brakes for flight testing was only a few months away.

Although John Warren had more or less turned the A7D over to Lawson, he knew of the difficulties Lawson had been experiencing. He had assured the younger engineer that the problem revolved around getting the right kind of lining material. Once that was found, he said, the difficulties would end.

Despite the evidence of the abortive tests and Lawson's careful computations, Warren rejected the suggestion that the four-disk brake was too light for the job. He knew that his superior had already told LTV, in rather glowing terms, that the preliminary tests on the A7D brake were very successful. Indeed, Warren's superiors weren't aware at this time of the troubles on the brake. It would have been difficult for Warren to admit not only that he had made a serious error in his calculations and original design but that his mistakes had been caught by a green kid, barely out of college.

Warren's reaction to a five-disk brake was not unexpected by Lawson, and, seeing that the four-disk brake was not to be abandoned so easily, he took his calculations and dismal test results one step up the corporate ladder.

At Goodrich, the man who supervises the engineers working on projects slated for production is called, predictably, the projects manager. The job was held by a short, chubby, bald man named Robert Sink. Some fifteen years before, Sink had begun working at Goodrich as a lowly draftsman. Slowly, he worked his way up. Despite his geniality, Sink was neither respected nor liked by the majority of the engineers, and his appointment as their supervisor did not improve their feelings toward him. He possessed only a high-school diploma, and it quite naturally rankled those who had gone through years of college to be commanded by a man whom they considered their intellectual inferior. But, though Sink had no college training, he had something even more useful: a fine working knowledge of company politics.

Puffing on a Meerschaum pipe, Sink listened gravely as young Lawson confided his fears about the four-disk brake. Then he examined Lawson's calculations and the results of the abortive tests. Despite the fact that he was not a qualified engineer, in the strictest sense of the word, it must certainly have been obvious to Sink that Lawson's calculations were correct and that a four-disk brake would never work on the A7D.

But other things of equal importance were also obvious. First, to concede that Lawson's calculations were correct would also mean conceding that Warren's calculations were incorrect. As projects manager, not only was he responsible for Warren's activities, but in admitting that Warren had erred, he would have to admit that he had erred in trusting Warren's judgment. It also meant that, as projects manager, it would be he who would have to explain the whole messy situation to the Goodrich hierarchy, not only at Troy but possibly on the corporate level at Goodrich's Akron offices. And having taken Warren's judgment of the four-disk brake at face value, he had assured LTV, not once but several times, that about all there was left to do on the brake was pack it in a crate and ship it out the door.

There's really no problem at all, he told Lawson. After all, Warren was an experienced engineer, and if he said the brake would work, it would work. Just keep on testing and probably, maybe even on the very next try, it'll work out just fine.

Lawson was far from convinced, but without the support of his superiors there was little he could do except keep on testing. By now, housings for the four-disk brake had begun to arrive at the plant, and

Lawson was able to build a production model of the brake and begin the formal qualification tests demanded by the military.

The first qualification attempts went exactly as the tests on the prototype had. Terrific heat developed within the brakes, and after a few short, simulated stops the linings crumbled. A new type of lining material was ordered and once again an attempt to qualify the brake was made. Again, failure.

Experts were called in from lining manufacturers, and new lining "mixes" were tried, always with the same result. Failure.

It was now the last week in March 1968, and flight tests were scheduled to begin in seventy days. Twelve separate attempts had been made to qualify the brake, and all had failed. It was no longer possible for anyone to ignore the glaring truth that the brake was a dismal failure and that nothing short of a major design change could ever make it work.

On April 4, the thirteenth attempt at qualification was begun. This time no attempt was made to conduct the tests by the methods and techniques spelled out in the military specifications. Regardless of how it had to be done, the brake was to be "nursed" through the required fifty simulated stops.

Fans were set up to provide special cooling. Instead of maintaining pressure on the brake until the test wheel had come to a complete stop, the pressure was reduced when the wheel had decelerated to around 15 mph, allowing it to "coast" to a stop. After each stop, the brake was disassembled and carefully cleaned, and after some of the stops, internal brake parts were machined in order to remove warp and other disfigurations caused by the high heat.

By these and other methods, all clearly contrary to the techniques established by the military specifications, the brake was coaxed through the fifty stops. But even using these methods, the brake could not meet all the requirements. On one stop the wheel rolled for a distance of 16,000 feet, or over three miles, before the brake could bring it to a stop. The normal distance required for such a stop was around 3,500 feet.

On April 11, the day the thirteenth test was completed, I became personally involved in the A7D situation.

I had worked in the Goodrich test laboratory for five years, starting first as an instrumentation engineer, then later becoming a data analyst and technical writer. As part of my duties, I analyzed the reams and reams of instrumentation data that came from the many testing machines in the lab, then transcribed all of it to a more usable form for the engineering department. When a new-type brake had successfully completed the required qualification tests, I would issue a formal qualification report.

Qualification reports are an accumulation of all the data and test logs compiled during the qualification tests and are documentary proof that a brake has met all the requirements established by the military specifications and is therefore presumed safe for flight testing. Before actual flight tests are conducted on a brake, qualification reports have to be delivered to the customer and to various government officials.

On April 11, I was looking over the data from the latest A7D test, and I noticed that many irregularities in testing had been noted on the test logs.

Technically, of course, there was nothing wrong with conducting tests in any manner desired, so long as the test was for research purposes only. But qualification test methods are clearly delineated by the military, and I knew that this test had been a formal qualification attempt. One particular notation on the test logs caught my eye. For some of the stops, the instrument that recorded the brake pressure had been deliberately miscalibrated so that, while the brake pressure used during the stops was recorded as 1,000 psi (pounds per square inch)—the maximum pressure that would be available on the A7D aircraft—the pressure had actually been 1,100 psi.

I showed the test logs to the test lab supervisor, Ralph Gretzinger, who said he had learned from the technician who had miscalibrated the instrument that he had been asked to do so by Lawson. Lawson, said Gretzinger, readily admitted asking for the miscalibration, saying he had been told to do so by Sink.

I asked Gretzinger why anyone would want to miscalibrate the data-recording instruments.

"Why? I'll tell you why," he snorted. "That brake is a failure. It's way too small for the job, and they're not ever going to get it to work. They're getting desperate, and instead of scrapping the damned thing and starting over, they figure they can horse around down here in the lab and qualify it that way."

An expert engineer, Gretzinger had been responsible for several innovations in brake design. It was he who had invented the unique brake system used on the famous XB70. "If you want to find out what's going on," said Gretzinger, "ask Lawson; he'll tell you."

Curious, I did ask Lawson the next time he came into the lab. He seemed eager to discuss the A7D and gave me the history of his months of frustrating efforts to get Warren and Sink to change the brake design. "I just can't believe this is really happening," said Lawson, shaking his head slowly. "This isn't engineering, at least not what I thought it would be. Back in school, I thought that when you were an engineer, you tried to do your best, no matter what it cost. But this is something else."

He sat across the desk from me, his chin propped in his hand. "Just wait," he warned. "You'll get a chance to see what I'm talking about. You're going to get in the act too, because I've already had the word that we're going to make one more attempt to qualify the brake, and that's it. Win or lose, we're going to issue a qualification report!"

I reminded him that a qualification report could be issued only after a brake had successfully met all military requirements, and therefore, unless the next qualification attempt was a success, no report would be issued.

"You'll find out," retorted Lawson. "I was already told that regardless of what the brake does on test, it's going to be qualified." He said he had been told in those exact words at a conference with Sink and Russell Van Horn.

This was the first indication that Sink had brought his boss, Van Horn, into the mess. Although Van Horn, as manager of the design engineering section, was responsible for the entire department, he was not necessarily familiar with all phases of every project, and it was not uncommon for those under him to exercise the what-he-doesn't-know-won't-hurt-him philosophy. If he was aware of the full extent of the A7D situation, it meant that Sink had decided not only to call for help but to look toward that moment when blame must be borne and, if possible, shared.

Also, if Van Horn had said, "regardless of what the brake does on test, it's going to be qualified," then it could only mean that, if necessary, a false qualification report would be issued. I discussed this possibility with Gretzinger, and he assured me that under no circumstances would such a report ever be issued.

"If they want a qualification report, we'll write them one, but we'll tell it just like it is," he declared emphatically. "No false data or false reports are going to come out of this lab."

On May 2, 1968, the fourteenth and final attempt to qualify the brake was begun. Although the same improper methods used to nurse the brake through the previous tests were employed, it soon became obvious that this too would end in failure.

When the tests were about half completed, Lawson asked if I would start preparing the various engineering curves and graphic displays that were normally incorporated in a qualification report. I flatly refused to have anything to do with the matter and immediately told Gretzinger what I had been asked to do. He was furious and repeated his previous declaration that under no circumstances would any false data or other matter be issued from the lab.

"I'm going to get this settled right now, once and for all," he declared. "I'm going to see Line[Russell Line, manager of the Goodrich Technical Services Section, of which the test lab was a part] and find out just how far this thing is going to go!" He stormed out of the room.

In about an hour, he returned and called me to his desk. He sat silently for a few moments, then muttered, half to himself, "I wonder what the hell they'd do if I just quit?" I didn't answer and I didn't ask him what he meant. I knew. He had been beaten down. He had reached the point when the decision had to be made. Defy them now while there was still time—or knuckle under, sell out.

"You know," he went on uncertainly, looking down at his desk, "I've been an engineer for a long time, and I've always believed that ethics and integrity were every bit as important as theorems and formulas, and never once has anything happened to change my beliefs. Now this. . . . Hell, I've got two sons I've got to put through school and I just . . ." His voice trailed off.

He sat for a few more minutes, then, looking over the top of his glasses, said hoarsely, "Well, it looks like we're licked. The way it stands now, we're to go ahead and prepare the data and other things for the graphic presentation in the report, and when we're finished, someone upstairs will actually write the report.

"After all," he continued, "we're just drawing some curves, and what happens to them after they leave here—well, we're not responsible for that."

I wasn't at all satisfied with the situation and decided that I too would discuss the matter with Russell Line, the senior executive in our section.

Tall, powerfully built, his teeth flashing white, his face tanned to a coffee-brown by a daily stint with a sunlamp, Line looked and acted every inch the executive. He had been transferred from the Akron offices some two years previously, and he commanded great respect and had come to be well liked by those of us who worked under him.

He listened sympathetically while I explained how I felt about the A7D situation, and when I had finished, he asked me what I wanted him to do about it. I said that as employees of the Goodrich Company we had a responsibility to protect the company and its reputation if at all possible. I said I was certain that officers on the corporate level would never knowingly allow such tactics as had been employed on the A7D.

"I agree with you," he remarked, "but I still want to know what you want me to do about it."

I suggested that in all probability the chief engineer at the Troy plant, H. C. "Bud" Sunderman, was unaware of the A7D problem and that he, Line, could tell him what was going on.

Line laughed, good-humoredly. "Sure, I could, but I'm not going to. Bud probably already knows about this thing anyway, and if he doesn't, I'm sure not going to be the one to tell him."

"But why?"

"Because it's none of my business, and it's none of yours. I learned a long time ago not to worry about things over which I had no control. I have no control over this."

I wasn't satisfied with this answer, and I asked him if his conscience wouldn't bother him if, say, during flight tests on the brake, something should happen resulting in death or injury to the test pilot.

"Look," he said, becoming somewhat exasperated, "I just told you I have no control over this. Why should my conscience bother me?"

His voice took on a quiet, soothing tone as he continued. "You're just getting all upset over this thing for nothing. I just do as I'm told, and I'd advise you to do the same."

I made no attempt to rationalize what I had been asked to do. It made no difference who would falsify which part of the report or whether the actual falsification would be by misleading numbers or misleading words. Whether by acts of commission or omission, all of us who contributed to the fraud would be guilty. The only question left for me to decide was whether or not I would become a party to the fraud.

Before coming to Goodrich in 1963, I had held a variety of jobs, each a little more pleasant, a little more rewarding than the last. At forty-two, with seven children, I had decided that the Goodrich Company would probably be my "home" for the rest of my working life. The job paid well, it was pleasant and challenging, and the future looked reasonably bright. My wife and I had bought a home and we were ready to settle down into a comfortable, middle-age, middle-class rut. If I refused to take part in the A7D fraud, I would have either to resign or be fired. The report would be written by someone anyway, but I would have the satisfaction of knowing I had had no part in the matter. But bills aren't paid with personal satisfaction, nor house payments with ethical principles. I made my decision. The next morning, I telephoned Lawson and told him I was ready to begin on the qualification report.

I had written dozens of qualification reports, and I knew what a "good" one looked like. Resorting to the actual test data only on occasion, Lawson and I proceeded to prepare page after page of elaborate, detailed engineering curves, charts, and test logs, which purported to show what had happened during the formal qualification tests. Where temperatures were too high, we deliberately chopped them down a few hundred degrees, and where they were too low, we raised them to a value that would appear reasonable to the LTV and military engineers. Brake pressure, torque values, distances, times—everything of consequence was tailored to fit.

Occasionally, we would find that some test either hadn't been performed at all or had been conducted improperly. On those occasions, we "conducted" the test—successfully, of course—on paper.

For nearly a month we worked on the graphic presentation that would be a part of the report. Meanwhile, the final qualification attempt had been completed, and the brake, not unexpectedly, had failed again.

We finished our work on the graphic portion of the report around the first of June. Altogether, we had prepared nearly two hundred pages of data, containing dozens of deliberate falsifications and misrepresentations. I delivered the data to Gretzinger, who said he had been instructed to deliver it personally to the chief engineer, Bud Sunderman, who in turn would assign someone in the engineering department to complete the written portion of the report. He gathered the bundle of data and left the office. Within minutes, he was back with the data, his face white with anger.

"That damned Sink's beat me to it," he said furiously. "He's already talked to Bud about this, and now Sunderman says no one in the engineering department has time to write the report. He wants us to do it, and I told him we couldn't."

The words had barely left his mouth when Russell Line burst in the door. "What the hell's all the fuss about this damned report?" he demanded.

Patiently, Gretzinger explained. "There's no fuss. Sunderman just told me that we'd have to write the report down here, and I said we couldn't. Russ," he went on, "I've told you before that we weren't going to write the report. I made my position clear on that a long time ago."

Line shut him up with a wave of his hand and, turning to me, bellowed, "I'm getting sick and tired of hearing about this damned report. Now, write the goddamn thing and shut up about it!" He slammed out of the office.

Gretzinger and I just sat for a few seconds looking at each other. Then he spoke.

"Well, I guess he's made it pretty clear, hasn't he? We can either write the thing or quit. You know, what we should have done was quit a long time ago. Now, it's too late."

Somehow, I wasn't at all surprised at this turn of events, and it didn't really make that much difference. As far as I was concerned, we were all up to our necks in the thing anyway, and writing the narrative portion of the report couldn't make me more guilty than I already felt myself to be.

Within two days, I had completed the narrative, or written portion, of the report. As a final sop to my own self-respect, in the conclusion of the report I wrote, "The B. F. Goodrich P/N 2-1162-3 brake assembly does not meet the intent or the requirements of the applicable specification documents and therefore is not qualified."

This was a meaningless gesture, since I knew that this would certainly be changed when the report went through the final typing process. Sure enough, when the report was published, the negative conclusion had been made positive.

One final and significant incident occurred just before publication.

Qualification reports always bear the signature of the person who has prepared them. I refused to sign the report, as did Lawson. Warren was later asked to sign the report. He replied that he would "when I receive a signed statement from Bob Sink ordering me to sign it."

The engineering secretary who was delegated the responsibility of "dogging" the report through publication told me later that after I, Lawson, and Warren had all refused to sign the report, she had asked Sink if he would sign. He replied, "On something of this nature, I don't think a signature is really needed."

On June 5, 1968, the report was officially published and copies were delivered by hand to the Air Force and LTV. Within a week flight tests were begun at Edwards Air Force Base in California. Searle Lawson was sent to California as Goodrich's representative. Within approximately two weeks, he returned because some rather unusual incidents during the tests had caused them to be canceled.

His face was grim as he related stories of several near crashes during landings—caused by brake troubles. He told me about one incident in which, upon landing, one brake was literally welded together by the intense heat developed during the test stop. The wheel locked, and the plane skidded for nearly 1,500 feet before coming to a halt. The plane was jacked up and the wheel removed. The fused parts within the brake had to be pried apart.

That evening I left work early and went to see my attorney. After I told him the story, he advised that, while I was probably not actually guilty of fraud, I was certainly part of a conspiracy to defraud. He advised me to go to the Federal Bureau of Investigation and offered to arrange an appointment. The following week he took me to the Dayton office of the FBI and after I had been warned that I would not be immune from prosecution, I disclosed the A7D matter to one of the agents. The agent told me to say nothing about the episode to anyone and to report any further incidents to him. He said he would forward the story to his superiors in Washington.

A few days later, Lawson returned from a conference with LTV in Dallas and said that the Air Force, which had previously approved the qualification report, had suddenly rescinded that approval and was demanding to see some of the raw test data. I gathered that the FBI had passed the word.

Omitting any reference to the FBI, I told Lawson I had been to an attorney and that we were probably guilty of conspiracy.

"Can you get me an appointment with your attorney?" he asked. Within a week, he had been to the FBI and told them of his part in the mess. He too was advised to say nothing but to keep on the job reporting any new development.

Naturally, with the rescinding of Air Force approval and the demand to see raw test data, Goodrich officials were in a panic. A conference was called for July 27, a Saturday morning affair at which Lawson, Sink, Warren, and I were present. We met in a tiny conference room in the deserted engineering department. Lawson and I, by now openly hostile to Warren and Sink, ranged ourselves on one side of the conference table while Warren sat on the other side. Sink, chairing the meeting, paced slowly in front of a blackboard, puffing furiously on a pipe.

The meeting was called, Sink began, "to see where we stand on the A7D." What we were going to do, he said, was to "level" with LTV and tell them the "whole truth" about the A7D. "After all," he said, "they're in this thing with us, and they have the right to know how matters stand."

"In other words," I asked, "we're going to tell them the truth?"

"That's right," he replied. "We're going to level with them and let them handle the ball from there."

"There's one thing I don't quite understand," I interjected. "Isn't it going to be pretty hard for us to admit to them that we've lied?"

"Now, wait a minute," he said angrily. "Let's don't go off half-cocked on this thing. It's not a matter of lying. We've just interpreted the information the way we felt it should be."

"I don't know what you call it," I replied, "but to me it's lying, and it's going to be damned hard to confess to them that we've been lying all along."

He became very agitated at this and repeated, "We're not lying," adding, "I don't like this sort of talk."

I dropped the matter at this point, and he began discussing the various discrepancies in the report.

We broke for lunch, and afterward, I came back to the plant to find Sink sitting alone at his desk, waiting to resume the meeting. He called me over and said he wanted to apologize for his outburst that morning. "This thing has kind of gotten me down," he confessed, "and I think you've got the wrong picture. I don't think you really understand everything about this."

Perhaps so, I conceded, but it seemed to me that if we had already told LTV one thing and then had to tell them another, changing our story completely, we would have to admit we were lying.

"No," he explained patiently, "we're not really lying. All we were doing was interpreting the figures the way we knew they should be. We were just exercising engineering license."

During the afternoon session, we marked some forty-three discrepant points in the report; forty-three points that LTV would surely spot as occasions where we had exercised "engineering license."

After Sink listed those points on the blackboard, we discussed each one individually. As each point came up, Sink would explain that it was probably "too minor to bother about," or that perhaps it "wouldn't be wise to open that can of worms," or that maybe this was a point that "LTV just wouldn't understand." When the meeting was over, it had been decided that only three points were "worth mentioning."

Similar conferences were held during August and September, and the summer was punctuated with frequent treks between Dallas and Troy and demands by the Air Force to see the raw test data. Tempers were short, and matters seemed to grow worse.

Finally, early in October 1968, Lawson submitted his resignation, to take effect on October 25. On October 18, I submitted my own resignation, to take effect on November 1. In my resignation, addressed to Russell Line, I cited the A7D report and stated: "As you are aware, this report contained numerous deliberate and willful misrepresentations which, according to legal counsel, constitute fraud and expose both myself and others to criminal charges of conspiracy to defraud . . . The events of the past seven months have created an atmosphere of deceit and distrust in which it is impossible to work . . ."

On October 25, I received a sharp summons to the office of Bud Sunderman. Tall and graying, impeccably dressed at all times, he was capable of producing a dazzling smile or a hearty chuckle or immobilizing his face into marble hardness, as the occasion required.

I faced the marble hardness when I reached his office. He motioned me to a chair. "I have your resignation here," he snapped, "and I must say you have made some rather shocking, I might even say irresponsible, charges. This is very serious."

Before I could reply, he was demanding an explanation. "I want to know exactly what the fraud is in connection with the A7D and how you can dare accuse this company of such a thing!"

I started to tell some of the things that had happened during the testing, but he shut me off saying, "There's nothing wrong with anything we've done here. You aren't aware of all the things that have been going on behind the scenes. If you had known the true situation, you would never have made these charges." He said that in view of my apparent "disloyalty" he had decided to accept my resignation "right now," and said it would be better for all concerned if I left the plant immediately. As I got up to leave he asked me if I intended to "carry this thing further."

I answered simply, "Yes," to which he replied, "Suit yourself." Within twenty minutes, I had cleaned out my desk and left. Forty-eight hours later, the B. F. Goodrich Company recalled the qualification report and the four-disk brake, announcing that it would replace the brake with a new, improved, five-disk brake at no cost to LTV.

Ten months later, on August 13, 1969, I was the chief government witness at a hearing conducted before Senator William Proxmire's Economy in Government Subcommittee. I related the A7D story to the committee, and my testimony was supported by Searle Lawson, who followed me to the witness stand. Air Force officers also testified, as well as a four-man team from the General Accounting Office, which had conducted an investigation of the A7D brake at the request of Senator Proxmire. Both Air Force and GAO investigators declared that the brake was dangerous and had not been tested properly.

Testifying for Goodrich was R. G. Jeter, vice-president and general counsel of the company, from the Akron headquarters. Representing the Troy plant was Robert Sink. These two denied any wrongdoing on the part of the Goodrich Company, despite expert testimony to the contrary by Air Force and GAO officials. Sink was quick to deny any connection with the writing of the report or directing of any falsifications, claiming to have been on the West Coast at the time. John Warren was the man who had supervised its writing, said Sink.

As for me, I was dismissed as a high-school graduate with no technical training, while Sink testified that Lawson was a young, inexperienced engineer. "We tried to give him guidance," Sink testified, "but he preferred to have his own convictions."

About changing the data and figures in the report, Sink said: "When you take data from several different sources, you have to rationalize among those data what is the true story. This is part of your engineering know-how." He admitted that changes had been made in the data, "but only to make them more consistent with the overall picture of the data that is available."

Jeter pooh-poohed the suggestion that anything improper occurred, saying: "We have thirty-odd engineers at this plant . . . and I say to you that it is incredible that these men would stand idly by and see reports changed or falsified. . . . I mean you just do not have to do that working for anybody. . . . Just nobody does that."

The four-hour hearing adjourned with no real conclusion reached by the subcommittee. But the following day the Department of Defense made sweeping changes in its inspection, testing, and reporting procedures. A spokesman for the DOD said the changes were a result of the Goodrich episode.

The A7D is now in service, sporting a Goodrich-made five-disk brake, a brake that works very well, I'm told. Business at the Goodrich plant is good. Lawson is now an engineer for LTV and has been assigned to the A7D project, possibly explaining why the A7D's new brakes work so well. And I am now a newspaper reporter.

At this writing, those remaining at Goodrich—including Warren—are still secure in the same positions, all except Russell Line and Robert Sink. Line has been rewarded with a promotion to production superintendent, a large step upward on the corporate ladder. As for Sink, he moved up into Line's old job.

Self-Interest

THOMAS HOBBES

OR THE MATTER, FORM, AND POWER OF A COMMONWEALTH, ECCLESIASTICAL AND CIVIL THE FIRST PART, OF MAN

CHAPTER VI
OF THE INTERIOR BEGINNINGS OF VOLUNTARY MOTIONS; COMMONLY CALLED THE PASSIONS

. . . That which men desire, they are also said to LOVE, and to HATE those things for which they have aversion. So that desire and love are the same thing; save that by desire, we always signify the absence of the object; by love, most commonly the presence of the same. So also by aversion, we signify the absence; and by hate, the presence of the object.

Of appetites and aversions, some are born with men; as appetite of food, appetite of excretion, and exoneration, which may also and more properly be called aversions, from somewhat they feel in their bodies; and some other appetites, not many. The rest, which are appetites of particular things, proceed from experience, and trial of their effects upon themselves or other men. For of things we know not at all, or believe not to be, we can have no further desire than to taste and try. But aversion we have for things, not only which we know have hurt us, but also that we do not know whether they will hurt us, or not.

. . . whatsoever is the object of any man's appetite or desire, that is it which he for his part calleth *good:* and the object of his hate and aversion, *evil;* and of his contempt, *vile* and *inconsiderable.* For these words of good, evil, and contemptible, are ever used with relation to the person that useth them: there being nothing simply and absolutely so; nor any common rule of good and evil, to be taken from the nature of the objects themselves; but from the person of the man, where there is no Commonwealth; or, in a Commonwealth, from the person that representeth it; or from an

From the *Leviathan* (1651; rpt. London: Oxford University Press, 1967), Part I, Chaps. VI and XIII, Part II, Chap. XVII.

arbitrator or judge, whom men disagreeing shall by consent set up, and make his sentence the rule thereof.

. . . Of pleasure or delights, some arise from the sense of an object present; and those may be called *pleasures of sense;* the word *sensual,* as it is used by those only that condemn them, having no place till there be laws. Of this kind are all onerations and exonerations of the body; as also all that is pleasant, in the *sight, hearing, smell, taste,* or *touch.* Others arise from the expectation, that proceeds from foresight of the end,or consequence of things; whether those things in the sense please or displease. And these are *pleasures of the mind* of him that draweth those consequences, and are generally called JOY. In the like manner, displeasures are some in the sense, and called PAIN; others in the expectation of consequences, and are called GRIEF. . . .

CHAPTER XIII

OF THE NATURAL CONDITION OF MANKIND
AS CONCERNING THEIR FELICITY AND MISERY

Nature hath made men so equal, in the faculties of the body, and mind; as that though there be found one man sometimes manifestly stronger in body, or of quicker mind than another, yet when all is reckoned together, the difference between man and man, is not so considerable, as that one man can thereupon claim to himself any benefit to which another may not pretend, as well as he. For as to the strength of body, the weakest has strength enough to kill the strongest, either by secret machination, or by confederacy with others, that are in the same danger with himself.

And as to the faculties of the mind, setting aside the arts grounded upon words, and especially that skill of proceeding upon general and infallible rules, called science; which very few have, and but in few things; as being not a native faculty born with us; nor attained, as prudence, while we look after somewhat else, I find yet a greater equality amongst men than that of strength. For prudence, is but experience; which equal time, equally bestows on all men, in those things they equally apply themselves unto. That which may perhaps make such equality incredible, is but a vain conceit of one's own wisdom, which almost all men think they have in a greater degree than the vulgar; that is, than all men but themselves, and a few others, whom by fame, or for concurring with themselves, they approve. For such is the nature of men, that howsoever they may acknowledge many others to be more witty, or more eloquent, or more learned; yet they will hardly believe there be many so wise as themselves; for they see their own wit at hand, and other men's at a distance. But this proveth rather that men are in that point equal, than unequal. For there is not ordinarily a greater sign of the equal distribution of anything, than that every man is contented with his share.

From this equality of ability, ariseth equality of hope in the attaining of our ends. And therefore if any two men desire the same thing, which nevertheless they cannot both enjoy, they become enemies; and in the way to their end, which is principally their own conservation, and sometimes their delectation only, endeavour to destroy or subdue one another. And from hence it comes to pass, that where an invader hath no more to fear, than another man's single power; if one plant, sow, build, or possess a convenient seat, others may probably be expected to come prepared with forces united, to dispossess, and deprive him, not only of the fruit of his labour, but also of his life or liberty. And the invader again is in the like danger of another.

And from this diffidence of one another, there is no way for any man to secure himself, so reasonable as anticipation; that is, by force, or wiles, to master the persons of all men he can, so long, till he see no other power great enough to endanger him: and this is no more than his own conservation requireth, and is generally allowed. Also because there be some, that taking pleasure in contemplating their own power in the acts of conquest, which they pursue farther than their security requires; if others, that otherwise would be glad to be at ease within modest bounds, should not by invasion increase their power, they would not be able, long time, by standing only on their defence, to subsist. And by consequence, such augmentation of dominion over men being necessary to a man's conservation, it ought to be allowed him.

Again, men have no pleasure, but on the contrary a great deal of grief, in keeping company, where there is no power able to overawe them all. For every man looketh that his companion should value him, at the same rate he sets upon himself: and upon all signs of contempt, or undervaluing, naturally endeavours as far as he dares (which amongst them that have no common power to keep them in quiet, is far enough to make them destroy each other), to extort a greater value from his contemners, by damage; and from others, by the example.

So that in the nature of man, we find three principal causes of quarrel. First, competition; secondly, diffidence; thirdly, glory.

The first maketh men invade for gain; the second, for safety; and the third, for reputation. The first use violence, to make themselves masters of other men's persons, wives, children, and cattle; the second, to defend them; the third, for trifles, as a word, a smile, a different opinion, and any sign of undervalue, either direct in their persons, or by reflection in their kindred, their friends, their nation, their profession, or their name.

Hereby it is manifest, that during the time men live without a common power to keep them all in awe, they are in that condition which is called WAR; and such a war, as is of every man, against every man. For WAR, consisteth not in battle only, or the act of fighting; but in a tract of time, wherein the will to contend by battle is sufficiently known: and therefore the notion of *time*, is to be considered in the nature of war, as it is in the nature of weather. For as the nature of foul weather, lieth not in a shower or two of rain, but in an inclination thereto of many days together; so the nature of war, consisteth not in actual fighting, but in the known disposition thereto, during all the time there is no assurance to the contrary. All other time is PEACE.

Whatsoever therefore is consequent to a time of war, where every man is enemy to every man, the same is consequent to the time wherein men live without other security, than what their own strength, and their own invention shall furnish them withal. In such condition, there is no place for industry, because the fruit thereof is uncertain, and consequently no culture of the earth; no navigation, nor use of the commodities that may be imported by sea; no commodious building; no instruments of moving, and removing, such things as require much force; no knowledge of the face of the earth; no account of time; no arts; no letters; no society; and, which is worst of all, continual fear, and danger of violent death; and the life of man, solitary, poor, nasty, brutish, and short. . . .

THE SECOND PART, OF COMMONWEALTH

CHAPTER XVII

OF THE CAUSES, GENERATIONS,
AND DEFINITION OF A COMMONWEALTH

The final cause, end, or design of men who naturally love liberty and dominion over others, in the introduction of that restraint upon themselves in which we see them live in commonwealths, is the foresight of their own preservation, and of a more contented life thereby; that is to say, of getting themselves out from that miserable condition of war, which is necessarily consequent . . . to the natural passions of men, when there is no visible power to keep them in awe, and tie them by fear of punishment to the performance of their covenants and observation of those laws of nature set down [previously].

. . . The only way to erect such a common power, as may be able to defend them from the invasion of foreigners and the injuries of one another, and thereby to secure them in such sort as that, by their own industry, and by the fruits of the earth, they may nourish themselves and live contentedly; is, to confer all their power and strength upon one man, or upon one assembly of men, that may reduce all their wills, by plurality of voices, unto one will: which is as much as to say, to appoint one man, or assembly of men, to bear their person; and everyone to own and acknowledge himself to be author of whatsoever he that so beareth their person, shall act or cause to be acted in those things which concern the common peace and safety; and therein to submit their wills, everyone to his will, and their judgments, to his judgment. This is more than consent, or concord; it is a real unity of them all, in one and the same person, made by covenant of every man with every man, in such manner as if every man should say to every man, *"I authorize and give up my right of governing myself to this man, or to this assembly of men, on this condition, that thou give up thy right to him, and authorize all his actions in like manner."* This done, the multitude so united in one person, is called a *commonwealth,* in Latin *civitas.* This is the generation of that great LEVIATHAN, or rather, to speak more reverently, of that *mortal god,* to which we owe under the *immortal God,* our peace and defense. For by this authority, given him by every particular man in the commonwealth, he hath the use of so much power and strength conferred on him, that by terror thereof he is enabled to perform the wills of them all, to peace at home and mutual aid against their enemies abroad. And in him consisteth the essence of the commonwealth; which, to define it, is *one person, of whose acts a great multitude, by mutual covenants one with another, have made themselves every one the author, to the end he may use the strength and means of them all, as he shall think expedient, for their peace and common defense.*

And he that carrieth this person, is called *sovereign,* and said to have sovereign power; and everyone besides, his *subject.*

The attaining to this sovereign power is by two ways. One, by natural force; as when a man maketh his children to submit themselves and their children to his government, as being able to destroy them if they refuse; or by war subdueth his enemies to his will, giving them their lives on that condition. The other, is when men agree amongst themselves to submit to some man, or assembly of men, voluntarily, on confidence to be protected by him against all others. This latter may be called a political commonwealth, or commonwealth by *institution;* and the former, a commonwealth by *acquisition.* . . .

Benevolence and Self-Interest

JOSEPH BUTLER

SERMON I
UPON THE SOCIAL NATURE OF MAN

The comparison will be between the nature of man as respecting self, and tending to private good, his own preservation and happiness; and the nature of man as having respect to society, and tending to promote public good, the happiness of that society. These ends do indeed perfectly coincide; and to aim at public and private good are so far from being inconsistent, that they mutually promote each other: yet in the following discourse they must be considered as entirely distinct; otherwise the nature of man as tending to one, or as tending to the other cannot be compared. There can no comparison be made, without considering the things compared as distinct and different.

From this review and comparison of the nature of man as respecting self, and as respecting society, it will plainly appear, that *there are as real and the same kind of indications in human nature, that we were made for society and to do good to our fellow-creatures, as that we were intended to take care of our own life*

From *Fifteen Sermons Preached at Rolls Chapel* (1726; rpt. London: Thomas Tegg & Son, 1835), selections from Sermons I and XI.

and health and private good: and that the same objections lie against one of these assertions, as against the other. For,

First, There is a natural principle of *benevolence*[1] in man; which is in some degree to *society,* what *self-love* is to the *individual.* And if there be in mankind any disposition to friendship; if there be any such thing as compassion, for compassion is momentary love; if there be any such thing as the paternal or filial affections; if there be any affection in human nature, the object and end of which is the good of another, this is itself benevolence, or the love of another. Be it ever so short, be it in ever so low a degree, or ever so unhappily confined; it proves the assertion, and points out what we were designed for, as really as though it were in a higher degree and more extensive. I must, however, remind you that though benevolence and self-love are different; though the former tends most directly to public good, and the latter to private: yet they are so perfectly coincident that the greatest satisfactions to ourselves depend upon our having benevolence in a due degree, and that self-love is one chief security of our right behaviour towards society. It may be added, that their mutual coinciding, so that we can scarce promote one without the other, is equally proof that we were made for both.

Secondly, This will further appear, from observing that the *several passions* and *affections,* which are distinct, both from benevolence and self-love, do in general contribute and lead us to *public* good as really as to *private.* It might be thought too minute and particular, and would carry us too great a length, to distinguish between and compare together the several passions or appetites distinct from benevolence, whose primary use and intention is the security and good of society; and the passions distinct from self-love, whose primary intention and design is the security and good of the individual.[2] It is enough to the present argument, that desire of esteem from others, contempt and esteem of them, love of society as distinct from affection to the good of it, indignation against successful vice, that these are public affections or passions; have an immediate respect to others, naturally lead us to regulate our behavior in such a manner as will be of service to our fellow-creatures. If any or all of these may be considered likewise as private affections, as tending to private good; this does not hinder them from being public affections too, or destroy the good influence of them upon society, and their tendency to public good. It may be added, that as persons without any conviction from reason of the desirableness of life, would yet of course preserve it merely from the appetite of hunger; so by acting merely from regard (suppose) to reputation, without any consideration of the good of others, men often contribute to public good. In both these instances they are plainly instruments in the hands of another, in the hands of Providence, to carry on ends, the preservation of the individual and good of society, which they themselves have not in their view or intention. The sum is, men have various appetites, passions, and particular affections, quite distinct both from self-love and from benevolence: all of these have a tendency to promote both public and private good, and may be considered as respecting others and ourselves equally and in common: but some of them seem most immediately to respect others, or tend to public good; others of them most immediately to respect self, or tend to private good: as the former are not benevolence, so the latter are not self-love: neither sort are instances of our love either to ourselves or others; . . .

Thirdly, There is a principle of reflection in men, by which they distinguish between, approve, and disapprove their own actions. We are plainly constituted such sort of creatures as to reflect upon our own nature. The mind can take a view of what passes within itself, its propensions, aversions, passions, affections, as respecting such objects, and in such degrees; and of the several actions consequent thereupon. In this survey it approves of one, disapproves of another, and towards a third is affected in neither of these ways, but is quite indifferent. This principle in man, by which he approves or disapproves his heart, temper, and actions, is conscience; for this is the strict sense of the word, though sometimes it is used so as to take in more. And that this faculty tends to restrain men from doing mischief to each other, and leads them to do good, is too manifest to need being insisted upon. Thus a parent has the affection of love to his children: this leads him to take care of, to educate, to make due provision for them: the natural affection leads to this; but the reflection that it is his proper business, what belongs to him, that it is right and commendable so to do, this added to the affection becomes a much more settled principle, and carries him on through more labour and difficulties for the sake of his children, then he would undergo from that affection alone, if he thought it, and the course of action it led to, either indifferent or criminal. This indeed is impossible, to do that which is good and not to approve of it; for which reason they are frequently not considered as distinct, though they really are; for men often approve of the actions of others, which they will not imitate, and likewise do that which they approve not. It cannot possibly be denied that there is this principle of reflection or conscience in human nature. Suppose a man to relieve an innocent person in great distress; suppose the same man afterwards, in the fury of anger, to do the greatest mischief to a person who had given no just cause of offence; to aggravate the injury, add the circumstances of former friendship, and obligation from the injured person; let the man who is supposed to have done these two different actions, coolly reflect upon them afterwards, without regard to their consequences to himself: to assert that any common man would be affected in the same way towards these different actions, that he would make no distinction between them, but approve or disapprove them equally, is too glaring a falsity to need being confuted. There is therefore this principle of reflection or conscience in mankind. It is needless to compare the respect it has to private good, with the respect it has to public; since it plainly tends as much to the latter as to the former, and is commonly thought to tend chiefly to the latter. This faculty is now mentioned merely as another part of the inward frame of man, pointing out to us in some degree what we are intended for, and as what will naturally and of course have some influence. The particular place assigned to it by nature, what authority it has, and how great influence it ought to have, shall be hereafter considered.

From this comparison of benevolence and self-love, of our public and private affections, of the courses of life they lead to, and of the principle of reflection or conscience as respecting each of them, it is as manifest, that *we were made for society, and to promote the happiness of it, as that we were intended to take care of our own life, and health, and private good. . . .*

The sum of the whole is plainly this. The nature of man considered in his single capacity, and with respect only to the present world, is adapted and leads him to attain the greatest happiness he can for himself in the present world. The nature of man considered in his public or social capacity leads him to a right behaviour in society, to that course of life which we call virtue. Men follow or obey their nature in both these capacities and respects to a certain degree but not entirely: their actions do not come up to the whole of what their nature leads them to in either of these capacities or respects: and they often violate their nature in both, *i.e.* as they neglect the duties they owe to their fellow-creatures, to which their nature leads them; and are injurious, to which their nature is abhorrent; so there is a manifest negligence in men of their real happiness or interest in the present world, when that interest is inconsistent with a present gratification; for the sake of which they negligently, nay, even knowingly, are the authors and instruments of their own misery and ruin. Thus they are as often unjust to themselves as to others, and for the most part are equally so to both by the same actions. . . .

SERMON XI
UPON THE LOVE OF OUR NEIGHBOUR

Every man hath a general desire of his own happiness; and likewise a variety of particular affections, passions, and appetites, to particular external objects. The former proceeds from, or is, self-love, and seems inseparable from all sensible creatures, who can reflect upon themselves and their own interest or happiness, so as to have that interest an object to their minds: what is to be said of the latter is, that they proceed from, or together make up, that particular nature, according to which man is made. The object the former pursues is somewhat internal, our own happiness, enjoyment, satisfaction; whether we have or have not a distinct particular perception what it is, or wherein it consists: the objects of the latter are this or that particular external thing, which the affections tend towards, and of which it hath always a particular idea or perception. The principle we call self-love never seeks anything external for the sake of the thing, but only as a means of happiness or good: particular affections rest in the external things themselves. One belongs to man as a reasonable creature reflecting upon his own interest or happiness; the other, though quite distinct from reason, are as much a part of human nature.

That all particular appetites and passions are towards *external things themselves,* distinct from the *pleasure arising from them,* is manifested from hence, that there could not be this pleasure, were it not for that prior suitableness between the object and the passion: there could be no enjoyment or delight for one thing more than another, from eating food more than from swallowing a stone, if there were not an affection or appetite to one thing more than another.

Every particular affection, even the love of our neighbour, is as really our own affection, as self-love; and the pleasure arising from its gratification is as much my own pleasure, as the pleasure self-love would have from knowing I myself should be happy some time hence, would be my own pleasure. And if, because every particular affection is a man's own, and the pleasure arising from its gratification his own pleasure, or pleasure to himself, such particular affection must be called self-love. According to this way of speaking, no creature whatever can possibly act merely from self-love; and every action and every affection whatever is to be resolved up into this one principle. But then this is not the language of mankind: or, if it were, we should want words to express the difference between the principle of an action, proceeding from cool consideration that it will be to my own advantage; and an action, suppose of revenge, or of friendship by which a man runs upon certain ruin, to do evil or good to another. It is manifest the principles of these actions are totally different, and so want different words to be distinguished by: all that they agree in is, that they both proceed from, and are done to gratify an inclination in a man's self. But the principle or inclination in one case is self-love; in the other, hatred, or love of another. There is then a distinction between the cool principle of self-love, or general desire of our own happiness, as one part of our nature, and one principle of action; and the particular affections towards particular external objects, as another principle of action. How much soever, therefore, is to be allowed to self-love, yet it cannot be allowed to be the whole of our inward constitution; because, you see, there are other parts or principles which come into it.

Further, private happiness or good is all which self-love can make us desire or be concerned about. In having this consists its gratification; it is an affection to ourselves—a regard to our own interest, happiness, and private good: and in the proportion a man hath this, he is interested, or a lover of himself. Let this be kept in mind, because there is commonly, as I shall presently have occasion to observe, another sense put upon these words. On the other hand, particular affections tend towards particular external things; these are their objects; having these is their end; in this consists their gratification: no matter whether it be, or be not, upon the whole, our interest or happiness. An action, done from the former of these principles, is called an interested action. An action, proceeding from any of the latter, has its denomination of passionate, ambitious, friendly, revengeful, or any other, from the particular appetite or affection from which it proceeds. Thus self-love, as one part of human nature, and the several particular principles as the other part, are themselves, their objects, and ends, stated and shown.

From hence it will be easy to see how far, and in what ways, each of these can contribute and be subservient to the private good of the individual. Happiness does not consist in self-love. The desire of happiness is no more the thing itself, than the desire of riches is the possession or enjoyment of them. People may love themselves with the most entire and unbounded affection, and yet be extremely miserable. Neither can self-love any way help them out, but by setting them on work to get rid of the causes of their misery, to gain or make use of those objects which are by nature adapted to afford satisfaction. Happiness or satisfaction consists only in the enjoyment of those objects which are by nature suited to our several particular appetites, passions, and affections. So that if self-love wholly engrosses us, and leaves no room for any other principle, there can be absolutely no such thing at all as happiness or enjoyment of any kind whatever; since happiness consists in the gratification of particular passions, which supposes the having of them. Self-love then does not constitute *this* or *that* to be our interest or good; but our interest or good being constituted by nature and supposed self-love, only puts us upon obtaining and securing it. Therefore, if it be possible that self-love may prevail and exert itself in a degree or manner which is not subservient to this end, then it will not follow that our interest will be promoted in proportion to the degree in which that principle engrosses us, and prevails over others. Nay, further, the private and contracted affection, when it is not subservient to this end, private good, may, for anything that appears, have a direct contrary tendency and effect. And if we will consider the matter, we shall see that it often really has. Disengagement is absolutely necessary to enjoyment; and a person may have so steady and fixed an eye upon his own interest, whatever he places it in, as may hinder him from attending to many gratifications within his reach, which others have their minds free and open to. Overfondness for a child is not generally thought to be for its advantage; and, if there be any guess to be from appearances, surely that character we call *selfish* is not the most promising for happiness. Such a temper may plainly be, and exert itself in a degree and manner which may give unnecessary and useless solicitude and anxiety, in a degree and manner which may prevent obtaining the means and materials of enjoyment, as well as the making use of them. Immoderate self-love does very ill consult its own interest; and how much soever a paradox it may appear, it is certainly true, that, even from self-love, we should endeavour to get over all inordinate regard to, and consideration of, ourselves. Every one of our passions and affections hath its natural stint and bound, which may easily be exceeded; whereas our enjoyments can possibly be but in a determinate measure and degree. Therefore such excess of the affection, since it cannot procure any enjoyment, must in all cases be useless, but is generally attended with inconveniences, and often is down-right pain and misery. This holds as much with regard to self-love as to all other affections. The natural degree of it, so far as it sets us on work to gain and make use of the materials of satisfaction, may be to our real advantage; but beyond or beside this, it is in several respects an inconvenience and disadvantage. Thus it appears that private interest is so far from being likely to be promoted in proportion to the degree in which self-love engrosses us, and prevails over all other principles, that *the contracted affection may be so prevalent as to disappoint itself and even contradict its own end, private good.* . . .

Self-love and interestedness was stated to consist in or be an affection to ourselves, a regard to our own private good: it is, therefore, distinct from benevolence, which is an affection to the good of our fellow-creatures. But that benevolence is distinct from, that is, not the same thing with self-love, is no reason for its being looked upon with any peculiar suspicion, because every principle whatever, by means of which self-love is gratified, is distinct from it. And all things, which are distinct from each other, are equally so. A man has an affection or aversion to another: that one of these tends to, and is gratified by doing good, that the other tends to, and is gratified by doing harm, does not in the least alter the respect which either one or the other of these inward feelings has to self-love.

. . . Thus the principles, from which men rush upon certain ruin for the destruction of an enemy, and for the preservation of a friend, have the same respect to the private affection, are equally interested, or equally disinterested: and it is of no avail, whether they are said to be one or the other. Therefore, to those who are shocked to hear virtue spoken of as disinterested, it may be allowed, that it is indeed absurd to speak thus of it; unless hatred, several particular instances of vice, and all the common affections and aversions in mankind, are acknowledged to be disinterested too. . . . Is desire of, and delight in the happiness of another any more a diminution of self-love, than desire of and delight in the esteem of another? They are both equally desire of and delight in somewhat external to ourselves: either both or neither are so. The object of self-love is expressed in the term self: and every appetite of sense, and every particular affection of the heart, are equally interested or disinterested, because the objects of them all are equally self or somewhat else. . . .

Thus it appears, that there is no peculiar contrariety between self-love and benevolence; no greater competition between these, than between any other particular affections and self-love. . . .

The short of the matter is no more than this. Happiness consists in the gratification of certain affections, appetites, passions, with objects which are by nature adapted to them. Self-love may indeed set us on work to gratify these: but happiness or enjoyment has no immediate connexion with self-love, but arises from such gratification alone. Love of our neighbour is one of those affections. This, considered as a virtuous principle, is gratified by a consciousness of endeavouring to promote the good of others: but considered as a natural affection, its gratification consists in the actual accomplishment of this endeavour. Now, indulgence or gratification of this affection, whether in that consciousness, or this accomplishment, has the same respect to interest, as indulgence of any other affection; they equally proceed from, or do not proceed from, self-love; they equally include or equally exclude, this principle. Thus it appears, that "benevolence and the pursuit of public good have at least as great respect to self-love and the pursuit of private good, as any other particular passions, and their respective pursuits."

. . . There is indeed frequently an inconsistence, or interfering between self-love or private interest, and the several particular appetites, passions, affections, or the pursuits they lead to. But this competition or interfering is merely accidental, and happens much oftener between pride, revenge, sensual gratifications, and private interest, than between private interest and benevolence. For nothing is more common than to see men give themselves up to a passion or an affection to their known prejudice and ruin, and in direct contradiction to manifest and real interest, and the loudest calls of self-love: whereas the seeming competitions and interfering between benevolence and private interest, relate much more to the materials or means of enjoyment, than to enjoyment itself.

Notes

1. Suppose a man of learning to be writing a grave book upon human nature, and to show in several parts of it that he had an insight into the subject he was considering; amongst other things, the following one would require to be accounted for: the appearance of benevolence or good-will in men towards each other in the instances of natural relation, and in others. (Hobbes, *On Human Nature*, c. ix. § 17.) Cautious of being deceived with outward show, he retires within himself, to see exactly what that is in the mind of man from whence this appearance proceeds; and, upon deep reflection, asserts the principle in the mind to be only the love of power, and delight in the exercise of it. Would not everybody think here was a mistake of one word for another? That the philosopher was contemplating and accounting for some other human actions, some other behaviour of man to man? And could any one be thoroughly satisfied, that what is commonly called benevolence or good-will was really the affection meant, but only by being made to understand that this learned person had a general hypothesis, to which the appearance of good-will could no otherwise be reconciled? That what has this appearance, is often nothing but ambition; that delight in superiority often (suppose always) mixes itself with benevolence, only makes it more specious to call it ambition than hunger, of the two: but in reality that passion does no more account for the whole appearance of good-will than this appetite does. Is there not often the appearance of one man's wishing that good to another, which he knows himself unable to procure him; and rejoicing in it, though bestowed by a third person? And can love of power any way possibly come in to account for this desire or delight? Is there not often the appearance of men's distinguishing between two or more persons, preferring one before another, to do good to, in cases where love of power cannot in the least account for the distinction and preference? For this principle can no otherwise distinguish between objects, than as it is a greater instance and exertion of power to do good to one rather than to another. Again, suppose good-will in the mind of man to be nothing but delight in the exercise of power; men might indeed be restrained by distant and accidental considerations; but these restraints being removed, they would have a disposition to, and delight in mischief, as an exercise and proof of power: And this disposition and delight would arise from, or be the same principle in the mind, as a disposition to, and delight in charity. Thus cruelty, as distinct from envy and resentment, would be exactly the same in the mind of man as good-will: That one tends to the happiness, the other to the misery

of our fellow creatures, is, it seems, merely an accidental circumstance, which the mind has not the least regard to. These are the absurdities which even men of capacity run into, when they have occasion to belie their nature, and will perversely disclaim that image of God which was originally stamped upon it; the traces of which, however faint, are plainly discernible upon the mind of man.

If any person can in earnest doubt whether there be such a thing as good-will in one man towards another (for the question is not concerning either the degree or extensiveness of it, but concerning the affection itself), let it be observed, that *whether man be thus or otherwise constituted, what is the inward frame in this particular,* is a mere question of fact or natural history, not provable immediately by reason. It is therefore to be judged of and determined in the same way other facts or matters of natural history are: By appealing to the external senses, or inward perceptions, respectively, as the matter under consideration is cognizable by one or the other: By arguing from acknowledged facts and actions; for a great number of actions of the same kind in different circumstances, and respecting different objects, will prove, to certainty, what principles they do not, and, to the greatest probability, what principles they do proceed from: And, lastly, by the testimony of mankind. Now, that there is some degree of benevolence amongst men, may be as strongly and plainly proved in all these ways as it could possibly be proved, supposing there was this affection in our nature. And should any one think fit to assert, that resentment in the mind of man was absolutely nothing but reasonable concern for our own safety, the falsity of this, and what is the real nature of that passion, could be shown in no other ways than those in which it may be shown, that there is such a thing, in *some degree,* as *real* good-will in man towards man. It is sufficient that the seeds of it be implanted in our nature by God. There is, it is owned, much left for us to do upon our own heart and temper; to cultivate, to improve, to call it forth, to exercise it in a steady uniform manner. This is our work: this is Virtue and Religion.

2. If any desire to see this distinction and comparison made in a particular instance, the appetite and passion now mentioned may serve for one. Hunger is to be considered as a private appetite; because the end for which it was given us is the preservation of the individual. Desire of esteem is a public passion; because the end for which it was given us is to regulate our behaviour towards society. The respect which this has to private good is as remote as the respect that it has to public good; and the appetite is no more self-love, than the passion is benevolence. The object and end of the former is merely food; the object and end of the latter is merely esteem: but the latter can no more be gratified, without contributing to the good of society, than the former can be gratified, without contributing to the preservation of the individual.

TRUTH TELLING

Case Study—Italian Tax Mores

ARTHUR L. KELLY

The Italian federal corporate tax system has an official, legal tax structure and tax rates just as the U.S. system does. However, all similarity between the two systems ends there.

The Italian tax authorities assume that no Italian corporation would ever submit a tax return which shows its true profits but rather would submit a return which understates actual profits by anywhere between 30 percent and 70 percent; their assumption is essentially correct. Therefore, about six months after the annual deadline for filing corporate tax returns, the tax authorities issue to each corporation an "invitation to discuss" its tax return. The purpose of this notice is to arrange a personal meeting between them and representatives of the corporation. At this meeting, the Italian revenue service states the amount of corporate income tax which it believes is due. Its position is developed from both prior years' taxes actually paid and the current year's return; the amount which the tax authorities claim is due is generally several times that shown on the corporation's return for the current year. In short, the corporation's tax return and the revenue service's stated position are the opening offers for the several rounds of bargaining which will follow.

The Italian corporation is typically represented in such negotiations by its *commercialista*, a function which exists in Italian society for the primary purpose of negotiating corporate (and individual) tax payments with the Italian tax authorities; thus, the management of an Italian corporation seldom, if ever, has to meet directly with the Italian revenue service and probably has a minimum awareness of the details of the negotiation other than the final settlement.

Both the final settlement and the negotiation are extremely important to the corporation, the tax authorities, and the *commercialista*. Since the tax authorities assume that a corporation *always* earned more money this year than last year and *never* has a loss, the amount of the final settlement, i.e., corporate taxes which will actually be paid, becomes, for all practical purposes, the floor for the start of next year's negotiations. The final

This case—prepared by Arthur L. Kelly (president and chief operating officer of LaSalle Steel Company; formerly vice-president—International of A. T. Kearney, Inc.)—was presented at Loyola University of Chicago at a Mellon Foundation symposium entitled "Foundations of Corporate Responsibility to Society," April 1977. Printed with the permission of Arthur L. Kelly.

settlement also represents the amount of revenue the Italian government will collect in taxes to help finance the cost of running the country. However, since large amounts of money are involved and two individuals having vested personal interests are conducting the negotiations, the amount of *bustarella*—typically a substantial cash payment "requested" by the Italian revenue agent from the *commercialista*—usually determines whether the final settlement is closer to the corporation's original tax return or to the fiscal authority's original negotiating position.

Whatever *bustarella* is paid during the negotiation is usually included by the *commercialista* in his lump-sum fee "for services rendered" to his corporate client. If the final settlement is favorable to the corporation, and it is the *commercialista*'s job to see that it is, then the corporation is not likely to complain about the amount of its *commercialista*'s fee, nor will it ever know how much of that fee was represented by *bustarella* and how much remained for the *commercialista* as payment for his negotiating services. In any case, the tax authorities will recognize the full amount of the fee as a tax deductible expense on the corporation's tax return for the following year.

About ten years ago, a leading American bank opened a banking subsidiary in a major Italian city. At the end of its first year of operation, the bank was advised by its local lawyers and tax accountants, both from branches of U.S. companies, to file its tax return "Italian-style," i.e., to understate its actual profits by a significant amount. The American general manager of the bank, who was on his first overseas assignment, refused to do so both because he considered it dishonest and because it was inconsistent with the practices of his parent company in the United States.

About six months after filing its "American-style" tax return, the bank received an "invitation to discuss" notice from the Italian tax authorities. The bank's general manager consulted with his lawyers and tax accountants who suggested he hire a *commercialista*. He rejected this advice and instead wrote a letter to the Italian revenue service not only stating that his firm's corporate return was correct as filed but also requesting that they inform him of any specific items about which they had questions. His letter was never answered.

About sixty days after receiving the initial "invitation to discuss" notice, the bank received a formal tax assessment notice calling for a tax of approximately three times that shown on the bank's corporate tax return; the tax authorities simply assumed the bank's original return had been based on generally accepted Italian practices, and they reacted accordingly. The bank's general manager again consulted with his lawyers and tax accountants who again suggested he hire a *commercialista* who knew how to handle these matters. Upon learning that the *commercialista* would probably have to pay *bustarella* to his revenue service counterpart in order to reach a settlement, the general manager again chose to ignore his advisors. Instead, he responded by sending the Italian revenue service a check for the full amount of taxes due according to the bank's American-style tax return even though the due date for the payment was almost six months hence; he made no reference to the amount of corporate taxes shown on the formal tax assessment notice.

Ninety days after paying its taxes, the bank received a third notice from the fiscal authorities. This one contained the statement, "We have reviewed your corporate tax return for 19___ and have determined that [the lira equivalent of] $6,000,000 of interest paid on deposits is not an allowable expense for federal tax purposes. Accordingly, the total tax due for 19___ is lira _____ ." Since interest paid on deposits is any bank's largest single expense item, the new tax assessment was for an amount many times larger than that shown in the initial tax assessment notice and almost fifteen times larger than the taxes which the bank had actually paid.

The bank's general manager was understandably very upset. He immediately arranged an appointment to meet personally with the manager of the Italian revenue service's local office. Shortly after the start of their meeting, the conversation went something like this:

General manager: "You can't really be serious about disallowing interest paid on deposits as a tax deductible expense."

Italian
Revenue Service: "Perhaps. However, we thought it would get your attention. Now that you're here, shall we begin our negotiations?"[1]

Questions

1. Would you, as the general manager of the Italian subsidiary of an American corporation, "when in Rome" do as other Italian corporations do or adhere strictly to U.S. tax reporting practices?
2. Would you, as chief executive officer of a publicly traded corporation (subject to Securities Exchange Commission rules, regulations, and scrutiny), advise the general manager of your Italian subsidiary to follow common Italian tax reporting practices or to adhere to U.S. standards?

Note

1. For readers interested in what happened subsequently, the bank was forced to pay the taxes shown on the initial tax assessment, and the American manager was recalled to the United States and replaced.

Ethical Duties Towards Others: "Truthfulness"

IMMANUEL KANT

The exchange of our sentiments is the principal factor in social inter-course, and truth must be the guiding principle herein. Without truth social intercourse and conversation become valueless. We can only know what a man thinks if he tells us his thoughts, and when he undertakes to express them he must really do so, or else there can be no society of men. Fellowship is only the second condition of society, and a liar destroys fellowship. Lying makes it impossible to derive any benefit from conversa-tion. Liars are, therefore, held in general contempt. Man is inclined to be reserved and to pretend. . . . Man is reserved in order to conceal faults and shortcomings which he has; he pretends in order to make others attribute to him merits and virtues which he has not. Our proclivity to reserve and concealment is due to the will of Providence that the defects of which we are full should not be too obvious. Many of our propensities and peculiarities are objectionable to others, and if they became patent we should be foolish and hateful in their eyes. Moreover, the parading of these objectionable characteristics would so familiarize men with them that they would themselves acquire them. Therefore we arrange our conduct either to conceal our faults or to appear other than we are. We possess the art of simulation. In consequence, our inner weakness and error is revealed to the eyes of men only as an appearance of well-being, while we ourselves develop the habit of dispositions which are conducive to good conduct. No man in his true senses, therefore, is candid. Were man candid, were the request of Momus[1] to be complied with that Jupiter should place a mirror in each man's heart so that his disposition might be visible to all, man would have to be better constituted and to possess good principles. If all men were good there would be no need for any of us to be reserved; but since they are not, we have to keep the shutters closed. Every house keeps its dustbin in a place of its own. We do not press our friends to come into our water-closet, although they know that we have one just like themselves. Familiarity in such things is the ruin of good taste. In the same way we make no exhibition of our defects, but try to conceal them. We try to conceal our mistrust by affecting a courteous demeanour and so accus-tom ourselves to courtesy that at last it becomes a reality and we set a good example by it. If that were not so, if there were none who were better than we, we should become neglectful. Accordingly, the endeavour to appear good ultimately makes us really good. If all men were good, they could be candid, but as things are they cannot be. To be reserved is to be restrained in expressing one's mind. We can, of course, keep absolute silence. This is the readiest and most absolute method of reserve, but it is unsociable, and

From *Lectures on Ethics*, trans. Louis Infield (1930; rpt. New York: Harper & Row, 1963), pp. 224-35. Reprinted by permission of the publishers.

a silent man is not only unwanted in social circles but is also suspected; every one thinks him deep and disparaging, for if when asked for his opinion he remains silent people think that he must be taking the worst view or he would not be averse from expressing it. Silence, in fact, is always a treacherous ally, and therefore it is not even prudent to be completely reserved. Yet there is such a thing as prudent reserve, which requires not silence but careful deliberation; a man who is wisely reserved weighs his words carefully and speaks his mind about everything excepting only those things in regard to which he deems it wise to be reserved.

We must distinguish between reserve and secretiveness, which is something entirely different. There are matters about which one has no desire to speak and in regard to which reserve is easy. We are, for instance, not naturally tempted to speak about and to betray our own misdemeanours. Every one finds it easy to keep a reserve about some of his private affairs, but there are things about which it requires an effort to be silent. Secrets have a way of coming out, and strength is required to prevent ourselves betraying them. Secrets are always matters deposited with us by other people and they ought not to be placed at the disposal of third parties. But man has a great liking for conversation, and the telling of secrets adds much to the interest of conversation; a secret told is like a present given; how then are we to keep secrets? Men who are not very talkative as a rule keep secrets well, but good conversationalists, who are at the same time clever, keep them better. The former might be induced to betray something, but the latter's gift of repartee invariably enables them to invent on the spur of the moment something non-committal.

The person who is as silent as a mute goes to one extreme; the person who is loquacious goes to the opposite. Both tendencies are weaknesses. Men are liable to the first, women to the second. Someone has said that women are talkative because the training of infants is their special charge, and their talkativeness soon teaches a child to speak, because they can chatter to it all day long. If men had the care of the child, they would take much longer to learn to talk. However that may be, we dislike anyone who will not speak: he annoys us; his silence betrays his pride. On the other hand, loquaciousness in men is contemptible and contrary to the strength of the male. All this by the way; we shall now pass to more weighty matters.

If I announce my intention to tell what is in my mind, ought I knowingly to tell everything, or can I keep anything back? If I indicate that I mean to speak my mind, and instead of doing so make a false declaration, what I say is an untruth, a *falsiloquium*. But there can be *falsiloquium* even when people have no right to assume that we are expressing our thoughts. It is possible to deceive without making any statement whatever. I can make believe, make a demonstration from which others will draw the conclusion I want, though they have no right to expect that my action will express my real mind. In that case I have not lied to them, because I had not undertaken to express my mind. I may, for instance, wish people to think that I am off on a journey, and so I pack my luggage; people draw the conclusion I want them to draw; but others have no right to demand a declaration of my will from me.

. . . Again, I may make a false statement, *(falsiloquium)* when my purpose is to hide from another what is in my mind and when the latter can assume that such is my purpose, his own purpose being to make a wrong use of the truth. Thus, for instance, if my enemy takes me by the throat and asks where I keep my money, I need not tell him the truth, because he will abuse it; and my untruth is not a lie *(mendacium)* because the thief knows full well that I will not, if I can help it, tell him the truth and that he has no right to demand it of me. But let us assume that I really say to the fellow, who is fully aware that he has no right to demand it, because he is a swindler, that I will tell him the truth, and I do not, am I then a liar? He has deceived me and I deceive him in return; to him, as an individual, I have done no injustice and he cannot complain; but I am none the less a liar in that my conduct is an infringement of the rights of humanity. It follows that a *falsiloquium* can be a *mendacium*—a lie—especially when it contravenes the right of an individual. Although I do a man no injustice by lying to him when he has lied to me, yet I act against the right of mankind, since I set myself in opposition to the condition and means through which any human society is possible. If one country breaks the peace this does not justify the other in doing likewise in revenge, for if it did no peace would ever be secure. Even though a statement does not contravene any particular human right it is nevertheless a lie if it is contrary to the general right of mankind. If a man spreads false news, though he does no wrong to anyone in particular, he offends against mankind, because if such a practice were universal man's desire for knowledge would be frustrated. For, apart from speculation, there are only two ways in which I can increase my fund of knowledge, by experience or by what others tell me. My own experience must necessarily be limited, and if what others told me was false, I could not satisfy my craving for knowledge.

. . .Not every untruth is a lie; it is a lie only if I have expressly given the other to understand that I am willing to acquaint him with my thought. Every lie is objectionable and contemptible in that we purposely let people think that we are telling them our thoughts and do not do so. We have broken our pact and violated the right of mankind. But if we were to be at all times punctiliously truthful we might often become victims of the wickedness of others who were ready to abuse our truthfulness. If all men were well-intentioned it would not only be a duty not to lie, but no one would do so because there would be no point in it. But as men are malicious, it cannot be denied that to be punctiliously truthful is often dangerous. This has given rise to the conception of a white lie, the lie enforced upon us by necessity—a difficult point for moral philosophers. For if necessity is urged as an excuse it might be urged to justify stealing, cheating and killing, and the whole basis of morality goes by the board. Then, again, what is a case of necessity? Everyone will interpret it in his own way. And, as there is then no definite standard to judge by, the application of moral rules becomes uncertain. Consider, for example, the following case. A man who knows that I have money asks me: "Have you any money on you?" If I fail to reply, he will conclude that I have; if I reply in the affirmative he will take it from me; if I reply in the negative, I tell a lie. What am I to do? If force is used to extort a confession from me, if any confession is improperly used against me, and if I cannot save myself by maintaining silence, then my lie is a weapon of defence. The misuse of a declaration extorted by force justifies me in defending myself. For whether it is my money or a confession that is extorted makes no difference. The forcing of a statement from me under conditions which convince me that improper use would be made of it is the only case in which I can be justified in telling a white lie. But if a lie does no harm to anyone and no one's interests are affected by it, is it a lie? Certainly. I undertake to express my mind, and if I do not really do so, though my statement may not be to the prejudice of the particular individual to whom it is made, it is none the less *in praejudicium humanitatis.* Then, again, there are lies which cheat. To cheat is to make a lying promise, while a breach of faith is a true promise which is not kept. A lying promise is an insult to the person to whom it is made, and even if this is not always so, yet there is always something mean about it. If, for instance, I promise to send some one a bottle of wine, and afterwards make a joke of it, I really swindle him. It is true that he has no right to demand the present of me, but in Idea it is already a part of his own property.

   . . . If a man tries to extort the truth from us and we cannot tell it [to] him and at the same time do not wish to lie, we are justified in resorting to equivocation in order to reduce him to silence and put a stop to his questionings. If he is wise, he will leave it at that. But if we let it be understood that we are expressing our sentiments and we proceed to equivocate we are in a different case; for our listeners might then draw wrong conclusions from our statements and we should have deceived them. . . . But a lie is a lie, and is in itself intrinsically base whether it be told with good or bad intent. For formally a lie is always evil; though if it is evil materially as well, it is a much meaner thing. There are no lies which may not be the source of evil. A liar is a coward; he is a man who has recourse to lying because he is unable to help himself and gain his ends by any other means. But a stout-hearted man will love truth and will not recognize a *casus necessitatis.* All expedients which take us off our guard are thoroughly mean. Such are lying, assassination, and poisoning. To attack a man on the highway is less vile than to attempt to poison him. In the former case he can at least defend himself, but, as he must eat, he is defenceless against the poisoner. A flatterer is not always a liar; he is merely lacking in self-esteem; he has no scruple in reducing his own worth and raising that of another in order to gain something by it. But there exists a form of flattery which springs from kindness of heart. Some kind souls flatter people whom they hold in high esteem. There are thus two kinds of flattery, kindly and treacherous; the first is weak, while the second is mean. People who are not given to flattery are apt to be fault-finders.

   If a man is often the subject of conversation, he becomes a subject of criticism. If he is our friend, we ought not invariably to speak well of him or else we arouse jealousy and grudge against him; for people, knowing that he is only human, will not believe that he has only good qualities. We must, therefore, concede a little to the adverse criticism of our listeners and point out some of our friend's faults; if we allow him faults which are common and unessential, while extolling his merits, our friend cannot take it in ill part. Toadies are people who praise others in company in the hope of gain. Men are meant to form opinions regarding their fellows and to judge them. Nature has made us judges of our neighbours so that things which are false but are outside the scope of the established legal authority should be arraigned before the court of social opinion. Thus, if a man dishonours some one, the authorities do not punish him, but his fellows judge and punish him, though only so far as it is within their right to punish him and without doing violence to him. People shun him, and that is punishment enough. If that were not so, conduct not punished by the authorities would go altogether unpunished. What then is meant by the enjoinder that we ought not to judge others? As we are ignorant of their dispositions we cannot tell whether they are punishable before God or not, and we cannot, therefore, pass an adequate moral judgment upon them. The moral dispositions of others are for God to judge, but we are competent judges of our own. We cannot judge the inner core of morality: no man can do that; but we are competent to judge its outer manifestations. In matters of morality we are not judges of our fellows, but nature has given us the right to form judgments about others and she also has ordained that we should judge ourselves in accordance with judgments that others form about us. The man who turns a deaf ear to other people's opinion of him is base and reprehensible. There is nothing that happens in this world about which we ought not to form an opinion, and we show considerable subtlety in judging conduct. Those who judge our conduct with exactness are our best friends. Only friends can be quite candid and open with each other. But in judging a man a further question arises. In what terms are we to judge him? Must we pronounce him either good or evil? We must proceed from the assumption that humanity is lovable, and, particularly in regard to wickedness, we ought never to pronounce a verdict either of condemnation or of acquittal. We pronounce such a verdict whenever we judge from his conduct that a man deserves to be condemned or acquitted. But though we are entitled to form opinions about our fellows, we have no right to spy upon them. Everyone has a right to prevent others from watching and scrutinizing his actions. The spy arrogates to himself the right to watch the doings of strangers; no one ought to presume to do such a thing. If I see two people whispering to each other so as not to be heard, my inclination ought to be to get farther away so that no sound may reach my ears. Or if I am left alone in a room and I see a letter lying open on the table, it would be contemptible to try to read it; a right-thinking man would not do so; in fact, in order to avoid suspicion and distrust he will endeavour not to be left alone in a room where money is left lying about, and he will be averse from learning other people's secrets in order to avoid the risk of the suspicion that he has betrayed them; other people's secrets trouble him, for even between the most intimate of friends suspicion might arise. A man who will let his inclination or appetite drive him to deprive his friend of anything, of his fiancée, for instance, is contemptible beyond a doubt. If he can cherish a passion for my sweetheart, he can equally well cherish a passion for my purse. It is very mean to lie in wait and spy upon a friend, or on anyone else, and to elicit information about him from menials by lowering ourselves to the level of our inferiors, who will thereafter not forget to regard themselves as our equals. Whatever militates against frankness lowers the dignity of man. Insidious, underhand conduct uses means which strike at the roots of society because they make frankness impossible; it is far viler than violence; for against violence we can defend ourselves, and a violent man who spurns meanness can be tamed to goodness, but the mean rogue, who has not the courage to come out into the open with his roguery, is devoid of every vestige of nobility of character. For that reason a wife who attempts to poison her husband in England is burnt at the stake, for if such conduct spread, no man would be safe from his wife.

As I am not entitled to spy upon my neighbour, I am equally not entitled to point out his faults to him; and even if he should ask me to do so he would feel hurt if I complied. He knows his faults better than I, he knows that he has them, but he likes to believe that I have not noticed them, and if I tell him of them he realizes that I have. To say, therefore, that friends ought to point out each other's faults, is not sound advice. My friend may know better than I whether my gait or deportment is proper or not, but if I will only examine myself, who can know me better than I can know myself? To point out his faults to a friend is sheer impertinence; and once fault finding begins between friends their friendship will not last long. We must turn a blind eye to the faults of others, lest they conclude that they have lost our respect and we lose theirs. Only if placed in positions of authority over others should we point out to them their defects. Thus a husband is entitled to teach and correct his wife, but his corrections must be well-intentioned and kindly and must be dominated by respect, for if they be prompted only by displeasure they result in mere blame and bitterness. If we must blame, we must temper the blame with a sweetening of love, good-will, and respect. Nothing else will avail to bring about improvement.

Note

1. CF. *Babrii fabulae Aesopeae,* ed. O. Cousins, 1897, Fable 59, p. 54.

Is Business Bluffing Ethical?

ALBERT Z. CARR

A respected businessman with whom I discussed the theme of this article remarked with some heat, "You mean to say you're going to encourage men to bluff? Why, bluffing is nothing more than a form of lying! You're advising them to lie!"

I agreed that the basis of private morality is a respect for truth and that the closer a businessman comes to the truth, the more he deserves respect. At the same time, I suggested that most bluffing in business might be regarded simply as game strategy—much like bluffing in poker, which does not reflect on the morality of the bluffer.

I quoted Henry Taylor, the British statesman who pointed out that "falsehood ceases to be falsehood when it is understood on all sides that the truth is not expected to be spoken"—an exact description of bluffing in poker, diplomacy, and business. I cited the analogy of the criminal court, where the criminal is not expected to tell the truth when he pleads "not guilty." Everyone from the judge down takes it for granted that the job of the defendant's attorney is to get his client off, not to reveal the truth; and this is considered ethical practice. I mentioned Representative Omar Burleson, the Democrat from Texas, who was quoted as saying, in regard to the ethics of Congress, "Ethics is a barrel of worms"[1]—a pungent summing up of the problem of deciding who is ethical in politics.

I reminded my friend that millions of businessmen feel constrained every day to say *yes* to their bosses when they secretly believe *no* and that this is generally accepted as permissible strategy when the alternative might be the loss of a job. The essential point, I said, is that the ethics of business are game ethics, different from the ethics of religion.

He remained unconvinced. Referring to the company of which he is president, he declared: "Maybe that's good enough for some businessmen, but I can tell you that we pride ourselves on our ethics. In 30 years not one customer has ever questioned my word or asked to check our figures. We're loyal to our customers and fair to our suppliers. I regard my handshake on a deal as a contract. I've never entered into price-fixing schemes with my competitors. I've never allowed my salesmen to spread injurious rumors about other companies. Our union contract is the best in our industry. And, if I do say so myself, our ethical standards are of the highest!"

He really was saying, without realizing it, that he was living up to the ethical standards of the business game—which are a far cry from those of private life. Like a gentlemanly poker player, he did not play in cahoots with others at the table, try to smear their reputations, or hold back chips he owed them.

But this same fine man, at that very time, was allowing one of his products to be advertised in a way that made it sound a great deal better than it actually was. Another item in his product line was notorious among dealers for its "built-in obsolescence." He was holding back from the market a much-improved product because he did not want it to interfere with sales of the inferior item it would have replaced. He had joined with certain of his competitors in hiring a lobbyist to push a state legislature, by methods that he preferred not to know too much about, into amending a bill then being enacted.

In his view these things had nothing to do with ethics; they were merely normal business practice. He himself undoubtedly avoided outright falsehoods—never lied in so many words. But the entire organization that he ruled was deeply involved in numerous strategies of deception.

PRESSURE TO DECEIVE

Most executives from time to time are almost compelled, in the interests of their companies or themselves, to practice some form of deception when negotiating with customers, dealers, labor unions, government officials, or even other departments of their companies. By conscious misstatements, concealment of pertinent facts, or exaggeration—in short, by bluffing—they seek to persuade others to agree with them. I think it is fair to say that if the individual executive refuses to bluff from time to time—if he feels obligated to tell the truth, the whole truth, and nothing but the truth—he is ignoring opportunities permitted under the rules and is at a heavy disadvantage in his business dealings.

But here and there a businessman is unable to reconcile himself to the bluff in which he plays a part. His conscience, perhaps spurred by religious idealism, troubles him. He feels guilty; he may develop an ulcer or a nervous tic. Before any executive can make profitable use of the strategy of the bluff, he needs to make sure that in bluffing he will not lose self-respect or become emotionally disturbed. If he is to reconcile personal integrity and high standards of honesty with the practical requirements of business, he must feel that his bluffs are ethically justified. The justification rests on the fact that business, as practiced by individuals as well as by corporations, has the impersonal character of a game—a game that demands both special strategy and an understanding of its special ethics.

The game is played at all levels of corporate life, from the highest to the lowest. At the very instant that a man decides to enter business, he may be forced into a game situation, as is shown by the recent experience of a Cornell honor graduate who applied for a job with a large company:

• This applicant was given a psychological test which included the statement, "Of the following magazines, check any that you have read either regularly or from time to time, and double-check those which interest you most. *Reader's Digest, Time, Fortune, Saturday Evening Post, The New Republic, Life, Look, Ramparts, Newsweek, Business Week, U.S. News & World Report, The Nation, Playboy, Esquire, Harper's, Sports Illustrated.*"

His tastes in reading were broad, and at one time or another he had
read almost all of these magazines. He was a subscriber to *The New
Republic,* an enthusiast for *Ramparts,* and an avid student of the pictures in
Playboy. He was not sure whether his interest in *Playboy* would be held
against him, but he had a shrewd suspicion that if he confessed to an
interest in *Ramparts* and *The New Republic,* he would be thought a liberal, a
radical, or at least an intellectual, and his chances of getting the job, which
he needed, would greatly diminish. He therefore checked five of the
more conservative magazines. Apparently it was a sound decision, for he
got the job.

He had made a game player's decision, consistent with business ethics.

A similar case is that of a magazine space salesman who, owing to a
merger, suddenly found himself out of a job:

• This man was 58, and, in spite of a good record, his chance of getting
a job elsewhere in a business where youth is favored in hiring practice was
not good. He was a vigorous, healthy man, and only a considerable
amount of gray in his hair suggested his age. Before beginning his job
search he touched up his hair with a black dye to confine the gray to his
temples. He knew that the truth about his age might well come out in time,
but he calculated that he could deal with that situation when it arose. He
and his wife decided that he could easily pass for 45, and he so stated his
age on his résumé.

This was a lie; yet within the accepted rules of the business game, no
moral culpability attaches to it.

THE POKER ANALOGY

We can learn a good deal about the nature of business by comparing it
with poker. While both have a large element of chance, in the long run the
winner is the man who plays with steady skill. In both games ultimate
victory requires intimate knowledge of the rules, insight into the psychology of the other players, a bold front, a considerable amount of
self-discipline, and the ability to respond swiftly and effectively to
opportunities provided by chance.

No one expects poker to be played on the ethical principles preached in
churches. In poker it is right and proper to bluff a friend out of the
rewards of being dealt a good hand. A player feels no more than a slight
twinge of sympathy, if that, when—with nothing better than a single ace in
his hand—he strips a heavy loser, who holds a pair, of the rest of his chips.
It was up to the other fellow to protect himself. In the words of an
excellent poker player, former President Harry Truman, "If you can't
stand the heat, stay out of the kitchen." If one shows mercy to a loser in
poker, it is a personal gesture, divorced from the rules of the game.

Poker has its special ethics, and here I am not referring to rules against
cheating. The man who keeps an ace up his sleeve or who marks the cards
is more than unethical; he is a crook, and can be punished as such—kicked
out of the game or, in the Old West, shot.

In contrast to the cheat, the unethical poker player is one who, while abiding by the letter of the rules, finds ways to put the other players at an unfair disadvantage. Perhaps he unnerves them with loud talk. Or he tries to get them drunk. Or he plays in cahoots with someone else at the table. Ethical poker players frown on such tactics.

Poker's own brand of ethics is different from the ethical ideals of civilized human relationships. The game calls for distrust of the other fellow. It ignores the claim of friendship. Cunning deception and concealment of one's strength and intentions, not kindness and openheartedness, are vital in poker. No one thinks any the worse of poker on that account. And no one should think any the worse of the game of business because its standards of right and wrong differ from the prevailing traditions of morality in our society. . . .

'WE DON'T MAKE THE LAWS'

Wherever we turn in business, we can perceive the sharp distinction between its ethical standards and those of the churches. Newspapers abound with sensational stories growing out of this distinction:

• We read one day that Senator Philip A. Hart of Michigan has attacked food processors for deceptive packaging of numerous products.[2]

• The next day there is a Congressional to-do over Ralph Nader's book, *Unsafe At Any Speed,* which demonstrates that automobile companies for years have neglected the safety of car-owning families.[3]

• Then another Senator, Lee Metcalf of Montana, and journalist Vic Reinemer show in their book, *Overcharge,* the methods by which utility companies elude regulating government bodies to extract unduly large payments from users of electricity.[4]

These are merely dramatic instances of a prevailing condition; there is hardly a major industry at which a similar attack could not be aimed. Critics of business regard such behavior as unethical, but the companies concerned know that they are merely playing the business game.

Among the most respected of our business institutions are the insurance companies. A group of insurance executives meeting recently in New England was startled when their guest speaker, social critic Daniel Patrick Moynihan, roundly berated them for "unethical" practices. They had been guilty, Moynihan alleged, of using outdated actuarial tables to obtain unfairly high premiums. They habitually delayed the hearings of lawsuits against them in order to tire out the plaintiffs and win cheap settlements. In their employment policies they used ingenious devices to discriminate against certain minority groups.[5]

It was difficult for the audience to deny the validity of these charges. But these men were business game players. Their reaction to Moynihan's attack was much the same as that of the automobile manufacturers to Nader, of the utilities to Senator Metcalf, and of the food processors to Senator Hart. If the laws governing their businesses change, or if public opinion becomes clamorous, they will make the necessary adjustments.

But morally they have in their view done nothing wrong. As long as they comply with the letter of the law, they are within their rights to operate their businesses as they see fit.

The small business is in the same position as the great corporation in this respect. For example:

• In 1967 a key manufacturer was accused of providing master keys for automobiles to mail-order customers, although it was obvious that some of the purchasers might be automobile thieves. His defense was plain and straightforward. If there was nothing in the law to prevent him from selling his keys to anyone who ordered them, it was not up to him to inquire as to his customers' motives. Why was it any worse, he insisted, for him to sell car keys by mail, than for mail-order houses to sell guns that might be used for murder? Until the law was changed, the key manufacturer could regard himself as being just as ethical as any other businessman by the rules of the business game.[6]

Violations of the ethical ideals of society are common in business, but they are not necessarily violations of business principles. Each year the Federal Trade Commission orders hundreds of companies, many of them of the first magnitude, to "cease and desist" from practices which, judged by ordinary standards, are of questionable morality but which are stoutly defended by the companies concerned.

In one case, a firm manufacturing a well-known mouthwash was accused of using a cheap form of alcohol possibly deleterious to health. The company's chief executive, after testifying in Washington, made this comment privately:

"We broke no law. We're in a highly competitive industry. If we're going to stay in business, we have to look for profit wherever the law permits. We don't make the laws. We obey them. Then why do we have to put up with this 'holier than thou' talk about ethics? It's sheer hypocrisy. We're not in business to promote ethics. Look at the cigarette companies, for God's sake! If the ethics aren't embodied in the laws by the men who made them, you can't expect businessmen to fill the lack. Why, a sudden submission to Christian ethics by businessmen would bring about the greatest economic upheaval in history!"

It may be noted that the government failed to prove its case against him.

CAST ILLUSIONS ASIDE

Talk about ethics by businessmen is often a thin decorative coating over the hard realities of the game:

• Once I listened to a speech by a young executive who pointed to a new industry code as proof that his company and its competitors were deeply aware of their responsibilities to society. It was a code of ethics, he said. The industry was going to police itself, to dissuade constituent companies from wrongdoing. His eyes shone with conviction and enthusiasm.

The same day there was a meeting in a hotel room where the industry's top executives met with the "czar" who was to administer the new code, a man of high repute. No one who was present could doubt their common attitude. In their eyes the code was designed primarily to forestall a move by the federal government to impose stern restrictions on the industry. They felt that the code would hamper them a good deal less than new federal laws would. It was, in other words, conceived as a protection for the industry, not for the public.

The young executive accepted the surface explanation of the code; these leaders, all experienced game players, did not deceive themselves for a moment about its purpose.

The illusion that business can afford to be guided by ethics as conceived in private life is often fostered by speeches and articles containing such phrases as, "It pays to be ethical," or, "Sound ethics is good business." Actually this is not an ethical position at all; it is a self-serving calculation in disguise. The speaker is really saying that in the long run a company can make more money if it does not antagonize competitors, suppliers, employees, and customers by squeezing them too hard. He is saying that oversharp policies reduce ultimate gains. That is true, but it has nothing to do with ethics. The underlying attitude is much like that in the familiar story of the shopkeeper who finds an extra $20 bill in the cash register, debates with himself the ethical problem—should he tell his partner?—and finally decides to share the money because the gesture will give him an edge over the s.o.b. the next time they quarrel.

I think it is fair to sum up the prevailing attitude of businessmen on ethics as follows:

We live in what is probably the most competitive of the world's civilized societies. Our customs encourage a high degree of aggression in the individual's striving for success. Business is our main area of competition, and it has been ritualized into a game of strategy. The basic rules of the game have been set by the government, which attempts to detect and punish business frauds. But as long as a company does not transgress the rules of the game set by law, it has the legal right to shape its strategy without reference to anything but its profits. If it takes a long-term view of its profits, it will preserve amicable relations, so far as possible, with those with whom it deals. A wise businessman will not seek advantage to the point where he generates dangerous hostility among employees, competitors, customers, government, or the public at large. But decisions in this area are, in the final test, decisions of strategy, not of ethics.

. . . If a man plans to make a seat in the business game, he owes it to himself to master the principles by which the game is played, including its special ethical outlook. He can then hardly fail to recognize that an occasional bluff may well be justified in terms of the game's ethics and warranted in terms of economic necessity. Once he clears his mind on this point, he is in a good position to match his strategy against that of the other players. He can then determine objectively whether a bluff in a given situation has a good chance of succeeding and can decide when and how to bluff, without a feeling of ethical transgression.

To be a winner, a man must play to win. This does not mean that he must be ruthless, cruel, harsh, or treacherous. On the contrary, the better his reputation for integrity, honesty, and decency, the better his chances of victory will be in the long run. But from time to time every businessman, like every poker player, is offered a choice between certain loss or bluffing within the legal rules of the game. If he is not resigned to losing, if he wants to rise in his company and industry, then in such a crisis he will bluff—and bluff hard.

Every now and then one meets a successful businessman who has conveniently forgotten the small or large deceptions that he practiced on his way to fortune. "God gave me my money," old John D. Rockefeller once piously told a Sunday school class. It would be a rare tycoon in our time who would risk the horse laugh with which such a remark would be greeted.

In the last third of the twentieth century even children are aware that if a man has become prosperous in business, he has sometimes departed from the strict truth in order to overcome obstacles or has practiced the more subtle deceptions of the half-truth or the misleading omission. Whatever the form of the bluff, it is an integral part of the game, and the executive who does not master its techniques is not likely to accumulate much money or power.

Notes

1. *The New York Times,* March 9, 1967.
2. *The New York Times,* November 21, 1966.
3. New York, Grossman Publishers, Inc., 1965.
4. New York, David McKay Company, Inc., 1967.
5. *The New York Times,* January 17, 1967.
6. Cited by Ralph Nader in "Business Crime," *The New Republic,* July 1, 1967, p. 7.

The Executive's Conscience

CLARENCE B. RANDALL

It must be admitted . . . that not all ethical questions in business can be sharply divided between black and white. Often there is a gray area within which honorable men may differ. When the question falls in that category the junior may properly accept the judgment of his superior, and carry

From *Harvard Business Review,* Jan.-Feb. 1968; from *The Executive in Transition* by Clarence B. Randall (New York: McGraw-Hill Book Company, 1967), pp. 137–38. Reprinted by permission of McGraw-Hill Book Company.

out his instruction. But where the action required is unqualifiedly repugnant to his own conscience he has no alternative. He must quit rather than go ahead. The consequences may be devastating in his own life. The threat to his financial security, and to the welfare of his family, may be almost beyond his power to cope with. Nevertheless the answer is clear. He must walk off the job and preserve his honor, no matter what the sacrifice.

The key . . . is the executive's personal sensitivity to ethical problems. Few men who are able and mature enough to carry significant responsibility in the business world transgress the general code of morality with the conscious intention of doing wrong. The difficulty is that the warning bell of their conscience does not ring as they take their decisions. They plunge into action without pausing to reflect upon the moral implications of the course to which they are committing themselves and their corporations. They have been carefully trained in engineering, cost accounting, pricing, human relations, and other phases of management, but not in ethics.

What industry needs to offset the growing atmosphere of public suspicion is new emphasis on conscience, new discussion of ethical problems at all levels, and greater awareness of the importance of moral considerations in the formation of management policy.

Showdown on Business Bluffing

TIMOTHY B. BLODGETT

FOREWORD

Few articles that HBR [*Harvard Business Review*] has published have aroused a response as great and as vociferous as Albert Z. Carr's "Is Business Bluffing Ethical?" (January-February 1968). Mr. Carr contended that business's ethical standards differ from society's and that, in business, deception is accepted and indeed necessary if one is to succeed. He likened this "game strategy" of the businessman to the poker player's bluffing. Quoting liberally from letters, Mr. Blodgett, Associate Editor of HBR, reports readers' reactions. . . .

> This article presents a very realistic and accurate account of the standards used in business decisions, at least for those companies and individuals who are subject to competitive pressures and therefore feel that they must take every legally permissible advantage in order to survive and grow.

> Fortunately, Mr. Carr's view does not appear to be the prevailing view, except, perhaps, along the few remaining frontiers of civilization, such as the upper Amazon.

These two quotations—the first from a letter written by Rawson L. Wood, Chairman of the Board of Arwood Corporation, Rockleigh, New Jersey, and the second from a letter by Leon P. Chemlen, who is on the marketing staff of Dynamics Research Corporation, Stoneham, Massachusetts—distill the contrasting reactions of HBR readers to Mr. Carr's article.

Of the many readers who responded, more than twice as many are critical of the article as are favorable to it. Many others seem uncertain or are noncommittal about Mr. Carr's position, devoting themselves mainly to discussion of the state of business ethics today.

The tone of the letters ranges from enthusiastic to shocked. Interestingly, a couple of the most favorable letters have come from persons in the advertising business, an endeavor not noted for understatement about the virtues and powers of goods being marketed.

A few correspondents question HBR's motives in publishing the article. One indignant writer gives this title to a lengthy dissertation: "Is the Article on Business Bluffing Ethical?" Another even questions the existence of "A. Z. Carr" and suggests that the Editors may have been playing an early April Fool's joke.

But most readers have been as serious and thoughtful in answering Mr. Carr as he was in presenting his view of the way things are.

'NO MEDALS FOR HONESTY'

Was Mr. Carr "telling it like it is" (in the current expression)? One reader who thinks so is Richard O. Lundquist, an underwriter in Washington, D.C., with The Equitable Life Assurance Society of the United States. He cites this case:

"A young manager was upset because his boss had told a prospective salesman, 'The minimum income a new man earned with us last year was $8,900.' That was about $2,000 from the truth. When the senior manager was questioned about this, he answered, 'Well, that's not important. We are just trying to attract him into the business.' "

Mr. Lundquist mentions two similar examples and then concludes:

"What is universal about these examples is that these managers, each functioning on a different corporate level, are concerned with one thing—*getting the job done.* Most companies give numerous awards for achievement and accomplishment, for sales, for growth, for longevity and loyalty; but there are no medals in the business world for honesty, compassion, or truthfulness." . . .

A MATTER OF 'MUTUAL TRUST'

Many readers have given careful thought to refutation of Mr. Carr's contention that deception is an integral part of the business "game." I shall try to present their views fairly by quoting representative selections from letters.

Some readers take particular exception to Mr. Carr's claim that deception succeeds:

"All of us in business know that 'playing the game' yields only short-term rewards. We'll admit our faults, but we'll not endorse them as part of our philosophy. To do so would bring the house of business down on itself." (John Valiant, New Product Manager, William H. Rorer, Inc., Fort Washington, Pennsylvania)

"My own experience in dealing with hundreds of companies has led me to believe that sharp dealing or the slightest prevarication on the part of a businessman usually results in informal excommunication to the back alleys of the business world or to obscurity." (Mark Rollinson, President, Greater Washington Industrial Investments, Inc., Washington, D.C.)

"I think a better strategy in business is to work hard, be honest, and be smarter than anyone else." (L.D. Barre, Vice President—Marketing, RTE Corporation, Waukesha, Wisconsin) . . .

Mr. Carr cited as an accurate description of "bluffing" in business and poker this utterance of a British statesman: "Falsehood ceases to be falsehood when it is understood on all sides that the truth is not expected to be spoken." This has moved Alan B. Potter, Vice President of the Dye Division (Dorval, Quebec) of Ciba Company Limited, to comment:

"But it is not at all the case that businessmen do not expect the truth to be spoken. On the contrary, almost all day-to-day business is conducted verbally or on the basis of nonlegal documents. The economic system would collapse without mutual trust on a practically universal scale among business executives.

"Mr. Carr apparently assumes that 'not telling the whole truth' is synonymous with 'telling a lie.' Businessmen know that it would be ridiculous to expect anything more than a straight answer to a straight question. Moreover, it is perfectly acceptable to withhold the truth by saying, 'I am sorry, I am not willing to discuss that subject.' There are many reasons of self-interest or discretion which would justify a refusal to answer any question, and businessmen do not expect that those reasons need be given."

Another recurrent theme in the letters is an insistence that business's ethics cannot be separated from those of society. Typical is the response of J. Douglas McConnell, Marketing Economist at Stanford Research Institute and Lecturer at San Francisco State College:

"Mr. Carr's argument would be sound if business functioned in a vacuum. Because business is an integral part of society, however, it will always be judged by societal criteria.

"It is inevitable that the ethics of business and those of society will always have a considerable degree of commonality. For one thing, business as a group is large and powerful in our society, and many of its values are accepted by society at large. Business's goal is to function at a profit, and to a considerable extent making money is also a value of society.

"Another point of commonality is that most people are members of several groups. The business executive is likely to be a veteran, a member of a school or college board, a member of a local church, or a committee-man for the Community Chest; and he and his family are also consumers. The norms of these other groups carry over to his business life to a greater or lesser extent.

"We live in a highly complex world, with diverse pressures and in-terests, where simple answers seldom fit simple questions such as 'Is business bluffing ethical?' Business's principal role is that of the wealth-generating group in society—and its ethics will always reflect this. How-ever, the other groups in society—such as education, health services, religion, the military, government, and the consumer—will occasionally be in conflict with these ethics, and there will be (as there is now) pressure to bring business ethics more into conformity with those of society." . . .

Several readers object to Mr. Carr's poker analogy on the ground that it oversimplifies the process of decision making and the nature of personal relationships in business. One of these correspondents is Henry Johnson, President of The Johnson Wire Works Limited of Montreal. After ac-knowledging that "there is a substantial element of truth" in likening business to a game in which "duplicity" is an accepted practice, he goes on:

"But the fact is that the businessman is engaged in many games at the same time, with vastly differing rules. At one end of the spectrum, he may be engaged in a labor negotiation where the rules are well known and the protestations of either side are never seriously regarded. At the other pole, the businessman is dealing with an individual employee or cus-tomer. These people are not playing games. Anything but straight-forward dealing should indeed cause the businessman some guilty in-somnia.

"In between lie the ethical question marks, and I do not think we can avoid them as easily as Mr. Carr implies, simply by reason of the fact that we are 'in the office.' Each matter that arises poses its own question: 'How much gamesmanship, if any, can I use here?"

"But it is surely the function of what we call conscience to extend the area where truth is used, and to 'play games' only on recognized playing fields."

Implicit or stated in many letters is the idea that Mr. Carr *approved* of what he called "game strategy" (a notion to which he vigorously objects). . . . The stricture of F. W. Henrici, Systems Analyst for Schering Corpo-ration, Bloomfield, New Jersey, is typical:

"What really bothers me is Mr. Carr's attempt to give businessmen something with which to salve their consciences. Almost everyone knows that one doesn't reach a position of power in business, or even in the church, without a little hanky-panky. So be it. But if you lust for power, or money, or success, so that you are willing to put up with hanky-panky, then at least suffer those pangs of conscience. Know that other men scorn you in some small way for the things you condone.

"Mr. Carr doesn't make his case for hanky-panky, either. Business is not a game where lying is right and proper. His only justification is that you must do it because everybody else does. Using that philosophy, one can justify anything from slave trading to today's Mafia-type of business ethics. And the fact that there is no law against it doesn't make something right, either. Your conscience will tell you whether it is right or not."

Robert S. Hower, a salesman in York, Pennsylvania, for the National Gypsum Company, takes Mr. Carr to task with this reflection:

"My advice to Mr. Carr would be to read Aristotle again, and he will find that Aristotle was correct in his observation that much of our being is formed by personal, self-imposed discipline. If we permit ourselves to be weak in one area, it flows into our personality in other areas. Man cannot make excuses in one area by saying this is a game, and then become a strong, moral creature in other things—we just were not made that way."
. . .

WHAT CAN BE DONE?

So if we have a problem—whether it can be defined in a broad frame of reference or only in the narrower one of business—what can we do about it? Graham R. Briggs, Executive Assistant to the First Vice President of Abex Corporation, New York City, offers this reflection:

"Business, like society, operates within a set of norms of acceptable behavior. A radical departure from these norms in either direction, toward idealism or toward complete immorality, spells trouble at least and ruin at worst. Moreover, it seems to me to be true that acceptable behavior in business includes much that would be unacceptable in one's personal life.

"However, Mr. Carr sidesteps the question of where an individual should draw the line between acceptable and immoral action. Every businessman is tempted to be just a little less moral than his competitors—not enough to be operating right outside the business 'moral code,' but enough to secure a competitive edge.

"Then how can the inevitable gradual decline of business morals to an eventual state of complete anarchy be prevented? The law is insufficient protection against this; it can cover only the most flagrant violations, it cannot change as quickly as circumstances nowadays require, and it is too easily circumvented by those who are quick-witted and prepared to take a risk.

"The only guard against a gradual decline in morals is the ideals of each businessman. All of us have (or if we do not, something is wrong with us) an ideal of how business should be conducted; how we would like to be able to behave, or, rather, how we wish we could rely on other businessmen to act. It is usually impossible to adhere to this ideal in practice, since we live in an imperfect world, but we should always have this ideal in mind, be prepared to make some sacrifices for its sake, and be conscious of what we are doing when we depart from it.

"Only in this way can we apply 'upward' pressure on business morality, which, if practiced by a sufficient number of businessmen, will tend over time to raise the level of business values closer to the ideal. Most of us would like to be able to trust our fellow businessmen more than we can now. I see no other way of ever achieving this result."

MR. CARR COMMENTS

I was especially struck by the high charge of emotion, ranging from fury to enthusiasm, in the letters received by HBR, as well as in a number of letters and even phone calls that have come directly to me. It may be significant that, of the *company heads* responding, a large majority ruefully agree that the state of business ethics portrayed in the article was accurate. The letters strongly suggest that the men who have "made it" are more willing to face the realities of the problem than are those farther down the ladder.

I have the distinct impression that many of HBR's more outraged respondents (one or two even burst into vituperative verse!) have not yet fully sensed the nature of the strategic questions confronting the men responsible for the profitability and growth of their companies.

Perhaps I can assuage some of the pain the article seems to have caused by listing below the main criticisms leveled against it, and appending a few comments of my own.

"Business is too important to be regarded as a game." This misses the point of the article, which is that—whether or not business ought to be regarded and conducted as a game—it is so regarded and conducted by many of its practitioners, including executives of great importance and high reputation. A businessman is certainly entitled to refuse to employ game strategy himself, but he may be at a severe disadvantage if he does not recognize that it is being used by others.

"The comparison to poker is unfair and inaccurate." Like all useful analogies, this one was intended to throw light on the subject, not to provide an exact parallel. The honorable poker player who, within the laws of the game, takes pleasure in outsmarting the other fellow has many a counterpart in the paneled offices of the corporate hierarchies. Again, it may be noted that there is no compulsion for any executive to mislead others, any more than there is for the poker player to bluff. The option is his; most players exercise it at one time or another.

"The article condones unethical practices." This complaint seems to me extraordinary. More than once, the article stresses the values of truth-telling and integrity in business, where, certainly, there are as many high-minded men as one will find in most walks of life. My point is that, given the prevailing ethical standards of business, an executive who accepts those standards and operates accordingly is guilty of nothing worse than conformity; he is merely playing the game according to the rules and the customs of society.

"A man cannot separate the ethics of his business life from the ethics of his home life." Over the long run, that is probably true. What happens is that, in too many instances, the ethical outlook of business comes to dominate in the home as well. Perhaps that accounts in part for the notorious instability of the middle-class home in our society, and the increasing revolt of the young against the corporate establishment. It may also explain why so many wives of businessmen have, like their husbands, been conscience-washed into undiscriminating acceptance of corporation policies.

58

"The article is one-sided and extreme in its description of what goes on in business." This I must deny. I regard the article as mild, objective, and, if anything, overdiscreet. If it had incorporated all the facts in my files, it would have curled HBR readers' hair. And I am talking now not about violations of law, but of decisions within the realm of business ethics—the so-called "gray area," where complexity so often provides the executive with a rationalization for doing what serves his interests.

"The article does not point out that if business fails to raise the moral level of its practices, it invites eventual reprisals from the public and the government." This thought was not within the scope of the article, but I could not agree with it more. As the article plainly conveys, sound long-range business strategy and ethical considerations are usually served by the same policy.

Beyond Fraud and Deception: The Moral Uses of Advertising

BURTON M. LEISER

Advertising is neither intrinsically good nor intrinsically evil, though one might be inclined to conclude that it is intrinsically tasteless. Practitioners of the art of advertising are evidently either unaware of the moral imperatives that relate to their profession or are so dedicated to the achievement of "success"—that is, more sales and higher profits—that all other considerations are shunted aside.

Plato's proposition that no one would ever do what he knows is wrong is dubious at best. However that may be, it appears that some of the most elementary distinctions that Plato drew more than two thousand years ago are unknown to some otherwise sophisticated businessmen. At a recent conference on business ethics, the founder and president of a high technology multinational corporation explained that a corporation is "a group of persons whose purpose is to provide goods and services to those who need them." This is surely a most commendable goal toward which to bend one's efforts. He then went on to explain that *needs* are whatever the public will buy in the marketplace. Now if people need whatever they buy, then a corporation is merely fulfilling its purpose if it sells those goods and services to them. And any corporation that helps a person acquire what he or she needs would be doing what anyone ought morally to do, for it is *prima facie* right for one person to strive to meet the needs of another

This paper was originally presented at the Loyola University of Chicago Mellon Foundation Lecture Series: "Socio-Ethical Issues in Business," February 6, 1978. Reprinted by permission of the author. All rights reserved.

whenever he can reasonably do so. But people *don't* always need what they buy. From the fact that a person buys a given item, it does not necessarily follow that he *needs* that item, though it is reasonable to conclude that he *wants* or *desires* it. Men walking down Broadway may be seduced into purchasing the services of a prostitute or a supply of heroin or cocaine. Although they clearly *desire* those goods or services when they pay for them, they can be said to *need* them only in the most extended sense of that word. In that same extended sense, purchasers of slaves in the eighteenth century needed the slaves they purchased. I trust that no one would argue that the slave traders performed a valuable or morally commendable service. By the same token, there are corporations that are failing to meet the most elementary standards of morality, though they are surely catering to their customers' desires (or creating those desires) and selling them products and services.

People need far more than such elementary necessities of life as food, drink, clothing, and shelter. The executive to whom I referred earlier has developed a remarkable plastic tube which can be implanted in the leg of a person whose circulation has been obstructed and serve as an artificial blood vessel, thus saving the leg from being amputated. People afflicted by grave circulatory disorders *need* that product, and he has performed a valuable service by inventing it and making it available to them. Unlike many advertisers who create the illusion of need in order to sell products that people would never seek on their own initiative if they were not seduced into purchasing them, he met a genuine need and has only to inform the right people that it exists in order to sell it.* An advertisement informing the public of such a life-saving product would perform a valuable service, for it might save the lives or limbs of persons who might otherwise undergo needless suffering. Like the insurance ad that induced a young man to purchase a policy just a few days before his untimely death, thus assuring his widow and small children of a modest income, such an advertisement would help to reduce the amount of suffering in the world and add to the sum of human happiness. By any utilitarian standard, it would clearly be moral.

Suppose, however (contrary to the facts), that the manufacturer of the artificial blood vessel decided to increase his profits by selling his products to people who did *not* need it. An appropriate strategy might be to direct a

---

*An example is the vaginal deodorant, which is totally unnecessary and potentially harmful to the user's health. Other examples abound, but the reader can find his own by considering classes of products that are most heavily advertised. Vendors of things people *need* don't advertise much except as a means of attracting business away from competitors. Thus, one never sees expensive advertising campaigns attempting to persuade people to buy fresh fruit or vegetables, meat, poultry, or bread, though one may see ads designed to persuade people to buy one particular brand of bread, for example, or enticing them to shop for their produce at a particular market. But ads for cigarettes, deodorants, prepared breakfast foods, over-the-counter drugs, and many other products are principally designed to persuade potential customers that they ought to purchase those products—and then to buy a particular brand of the product they have been induced to buy.

well-organized advertising campaign at the medical profession, designed to persuade physicians that circulatory bypass ought to be employed in many conditions that are presently treated by chemical means. By offering large research grants to university professors interested in pursuing projects related to circulatory disorders, he might succeed in commissioning a number of studies that could be cited in his ads in support of his product. By offering entering medical students new instruments with his company's logo, and by sending them small gifts throughout their careers, he would attempt to build loyalty to his firm among those most likely to be using or prescribing his products. And finally, by having a professional agency prepare lavish layouts to be published in medical journals and circulars to be distributed to physicians, while his salesmen drop subtle hints about the financial advantages the physician would enjoy if he were to perform circulatory bypass surgery more often, he would attempt to sell his product at the expense of persons who don't need it and would be endangered by being subjected to unnecessary surgery.*

Such an advertising campaign would be immoral, for it would contribute to the corruption of scientific researchers upon whom other persons rely in making decisions that can affect the life and health of the communities in which they live and—in the long run—contribute to public cynicism about the reliability of science and the trustworthiness of the academic community. It would also contribute to the corruption of the medical profession by using petty bribery and commercial chicanery and dangling the enticement of personal financial rewards, thereby substituting commercial considerations for professional judgment. If successful, it would subject numerous patients to needless and potentially dangerous surgery with the expense, suffering, and possible loss of life that that entails. In earlier times, when people had a simpler way of judging one another's motivations, those responsible would simply have been called *greedy*.

Although this case is fictional, the devices I have described are not. All of them are regularly employed by the largest and most respected pharmaceutical firms.[1]

This case illustrates the contrast between advertising that fulfills the conditions of morality (that it be truthful and honest, and that it contribute to human happiness and diminish human suffering) and that which does not (for it is untruthful, deceitful, corrupting, and damaging to innocent persons). However, the advertiser's motives are not especially important, for in general, motives have little, if anything, to do with the moral quality of acts. The term *greed,* for example, is not especially helpful, for it contains a moral condemnation. Only *after* a moral judgment has been rendered would one be able to determine whether one was greedy. The inventor of the artificial blood vessel readily conceded that he was motivated by a desire to make a profit. The profit motive does not

---

*I reiterate that this is purely fictitious. As far as I know, the artificial blood vessel had never been marketed in this fashion.

render the invention and marketing of such a marvelous life-saving device immoral or amoral. One's motive is not a sufficient determinant of the moral quality of one's act. The actor must be judged on the bases of the act itself, and not on his psychological attitudes.* Whereas a person may have invented such a device out of pure and unselfish motives, it is the devices that save lives, not pure motives. Since they cannot perform their intended function without being marketed and advertised, there can be no doubt of the moral desirability of advertising them, however much the manufacturer may be motivated by the desire for profit. After all, that desire is not evil in itself. Greed is an unrestrained desire for money, regardless of the harm its acquisition may do to others, and is condemned for that reason. It should not be confused with the desire for profit.

As products and services are advertised, competition is usually enhanced and costs decline. Thus, the standard of living of the entire population or a significant segment thereof can rise. On the other hand, restraints upon the freedom to advertise often result in higher prices. Moreover, advertising fills the important public function of informing those who can least afford high prices of essential products of the availability of identical or similar ones at less cost.†

More important, perhaps, is the fact that certain goods and services cannot be made available at all without appropriate advertising. If it is morally right for women, under some circumstances, to seek abortions, then it is also morally right to inform them of the availability of safe abortions. If the decimation of fur-bearing animals is wrong, then it is right for the public to be informed of the availability of artificial furs. The advertisement by a domestic manufacturer of products whose purchase can contribute to a drop in unemployment and a rise in the standard of living is at least offering potential buyers information without which they would not be able to make informed, independent moral decisions about purchases they are thinking of making.‡ And where there is no advertising, people may be unaware of the availability of services that may deci-

---

*A detailed discussion of this thesis would lead us too far from the principal topic of this article, but it is obvious that the husband who has sexual relations with a woman he mistakenly thinks is not his wife may have committed adultery in his heart, whatever that is, but he has certainly not committed adultery.

†Numerous studies have demonstrated enormous price differences in prescription drugs, for example, which aged and poor persons could not take advantage of because pharmacists were not permitted to advertise. Cf. Justice Blackmun's majority opinion in *Virginia State Board of Pharmacy* v. *Citizens Consumer Council*, 96 S. Ct. 1817 (1976), at 1821–1822, and n. 11 there. Other studies have revealed that the prices of eyeglasses are significantly lower where optometrists are permitted to advertise.

‡I am not addressing myself to the question of the desirability of preferential purchases of domestic over foreign goods. I am merely pointing out that important moral questions are involved and that ads can help the consumer make more informed decisions.

sively enhance the quality of their lives. Many poor persons, for example, would be far better off if they could be professionally advised of their legal rights as tenants, consumers, and employees and helped in writing contracts, wills, and other documents. Legal advertisements could help make them aware of the availability of such advice.[2]

Some professional organizations have banned all forms of advertising, presumably because the practice is "unbecoming" to professional persons, but more realistically because it is likely to lead to price competition. The American Bar Association has argued that competitive advertising would "encourage extravagant, artful, self-laudatory brashness in seeking business and thus could mislead the layman. . . . It would inevitably produce unrealistic expectations . . . and bring about distrust of the law and lawyers."[3] Pharmacists contend that advertising would force them to cut down on professional services and would reduce their image to that of mere retailers.[4] Physicians insist that ads by members of their profession would be confusing, however truthful they might be, since patients are incapable of understanding fee information; such ads should be banned, they say, because people would select doctors on the basis of cost rather than quality of professional care.[5] The courts have held that these contentions are based upon the assumption that people are ignorant, that they must be protected from exploitation by knowledgable professionals, and that the professionals themselves are not to be trusted. As the court in the *ABA* case put it, the ABA is assuming that "the public will not be able to accurately evaluate its [the advertising's] content, for either they are intellectually incapable of legal services or they will fall prey to every huckster with a promise, law license, and a law book." If the public is so likely to fall prey to hucksters, the court said, that is all the more reason for giving it more rather than less information. In the pharmacy case, the court concluded that an alternative to the "highly paternalistic approach" of the professionals was "to assume that this information is not in itself harmful, that people will perceive their own best interests if only they are well enough informed, and that the best means to that end is to open the channels of communication rather than to close them."

In short, the utility of advertisements rests upon the fact that potentially valuable information is passed from one person to another. The right of the advertiser to hawk his wares is parallel to the consumer's right to hear the advertiser's message. Although such communication may not be deserving of the broad protection that John Stuart Mill and the U.S. Constitution have conferred upon other forms of speech and artistic presentations, similar considerations justify granting advertisers relatively broad rights—rights which have recently gained some degree of recognition in American courts.[6]

On the other hand, some kinds of advertisements are immoral on their face, for they promote personally or socially harmful products or services. From the point of view of an antiabortionist, an advertisement informing pregnant women of the availability of abortions itself may be immoral. The advertisement of cock fights or dog fights or other cruel exhibitions, or of slave auctions (when slavery was legal), insofar as they are encouraging, aiding, and abetting wrongful behavior, are wrong in themselves. If racism and sexism are immoral, then help-wanted ads that specify racial, religious, or sexual preferences or exclusions are clearly immoral.*

In addition to such socially harmful advertisements, dangerous articles are sometimes advertised in a particularly irresponsible fashion. In a free market, it may be proper to permit any product to be sold, as long as the prospective purchaser is fully informed of the hazards of the product he is buying. As Mill stated in Chapter 5 of *On Liberty*, the most deadly poisons may be sold over the counter in a free society, as long as the merchant labels them clearly and refrains from selling them to children or other persons who are unable to appreciate the significance of the warnings. But some American advertisers not only fail to warn those who view their messages of such dangers. They deliberately conceal them, and they also deliberately aim their messages at the weakest and most vulnerable audiences: children.

Ultra-Sheen Permanent Creme Relaxer, for example, was advertised as "truly gentle," "cool," and easy to use for persons wanting to straighten curly hair. According to the Federal Trade Commission, its active ingredient is sodium hydroxide—lye—which works by "breaking down the cells of the hair shaft," sometimes causing "partial or total hair loss." It is "caustic to skin and . . . causes skin and scalp irritation and burns, which may produce scars and permanent follicle damage." It also "may impair vision."[7]

In the fall of 1976, the FTC issued a consent order against the Hudson Pharmaceutical Corporation, enjoining the company from promoting a vitamin and mineral preparation with the popular comic strip and television hero, Spiderman. Under the influence of the company's ads, children were led to believe that Spiderman vitamins would confer supernatural strength and agility upon them. Small children, assuming that many pills are better than one, consumed entire bottles of pills or shared them with their baby brothers and sisters. Each bottle contained five to ten

---

*Some periodicals continue to carry help-wanted advertising that is discriminatory, despite the fact that it is contrary to American public policy. The *Chronicle of Higher Education*, for example, publishes notices of academic vacancies in certain Arab universities that obviously indicate that Jewish applicants will not be accepted. In a letter to the author of this article, the managing editor of the *Chronicle* has explained that since such discrimination is not contrary to the law of the states which place the ads, the ads do not violate any American law, and will therefore continue to be run in the *Chronicle*'s columns. This legal point has nothing whatever to do with the moral question, whether such ads ought to be accepted by journals that presumably oppose racism and subscribe to the principles of liberty and equality for all. It is doubtful, incidentally, whether the *Chronicle* would accept a notice from a South African or Rhodesian university indicating that black applicants would not be considered. In some circles, it seems, discrimination against blacks is considered to be more pernicious than anti-Semitism.

times the lethal dose of ferrous sulfate for children, in brightly colored candy-coated tablets. In 1973 alone, vitamins and minerals accounted for more than 5,000 cases of poisoning among children under the age of five. Iron poisoning can result in death from shock within four to six hours. Where death does not occur, complications can include convulsions, hyperthermia, anuria, and cirrhosis of the liver.[8] The sale of such products through ads directed to children, and the encouragement of excessive consumption through such techniques, is morally indefensible. But the bottom-line mentality, which justifies everything on the basis of net profits and growth, may be impervious to such considerations. The simple fact is that such advertising campaigns work.

Corporate officers and their public relations staffs are citizens as well as businessmen. They have duties as citizens as well as those they owe to the firms for which they work. Even the most unexceptionable advertisement for the most innocuous product or service may indirectly damage important interests or harm innocent persons, and therefore be morally objectionable. An ad placed in publications of the American Nazi Party, for example, would help to further the racist and totalitarian aims of that organization, since the revenue from the ad would help to support the organization's activities. On a rather different level, ads placed in the *Christian Yellow Pages,* a directory which accepts the business of "born-again Christians" only and urges its users to patronize them to the exclusion of all others, further a consumer boycott against nonevangelical Christians, Jews, and all other non-Christians. The power and wealth of corporations ought not to be used in such a way as to harm innocent persons or to support causes or movements that are antidemocratic or inconsistent with the principles of decency, justice, and fairness.

Corporate responsibility in the promotion of goods and services is not exhausted by the requirement that advertisements not be fraudulent. Corporations have the power to corrupt scientists and professional persons for their own selfish ends; they can promote their products in such a way as to pose grave hazards to the health and safety of those who use them; they can promote products that are in themselves personally or socially harmful; and they can support media that are arms of organizations dedicated to sinister or maleficent objectives. On the other hand, advertisements can promote the well-being of society and increase the standard of living of all who live within it by making information about beneficial goods and services widely available. While promoting their products, advertisers can also perform valuable communal services, such as supporting artistic and humanistic endeavors. Like every other tool, advertising can be turned to good or to ill uses. Such distinctions as those between needs and desires are vital to the rendering of informed corporate decisions. If advertisers would devote more attention to such distinctions and to questions having to do with their duties toward their fellow citizens, they might find that it is possible, not only to achieve respectable earnings, but also to enjoy the satisfactions that come from making a contribution to the well-being of their communities and their fellow citizens.

Notes

1. Cf. *Action for Children's Television Petition before the FTC,* October, 1975 (hereinafter referred to as *ACT*), *passim.*
2. Cf. *Consumers Union* v. *American Bar Association,* 427 F. Supp. 506 (E.D. Va., 1976), at 520–521.
3. *Ibid.*
4. *Virginia State Board of Pharmacy* v. *Virginia Citizens Consumer Council,* 96 S.Ct. 1817 (1976).
5. *Health Systems Agency of Northern Virginia* v. *State Board of Medicine,* 424 F. Supp. 267 (E.D. Va., 1976).
6. See cases cited above.
7. *FTC in the Matter of Johnson Products Co., Inc., and Bozell & Jacobs, Inc.,* Docket no. C-2788.
8. *ACT,* esp. Appendix G.

ETHICAL RELATIVISM

Case Study—Lockheed Aircraft Corporation

A. Carl Kotchian

My initiation into the chill realities of extortion, Japanese style, began in 1972. In August of that year I flew to Tokyo to work for the sale to a Japanese airline of Lockheed's wide-bodied TriStar passenger plane.

Soon after landing I found myself deep in conversation with Toshiharu Okubo, an official of Marubeni, the trading company that was serving as Lockheed's representative and go-between in the already ongoing TriStar negotiations.

Beaming, Okubo reviewed Marubeni's efforts on behalf of TriStar, then gave me the good news that "tomorrow at seven-thirty A.M., we are seeing Prime Minister Tanaka" about the matter. I was quite impressed with and encouraged by the "power of Marubeni"—power that made it possible to make an appointment with the prime minister only 24 hours after I had asked Marubeni to set up such a meeting. Then came an unexpected development: when we began to discuss in detail how to bring about the sale of TriStar, Okubo suddenly suggested that I make a "pledge" to pay money for a major favor like this. Though the proposal did not appall and outrage me, I was nonetheless quite astonished that the question of money had been brought up so abruptly—especially since in broaching the idea Okubo mentioned the name of the prime minister's secretary, Toshio Enomoto.

"How much money do we have to pledge?" I asked.

"The going rate when asking for a major favor is usually five hundred million yen [roughly $1.7 million]. It can be smaller. . . ."

I was now faced with the problem of whether to make a payment to Japan's highest government office. If I refused, declining Marubeni's advice, and should our sale fail, I was certain that the full responsibility would be placed squarely upon me by Marubeni's officials, who could say to me, "We told you so. You did not listen to us."

Sensing my hesitation, Okubo reiterated, "If you wish to be successful in selling the aircraft, you would do well to pledge five hundred million yen."

From *Saturday Review*, July 9, 1977. Mr. Kotchian was president of Lockheed Corporation from 1967 to 1975.

During this exchange, Okubo never mentioned for whom the money was intended. But we both knew that our whole conversation had been about the meeting between Prime Minister Tanaka and Chairman Hiyama of Marubeni, scheduled for early in the morning of the next day. Stalling for time and hoping to discover for whom the money was intended, I asked, "How do you deliver that money?"

"We do not have to worry about it," Okubo assured me, "because Mr. Ito [Hiroshi Ito, another executive of Marubeni] is very close to Mr. Enomoto, the prime minister's secretary."

This exchange left me with no doubt that the money was going to the office of Japan's prime minister. Then, in response to my further questions, Okubo concretely spelled out the details of the arrangement—the amount, 500 million yen; the way it had to be put together, in Japanese yen, cash; the fact that it had to be ready when we were given the signal; and the way the delivery of the money was to be accomplished, through the prime minister's secretary. This, then, was how I got involved in the now much publicized secret payments to Japanese government officials.

And "involved" is the word, for later that day I had a meeting near Tokyo's Sony Building with Yoshio Kodama, Lockheed's confidential consultant in Japan. So Byzantine were the TriStar maneuverings that Marubeni, our "above ground" agents and consultants, had no idea that Kodama was on Lockheed's payroll! In keeping with the air of mystery surrounding these dealings, Kodama always insisted on meeting me in the evening, because, I gather, he did not want employees in the other offices to see a highly conspicuous, six-foot-tall *gaijin*—a Japanese word for "foreigner"—going in and out of his office.

During the meeting, I asked about the chances of Lockheed's enlisting the support of Kenji Osano, an intimate of Prime Minister Tanaka whom some people had urged on me as an adviser, since he was "the most influential person in Japan." On this point, Kodama told me without hesitation, "In order to include Mr. Osano, we need an extra five hundred million yen." Frankly, I was quite surprised that he had come up with this figure so readily, as though it had already been decided on well in advance.

So my education in Japanese business practices was proceeding apace: it was the second time that day that I had been asked for "five hundred million yen." I felt that this particular figure must be used quite often in Japan!

In fact, as I thought about it back in my room at the Hotel Okura, I had now had *three* requests for around 500 million yen—520 million yen for Kodama on our contract with him, a second 500 million yen requested by Okubo to make a "payment pledge," and finally the third 500 million yen requested by Kodama for the inclusion of Osano in our campaign. I could not help thinking about these payments while I was having a room service dinner with my wife, Lucy. I was in fact thinking of calling Okubo to stop the 500 million yen that I had promised to pledge; but if I did that, I thought, I would have to tell him about the 500 million yen requested by Kodama. I decided at the last minute not to do that.

But why, you may wonder, did Lockheed put up at all with these under-the-counter demands? Why not just throw up our hands and try to sell our planes in some other country?

The truth is that—for the moment, at least—Lockheed had nowhere else to go *but* Japan. Although our planes were, and still are, first-rank products, fully competitive with if not superior to any other planes in the world, we had just come off a run of bad luck in the European market. To our chagrin and dismay, we had lost out on contract after airline contract—especially with Italy's Alitalia, Germany's Lufthansa, and Belgium's Sabena airlines.

Further, we were having difficulties with U.S. Defense Department contracts for the "Cheyenne" helicopter and the giant C5A Galaxie transport plane.

This bleak situation all but dictated a strong push for sales in the biggest untapped market left—Japan. This push, if successful, might well bring in revenues upwards of $400 million. Such a cash inflow would go a long way toward helping to restore Lockheed's fiscal health, and it would, of course, save the jobs of thousands of the firm's employees.

Against this background, I could hardly afford simply to fly away in disgust at the mere mention of these payments—payments which were in any case not forbidden under U.S. law. Realistically, the best I could hope for was to bend a bit in the face of these demands, while keeping our payments to a minimum percentage of any sale that went through.

While I was working in the Lockheed office at about 10:00 A.M. the next day, August 23, I received a telephone call from Okubo. He asked me to come to his office.

When I got there an hour or so later, I found him in a very jovial mood. He told me, "I accompanied Mr. Hiyama, Marubeni's chairman, to Prime Minister Tanaka's residence this morning."

According to Okubo, the two men had seen Prime Minister Tanaka briefly, and then Okubo left while Hiyama stayed to talk with the prime minister. He did not tell me what the three of them talked about or what Hiyama talked about with the prime minister. But then Okubo confided: "That pledge has been made, too."

I do not know specifically how the pledge was made to the office of the prime minister, since these transactions seemed to be such a uniquely Japanese method. All I know is that I was given no paper saying, for instance, "If Lockheed is successful, we will pay 500 million yen," and the like. First of all, it was not clear whether the pledge was made to the prime minister himself or to his secretary. But I did not ask Okubo about this point, nor did I have any intention of doing so. I knew from the beginning that this money was going to the office of the prime minister and there was no need for me to have to pin down exactly to whom it was going or how the money was going to be delivered.

For the next few months, as summer passed over into fall, I stayed on in Tokyo, trying with little success to force-feed the situation, while delays, diversions, and frustrations piled up.

Then, to make things worse, late in October I was knocked flat by the pain and fever of a severe "bug" infection. Doctors, antibiotics, and bed rest seemed to do me no good: all I could do was lie there in my hotel suite, aching and perspiring and thinking darkly about jumping out the window. I suspect that it was only my wife's comforting presence that kept me from doing something drastic.

On October 29, when I was at my lowest ebb physically and mentally, our telephone started ringing. I picked up the receiver thinking, Who can it be at this time on a Sunday night? It was Okubo. Judging from the way his voice sounded, he seemed to be telephoning from a faraway place. After we exchanged pleasantries, he pointed out that the final decision by All Nippon Airlines (ANA)—the largest Japanese domestic carrier— would be made very shortly and said:

"If you do three things, Mr. Kotchian, you will definitely succeed in selling the TriStar."

I was struck with the importance of what Okubo was trying to say to me, and I straightened out the receiver in my hand and asked him, like a pupil asking questions of a teacher, "What are these three things that I have to do?" There was a tension in Okubo's voice, and for my part I listened to him with the phone pressed hard against my ear.

His first few stipulations were relatively minor, having to do with the maintenance of any planes Lockheed might sell to All Nippon Airlines. I readily agreed to them. And then came the "hook." According to Okubo, I had to get together as soon as possible $400,000—that is, 120 million Japanese yen—cash. "If possible, the first thing tomorrow morning, it has to be ready," Okubo urged me. As I'm sure he knew, it would have been impossible to have such a large sum of money ready on such short notice. I began asking questions; above all, What is the money for?

"To give three hundred thousand dollars [90 million yen] to Mr. Wakasa, president of All Nippon Airlines," Okubo blandly explained, "and also to make payments to six politicians."

As Okubo mentioned the six politicians by name, I wrote the names down on a hotel memo pad.

"If we give three hundred thousand dollars to Mr. Wakasa and to each of the six politicians, won't that make two million one hundred thousand dollars—six hundred thirty million yen?" I asked.

Suffering from a high fever and pain, I really became sick at the thought of such a preposterous sum. Okubo had, I reflected, already asked me for 500 million yen in August and I had agreed to make the pledge. Now he's asking more money for payments to politicians. What is he trying to do to me? Okubo hurriedly objected to my 630-million-yen figure: "No, not such a large sum."

"Is it, then, three hundred thousand dollars altogether, including the payments to the politicians?"

"No, that is not correct either. What I'm trying to say is. . . ."

In the end, it came down to this: the amount of money that had to be delivered to Mr. Wakasa, the president of ANA, was $300,000 altogether. This amount was calculated on the basis of $50,000 for each of the six airplanes ANA planned to purchase initially. In addition to this $300,000 for ANA, Okubo mentioned that an additional $100,000 should be prepared in Japanese yen—cash—and that this money should go to the following six politicians:

Tomisaburo Hashimoto, secretary-general of the Liberal Democratic party.

Susumu Nikaido, chief cabinet secretary.

Hideyo Sasaki, minister of transportation.

Kazuomi Fukunaga, chairman of the Liberal Democratic party's special committee on aviation.

Takayuki Sato, former parliamentary vice-minister of transportation.

Mutsuki Kato, present parliamentary vice-minister of transportation.

Of the six politicians, I had not heard of Kazuomi Fukunaga and Mutsuki Kato. Of the remaining four, I had never met or talked with even one (and have never met them since, either); but I had heard of them and had seen their names in the newspapers. The hotel's telephone memo paper, on which I jotted down their names in romanized Japanese, was the so-called "memo" that had the names of the high Japanese government officials; it is this memo that became a great subject of curiosity when the Lockheed incident was disclosed in the United States.

As for the breakdown of this money for the politicians, Okubo expressed the intention of distributing the money as follows: 7 million yen each to Hashimoto and Nikaido, and 4 million yen each to Sasaki, Fukunaga, Sato, and Kato.

"If you do this first thing tomorrow morning," said Okubo, full of confidence, "we can formally get ANA's order tomorrow without fail." I had a feeling that these figures and the names must have been carefully thought about by someone. The problem, however, was that it was already past midnight and it was going to be very difficult to prepare such a large sum of money so quickly.

"By what time do we have to prepare this amount?" I asked.

"I would like you to have the whole sum of money ready by ten A.M. tomorrow," responded Okubo.

"That is impossible. I could not have it ready so quickly."

"The thirty million yen [for the politicians] is highly important. Couldn't you have that much ready at least?"

"Well, I'll try to do my best," I responded, adding, "and I will have the remaining ninety million yen ready at the earliest possible date. I will let you know on this remaining amount tomorrow morning."

If some third party had heard this conversation, he could ask why I responded to this request for secret payments. However, I must admit that it was extremely persuasive and attractive at that time to have someone come up to me and confidently tell me, "If you do this, you will surely get ANA's order in twenty-four hours." What businessman who is dealing with commercial and trade matters could decline a request for certain amounts of money when that money would enable him to get the contract? For someone like myself, who had been struggling against plots and severe competition for over two months, it was almost impossible to dismiss this opportunity.

At about 10:00 A.M. the next day, a Lockheed representative in Toyko called to tell me that—pursuant to my instructions—he had delivered the 30 million yen to Okubo. (As for the remaining 90 million yen, I believe it was delivered on November 6, after I left Japan.)

Later that day, a group of us who had been working on the TriStar sale met in the lobby of the Kasumigaseki Building; Mr. Matsui of Marubeni got into the elevator with us, and together we went up to the head office of All Nippon Airlines. When we were ushered into one of the conference rooms in the main office, the top management of ANA had already assembled. I was told, "Congratulations, Mr. Kotchian, you have won the contract."

Feverish and light-headed though I was from my illness, I nonetheless felt very happy when I heard this and had a warm feeling inside me. I came back to the hotel at about seven o'clock and waited a little bit longer until it was Monday morning, California time. Then I called up our main office in Burbank and informed Mr. Haughton, our chairman, of the good news. He was delighted and told me that on my return they were going to have a big celebration party for all of us who had worked on the sale.

Now, finally, I began to feel a sense of victory after the most intense sales campaign of my life. It was a victory of pain after 70 straight days of battle in which I had literally run around the great city of Tokyo without getting a chance to know it at all. At about seven o'clock on the evening of October 31, our suite was filled with happy Lockheed men and women who had worked many weeks for this occasion. Everybody's face looked so happy and bright; champagne was opened, one bottle after another. I even poured champagne over the head of Peter Mingrone, a Lockheed executive who had helped enormously in the sales campaign.

After returning to the States, I began to take care of the areas of my responsibility other than Japan. Having completed the official signing of the contract document, I thought that the sales campaign of the TriStar in Japan had been completed.

I believe it was around June 25, 1973, although I do not specifically remember the date, that I received an unexpected telephone communication from Okubo, who said, "Now is the time for you to honor that pledge."

For one second, I wondered what he was talking about, but then I realized that by the word *pledge,* he was talking about the pledge of 500 million yen that we made to the office of Prime Minister Tanaka the previous August. The word *pledge* had been used frequently at that time in Okubo's office when we were talking about the subject. Nevertheless, there had been a ten-month lapse since August. It had been almost half a year since Lockheed and ANA officially signed the formal contract in January. I wondered why he was bringing this up now, when the sales campaign of the TriStar to ANA had long ago been completed.

"I am very surprised, Mr. Okubo, because it all happened six or eight months ago; and we haven't heard anything about it. Frankly, as our

campaign has been completed, I don't have that kind of budget now," I
told him.

"Yes, but that is the pledge that you agreed upon and accepted,"
Okubo insisted.

"But you have not communicated with us for such a long time on this
matter. The whole deal was completed six months ago," I repeated.

I expressed strong opposition to doing this kind of thing this late.
Therefore I asked him: "Are you sure it's necessary, Mr. Okubo?"

Okubo said, "Let me check into it. If it's really necessary, I'll get back to
you."

This is how our telephone conversation ended on that day. Three days
later, Okubo called me again and said: "This is very serious, Mr. Kotchian,
and you must carry out that pledge."

Okubo *sounded* very serious and worried. He said that he had talked to
Mr. Hiyama, the chairman of the board of Marubeni, on this matter, and
that Mr. Hiyama asked him to tell me that if Lockheed did not stand by its
pledge, we would never be able to sell anything in Japan again. Worse
still, Okubo said, if the pledge was not honored, "Mr. Hiyama will have
to leave Japan."

It was quite shocking for me to hear that the chairman of Marubeni
would have to leave Japan. I interpreted this as meaning that Hiyama
would be forced into exile.

"You have convinced me, Mr. Okubo, that the matter is indeed serious," I told him, promising that I would get in touch with him early the
next week.

After hanging up the telephone, I went home and thought about the
matter overnight. I decided on the basis of what Okubo had told me that
we could not possibly risk any retaliation against Lockheed or against
Marubeni. If we did not make the payment on this matter, Hiyama would
be forced into exile, Lockheed might not be able to sell anything in Japan
again, and our relations with Marubeni might be completely disrupted.
Consequently, the more I thought about it, the more I was convinced that
there was no alternative but to make the payment. In the end, after talking
it over with other Lockheed executives, I called Okubo and told him we
would honor the pledge.

Throughout these three international telephone calls on this matter,
Okubo never once mentioned the name of the person for whom the
money was intended, or the amount; and neither did I. Perhaps we were
both mindful of the fact that the conversation was going through the
telephone exchange and we did not want to be overheard by anybody; but
more than anything else, we were both aware that this 500 million yen was
going to the office of the prime minister. I never asked why the payment
was necessary at this particular stage, after so many months had passed.
All I know is that the designated amount was paid—spread over the
remainder of 1973 to early 1974. I did not know then that it was made in
four shipments or when it was paid specifically.

When I visited Japan in October 1973, on my way back from Iran, to arrange the date for the delivery of the first plane, All Nippon Airlines had already decided to make a firm order for the additional eight TriStars on which they had an option. After this second contract was concluded, Okubo again demanded $400,000 from us, calculated on the basis of $50,000 per plane for eight planes, to be delivered to Mr. Wakasa, the president of ANA, as a secret payment.

When Okubo called me by international telephone from Tokyo and demanded this amount, I responded rather harshly, saying, "Wasn't it a one-time expenditure at that time only?"

"No," Okubo said emphatically. "I'm sure I told you these payments were necessary for all of the planes—all of the twenty-one planes."

I had no intention of paying this kind of money until the actual order was made and the initial down payment for the next eight planes was made to Lockheed, and I told this to Okubo. Here again, I could have declined. However, if I had declined and they had said, "Well, we will not order any more planes from Lockheed," what would we do?

The most I could say to this additional demand for money was: "When the initial down payment is received, we will pay what we have to."

The down payment started coming in, and by August of the next year, 1974, down payment for the first four of the eight planes had been received by Lockheed. I thought that if I paid the $400,000 requested by Okubo at that stage I would expedite the down payment for the remaining four planes. So it was around this time that I finally approved the payment of $400,000 to ANA and instructed our representative to arrange such a delivery per instructions from Okubo. I don't know how this money was paid, where, and in what manner—or what kind of receipts were used.

As for the purpose of the $700,000 (calculated on the basis of $50,000 per plane for the 14 planes), Okubo never explained it to me, nor did I ask any questions about it. It could be inferred, however, from the way that Okubo spoke that the money was to be used at the discretion of the top management of ANA, although none of the ANA people ever talked about this in our meetings.

Such were some of the payments for the sale of the TriStar in Japan, viewed from my perspective. Above all, there are three things I would like to stress about the whole sequence I have described.

The *first* is that the Lockheed payments in Japan, totaling about $12 million, were worthwhile from Lockheed's standpoint, since they amounted to less than 3 percent of the expected sum of about $430 million that we would receive from ANA for 21 TriStars. Further, as I've noted, such disbursements *did not violate American laws*. I should also like to stress that my decision to make such payments stemmed from my judgment that the TriStar payments to ANA would provide Lockheed workers with jobs and thus redound to the benefit of their dependents, their communities, and stockholders of the corporation.

Secondly, I should like to emphasize that the payments to the so-called "high Japanese government officials" were all requested by Okubo and were *not brought up from my side*. When he told me "five hundred million yen is necessary for such sales," from a purely ethical and moral standpoint I would have declined such a request. However, in that case, I would *most certainly* have sacrificed commercial success.

Finally, I want to make it clear that I never discussed money matters with Japanese politicians, government officials, or airline officials.

It would be simple if selling were merely a matter of presenting a product on its merits. Lockheed conducted its business in Japan much as other aircraft companies, its competitors, had done over the years. All have found it helpful to have nationals advise them, in Japan as in many other countries. Much has been made in press accounts in both Japan and the United States of secret agents and secret channels for sales efforts. Of course these consultations with advisers were secret: competitors do not tell each other their strategy or even their sales targets.

And if Lockheed had not remained competitive by the rules of the game as then played, we would not have sold the TriStar and would not have provided work for tens of thousands of our employees or contributed to the future of the corporation. Nor would ANA have had the services of this excellent airplane.

From my experience in international sales, I knew that if we wanted our product to have a chance to win on its own merits, we had to follow the functioning system. If we wanted our product to have a chance, we understood that we would have to pay, or pledge to pay, substantial sums of money in addition to the contractual sales commissions. We never *sought* to make these extra payments. We would have preferred not to have the additional expenses for the sale. But, always, they were recommended by those whose experience and judgment we trusted and whose recommendations we therefore followed.

Every investigation campaign requires an "example," a "scapegoat," and Lockheed is that today in the current international climate of reform. The requirement to assess responsibility in Japan has brought the embarrassment of public accusation to some persons associated with the company. To others it has brought the humiliation of arrest and imprisonment. We, too, have suffered. We are anguished that some of our friends and their families have had to bear this agony. We hope it will not have been without benefit.

Ethical Relativism

RICHARD BRANDT

ARE THERE ULTIMATE DISAGREEMENTS
ABOUT ETHICAL PRINCIPLE?

No one seriously doubts that there are differences of ethical principle.
. . . However, there is a question about these differences, and its answer
is controversial. In order to mark this question, let us use the phrase
"*ultimate* difference of ethical principle," . . .

What is meant by an "ultimate" difference of principle? Consider first
an example of conflicting evaluations of a particular action. Suppose
Smith gives his father an overdose of sleeping pills, resulting in death.
Suppose further that Jones hears of this event, but thinks no worse of
Smith for this reason, because he knows that Smith's father was dying
from cancer and in a very painful condition, and he believes Smith's act
was done as an act of mercy. We might say he thinks Smith's act was right,
because it was of the kind *ABC*. Suppose, now, that Brown also learns of
Smith's act, but, unlike Jones, he thinks it was wrong. Brown knows that
Smith's father was wealthy and that Smith was penniless, and he believes
Smith's act was done to expedite the transfer of his father's property to
him. Brown, then, thinks Smith's act was wrong, since he assumes that it
was of the kind *ADE*. Brown and Jones, then, differ in their appraisal of
the act, but possibly they do not differ at all in their ethical principles,
but only in their factual beliefs about the properties of the act. It may
well be that Brown and Jones both agree that all acts of the kind *ABC* are
right, and that all acts of the kind *ADE* are wrong. In this case, we do not
wish to say there was any *ultimate* disagreement between them.

Let us now turn to disagreements about ethical principles. . . . the
Romans decidedly did not think it right to put one's parents to death. In
some of the Eskimo groups, however, this is thought proper. One ob-
server has told of an Eskimo who was getting ready to move camp, and was
concerned about what to do with his blind and aged father, who was a
burden to the family. One day the old man expressed a desire to go
seal-hunting again, something he had not done for many years. His son
readily assented to this suggestion, and the old man was dressed warmly
and given his weapons. He was then led out to the seal grounds and was
walked into a hole in the ice, into which he disappeared.[1] The Romans, we
may expect, would have been shocked at this deed. The Eskimos think it
right, in general, to drown a parent who is old and a burden; the Romans,
we guess, think this is wrong. The Romans, we may say, think that all acts
of the kind *ABC* are wrong; the Eskimos deny this.

But may it not be that the Eskimos and the Romans in some sense have

From Richard Brandt, *Ethical Theory* (Englewood Cliffs, N.J.: Prentice-Hall, Inc., 1959);
reprinted by permission of the publisher.

different acts in mind? Suppose that Eskimos, through their experience with the hardships of living, think of parricide as being normally the merciful cutting short of a miserable, worthless, painful old age. And suppose the Romans think of parricide as being normally the getting rid of a burden, or a getting one's hands on the parent's money—an ungrateful, selfishly motivated aggression against one whose care and sacrifices years ago have made the child's life a rich experience. The Eskimos are more-or-less unconsciously taking for granted that putting a parent to death is euthanasia under extreme circumstances; the Romans are more-or-less unconsciously taking for granted that putting a parent to death is murder for gain. In this case, although the Romans and the Eskimos may use the very same words to describe a certain sort of act— and then may express conflicting ethical appraisals of it—actually in some sense they have in mind quite different things. The Eskimos, perhaps, are accepting something of the kind *ABCD;* the Romans are condemning something of the kind *ABFG.* In this situation, we do not want to say there is necessarily any ultimate disagreement of principle between them. . . .

It is not easy to answer the question whether there is ultimate disagreement on ethical principles between different groups. Most of the comparative material assembled . . . is of little value for this purpose, for in large part what it tells us is simply whether various peoples approve or condemn lying, suicide, industry, cleanliness, adultery, homosexuality, cannibalism, and so on. But this is not enough. We need, for our purpose, to know how various peoples *conceive* of these things. Do they eat human flesh because they like its taste, and do they kill slaves merely for the sake of a feast? Or do they eat flesh because they think this is necessary for tribal fertility, or because they think they will then participate in the manliness of the person eaten? Perhaps those who condemn cannibalism would not do so if they thought that eating the flesh of an enemy is necessary for the survival of the group. If we are to estimate whether there is ultimate disagreement of ethical principle, we must have information about this, about the beliefs, more or less conscious, of various peoples, about what they do. However, the comparative surveys seldom give us this.

In view of the total evidence, then, is it more plausible to say that there is ultimate disagreement of ethical principle, or not? Or don't we really have good grounds for making a judgment on this crucial issue?

. . . The writer inclines to think there is ultimate ethical disagreement, and that it is well established. Maybe it is not very important, or very pervasive; but there is some. Let us look at the matter of causing suffering to animals. It is notorious that many peoples seem quite indifferent to the suffering of animals. We are informed that very often, in Latin America, a chicken is *plucked alive,* with the thought it will be more succulent on the table. The reader is invited to ask himself whether he would consider it justified to pluck a chicken alive, for this purpose. Or again, take the "game" played by Indians of the Southwest (but learned from the Spaniards, apparently), called the "chicken pull." In this "game," a chicken is buried in the sand, up to its neck. The contestants ride by on horseback, trying to grab the chicken by the neck and yank it from the sand. When someone succeeds in this, the idea is then for the other contestants to take away from him as much of the chicken as they can. The "winner" is the one who ends up with the most chicken. The reader is invited to ask himself whether he approves of this sport. The writer had the decided impression that the Hopi disapproval of causing pain to animals is much milder than he would suppose typical in suburban Philadelphia—certainly much milder than he would feel himself. For instance, children often catch birds and make "pets" of them. A string is tied to their legs, and they are then "played" with. The birds seldom survive this "play" for long: their legs are broken, their wings pulled off, and so on. One informant put it: "Sometimes they get tired and die. Nobody objects to this." Another informant said: "My boy sometimes brings in birds, but there is nothing to feed them, and they die."[2] Would the reader approve of this, or permit his children to do this sort of thing?

Of course, these people might believe that animals are unconscious automata, or that they are destined to be rewarded many times in the afterlife if they suffer martyrdom on this earth. Then we should feel that our ethical principles were, after all, in agreement with those of these individuals. But they believe no such thing. The writer took all means he could think of to discover some such belief in the Hopi subconscious, but he found none. So probably—we must admit the case is not definitively closed—there is at least one ultimate difference of ethical principle. How many more there are, or how important, we do not say at present.

It is obvious that if there is *ultimate* disagreement of ethical opinion between two persons or groups, there is also disagreement in *basic* principles—if we mean by "basic ethical principle" . . . the principles we should have to take as a person's ethical premises, if we represented his ethical views as a deductive system. We have so defined "ultimate disagreement" that a difference in the ethical theorems of two persons or groups does not count as being "ultimate" if it can be explained as a consequence of identical ethical premises but different factual assumptions of the two parties. Since ultimate ethical disagreements, then, cannot be a consequence of the factual assumptions of the parties, it must be a consequence of their ethical premises. Hence, there is also disagreement in "basic" principles. Our conclusion from our total evidence, then, is that different persons or groups sometimes have, in fact, conflicting basic ethical principles. . . .

ARE CONFLICTING ETHICAL OPINIONS EQUALLY VALID?

A Greek philosopher who lived in the fifth century B.C., named Protagoras, seems to have believed two things: first, that moral principles cannot be shown to be valid for everybody; and second, that people ought to follow the conventions of their own group.[3] Something like this combination of propositions probably had been thought of before his time. Primitive people are well aware that different social groups have different standards, and at least sometimes doubt whether one set of standards can really be shown to be superior to others. Moreover, probably in many groups it has been thought that a person who conforms conscientiously to the standards of his own group deserves respect.

Views roughly similar to those of Protagoras may be classified as forms of *ethical relativism*. The term "ethical relativism," however, is used in different senses, and one should be wary when one comes across it. Sometimes one is said to be a relativist if he thinks that an action that is wrong in one place might not be in another, so that one is declared a relativist if he thinks it wrong for a group of Eskimos to strip a man of his clothing twenty miles from home on January 1, but not wrong for a tribe at the equator. If "relativism" is used in this sense, then practically everyone is a relativist, for practically everyone believes that particular circumstances make a difference to the morality of an act—that, for instance, it is right to lie in some circumstances but wrong in others. Again, one is sometimes said to be a relativist if he asserts a pair of causal propositions: that different social groups sometimes have different values (ethical opinions) as a result of historical developments; and that an individual's values are near-replicas of the tradition of his group, however strongly he may feel that they are "his own" or that they are "valid" and can be supported by convincing reasons. We shall not use "ethical relativism" for either of these views, but reserve it for a theory at least fairly close to that of Protagoras. . . .

It is clarifying to substitute, in place of our initial statement of Protagoras' view, the following, as a brief formulation of the relativist thesis in ethics: *"There are conflicting ethical opinions that are equally valid."* But this formulation requires discussion in order to be clear.

The first thing to notice—although the fact will not be obvious until we have explained the phrase "equally valid"—is that the statement is *about* ethical opinions or statements, but is not an ethical statement itself. It is not like saying, "Nothing is right or wrong!" or "Some things are both right and wrong!" It is a metaethical theory.

Next, the statement is cautious. It does not say that no ethical opinions are valid for everybody. It says only that some ethical opinions are not more valid than some other ethical opinions that conflict with them.

Third, our relativist thesis is not merely the claim that different individuals sometimes in fact have conflicting ethical opinions. It does assert this, but it goes further. It holds that the conflicting ethical opinions are *equally valid.*

. . . Now, the ethical relativist is not merely making the uninteresting claim, when he says two conflicting ethical statements are equally valid, that the two statements are equally plausible in the light of the facts known at present. He is saying something much more radical, about what would happen if one were testing these statements by the best possible ethical methodology, and in the light of a complete system of factual or nonethical knowledge. In other words, he is saying that the application of a "rational" method in ethics would support, equally, two conflicting ethical statements even if there were available a complete system of factual knowledge—or else that there is no "rational" method in ethics comparable to an ideal inductive method for empirical science. . . .

We can now explain exactly what it means to say that two conflicting ethical statements are "equally valid." What it means to say this, is that *either* there is *no* unique rational or justified method in ethics, *or* that the use of the unique rational method in ethics, in the presence of an ideally complete system of factual knowledge, would still not enable us to make a distinction between the ethical statements being considered.

The ethical relativist asserts that there are at least *some* instances of conflicting ethical opinions that are equally valid in this sense. . . .

The facts of anthropology are also relevant to our question, and in the following way. In the first place . . . studies of cultural change in primitive societies suggest that facts like personal conflicts and maladjustments, the attitudes of one's close relatives (for example, whether favorably oriented toward White civilization), and personal success in achieving status in one's group or outside one's group (for example, with White men) play an important role in the development of the values of adults. This finding is some support for our reading of the observational evidence of psychology. In the second place, there is the fact that various groups have different values. The mere fact that different ethical standards exist in different societies, of course, by itself proves nothing relevant to our present problem. Nevertheless, something important is proved if the facts bear testimony that different standards can prevail even if different groups have the *same beliefs* about the relevant event or act, and if there is no reason to suppose that the group standards reflect group differences in respect of other "qualifications." (We must remember that attitudes common to a group cannot usually be discounted as being a result of personal interest or of an abnormal frame of mind.) The fact of variation of group standards, in these circumstances, would tend to show that attitudes are a function of such variables, that attitudes could differ even if our "ideal qualifications" were all met.

Is there such variation of group standards? We have seen that there is one area of ethical opinion where there is diversity in appraisal and at the same time possible identity of belief about the action—that about the treatment of animals. On the whole, primitive groups show little feeling that it is wrong to cause pain to animals, whereas the columns of *The New York Times* are testimony to the fact that many persons in the U.S.A. take a vigorous interest in what goes on in slaughterhouses. . . . Nevertheless, we cannot be sure that attitudes of the groups here in question really do fulfill our "qualifications" equally well. Primitive peoples rarely make pets of the animals they maltreat. There is at least some question whether they have a vivid imagination of what the suffering of an animal is like, comparable to that of the authors of letters to the *Times*. The writer has assured himself by personal investigation that there is no definite discrepancy between the Hopi *beliefs*, about the effects of maltreating animals, and those of what seems a representative sample of educated White Americans. Degrees of *vividness* of belief, however, do not lend themselves to objective investigation, and it is not clear how we may definitely answer questions about them, either way. Perhaps the sanest conclusion is just to say that, as far as can be decided objectively, groups do sometimes make divergent appraisals when they have identical beliefs about the objects, but that the difficulties of investigation justify a healthy degree of skepticism about the conclusiveness of the inquiry.

The fact that objective inquiry is difficult naturally works both ways. It prevents us from asserting confidently that, where there are differences of appraisal, there is still identity of factual belief. But equally it prevents us from denying confidently that there is identity of belief, where appraisals differ.

The anthropological evidence, taken by itself, then, does not give a *conclusive* answer to our question. At the present time, the anthropologist does not have two social groups of which he can say definitely: "These groups have exactly the same beliefs about action A, on all points that could be seriously viewed as ethically relevant. But their views—attitudes—about the morality of the acts are vastly different." Whether, everything considered, the relativist reading of the facts is not the more balanced judgment, is another question. The writer is inclined to think it is the better judgment.

If we agree that the ethical standards of groups are not a function solely of their beliefs (or the vividness of these), it is reasonable to suppose that "ideally qualified" attitudes may well conflict with respect to the very same act or event. . . .

Notes

1. G. de Poncins, *Kabloona* (New York: Reynal & Hitchcock, 1941).
2. See the writer's *Hopi Ethics* [(Chicago: University of Chicago Press, 1954)], pp. 213–15, 245–46, 373; and Wayne Dennis, *The Hopi Child* (New York: Appleton-Century-Crofts, Inc., 1940).
3. For Protagoras' views, see Plato, *Theaetetus,* pp. 166ff.; and F. J. Copleston, *A History of Philosophy*, I (London: Burns Oates & Washbourne Ltd., 1956), pp. 87–90.

Ethical Relativity and
Ethical Absolutism

WALTER TERENCE STACE

Any ethical position which denies that there is a single moral standard which is equally applicable to all men at all times may fairly be called a species of ethical relativity. There is not, the relativist asserts, merely one moral law, one code, one standard. There are many moral laws, codes, standards. What morality ordains in one place or age may be quite different from what morality ordains in another place or age. The moral code of Chinamen is quite different from that of Europeans, that of African savages quite different from both. Any morality, therefore, is relative to the age, the place, and the circumstances in which it is found. It is in no sense absolute.

This does not mean merely—as one might at first sight be inclined to suppose—that the very same kind of action which is *thought* right in one country and period may be *thought* wrong in another. This would be a mere platitude, the truth of which everyone would have to admit. Even the absolutist would admit this—would even wish to emphasize it—since he is well aware that different peoples have different sets of moral ideas, and his whole point is that some of these sets of ideas are false. What the relativist means to assert is, not this platitude, but that the very same kind of action which is right in one country and period may *be* wrong in another. And this, far from being a platitude is a very startling assertion.

It is very important to grasp thoroughly the difference between the two ideas. . . . We fail to see that the word "standard" is used in two different senses. It is perfectly true that, in one sense, there are many variable moral standards. We speak of judging a man by the standard of his time. And this implies that different times have different standards. And this, of course, is quite true. But when the word "standard" is used in this sense it means simply the set of moral ideas current during the period in question. It means what people *think* right, whether as a matter of fact it is right or not. On the other hand when the absolutist asserts that there exists a single universal moral "standard," he is not using the word in this sense at all. He means by "standard" what *is* right as distinct from what people merely think right. His point is that although what people think right varies in different countries and periods, yet what actually is right is everywhere and always the same. And it follows that when the ethical relativist disputes the position of the absolutist and denies that any universal moral standard exists he too means by "standard" what actually is right. . . .

To sum up, the ethical relativist consistently denies, it would seem, whatever the ethical absolutist asserts. For the absolutist there is a single

From W. T. Stace, *The Concept of Morals* (New York: The Macmillan Co., 1937); renewed 1965 by Walter T. Stace; reprinted by permission of The Macmillan Co.

universal moral standard. For the relativist there is no such standard. There are only local, ephemeral, and variable standards. For the absolutist there are two senses of the word "standard." Standards in the sense of sets of current moral ideas are relative and changeable. But the standard in the sense of what is actually morally right is absolute and unchanging. For the relativist no such distinction can be made. There is only one meaning of the word standard, namely, that which refers to local and variable sets of moral ideas.

Finally—though this is merely saying the same thing in another way— the absolutist makes a distinction between what actually is right and what is thought right. The relativist rejects this distinction and identifies what is moral with what is thought moral by certain human beings or groups of human beings. . . .

I shall now proceed to consider, first, the main arguments which can be urged in favour of ethical relativity; and secondly, the arguments which can be urged against it. . . .

There are, I think, [two] main arguments in favour of ethical relativity. The first is that which relies upon the actual varieties of moral "standards" found in the world. . . .

The investigations of anthropologists have shown that there exist side by side in the world a bewildering variety of moral codes. On this topic endless volumes have been written, masses of evidence piled up. Anthropologists have ransacked the Melanesian Islands, the jungles of New Guinea, the steppes of Siberia, the deserts of Australia, the forests of central Africa, and have brought back with them countless examples of weird, extravagant, and fantastic "moral" customs with which to confound us. We learn that all kinds of horrible practices are, in this, that, or the other place, regarded as essential to virtue. We find that there is nothing, or next to nothing, which has always and everywhere been regarded as morally good by all men. Where then is our universal morality? Can we, in face of all this evidence, deny that it is nothing but an empty dream?

This argument, taken by itself, is a very weak one. It relies upon a single set of facts—the variable moral customs of the world. But this variability of moral ideas is admitted by both parties to the dispute, and is capable of ready explanation upon the hypothesis of either party. The relativist says that the facts are to be explained by the non-existence of any absolute moral standard. The absolutist says that they are to be explained by human ignorance of what the absolute moral standard is. And he can truly point out that men have differed widely in their opinions about all manner of topics including the subject-matters of the physical sciences— just as much as they differ about morals. And if the various different opinions which men have held about the shape of the earth do not prove that it has no one real shape, neither do the various opinions which they have held about morality prove that there is no one true morality.

Thus the facts can be explained equally plausibly on either hypothesis. There is nothing in the facts themselves which compels us to prefer the relativistic hypothesis to that of the absolutist. And therefore the argument fails to prove the relativist conclusion. If that conclusion is to be established, it must be by means of other considerations. . . .

The [second] argument in favour of ethical relativity is a very strong one. . . . It consists in alleging that no one has ever been able to discover upon what foundation an absolute morality could rest, or from what source a universally binding moral code could derive its authority.

If, for example, it is an absolute and unalterable moral rule that all men ought to be unselfish, from whence does this *command* issue? For a command it certainly is, phrase it how you please. There is no difference in meaning between the sentence "You ought to be unselfish" and the sentence "Be unselfish." Now a command implies a commander. An obligation implies some authority which obliges. Who is this commander, what this authority? Thus the vastly difficult question is raised of *the basis of moral obligation.* Now the argument of the relativist would be that it is impossible to find any basis for a universally binding moral law; but that it is quite easy to discover a basis for morality if moral codes are admitted to be variable, ephemeral, and relative to time, place, and circumstance.

No such easy solution of the problem of the basis of moral obligation is open to the absolutist. He believes in moral commands, obedience to which is obligatory on all men, whether they know it or not, whatever they feel, and whatever their customs may be. Such uniform obligation cannot be founded upon feelings, because feelings are—or are said to be— variable. And there is no set of customs which is more than local in its operation. The will of God as the source of a universal law is no longer a feasible suggestion. . . . Where then is the absolutist to turn for an answer to the question? And if he cannot find one, he will have to admit the claims of the ethical relativist; or at least he will have to give up his own claims. . . .

This argument is undoubtedly very strong. It is absolutely essential to solve the problem of the basis of moral obligation if we are to believe in any kind of moral standards other than those provided by mere custom or by irrational emotions. It is idle to talk about a universal morality unless we can point to the source of its authority—or at least to do so is to indulge in a faith which is without rational ground. To cherish a blind faith in morality may be, for the average man whose business is primarily to live aright and not to theorize, sufficient. Perhaps it is his wisest course. But it will not do for the philosopher. His function, or at least one of his functions, is precisely to discover the rational grounds of our everyday beliefs—if they have any. Philosophically and intellectually, then, we cannot accent belief in a universally binding morality unless we can discover upon what foundation its obligatory character rests.

But in spite of the strength of the argument thus posed in favour of ethical relativity, it is not impregnable. For it leaves open one loop-hole. It is always possible that some theory, not yet examined, may provide a basis for a universal moral obligation. The argument rests upon the negative proposition that *there is no theory which can provide a basis for a universal morality.* But it is notoriously difficult to prove a negative. How can you prove that there are no green swans? All you can show is that none have been found so far. And then it is always possible that one will be found tomorrow. So it is here. The relativist shows that no theory of the basis of moral obligation has yet been discovered which could validate a universal morality. Perhaps. But it is just conceivable that one might be discovered in the course of this book.

It is time that we turned our attention from the case in favour of ethical relativity to the case against it. Now the case against it consists, to a very large extent, in urging that, if taken seriously and pressed to its logical conclusion, ethical relativity can only end in destroying the conception of morality altogether, in undermining its practical efficacy, in rendering meaningless many almost universally accepted truths about human affairs, in robbing human beings of any incentive to strive for a better world, in taking the life-blood out of every ideal and every aspiration which has ever ennobled the life of man. . . .

First of all, then, ethical relativity, in asserting that the moral standards of particular social groups are the only standards which exist, renders meaningless all propositions which attempt to compare these standards with one another in respect of their moral worth. And this is a very serious matter indeed. We are accustomed to think that the moral ideas of one nation or social group may be "higher" or "lower" than those of another. We believe, for example, that Christian ethical ideals are nobler than those of the savage races of central Africa. Probably most of us would think that the Chinese moral standards are higher than those of the inhabitants of New Guinea. In short we habitually compare one civilization with another and judge the sets of ethical ideas to be found in them to be some better, some worse. The fact that such judgments are very difficult to make with any justice, and that they are frequently made on very superficial and prejudiced grounds, has no bearing on the question now at issue. The question is whether such judgments have any *meaning*. We habitually assume that they have.

But on the basis of ethical relativity they can have none whatever. For the relativist must hold that there is no *common* standard which can be applied to the various civilizations judged. Any such comparison of moral standards implies the existence of some superior standard which is applicable to both. And the existence of any such standard is precisely what the relativist denies. According to him the Christian standard is applicable only to Christians, the Chinese standard only to Chinese, the New Guinea standard only to the inhabitants of New Guinea.

What is true of comparisons between the moral standards of different races will also be true of comparisons between those of different ages. It is not unusual to ask such questions as whether the standard of our own day is superior to that which existed among our ancestors five hundred years ago. And when we remember that our ancestors employed slaves, practiced barbaric physical tortures, and burnt people alive, we may be inclined to think that it is. At any rate we assume that the question is one which has meaning and is capable of rational discussion. But if the ethical relativist is right, whatever we assert on this subject must be totally meaningless. For here again there is no common standard which could form the basis of any such judgments.

There is indeed one way in which the ethical relativist can give some sort of meaning to judgments of higher or lower as applied to the moral ideas of different races or ages. What he will have to say is that we assume *our* standards to be the best simply because they are ours. And we judge other standards by our own. If we say that Chinese moral codes are better than those of African cannibals, what we *mean* by this is that they are better *according to our standards.* We mean, that is to say, that Chinese standards are *more like our own* than African standards are. "Better" accordingly *means* "more like us." "Worse" means "less like us." It thus becomes clear that judgments of better and worse in such cases do not express anything that is really true at all. They merely give expression to our perfectly groundless satisfaction with our own ideas. In short, they give expression to nothing but our egotism and self-conceit. Our moral ideals are not really better than those of the savage. We are simply deluded by our egotism into thinking they are. The African savage has just as good a right to think his morality the best as we have to think ours the best. His opinion is just as well grounded as ours, or rather both opinions are equally groundless. . . .

Thus the ethical relativist must treat all judgments comparing different moralities as either entirely meaningless; or, if this course appears too drastic, he has the alternative of declaring that they have for their meaning-content nothing except the vanity and egotism of those who pass them. . . .

I come now to a second point. Up to the present I have allowed it to be taken tacitly for granted that, though judgments comparing different races and ages in respect of the worth of their moral codes are impossible for the ethical relativist, yet judgments of comparison between individuals living within the same social group would be quite possible. For individuals living within the same social group would presumably be subject to the same moral code, that of their group, and this would therefore constitute, as between these individuals, a common standard by which they could both be measured. We have not here, as we had in the other case, the difficulty of the absence of any common standard of comparison. It should therefore be possible for the ethical relativist to say quite meaningfully that President Lincoln was a better man than some criminal or moral imbecile of his own time and country, or that Jesus was a better man than Judas Iscariot.

But is even this minimum of moral judgment really possible on relativist grounds? It seems to me that it is not. For when once the whole of humanity is abandoned as the area covered by a single moral standard, what smaller areas are to be adopted as the loci of different standards? Where are we to draw the lines of demarcation? We can split up humanity, perhaps—though the procedure will be very arbitrary—into races, races into nations, nations into tribes, tribes into families, families into individuals. Where are we going to draw the *moral* boundaries? Does the *locus* of a particular moral standard reside in a race, a nation, a tribe, a family, or an individual? Perhaps the blessed phrase "social group" will be dragged in to save the situation. Each such group, we shall be told, has its own moral code which is, for it, right. But what *is* a "group"? Can anyone define it or give its boundaries? . . .

. . . Does the American nation constitute a "group" having a single moral standard? Or does the standard of what I ought to do change continuously as I cross the continent in a railway train? Do different States of the Union have different moral codes? Perhaps every town and village has its own peculiar standard. This may at first sight seem reasonable enough. "In Rome do as Rome does" may seem as good a rule in morals as it is in etiquette. But can we stop there? Within the village are numerous cliques each having its own set of ideas. Why should not each of these claim to be bound only by its own special and peculiar moral standards? And if it comes to that, why should not the gangsters of Chicago claim to constitute a group having its own morality, so that its murders and debaucheries must be viewed as "right" by the only standard which can legitimately be applied to it? And if it be answered that the nation will not tolerate this, that may be so. But this is to put the foundation of right simply in the superior force of the majority. In that case whoever is stronger will be right, however monstrous his ideas and actions. And if we cannot deny to any set of people the right to have its own morality, is it not clear that, in the end, we cannot even deny this right to the individual? Every individual man and woman can put up, on this view, an irrefutable claim to be judged by no standard except his or her own.

If these arguments are valid, the ethical relativist cannot really maintain that there is anywhere to be found a moral standard binding upon anybody against his will. And he cannot maintain that, even within the social group, there is a common standard as between individuals. And if that is so, then even judgments to the effect that one man is morally better than another become meaningless. All moral valuation thus vanishes. There is nothing to prevent each man from being a rule unto himself. The result will be moral chaos and the collapse of all effective standards.

Perhaps, in regard to the difficulty of defining the social group, the relativist may make the following suggestion. If we admit, he may say, that it is impossible or very difficult to define a group territorially or nationally or geographically, it is still possible to define it logically. We will simply define an ethical group as any set of persons (whether they live together in one place or are scattered about in many places over the earth) who recognizes one and the same moral standard. As a matter of fact such groups will as a rule be found occupying each something like a single locality. The people in one country, or at least in one village, tend to think much alike. But theoretically at least the members of an ethical group so defined might be scattered all over the face of the globe. However that may be, it will now be possible to make meaningful statements to the effect that one individual is morally better or worse than another, so long as we keep within the ethical group so defined. For the individuals of the ethical group will have as their common standard the ethical belief or beliefs the acknowledgment of which constitutes the defining characteristic of the group. By this common standard they can be judged and compared with one another. Therefore it is not true that ethical relativity necessarily makes all such judgments of moral comparison between individuals meaningless.

I admit the logic of this. Theoretically judgments of comparison can be given meaning in this way. Nevertheless there are fatal objections to the suggestion. . . .

. . . Even if we assume that the difficulty about defining moral groups has been surmounted, a further difficulty presents itself. Suppose that we have now definitely decided what are the exact boundaries of the social group within which a moral standard is to be operative. And we will assume—as is invariably done by relativists themselves—that this group is to be some actually existing social community such as a tribe or nation. How are we to know, even then, what actually *is* the moral standard within that group? How is anyone to know? How is even a member of the group to know? For there are certain to be within the group—at least this will be true among advanced peoples—wide differences of opinion as to what is right, what wrong. Whose opinion, then, is to be taken as representing *the* moral standard of the group? Either we must take the opinion of the majority within the group, or the opinion of some minority. If we rely upon the ideas of the majority, the results will be disastrous. Wherever there is found among a people a small band of select spirits, or perhaps one man, working for the establishment of higher and nobler ideals than those commonly accepted by the group, we shall be compelled to hold that, for that people at that time, the majority are right, and that the reformers are wrong and are preaching what is immoral. . . .

The ethical relativists are great empiricists. *What* is the actual moral standard of any group can only be discovered, they tell us, by an examination on the ground of the moral opinions and customs of that group. But will they tell us how they propose to decide, when they get to the ground, which of the many moral opinions they are sure to find there is *the* right one in that group? To some extent they will be able to do this for the Melanesian Islanders—from whom apparently all lessons in the nature of morality are in future to be taken. But it is certain that they cannot do it for advanced peoples whose members have learnt to think for themselves and to entertain among themselves a wide variety of opinions. They cannot do it unless they accept the calamitous view that the ethical opinion of the majority is always right. We are left therefore once more with the conclusion that, even within a particular social group, anybody's moral opinion is as good as anybody else's, and that every man is entitled to be judged by his own standards.

Finally, not only is ethical relativity disastrous in its consequences for moral theory. It cannot be doubted that it must tend to be equally disastrous in its impact upon practical conduct. If men come really to believe that one moral standard is as good as another, they will conclude that their own moral standard has nothing special to recommend it. They might as well then slip down to some lower and easier standard. It is true that, for a time, it may be possible to hold one view in theory and to act practically upon another. But ideas, even philosophical ideas, are not so ineffectual that they can remain for ever idle in the upper chambers of the intellect.

In the end they seep down to the level of practice. They get themselves acted on.

These, then, are the main arguments which the anti-relativist will urge against ethical relativity. And perhaps finally he will attempt a diagnosis of the social, intellectual, and psychological conditions of our time to which the emergence of ethical relativism is to be attributed.

MORALITY AND ORGANIZATIONS

Case Study—Campaign to Make General Motors Responsible

JOHN W. COLLINS

In the fall of 1969 a few young Washington attorneys began an organization which they called the "Project on Corporate Responsibility." They had in mind several strategies for encouraging social responsibility by business, e.g., statements at stockholder meetings, campaigns to withhold proxies, shareholder initiated resolutions, election of directors, participate in contests for corporate control, litigation and negotiation.

The project has put several of these strategies into operation. But without doubt the most publicized of these efforts was its "Campaign to Make General Motors Responsible." Campaign GM was introduced publicly at a press conference on February 7, 1970, by Ralph Nader. Mr. Nader released the following statement to the press at that time:

> Today is announced an effort to develop a new kind of citizenship around an old kind of private government—the large corporation. It is an effort which rises from the shared concern of many citizens over the role of the corporation in American society and the uses of its complex powers. It is an effort which is dedicated toward developing a new constituency for the corporation that will harness these powers for the fulfillment of a broader spectrum of democratic values. . . .
>
> I am informed that a new organization called the Project on Corporate Responsibility, record holder presently of 12 shares of GM stock, is mailing to its company three shareholder resolutions with the request that they be included in the proxy statement to be sent by GM to its shareholders in April, preparatory for the annual meeting in Detroit on May 22, 1970.
>
> The first of these resolutions proposes an amendment to GM's charter which would limit the business purposes of the corporation to those purposes which are not detrimental to the public health, safety, and welfare.
>
> The second resolution proposes that a shareholders' committee for corporate responsibility be established. This committee, to be appointed jointly by a representative from GM, the campaign committee, and the United Auto Workers, would prepare a study on the corporate impact of GM on its workers, the environment, transport safety and efficiency, and

From case prepared by John W. Collins, Syracuse University School of Management. Reprinted from *Business and Society*, ed. Robert D. Hay, Edmund R. Gray, and James E. Gates (Cincinnati, Ohio: South-Western Publishing Co., 1976). Reprinted with permission from the publisher and the author.

the public welfare. It will recommend new priorities for the corporation to pursue. The committee will render a report to the shareholders in time for shareholder action at the next meeting. To permit such a task to be accomplished, the committee would have access to all of GM's files.

The third resolution proposes to amend the bylaws of the corporation to increase the size of the Board of Directors from 23 to 26 members. The purpose of this action, as explained in the statement supporting the resolution, would be to make room on the Board for three representatives of the public without displacing anyone now on the Board of Directors.

Three knowledgeable and public-spirited citizens have agreed to stand for election as public representatives on the Board. They are Professor Rene Dubos, Miss Betty Furness, and the Rev. Channing Phillips. . . . The assumption to the Board of these three Americans and the adoption of the aforementioned resolutions will go a long way toward making the days of GM executives less daily and less inimical to the short- and long-run public interest.

This campaign will seek to win public and shareholder support for these resolutions and candidates. The drive will be run by the Campaign to Make GM Responsible Committee, a Washington-based organization with four coordinators—Philip Moore, executive secretary, Geoffrey Cowan, Joseph N. Onek, and John C. Esposito. The coordinators will undertake a nationwide effort to raise many of the issues relating to the public impact of GM's private decision-making.

A basic thrust of the campaign will be alerting and informing the public about their omnipresent neighbor—General Motors—and how it behaves. It will ask citizens to make their views known to both shareholders and management. It will go to institutions that own GM stock and, if they decline to respond, the constituents of those institutions will be contacted. The campaign will reach to the Universities and their students and faculty, to the banks and their depositors and fiduciaries, to churches and their congregations, to insurance companies and their policyholders, to union and company pension funds and their membership, and to other investors. Not only is everyone affected by General Motors, whether a car owner or not, but almost everyone could exert some influence on some aspect of the company's operations. The totality of such influence may be productive of a sustained momentum. At its annual meeting on May 22, 1970, GM may be the host for a great public debate on the giant corporation rather than a wooden recital of aggregate financial data. Putting the people back into People's Capitalism, as the New York Stock Exchange once phrased it before small investors were desired to go out of style, is no easy task. But then it never was for any period in our history. Increasingly the looming issue is that the choices no longer include the luxury of deferral. Rather they demand the urgency of unyielding reform.

The proposals mentioned in Mr. Nader's statements were delivered to General Motors early in February.

On February 17, 1970, the project sent additional proposals to GM, as follows:

RESOLVED:

That General Motors announce and act upon a commitment to a greatly increased role for public mass transportation—by rail, by bus, and by methods yet to be developed.

92 PHILOSOPHICAL ISSUES IN BUSINESS ETHICS

STATEMENT IN SUPPORT:

General Motors is publicly opposed to diverting to public transportation any part of the more than thirteen billion dollars annually generated in automobile-related taxes. While GM lobbies with the government, our cities are being destroyed by too much pollution, pavement, and traffic. With imaginative mass transit, travel would be faster, more convenient, and less costly to society. As the nation's largest transportation corporation, GM should take the lead in helping to develop new modes of mass transit.

RESOLVED:

That, by January 1, 1974, all General Motors vehicles be designed so as to be capable of being crash-tested—front, rear, and side—against a solid barrier at sixty miles per hour, without causing any harm to passengers wearing shoulder restraints.

STATEMENT IN SUPPORT:

The National Highway Safety Bureau has already crash-tested domestically manufactured vehicles with "marked modifications" at forty-seven miles per hour, without harming passengers, according to Robert Carter, chief of the Vehicle Structures Division. These cars, with much-strengthened frames, are not immediately marketable because of lead time required for design, Carter says. But the technology exists, and Carter expects successful tests at sixty miles per hour within one year. General Motors should have developed such a car itself. Now, it should at least make the necessary modifications on all its cars by 1974.

RESOLVED:

First, that General Motors support and commit whatever funds and manpower are necessary to comply with the vehicle emission standards recently recommended by the National Air Pollution Control Administration for the 1975 model year, and to comply with these standards before 1975 if in the course of developing the emission controls this is shown to be technologically feasible. Second, that General Motors commit itself to an extensive research program (with an annual budget as large as its present advertising budget of about a quarter billion dollars) on the long-range effects on health and the environment of all those contaminants released into the air by automobiles which are not now regulated by government. These would include, but not be limited to, asbestos and particulate matter from tires. The results of this research would be periodically published.

STATEMENT IN SUPPORT:

Experts in the National Air Pollution Control Administration consider its recommended standards technologically feasible by the 1975 model year: General Motors should do everything possible to develop the necessary devices, and to make sure they continue to control emissions after 50,000 miles, with the tune-ups at 25,000, which their present cars often do not do. But the government's regulations cover only three pollutants—hydrocarbons, carbon monoxide, and oxides of nitrogen. General Motors is not known to have spent anything studying potentially serious pollutants not regulated by the government, like asbestos and tire particulate matter. GM should start regulating itself.

RESOLVED:

That first, the warranty for all General Motors cars and trucks produced after January 1, 1971, be written to incorporate the following:

1. General Motors warrants that the vehicle is fit for normal and anticipated uses for a period of five years or 50,000 miles, whichever occurs first.
2. General Motors will bear the cost of remedying any defects in manufacture or workmanship whenever or wherever they appear, for the life of the vehicle. Neither time nor mileage limitations nor exclusions of successive purchasers nor other limitations shall apply with respect to such defects.
3. General Motors accepts responsibility for loss of use of vehicles, loss of time, and all other incidental and consequential personal inquiries shown to have resulted from such defects.

Second, General Motors raise its reimbursement rates to dealers on warranty work, making them competitive with other repair work.

STATEMENT IN SUPPORT:

Inevitably, some cars are so bad that replacing parts won't help. At present, GM bears no responsibility for such "lemons." Under (1) GM would replace these cars; (2) and (3) are revisions of present warranty provisions, aimed at relieving the heavy burden now imposed on car owners through no fault of their own. The second part, on raising reimbursement rates, would make dealers less reluctant to take on warranty work than a 1968 FTC staff report indicates they now are.

RESOLVED:

That General Motors undertake to monitor daily the in-plant air contaminants and other environmental hazards to which employees are exposed in each plant owned or operated by General Motors; that the Corporation report weekly the results of its monitoring to a safety committee of employees in each plant; that if such monitoring discloses a danger to the health or safety of the workers in any plant, or in any part of a plant, the Corporation shall take immediate steps to eliminate such hazard, and that no employee shall be required to work in the affected area so long as the hazard exists.

STATEMENT IN SUPPORT

For the most part, General Motors has been an industry leader in providing health and safety mechanisms to its employees. But often the need for safety improvements has been subordinated to the Corporation's concern for production and profit. To date, GM has given too little consideration to the effects of in-plant air contamination which may harm both workers and the immediate community near the plant. Employees must be informed of potential hazards in order to take effective action to help prevent or eliminate them. If adopted, this resolution will enable employees to participate directly in alleviating these health hazards.

RESOLVED:

That General Motors take immediate and effective action to allot a fair proportion of its franchised new car dealerships to minority owners: furthermore, that General Motors act to increase significantly the proportion of minority employees of General Motors in managerial and other skilled positions.

STATEMENT IN SUPPORT:

As of January, 1970, GM had seven nonwhite dealers out of an estimated 13,000. GM would have to increase this number sixtyfold—to cover 400—to achieve the ratio of nonwhite businesses to all U.S. businesses. A fair proportion would be larger still—perhaps approximating the percentage of nonwhites in the population. Also, while GM in recent years has hired many more nonwhites proportionately than before for unskilled and semi-skilled positions, its record in skilled and managerial jobs remains poor. The most recent public study indicates that in 1966 GM trailed both Chrysler and Ford in these categories.

On February 27, 1970, General Motors Corporation wrote to the Securities and Exchange Commission stating that it intended "to omit all nine proposals from its proxy material for the 1970 annual meeting. . . ." It stated a variety of legal reasons why it felt such a move to be proper. The primary reason was that "the Commission for many years has rightly required that in order for a proposal to be required to be included in the management's proxy soliciting material it must concern a matter of common interest to shareholders *qua* shareholders, as distinguished from matters which might equally be the concern of an interested group of citizens who are not shareholders." . . .

Early in April General Motors sent out its proxy soliciting material to all shareholders. The cover of the notice and proxy statement carried the following message:

Dear Stockholder

You are cordially invited to attend the annual meeting of stockholders which will be held at 2:00 p.m. on Friday, May 22, 1970, at Cobo Hall, 1 Washington Boulevard, Detroit, Michigan. Notice of Meeting and Proxy Statement are attached which you are urged to read for further information.

It is important that your shares be represented at the meeting whether or not you are personally able to attend; therefore, you are urged to sign, date and mail the enclosed proxy promptly.

Stockholders will be asked to elect directors and to ratify the appointment of auditors (Proposal No. 1). We recommend a vote in favor of the directors and "FOR" Proposal No. 1.

There are also four stockholder proposals (Nos. 2, 3, 4 and 5) to be voted upon. Proposal No. 2 relates to limitation of annual executive compensations. It has been presented at eight previous meetings and was defeated overwhelmingly by the stockholders each time. Proposal No. 3 relates to cumulative voting and has been overwhelmingly defeated each of the three times it has been presented. For the reasons explained in the proxy statement we again recommend a vote "AGAINST" each of these proposals.

Stockholder Proposals Nos. 4 and 5 seek the formation of a so-called "Committee for Corporate Responsibility" and an increase in the number of directors of the Corporation. It is important for you to know that these proposals are put forth by a group of seven individuals calling themselves The Project on Corporate Responsibility, Inc. This group purchased its 12 shares of common stock in January 1970 for the purpose of promoting its own particular economic and social views. The group has implied that the efforts of General Motors have not been adequate in fulfilling its responsibilities to the community as a whole.

The Board of Directors sincerely believes that General Motors could not have achieved its record of growth and progress unless it had well served the interests of the public and the stockholders. We are proud of GM's excellent record of leadership in meeting its public responsibilities. A summary of some of GM's achievements in automotive safety, air pollution control, mass transit, plant safety and social welfare is given in the enclosed booklet "GM's Record of Progress," which we urge you to read.

If General Motors is to fulfill its responsibilities in the future, it must continue to prosper and grow. Indeed, a corporation can only discharge its obligations to society if it continues to be a profitable investment for its stockholders. We are convinced that Proposals Nos. 4 and 5 would restrict management's ability to meet its responsibilities to the stockholders and the public. Accordingly, we recommend a vote "AGAINST" both proposals.

So that we may make suitable preparations for the meeting, if you wish to attend please enclose a note with your proxy. A reservation card will be mailed to you promptly to facilitate your admittance. We again urge you to support your management by signing, dating and mailing the enclosed proxy at your earliest convenience. Your cooperation will be appreciated.

Cordially,

E. N. Cole
President

J. M. Roche
Chairman

The proxy statement contained the following information regarding the proposals which were approved by the SEC:

The Project on Corporate Responsibility, Inc., 2008 Hilyer Place, N.W., Washington, D.C. 20009, which is the owner of record of 12 shares of the common stock of the Corporation, has given notice that it intends to present for action at the annual meeting the following two proposals, designated herein as Proposal Number 4 and Proposal Number 5, respectively.

PROPOSAL NUMBER 4

Whereas the shareholders of General Motors are concerned that the present policies and priorities pursued by the management have failed to take into account the possible social impact of the Corporation's activities, it is resolved that:

1. There be established the General Motors Shareholders Committee for Corporate Responsibility.
2. The Committee for Corporate Responsibility shall consist of no less than fifteen and no more than twenty-five persons, to be appointed by a representative of the Board of Directors, a representative of the Campaign to Make General Motors Responsible, and a representative of

United Auto Workers, acting by majority vote. The members of the Committee for Corporate Responsibility shall be chosen to represent the following: General Motors management, the United Auto Workers, environmental and conservation groups, consumers, the academic community, civil rights organizations, labor, the scientific community, religious and social service organizations, and small shareholders.

3. The Committee for Corporate Responsibility shall prepare a report and make recommendations to the shareholders with respect to the role of the corporation in modern society and how to achieve a proper balance between the rights and interests of shareholders, employees, consumers and the general public. The Committee shall specifically examine, among other things:

    A. The Corporation's past and present efforts to produce an automobile which:
        (1) is nonpolluting
        (2) reduces the potentiality for accidents
        (3) reduces personal injury resulting from accidents
        (4) reduces property damage resulting from accidents
        (5) reduces the cost of repair and maintenance whether from accidents or extended use.

    B. The extent to which the Corporation's policies towards suppliers, employees, consumers, and dealers are contributing to the goals of providing safe and reliable products.

    C. The extent to which the Corporation's past and present efforts have contributed to a sound national transportation policy and an effective low cost mass transportation system.

    D. The manner in which the Corporation has used its vast economic power to contribute to the social welfare of the nation.

    E. The manner by which the participation of diverse sectors of society in corporate decision-making can be increased including nomination and election of directors and selection of members of the committees of the Board of Directors.

4. The Committee's report shall be distributed to the shareholders and to the public no later than March 31, 1971. The Committee shall be authorized to employ staff members in the performance of its duties. The Board of Directors shall allocate to the Committee those funds the Board of Directors determines reasonably necessary for the Committee to accomplish its tasks. The Committee may obtain any information from the Corporation and its employees reasonably deemed relevant by the Committee, provided, however, that the Board of Directors may restrict the information to be made available to the Committee to information which the Board of Directors reasonably determines to be not privileged for business or competitive reasons.

The stockholder has submitted the following statement in support of such resolution:

Reasons: The purpose of this resolution is to enable shareholders to assess the public impact of the Corporation's decisions, and to determine the proper role of the Corporation in society. Past efforts by men such as Ralph Nader to raise these issues have been frustrated by the refusal of management to make its files and records available either to the shareholder or the public. Only a committee representing a broad segment of the public with adequate resources and access to information can prepare a report which will accomplish these objectives.

The Board of Directors favors a vote *AGAINST* this resolution for the following reasons:

This resolution and Proposal Number 5 by the same sponsor are parts of an attack on the General Motors Board of Directors and management and on what General Motors had achieved on behalf of its stockholders and the public. In the opinion of the Board of Directors and management the attack is based on false conceptions and assumptions. It was launched by a stock-holder (the Project), composed of seven members, which purchased 12 shares of General Motors stock in January 1970 for the express purpose of this attack. The Project has announced that while General Motors is its first target, similar attacks will be made on other large corporations.

The Project is a nonprofit corporation organized this year under the laws of the District of Columbia. Its formation was announced by Ralph Nader. Although he has stated that he is "not a formal participant in the Project" and that the "program" affecting General Motors is one "undertaken by a number of other young attorneys in Washington," he has promoted the Project and the Campaign to Make General Motors Responsible (Campaign GM) by press interview, television appearance and otherwise. For many years he has been identified with various campaigns against General Motors and was a prominent participant in a demonstration against the Corpora-tion at the General Motors Building in New York in December 1969.

The names "Committee for Corporate Responsibility" and "Campaign to Make General Motors Responsible" together with this resolution which would establish a Committee for Corporate Responsibility and the state-ments in support of the resolution suggest that management's decisions "have failed to take into account the possible adverse social impact of the Corporation's activities. . . ." This simply is not true. The true facts in regard to the concern and responsibility with which General Motors has pursued goals of social and public policy are set forth in detail in the enclosed booklet, "GM's Record of Progress." We are proud of this record and all stockholders are urged to read the booklet.

The objective of the resolution is to interpose a body unknown to cor-porate law or practice (the Committee for Corporate Responsibility)— purportedly investigatory in nature but structured for harassment and publicity—between the stockholders and the Board of Directors. The estab-lishment of such a Committee would seriously hamper the Board of Direc-tors in representing the stockholders and in carrying out its responsibilities to manage the business and affairs of the Corporation.

The proposed Committee, far from achieving "a proper balance be-tween the rights and interest of shareholders, employees, consumers and the general public," is proposed to be appointed "by majority vote" of (1) a representative of "Campaign GM," which is the creature of the proponent of the resolution, (2) a representative of the United Auto Workers, and (3) a representative of the Board of Directors. This permits the crucial "majority vote," with power to elect the entire Committee, to be supplied by a rep-resentative of "Campaign GM" (which itself owns no General Motors stock) and by a representative of the United Auto Workers. Members of the Committee would not be required to be stockholders of General Motors and would be chosen to represent General Motors management, the UAW, environmental and conservation groups, consumers, the academic community, civil rights organizations, labor, the scientific community, religious and social service organizations, and small stockholders. It is obvious that the proponent of the resolution seeks this Committee to pursue its special interests.

The proposed method of appointing the proposed Committee makes it clear that its purpose is to harass the Corporation and its management and to promote the particular economic and social views espoused by the proponent of the resolution. The Board of Directors believes that this resolution, if adopted, would do serious damage to General Motors and to its stockholders and, in fact, to the general public.

The Board of Directors favors a vote *AGAINST* this Proposal Number 4. Proxies solicited by the Board of Directors will be so voted unless stockholders specify in their proxies a contrary choice.

PROPOSAL NUMBER 5

Resolved: That Number 15 of the By-Laws of the Corporation be amended to read as follows:

15. The business of the Corporation shall be managed by a board of twenty-six members.

The stockholder has submitted the following statement in support of such resolution:

Reasons: This amendment will expand the number of directors to enable representatives of the public to sit on the Board of Directors without replacing any of the current nominees of management. The proponents of this amendment believe that adding representatives of the public to the Board is one method to insure that the Corporation will consider the impact of its decisions on important public issues, including auto safety, pollution, repairs, mass transportation, and equal employment opportunities.

The Board of Directors favors a vote *AGAINST* this resolution for the following reasons:

The Board of Directors finds no valid reason why the number of directors should be increased at the present time. Any suggestion that General Motors Corporation has been deficient in considering the interest of the public in such matters as auto safety, pollution, mass transportation and the like is entirely contrary to fact; the Company's record in this regard is set forth in the enclosed booklet.

The Board of Directors believes that each director, in addition to his responsibility to represent all the stockholders, has a very important responsibility to customers, employees, the public, and society generally. This is in accord with the development of the modern American corporation and corporate theory to which General Motors whole-heartedly subscribes and in accordance with which it operates. But that is very different from having as members of the Board individuals, no matter how worthy, who would be elected to represent special interests and who would feel obliged to concentrate attention on those special interests whether or not the effect would be to disrupt the proper and effective functioning of the Board.

Moreover, the Board of Directors continues to believe that for a board of directors to be effective each member must feel a responsibility to represent all the stockholders. In fact, representation of special groups introduces the possibility of partisanship among board members which would impair the ability to work together, a requirement essential to the efficient functioning of a board of directors.

Stockholders should recognize that the resolution to amend the By-Laws to increase the number of Directors is not a simple, innocuous proposal. The real issue posed by this proposal is whether an opportunity should be created to inject into the Corporation's Board of Directors three additional directors who are selected not on the basis of their interest in the success of the Corporation but rather on the basis of their sympathy with the special interests of the proponent of the resolution. This is proposed under the guise that as "representatives of the public" they would insure that the Corporation "will consider the impact of its decisions on important public issues." The proposal is a reflection upon the service rendered to the Corporation and its stockholders by the present members of the Board of Directors who were elected because of their integrity and broad experience in many fields including public service. The suggestion that they have not taken into account the impact of their decisions upon the public has no basis in fact. The objective of Proposal No. 5 is substantially the same as that of Proposal No. 4. If the proponent should be successful in increasing the number of directors and thereafter electing its nominees, the Board of Directors believes there would be similar internal harassment to the detriment of General Motors, its stockholders, and the public.

The Board of Directors favors a vote *AGAINST* this Proposal Number 5. Proxies solicited by the Board of Directors will be so voted unless stockholders specify in their proxies a contrary choice.

The proxy material was accompanied by a 21-page booklet entitled "GM's Record of Progress in Automotive Safety, Air Pollution Control, Mass Transit, Plant Safety, Social Welfare."

Prior to the May 22 stockholders meeting both GM and the project were active in seeking support, as is indicated in the following article from the May 21, 1970, issue of *The Wall Street Journal.*[1]. . .

Case of Overkill

. . . Shareholders, including individuals, banks, churches, universities, and other institutional investors, are being wooed by management as though a major proxy fight were on. "We're being treated to a classic example of corporate overkill," says one bank trust officer who has had intimate exposure to the GM efforts.

"We're not doing anything that we haven't done before," protests a GM spokesman. Mrs. Helen Faust, an Ionia, Mich. housewife and mother of nine, tells a different story. A few weeks ago a GM employee called, asking if she had received a proxy statement for her 3,150 shares.

"Did she plan to return the proxy or vote it herself at the annual meeting?" the caller inquired. Charles Greb, the GM stock transfer agent who made the call from his New York City office, says he has been calling shareholders because they have been having a little difficulty with the mails and wanted to make sure that the proxy statements had been received.

But Mrs. Faust, who has owned her shares for 12 years, says, "I don't believe for a moment that he was calling to see if the proxy was lost. I have failed to return GM proxies in the past and have never been favored with such concern." She thinks Mr. Greb found out what he wanted to know "when I told him I was voting my shares for the project."

GM's president, Edward N. Cole, concedes that he isn't "concerned that they [the project] will take over the company." Rather, he says, GM is "worried about the principles" the project espouses.

The project's Mr. Moore says, "GM hopes that by crushing us this time we will go away and won't come back. Such thinking is silly. Although we will lose the vote, we have succeeded in forcing many GM stockholders to think about the corporation's responsibility to society for the first time." . . .

At the meeting Proposal No. 4, to establish the committee on corporate responsibility, was defeated. It received 6.4 million votes (2.7%) from 62,000 shareholders (7.1%). Proposal No. 5, to increase the size of the board of directors, was also defeated, receiving 5.7 million votes (2.4%) from 53,000 shareholders (6.2%). . . .

EPILOGUE: The following article appeared on page one of the September 1, 1970, edition of the *New York Times*.[2]

DETROIT. Aug. 31—The General Motors Corporation announced today the establishment of a "public policy committee" to advise the giant concern on matters that affect the general public.

General Motors, the world's largest corporation, has become a major target of leaders of environmental and consumer movements. The committee is designed to give the board of directors expert advice on how to deal with such issues as pollution and safety.

The committee is made up of five members of the 23-member board of directors of GM, four of whom are not officers in the company and one of whom is a former vice chairman of the corporation.

James M. Roche, chairman of the board of directors, said the five men "have a broad and diverse background reflecting their deep interest in social, environmental and other concerns." He added that this combination would enable the committee "to act in the best interest of our stockholders as well as the broader community in which we operate."

The members on the committee are:

John A. Mayer, chairman of the committee. He is also chairman of the Mellon National Bank and Trust Company of Pittsburgh and a trustee of Carnegie-Mellon University, the Carnegie Institute, and the University of Pennsylvania.

James R. Killian, chairman of the corporation of the Massachusetts Institute of Technology and former United States Presidential Assistant for Science and Technology.

John T. Connor, chairman of the Allied Chemical Corporation and former Secretary of Commerce.

George Russel, former vice chairman of General Motors and a trustee and national campaign director for Meharry Medical College in Nashville.

Gerald A. Sivage, president of Marshall Field & Co. of Chicago and a trustee of Northwestern University and Carroll College.

The committee, which will report directly to the board of directors, is

GM's apparent answer to demands made by a group of critics at the last stockholder meeting on May 22. The critics, organized in a group called Campaign GM, had submitted two proposals to make the corporation more responsive to the general public.

One proposal would have added three more members of the board of directors to represent the public interest. The other would have set up a committee of "corporate responsibility" drawn from management, the United Auto Workers Union, and civic groups to report on how the company was dealing with such issues as pollution, safety, and mass transportation. The two proposals were overwhelmingly defeated in the proxy balloting, getting less than 3 percent of the votes.

Ralph Nader, the consumer advocate who helped start Campaign GM but did not directly involve himself in the effort, said in an interview that the new committee was "genuinely preposterous."

"The fact that they couldn't go outside of the company for the men is an indication of GM's insecurity. It's so ridiculous that it will backfire on them."

Mr. Nader added that Mr. Connor could not possibly deal fairly with such problems as pollution because he said Mr. Connor's company, Allied Chemical, was one of the biggest polluters in the nation.

Mr. Killian, he said, also could not act independently because GM was a big contributor to Massachusetts Institute of Technology and "MIT has never let out a peep against GM."

Notes

1. Norman Pearlstine, "Activist Shareholders Provoke GM Offensive for Its Annual Meeting," *The Wall Street Journal* (May 21, 1970), p. 1.
2. Reprinted with permission of the *New York Times,* from "GM Names 5 Directors as Public-Issue Advisers," by Agis Salpukis. Copyright Sept. 1, 1970, by the New York Times Company.

Morality and the Ideal of Rationality in Formal Organizations

JOHN LADD

I. INTRODUCTORY

The purpose of this paper is to explore some of the moral problems that arise out of the interrelationships between individuals and formal organizations (or bureaucracies) in our society. In particular, I shall be concerned with the moral implications of the so-called ideal of rationality of formal organizations with regard to, on the one hand, the obligations of individuals both inside and outside an organization to that organization and, on the other hand, the moral responsibilities of organizations to individuals and to the public at large. I shall argue that certain facets of the organizational ideal are incompatible with the ordinary principles of morality and that the dilemma created by this incompatibility is one source of alienation in our contemporary, industrial society. The very conception of a formal organization or bureaucracy presents us with an ideological challenge that desperately needs to be met in some way or other.

The term "formal organization" will be used in a more or less technical sense to cover all sorts of bureaucracies, private and public. A distinctive mark of such organizations is that they make a clear-cut distinction between the acts and relationships of individuals in their official capacity within the organization and in their private capacity. Decisions of individual decision-makers in an organization are attributed to the organization and not to the individual. In that sense, they are impersonal. Individual office-holders are in principle replaceable by other individuals without affecting the continuity or identity of the organization. In this sense, it has sometimes been said that an organization is "immortal."

This kind of impersonality, in particular, the substitutability of individuals, is one way in which formal organizations differ from other kinds of social systems, e.g. the family, the community or the nation, which are collectivities that are dependent for their existence on specific individuals or groups of specific individuals and that change when they change. . . .

Social critics, e.g. W. H. Whyte, use phrases like the "smothering of the individual" to describe the contemporary situation created by organizations. It is not my purpose here to decry once more the unhappy condition of man occasioned by his submergence as an individual in the vast social, economic and political processes created by formal organizations. Instead, I shall try to show that the kind of alienation that we all feel and

Selections from the *Monist*, Vol. 54 (1970), reprinted with permission of the author and publisher.

complain about is, at least in part, a logical necessity flowing from the concept of formal organizations itself, that is, it is a logical consequence of the particular language-game one is playing in organizational decision-making. My analysis is intended to be a logical analysis, but one that also has important ethical implications. . . .

Here we may find the concept of a language-game, as advanced by Wittgenstein and others, a useful tool of analysis. The point about a language-game is that it emphasizes the way language and action are interwoven: "I shall call the whole, consisting of language and the actions into which it is woven, the language-game."[1] A language-game is thus more than simply an abstract set of propositions constituting, say, a formal system. The game not only determines what should and what should not be done, but also sets forth the goals and the moves by which they are to be attained. More important even than these, a particular language-game determines how the activities within it are to be conceptualized, prescribed, justified and evaluated. Take as an example what is meant by a "good" move in chess: we have to refer to the rules of chess to determine what a "move" is, how to make one, what its consequences will be, what its objective is and whether or not it is a good move in the light of this objective.[2] Finally, this system of rules performs the logical function of defining the game itself. . . .

If we pursue the game-analogy one step further, we find that there may be even more striking similarities between the language-game of formal organizations and the language-game of other types of games. For instance, the rules and rationale obtaining in most typical games like chess and baseball tend to make the activity logically autonomous, i.e. the moves, defenses and evaluations are made independently of external considerations. In this sense they are self-contained. Furthermore, while playing a game it is thought to be "unfair" to challenge the rules. Sometimes it is even maintained that any questioning of the rules is unintelligible. In any case, there is a kind of sanctity attached to the rules of a game that renders them immune to criticism on the part of those engaged in playing the game. The resemblance of the autonomy of the activity and the immunity of the rules governing the game to the operations of bureaucracies can hardly be coincidental![3]

II. THE CONCEPTS OF SOCIAL DECISION AND SOCIAL ACTION

Let us take as our point of departure Herbert Simon's definition of a formal organization as a "decision-making structure."[4] The central concept with which we must deal is that of a decision (or action) that is attributable to the organization rather than to the individuals who are actually involved in the decisional process. The decision is regarded as the organization's decision even though it is made by certain individuals acting as its representatives. The latter make the decision only for and on behalf of the organization. Their role is, i.e. is supposed to be, impersonal. Such nonindividual decisions will be called *social decisions,* choices or actions. (I borrow the term "social choice" from Arrow, who uses it to refer to a choice made on behalf of a group as distinct from the aggregate of individual choices.)[5]

The officials of an organization are "envisaged as more or less ethically neutral . . . (and) the values to be taken as data are not those which would guide the individual if he were a private citizen. . . ."[6] When the official decides for the organization, his aim is (or should be) to implement the objectives of the organization *impersonally,* as it were. The decisions are made for the organization, with a view to its objectives and not on the basis of the personal interests or convictions of the individual official who makes the decision. This is the theory of organizational decision-making.

One might be tempted to call such organizational decisions "collective decisions," but that would be a misnomer if we take a collective decision to be a decision made by a collection of individuals. Social decisions are precisely decisions (or actions) that are to be *attributed* to the organizations themselves and not to collections of individuals. In practice, of course, the organizational decisions made by officials may actually be collective decisions. But in theory the two must be kept separate; for the "logic" of decisions attributed to organizations is critically different from the "logic" of collective decisions, i.e. those attributed to a collection of individuals.

Underlying the concept of social decisions (choices, actions) as outlined here is the notion that a person (or group of persons) can make decisions that are not his, i.e. are not attributable to him. He makes the decisions on behalf of someone else and with a view to the latter's interest, not his own. In such cases, we ordinarily consider the person (or group) that acts to be a representative or agent of the person or thing he is acting for. . . .

Accordingly, a social decision, as intended here, would be an action performed by an official as actor but owned by the organization as author. For all the consequences of the decision so made are imputed to the organization and not to the individual decision-maker. The individual decision-making official is not personally bound by the agreements he makes for the organization, nor is he personally responsible for the results of these decisions.

The theory of social decision-making that we are considering becomes even clearer if we examine the theory of organizational authority with which it is conjoined. Formal organizations are hierarchical in structure, that is, they are organized along the principle that superiors issue commands to those below them. The superior exercises authority over the subordinates. . . .

In summary, then, the organizational order requires that its social decisions be attributed to the organization rather than to the individual decision-maker, the "decision is to be made nonpersonally from the point of view of its organization effect and its relation to the organizational purpose,"[7] and the officials, as its agents, are required to abdicate their choice in obedience to the impersonal organizational order.

We now turn to another essential facet of the organizational language-game, namely, that every formal organization must have a goal, or a set of goals. In fact, organizations are differentiated and defined by reference to their aims or goals, e.g. the aim of the Internal Revenue Service is to collect taxes. The goal of most business ventures is to maximize profits, etc. We may find it useful to distinguish between the real and stated goals of an organization. Thus, as Galbraith has pointed out, although the stated goal of large industrial organizations is the maximization of profits, that is a pure myth; their actual, operative goals are the securing of their own survival, autonomy and economic growth.[8] There may, indeed, be a struggle over the goals of an organization, e.g. a power play between officials.[9]

For our present purposes, we may consider the real goal of an organization to be that objective (or set of objectives) that is used as a basis for decision-making, i.e. for prescribing and justifying the actions and decisions of the organization itself, as distinct from the actions and decisions of individual persons within the organization. As such, then, the goal is an essential element in the language-game of a formal organization's activities in somewhat the same way as the goal of checkmating the king is an essential element in the game of chess. Indeed, formal organizations are often differentiated from other kinds of social organizations in that they are "deliberately constructed and reconstructed to seek specific goals."[10]

The logical function of the goal in the organizational language-game is to supply the value premises to be used in making decisions, justifying and evaluating them. "Decisions in private management, like decisions in public management, must take as their ethical premises the objectives that have been set for the organization."[11]

It follows that any considerations that are not related to the aims or goals of the organization are automatically excluded as irrelevant to the organizational decision-making process. This principle of the exclusion of the irrelevant is part of the language-game. It is a logical requirement of the process of prescribing, justifying and evaluating social decisions. Consequently, apart from purely legal considerations, decisions and actions of individual officers that are unrelated to the organization's aims or goals are construed, instead, as actions of those individuals rather than of the organization. If an individual official makes a mistake or does something that fails to satisfy this criterion of social decision, he will be said to have "exceeded his authority," and will probably be sacked or made a vice-president! Again, the point is a logical one, namely, that only those actions that are related to the goal of the organization are to be attributed to the organization; those actions that are inconsistent with it are attributed to the individual officers as individuals. The individual, rather than the organization, is then forced to take the blame for whatever evil results.

Thus, for example, a naval officer who runs his ship aground is court-martialed because what he did was inconsistent with the aims of the naval organization; the action is attributed to him rather than to the Navy. On the other hand, an officer who successfully bombards a village, killing all of its inhabitants, in accordance with the objectives of his organization, is performing a social action, an action that is attributable to the organization and not to him as an individual. Whether or not the organization should take responsibility in a particular case for the mistakes of its officials is a policy decision to be made in the light of the objectives of the organization.

In other words, the concept of a social decision or action is bound up logically with the notion of an organizational aim. The consequence of this co-implication of action and aim is that the notion of an action or decision taken by an organization that is not related to one of its aims makes no sense. It is an unintelligible notion within the language-game of formal organizations. Within that language-game such an action would be as difficult to understand as it would be to understand how a man's knocking over the pieces in a chess game can be part of playing chess.

We finally come to the concept of "rationality," the so-called "ideal of pure rationality."[12] From the preceding observations concerning the organizational language-game, it should be clear that the sole standard for the evaluation of an organization, its activities and its decisions, is its effectiveness in achieving its objectives—within the framework of existing conditions and available means. This kind of effectiveness is called "rationality." Thus, rationality is defined in terms of the category of means and ends. . . .

"Rationality," so construed, is relative, that is, to be rational means to be efficient in pursuing a desired goal, whatever that might be. In the case of organizations, "a decision is 'organizationally' rational if it is oriented to the organization's goals."[13] Rationality is consequently neutral as to "what goals are to be attained."[14] Or to be more accurate, "rationality" is an incomplete term that requires reference to a goal before it is completely intelligible. . . .

Let us return to the organizational language-game. It was observed that within that game the sole standard of evaluation of, e.g. a decision, is the "rational" one, namely, that it be effective in achieving the organization's goal. Hence, any considerations that are taken into account in deliberation about these social decisions and in the evaluation of them are relevant only if they are related to the attainment of the organization's objectives. Let us suppose that there are certain factual conditions that must be considered in arriving at a decision, e.g. the available means, costs, and conditions of feasibility. The determination of such conditions is presumably a matter of empirical knowledge and a subject for empirical investigation. Among these empirical conditions there is a special class that I shall call *limiting operating conditions.* These are conditions that set the upper limits to an organization's operations, e.g. the scarcity of resources, of equipment, of trained personnel, legal restrictions, factors involving employee morale. Such conditions must be taken into account as *data,* so to speak, in organizational decision-making and planning. In this respect information about them is on a par logically with other information utilized in decision-making, e.g. cost-benefit computations.

Now the only way that moral considerations could be relevant to the operations of a formal organization in the language-game that I have been describing is by becoming limiting operating conditions. Strictly speaking, they could not even be introduced as such, because morality is itself not a matter of empirical knowledge. Insofar as morality in the strict sense enters into practical reasoning it must do so as an "ethical" premise, not as an empirical one. Hence morality as such must be excluded as irrelevant in organizational decision-making—by the rules of the language-game. The situation is somewhat parallel to the language-game used in playing chess: moral considerations are not relevant to the decisions about what move to make there either.

Morality enters in only indirectly, namely, as moral opinion, what John Austin calls "positive morality."[15] Obviously the positive morality, laws and customs of the society in which the organization operates must be taken into account in decision-making and planning. The same thing goes for the religious beliefs and practices of the community. A decision-maker cannot ignore them, and it makes no difference whether he shares them or accepts them himself personally. But the determination of whether or not there are such limiting conditions set by positive morality, customs, law, and religion is an empirical matter. Whether there are such limitations is simply a matter of fact and their relevance to the decision-making is entirely dependent upon how they affect the efficiency of the organization's operations.

Social decisions, then, are not and cannot be governed by the principles of morality, or, if one wishes, they are governed by a different set of moral principles from those governing the conduct of individuals as individuals. For, as Simon says: "Decisions in private management, like decisions in public management, must take as their ethical premises the objectives that have been set for the organization."[16] By implication, they cannot take their ethical premises from the principles of morality.

Thus, for logical reasons it is improper to expect organizational conduct to conform to the ordinary principles of morality. We cannot and must not expect formal organizations, or their representatives acting in their official capacities, to be honest, courageous, considerate, sympathetic, or to have any kind of moral integrity. Such concepts are not in the vocabulary, so to speak, of the organizational language-game. (We do not find them in the vocabulary of chess either!) Actions that are wrong by ordinary moral standards are not so for organizations; indeed, they may often be required. Secrecy, espionage and deception do not make organizational action wrong; rather they are right, proper and, indeed, *rational,* if they serve the objectives of the organization. They are no more or no less wrong than, say, bluffing is in poker. From the point of view of organizational decision-making they are "ethically neutral."

Of course, I do not want to deny that it may be in the best interests of a formal organization to pay lip service to popular morality (and religion). That is a matter of public relations. But public relations operations themselves are evaluated and justified on the same basis as the other operations of the organization. The official function of the public relations officer is to facilitate the operations of the organization, not to promote morality. . . .

The upshot of our discussion so far is that actions are subject to two entirely different and, at times, incompatible standards: social decisions are subject to the standard of rational efficiency (utility) whereas the actions of individuals as such are subject to the ordinary standards of morality. An action that is right from the point of view of one of these standards may be wrong from the point of view of the other. Indeed, it is safe to say that our own experience attests to the fact that our actual expectations and social approvals are to a large extent based on a tacit acceptance of a double-standard—one for the individual when he is in his office working for the company and another for him when he is at home among friends and neighbors. Take as an example the matter of lying: nobody would think of condemning Joe X, a movie star, for lying on a TV commercial about what brand of cigarettes he smokes, for it is part of his job. On the other hand, if he were to do the same thing in private among friends, we should consider his action to be improper and immoral. Or again, an individual who, acting in his official capacity, refuses help to a needy suppliant, would be roundly condemned if he were to adopt the same course of action in his private life.

III. THE MORAL RELATIONSHIP
OF INDIVIDUALS TO ORGANIZATIONS

It follows from what has already been said that the standard governing an individual's relationship to an organization is likely to be different from the one governing the converse relationship, i.e. of an organization to individuals. The individual, for his part, is supposed to conduct himself in his relationship to an organization according to the same standards that he would employ in his personal relationships, i.e. the standards of ordinary morality. Thus, he is expected to be honest, open, respectful, conscientious, and loyal towards the organization of which he is a member or with which he has dealings. The organization, represented by its officials, can, however, be none of these in return. "Officials are expected to assume an impersonal orientation. . . . Clients are to be treated as cases . . . and subordinates are to be treated in a similar fashion."[17]

The question I now want to explore is whether or not the individual is justified in applying the standard of individual morality to his relations with formal organizations. It will, of course, generally be in the interest of the formal organizations themselves to encourage him to do so, e.g. to be honest, although the organization as such cannot "reciprocate." But we must ask this question from the point of view of the individual or, if you wish, from the moral point of view: what good moral reasons can be given for an individual to assume a moral stance in his conduct and relations with formal organizations, in contradistinction, say, to his conduct and relations with individuals who happen to be employees of such an organization?

The problem, which may be regarded as a question of loyalty and fidelity, puts the age-old problem of authority and obedience in a new light. Authority has become diffused, as I have already pointed out, and the problem of obedience can no longer be treated in terms of the personal relationship of an individual to his sovereign lord. The problem today is not so easily focused on one relationship; for the demands of authority, as represented in modern organizations, are at once more extensive, more pervasive and less personal. The question we face today is, for example, why should I, as an individual, comply with the mass of regulations laid down by an impersonal order, a bureaucratic organization? Why, for example, should I comply with draft-registration procedures? with passport regulations? with income-tax requirements? with mortage, credit, licensing, fair-trade regulations or with anti-trust laws? Or, indeed, has the individual any moral obligation at all to comply with them?[18]

It might be thought that, before trying to answer such questions, we must be careful to distinguish between individuals within an organization, e.g. officials and employees, and those outside it who have dealings with it, e.g. clients and the general public: what each of these classes ought to do is different. Granting that the specific demands placed on individuals in these various categories may be quite different, they all involve the question of authority in one way or another. Hence, for our purposes, the distinction is unimportant. For example, the authority, or the claims to it, of governmental bureaucracies extends far beyond those who are actually in their employ, e.g. the Internal Revenue Service. For convenience, I shall call those who come under the authority of an organization in some capacity or other, directly or indirectly, the *subjects* of the organization. Thus, we are all subjects of the IRS.

Can any moral reasons be given why individual subjects should comply with the decisions of organizations? Or, what amounts to the same thing, what is the basis of the authority of organizations by virtue of which we have an obligation to accept and obey their directives? And why, if at all, do we owe them loyalty and fidelity?

The most obvious answer, although perhaps not the most satisfactory one ethically, is that it is generally expedient for the individual to go along with what is required by formal organizations. If I want a new automobile, I have to comply with the financing requirements. If I want to avoid being harassed by an internal revenue agent, I make out my income tax form properly. If I want to be legally married, I comply with the regulations of the Department of Public Health. In other words, I comply from practical necessity, that is, I act under a hypothetical imperative.

Still, this sort of answer is just as unsatisfactory from the point of view of moral philosophy as the same kind of answer always has been with regard to political obligation, namely, it fails to meet the challenge of the conscientious objector.

Furthermore, there are many occasions and even whole areas where self-interest is not immediately or obviously involved in which, nevertheless, it makes good sense to ask: why comply? The traditional Lockian argument that our acceptance of the benefits of part of the social and political order commits us morally to the acceptance and conformity with the rest of it rests on the dubious assumption that the social and political order is all of one piece, a seamless web. But when we apply the argument to formal organizations it becomes especially implausible, because there are so many competing claims and conflicting regulations, not to mention loyalties. Not only logically, but as a matter of practicality, it seems obvious that accepting the benefits of one bureaucratic procedure, e.g. mailing letters, does not, from the moral point of view, *eo ipso* bind us to accept and comply with all the other regulations and procedures laid down by the formal organization and, much less, those laid down by formal organizations in general. . . .

In sum, we cannot make compacts with organizations because the standard of conduct which requires that promises be honored is that of individual conduct.[19] It does not and cannot apply to formal organizations. This follows from the fact of a double standard. . . .

I have been able to touch only on some very limited aspects of the relationship of individuals to organizations. I hope, however, that it is now abundantly clear that some sort of crisis is taking place in our moral relationships, and in particular in our conceptions of authority, and that this crisis is due not only to complex historical, psychological and sociological factors, but also to an inherent *logical* paradox in the foundations of our social relations.

IV. THE MORAL RELATIONSHIP OF ORGANIZATIONS TO INDIVIDUALS

For logical reasons that have already been mentioned, formal organizations cannot assume a genuine moral posture towards individuals. Although the language-game of social decision permits actions to be attributed to organizations as such, rather than to the officials that actually make them, it does not contain concepts like "moral obligation," "moral responsibility," or "moral integrity." For the only relevant principles in rational decision-making are those relating to the objectives of the organization. Hence individual officers who make the decisions for and in the name of the organization, as its representatives, must decide solely by reference to the objectives of the organization.

According to the theory, then, the individuals who are officers of an organization, i.e. those who run it, operate simply as vehicles or instruments of the organization. The organization language-game requires that they be treated as such. That is why, in principle at least, any individual is dispensable and replaceable by another. An individual is selected for a position, retained in it, or fired from it solely on the grounds of efficiency, i.e. of what will best serve the interests of the organization. The interests and needs of the individuals concerned, as individuals, must be considered only insofar as they establish limiting operating conditions. Organizational rationality dictates that these interests and needs must not be considered in their own right or on their own merits. If we think of an organization as a machine, it is easy to see why we cannot reasonably expect it to have any moral obligations to people or for them to have any to it.

For precisely the same reason, the rights and interests of persons outside the organization and of the general public are *eo ipso* ruled out as logically irrelevant to rational organizational decision, except insofar as these rights and interests set limiting conditions to the effectiveness of the organization's operations or insofar as the promoting of such rights and interests constitutes part of the goal of the organization. Hence it is fatuous to expect an industrial organization to go out of its way to avoid polluting the atmosphere or to refrain from making napalm bombs or to desist from wire-tapping on purely moral grounds. Such actions would be irrational.

It follows that the only way to make the rights and interests of individuals or of the people logically relevant to organizational decision-making is to convert them into pressures of one sort or another, e.g. to bring the pressure of the law or of public opinion to bear on the organizations. Such pressures would then be introduced into the rational decision-making as limiting operating conditions. . . .

Since, as I have argued in some detail, formal organizations are not moral persons, and have no moral responsibilities, they have no moral rights. In particular, they have no *moral* right to freedom or autonomy. There can be nothing morally wrong in exercising coercion against a formal organization as there would be in exercising it against an individual. Hence, the other side of the coin is that it would be irrational for us, as moral persons, to feel any moral scruples about what we do to organizations. (We should constantly bear in mind that the officials themselves, as individuals, must still be treated as moral persons with rights and responsibilities attached to them as individuals.) . . .

V. UTILITARIANISM AND ALIENATION

It is abundantly evident that the use of a double standard for the evaluation of actions is not confined to the operations of formal organizations, as I have described them. The double standard for social morality is pervasive in our society. For almost all our social decisions, administrative, political and economic, are made and justified by reference to the "rational" standard, which amounts to the principle that the end justifies the means; and yet as individuals, in our personal relations with one another, we are bound by the ordinary principles of morality, i.e. the principles of obligation, responsibility and integrity. . . .

A great deal more needs to be said about the effects of working from a double standard of morality. In our highly organized (and utilitarian) society, most of us, as individuals, are forced to live double lives, and in order to accommodate ourselves to two different and incompatible standards, we tend to compartmentalize our lives, as I have already pointed out. For the most part, however, the organizational (or utilitarian) standard tends to take over.

Accordingly, our actions as individuals are increasingly submerged into social actions, that is, we tend more and more to use the social standard as a basis for our decisions and to evaluate our actions. As a result, the individual's own decisions and actions become separated from himself as a person and become the decisions and actions of another, e.g.

of an organization. They become social decisions, not decisions of the
individual. And in becoming social decisions, they are, in Hobbes's terms,
no longer "his," they are "owned" by another, e.g. an organization or
society.

This is one way of rendering the Marxian concept of alienation. As his
actions are turned into social decisions, the individual is alienated from
them and is *eo ipso* alienated from other men and from morality. In
adopting the administrator's point of view (or that of a utilitarian) and so
losing his actions, the individual becomes dehumanized and demoralized.
For morality is essentially a relation between men, as individuals, and in
losing this relation, one loses morality itself.

IV. CLOSING REMARKS
ON THE SOURCE OF THE PARADOX

It is unnecessary to dwell on the intolerable character of the moral
schizophrenia in which we find ourselves as the result of the double
standard of conduct that has been pointed out. The question is: what can
be done about it? The simplest and most obvious solution is to jettison one
of the conflicting standards. But which one? The choice is difficult, if not
impossible. If we give up the standard of "rationality," e.g. of organizational operations, then we surrender one of the chief conditions of
civilized life and progress as well as the hope of ever solving mankind's
perennial practical problems, e.g. the problems of hunger, disease, ignorance and overpopulation. On the other hand, if we give up the standard
of ordinary moral conduct, then in effect we destroy ourselves as moral
beings and reduce our relationships to each other to purely mechanical
and materialistic ones. To find a third way out of the dilemma is not only a
practical, political and sociological necessity, but a moral one as well. . . .

Notes

1. Ludwig Wittgenstein, *Philosophical Investigations* (New York: Macmillan
   Company, 1953), p. 7.
2. These rules are called "constitutive rules" by John Searle. See his *Speech Acts*
   (Cambridge: The University Press, 1969), Ch. 2, Sec. 5.
3. For further discussion of the game-model and this aspect of rules, see my
   "Moral and Legal Obligation," in J. Roland Pennock and John W. Chapman,
   editors, *Political and Legal Obligations, Nomos,* 12 (New York: Atherton Press,
   1970).
4. Herbert A. Simon, *Administrative Behavior,* 2nd ed. (New York: Free Press,
   1965), p. 9. Hereinafter cited as Simon, AB. For a useful survey of the
   subject of formal organizations, see Peter M. Blau and W. Richard Scott,
   Formal Organizations (San Francisco: Chandler Publishing Company, 1962).
   [p. 36.] Hereinafter cited as Blau and Scott, FO.

5. See Kenneth Arrow, *Social Choice and Individual Values* (New York: John Wiley, 1951), *passim*.
6. Quoted from A. Bergson by Kenneth Arrow in "Public and Private Values," in *Human Values and Economic Policy*, ed. S. Hook (New York: New York University Press, 1967), p. 14.
7. Quoted from Chester I. Barnard in Simon, AB, p. 203.
8. See John Kenneth Galbraith, *The New Industrial State* (Boston: Houghton Mifflin, 1967), pp.171-78. Hereinafter cited as NIS.
9. Amitai Etzioni, *Modern Organizations* (Englewood Cliffs, N.J.: Prentice-Hall, 1964), p. 4. Hereinafter cited as MO.
10. Etzioni, MO, p. 3. See also Blau and Scott, FO, p. 5. In a forthcoming article on "Community," I try to show that communities, as distinct from formal organizations, do not have specific goals. Indeed, the having of a specific goal may be what differentiates a *Gesellschaft* from a *Gemeinschaft* in Tönnies' sense. See Ferdinand Tönnies, *Community and Society*, trans. Charles P. Loomis (New York: Harper and Row, 1957), *passim*.
11. Simon, AB, p. 52.
12. "The ideal of pure rationality is basic to operations research and the modern management sciences." Yehezkel Dror, *Public Policymaking Reexamined* (San Francisco: Chandler Publishing Company, 1968), p. 336. Dror gives a useful bibliography of this subject on pp. 336-40.
13. Simon, AB, p. 77.
14. Simon, AB, p. 14.
15. "The name *morality*, when standing unqualified or alone, may signify the human laws which I style positive morality, without regard to their goodness or badness. For example, such laws of the class as are peculiar to given age, or such laws of the class as are peculiar to a given nation, we style the morality of that given age or nation, whether we think them good or bad, etc." John Austin, *Province of Jurisprudence Determined*, ed. H.L.A. Hart (New York: Noonday Press, 1954), p. 125. The study of positive moralities belongs to what I call "descriptive ethics." See my *Structure of a Moral Code* (Cambridge, Mass: Harvard University Press, 1957).
16. Simon, AB, p. 52.
17. Blau and Scott, FO, p. 34.
18. See my "Moral and Legal Obligation," referred to in note [3].
19. The fact that promising involves an extremely personal relation between individuals is almost universally overlooked by philosophers who discuss promises.

Morality and Organizations

KENNETH E. GOODPASTER

I

In what follows, I propose to examine the applicability (and desirability of *rendering* applicable) such notions as 'virtue' and 'moral responsibility' to formal organizational agents (paradigmatically, business corporations and government agencies) in the face of certain conceptual barriers which have been thought to attend such a move. Motivation for such an inquiry stems from several sources. The last decade of American life has witnessed a deep intensification of concern about the quantity and quality of large-scale technological growth, in terms of both social and environmental impact. Clearly the vehicles of this growth have been corporate and bureaucratic agents whose presence in modern society is as ethically mysterious as it is pervasive. Ethics, as traditionally conceived, is a discipline which concentrates on the values and proprieties of individual conduct. That corporate conduct has in fact come to dominate the lives of individuals is only slowly beginning to occur to the moral philosophical community, together with an attendant imperative to accommodate this fact to ethical theory. One important stage in this accommodation process includes a shift in levels of agency (and consequently, moral responsibility or virtue) from the individual to the corporate or organizational decision-maker. On the face of it, what is demanded is a rather straightforward inversion of Plato's avowed methodology in the *Republic*. Instead of taking our cues from the macrocosmic or organizational level in the quest for a deeper understanding of virtue on the microcosmic or individual level, we seem to be faced with the task of searching for clarity about corporate moral responsibility through a close scrutiny of its necessary and sufficient conditions in the lives of ordinary human agents. This is, at least, the strategy that has suggested itself to more than one laborer in the vineyard of "technology and values" including the present writer.[1] Christopher D. Stone, in a recent and important book on law and the corporation has summarized the strategy nicely:

> If people are going to adopt the terminology of 'responsibility' (with its allied concepts of corporate conscience) to suggest new, improved ways of dealing with corporations, then they ought to go back and examine in detail what 'being responsible' entails—in the ordinary case of the responsible human being. Only after we have considered what being responsible calls for in general does it make sense to develop the notion of a corporation being responsible.[2]

Paper originally presented at the Bentley College Second National Conference on Business Ethics; reprinted in the *Proceedings of the Second National Conference on Business Ethics,* ed. Michael Hoffman (Waltham, Mass.: Center for Business Ethics, 1977); reprinted by permission of the editor and the author.

Thus the picture which emerges sets a clear, if not widely appreciated and accepted, project: if certain current social and environmental problems are related to the conduct of large-scale technological agents, we need to provide both a descriptive-explanatory account of the ethical style of such agents as well as a normative account of what moral responsibility for such agents might amount to. I have elsewhere labeled this double-purpose enterprise "ethical diagnostics"—invoking both the descriptive-explanatory and the therapeutic suggestions of the medical metaphor.[3]

This project (with its strategy) has been challenged, however. Usually the challenge is implicit and subtle, as in the context I shall focus on presently. But sometimes it is overt. Quotations from corporate executives such as the following carry the message:

> The social responsibility of business is to make profits.
>
> The owners of each business enterprise should define the social responsibility of their enterprise as they see fit. This is the only way compatible with the rights of their owners.
>
> I can't believe that social responsibility was ever invented by a businessman; it must have been made up by a sociologist.[4]

The idea that corporate agents should be thought of in the categories of ethical theory at all is what seems to be at stake in these remarks. And the challenge which this provides to the project sketched above is apparent. What should be noted, however, is that though the challenge is significant, it is at least *manageable* in the sense that it represents a difference in viewpoint of a quasiethical sort (sometimes ethical disagreements are actually to be preferred to other sorts!). That is, the disagreement seems to turn on whether we *should* think of or treat organizational agents as morally responsible beings. And we can entertain arguments and counterarguments in an effort to resolve such a disagreement.

But there is a more subtle and deeply rooted challenge to the project to which I propose to devote most of my attention in this essay. It does not come from the business world, but from ethical theory and allied disciplines. And the issue appears *not* to be the *advisability* of construing organizational agents in ethical terms, but rather the very *intelligibility* of doing so. The sort of view I have in mind here is paradigmatically articulated by John Ladd in a penetrating article entitled "Morality and the Ideal of Rationality in Formal Organizations."[5] Ladd's thesis, if I read him correctly, is that there is a logical or conceptual barrier to the project of ethical diagnostics and its moral intent. According to Ladd, if one expects corporate or organizational agents

> . . . to conform to the principles of morality, he is simply committing a logical mistake, perhaps even what Ryle calls a category mistake. In a sense, . . . organizations are like machines, and it would be a category mistake to expect a machine to comply with the principles of morality. By the same token, an official or agent of a formal organization is simply violating the basic rules of organizational activity if he allows his moral scruples rather than the objectives of the organization to determine his decision.[6]

Ladd bases his contention in part on a rather uncompromising account of the ideal of rationality in formal organizations gleaned from organization theorists like Herbert Simon,[7] Chester Barnard,[8] and, more indirectly, Max Weber. Essentially, the picture is that of organizational decision-making involving

    (A) Imputation of joint decisions to the organization;
    (B) A set of constitutive goals in terms of which the organization is defined and its rationality is assessed; and
    (C) The exclusiveness of a means-ends conception of rational decisions in the "language game" of the organization.

And one of the most significant results of the pervasiveness of this organizational standard, in Ladd's view, is a kind of moral schizophrenia which sets in upon participants (and recipients). For standards of moral responsibility are binding on individuals as individuals, whereas the corporate agents in which and toward which individuals operate are (logically) marching to the beat of a nonmoral drummer.

This last point needs expansion, for it contains by implication the other main part of Ladd's basis for his general contention. Besides the account of rationality in formal organizations, there is also an account of the nature of moral responsibility at work in Ladd's discussion which is broadly Kantian in character. Though it is not set out explicitly in the essay under discussion, the reader can piece it together in outline, at least as containing the following elements:

    (A′) Moral decisions are imputed to the individual agents who are their authors, not to (or from) something else;
    (B′) Moral responsibility is not (simply?) a matter of pursuing efficiently a goal or set of goals, i.e., it is not essentially instrumental in character; and
    (C′) Morality involves a conception of rationality in which respect for the integrity and freedom of persons is central.

Thus Ladd embraces the interesting, if controversial, view that standard utilitarian-style approaches to decision-making are, as a matter of logic, incompatible with morally responsible decision-making, at least as it is ordinarily understood. Expediency and moral responsibility are like oil and water.

The upshot, then, in light of the fact that organizations are such an integral part of modern civilized life, is that we find ourselves in a practical, ongoing dilemma which is rooted in a *conceptual* impasse between individual and institutional forms of rational agency.

II

Now, though much more could and should be said to do justice to Ladd's provocative discussion, perhaps enough has been set out for my present purposes. For if one is reluctant, as I am, to permit the project described at the outset to run aground in the face of what appears to be a challenge to its intelligibility, the alternatives become relatively clear: It would appear that we must either

    (1) Abandon Ladd's account of the ideal of rationality in formal organizations, or

(2) Abandon Ladd's implicit views as to the nature of moral responsibility, or
(3) Abandon both (in whole or in part).

The problem is that none of these courses is, in my opinion, easy.

Alternative (1) might seem at first glance to be the most appropriate on several counts. For one thing, it is phrased in terms of an "ideal" of rationality, and the natural response is: *Whose* ideal? After all, if we are simply dealing with certain idiosyncratic conceptions of what it is reasonable for an organization to do, then this should give us no pause in trying to articulate a ("therapeutic") model of what organizations ought to do morally. The problem with this response is that Ladd's account of the ideal of rationality in formal organizations is *not* idiosyncratic, either in terms of popular opinion or in terms of social scientific theories. It undoubtedly represents the dominant model of organizational behavior, both in terms of descriptive-explanatory studies of that behavior and in terms of people's expectations (if not ultimate appraisals) of that behavior.

There is, however, an important respect in which this account is incomplete, and I propose to argue that it is this fact which provides some flexibility in what is otherwise a tense dichotomy between corporate rationality and moral responsibility. In outlining the "ideal" of rationality for formal organizations, Ladd, drawing largely upon H.A. Simon, emphasizes the analogy with game rules (e.g., chess). The constitutive conditions which define what is a 'move' and what is not are compared to the decision-making premises ("organizational goals") which define what is and what is not a genuine organizational decision (as against, say, a personal decision by a member of an organization). But there is a crucial disanalogy here which is not emphasized. It is that, for the most part, game rules are static while organizational premisses tend to be more dynamic. In other words, though we are dealing perhaps with differences of degree, the irrelevance of morality to chess is of a different order of magnitude from the irrelevance of morality to organizational rationality. For organizational mandates and goals (the decision-making premisses) are subject to constant stress, even evolution, in the presence of complex pressures both from within and from outside the corporate coalition. The limits of willing identification and cooperation among managers, stockholders, workers, customers, and the general public (in the case of private organizations) and legislators, administrators, staff, voters, etc. (in the case of public organizations) result in considerable, though possibly incremental, changes in organizational premisses. By contrast, it would be surprising to find such changes in the rules or objectives of chess over time.[9] And the explanation is not hard to discern. Chess, unlike organizational decision-making, is pretty clearly insulated from morally significant impact. My guess is that one could think of limiting cases of game rules which do exhibit developmental characteristics due to their impact on human life (e.g., rules of war, or rules of language or rules of etiquette). But for the most part, the moral irrelevance of constitutive rules varies in direct proportion to the 'artificiality' or 'abstractness' of the games which they constitute. Thus we should expect that the stark separation between organizational rationality and moral responsibility is overstated. Organizational rationality, to be sure, includes a purely 'means-to-ends' component, but the 'ends' which are often taken as 'givens' are rarely taken as unalterable. This being the case, *efficiency* can only exhaust the concept of rationality in formal organizations *if it is also rational for such organizations to abdicate control over the development or change of those ends.* If it is not rational to do this, and I hazard the opinion that it is not, then the ideal of rationality in formal organizations must include more than the efficient pursuit of given or static decision-premises (by analogy with games like chess[10]). It must include criteria for the scrutiny and modification of those premises ('ends') themselves. And it seems less likely that a case can be made for the irrelevance of morality to *these* criteria than for the irrelevance of morality to any (*given*) premisses or ends.

Simon himself seems to me to acknowledge this perception implicitly when he writes:

> . . . although it is correct to say that organization behavior is oriented toward the organization objective, this is not the whole story; for the organization objective itself changes in response to the influence of those for whom the accomplishment of that objective secures personal values.[11]

Thus, though Ladd seems right in interpreting organizational theorists as less sensitive than they might be to the ramifications of controlled adaption of organizational goals or premises, he goes too far in inferring from remarks about the givenness of organizational goals[12] such conclusions as that:

> —organizational decisions "cannot take their ethical premisses from the principles of morality" and
> —"for logical reasons it is improper to expect organizational conduct to conform to the ordinary principles of morality."[13]

What is crucial is that it is an *empirical* question whether the principles of morality find their way into organizational premisses, and that the "givenness" of those premisses is only a *part* of what is involved in the ideal of rationality for formal organizations.

I conclude, then, that we must enrich the account of rationality for formal organizations to accommodate the phenomenon of controlled adaptation of organizational goals or decision-premises. This modification permits us to conceive of moral principles as candidates for organizational premisses, or at least as criteria for the control of those premisses, in a way which Ladd's account precludes due to its emphasis on the static "givenness" of those premisses. With respect to alternative (1) above, then, it seems unreasonable to abandon Ladd's account altogether, though it seems reasonable to do so in part.

III

Let us now turn to alternative (2). Here we find difficulties of a procedural sort, since Ladd does not develop explicitly an account of morally responsible decision-making. Determining whether to abandon it in whole or in part, then, is problematic. My strategy will be simply to isolate one feature of the account and suggest that it is overstated as it stands, and then trace the implications of this fact for Ladd's general argument.

As I pointed out earlier (B'), a key element in Ladd's contrast between organizational rationality and morality is the issue of *instrumentality*. As Ladd puts it, instrumental rationality

> . . . reduces the relationship between human beings to the category of means to an end, a category in which they do not belong. It makes the only point of a rational action the function that it plays in 'means-ends' chains. The only point of keeping a promise, for instance, is the effect that doing so will have on my ends or the ends of others. This way of looking at rationality reflects what seems to me to be essentially an amoral position, for it reduces morality, which is a matter of the relations between human beings, to what is useful or expedient for some purpose or other.[14]

Now, I have no desire to maintain that a non-instrumentalist conception of moral responsibility is untenable, quite the contrary. But I do wish to point out that there are two importantly different interpretations or versions of what has come to be called "deontological" morality. On the first, consideration of consequences for persons' ends is held to be *relevant* but *insufficient* for morally responsible decision-making, while on the second, such consideration of consequences is held to be *irrelevant* and *unnecessary*.[15] To the extent that Ladd is embracing the latter, more radical, view of morally responsible decision-making, his thesis of incompatibility between morality and organizational rationality is enhanced. To the extent that he is embracing the former, more moderate, view the incompatibility thesis becomes less plausible. For on the moderate view, there is a definite, even essential, place for consequential "means-ends" reasoning in moral decision-making—even if this sort of reasoning does not *exhaust* morality. This observation, joined to my earlier point about the place for controlled adaptation in organizational rationality, begins to complete the picture of a reconciliation where Ladd seems to have seen only conceptual impasse.

The question in the present context, then, becomes: Which of the two general forms of deontological morality is more plausible, if we assume with Ladd that a purely teleological account of morality will not do?[16] It seems to me that we have to answer in favor of the moderate form. The implications of relegating consequences to *irrelevance* are simply intolerable. In terms of Ladd's example of promise-keeping, it is salutary to be reminded that there is more, morally, to our responsibilities in this matter than expediency, but this is no reason for thinking that the effects on persons' ends of keeping or breaking a promise make no moral difference *at all*.[17] The moral ambiguity at work in such slogans as "whatever the consequences" has been too amply demonstrated (to most philosophers) to bear the weight that the radical deontologist wishes to place on it.

I conclude, then, that Ladd's account of the general nature of moral responsibility needs a moderation which is not clearly present, and that with this moderation we again perceive a lessening of the tension between the ideals of organizational rationality and the demands of morality. Thus alternative (2), though too strong, leads us to alternative (3).

The pattern which emerges is as follows. The project of "ethical diagnostics" and its point, the molding of corporate "conscience," appeared to
be threatened at the outset by what was claimed to be a logical or conceptual barrier. The ideal of rationality in formal organizations was simply
inconsistent with the ideal of morally responsible decision-making. On
examining Ladd's accounts of the respective ideals, however, I argued
that each required modification. Organizational rationality cannot be
conceived as *purely* instrumental with no criteria for guiding the development of the goals or premises from which efficiency departs. Nor can
moral responsibility be conceived as purely non-instrumental with no
attention to the consequences of conduct on the ends or interests of those
affected by it (including, I might add, the agent himself). Thus what I
claim to have provided so far is rather negative: a kind of *space* for the
working out of a solution to our problem. The logical or conceptual
barriers to describing and developing formal organizations through
moral categories were seen to depend upon unduly strong construals of
ideal rationality and ideal morality, respectively. The moderation of these
ideals (or better, the clarification of them) relaxes the barriers a bit and
allows for the possibility that rationality might be moralized and morality
rationalized.

But it is important not to overstate the case. Though perhaps exagger-
ated, Ladd's approach is a healthy caution to a naive conception of
corporate (or organizational) description and reform. There is, in other
words, a clear tension between the joint demands of efficiency and adaptation in decision-making, not to mention complications involved in the
proper understanding of each demand taken separately. My own view is
that this tension (not inconsistency) represents an essential structural
feature of rational as well as responsible agency. Both for purposes of
empirical analysis and for purposes of reform, our conception of corporate agency (like our conception of individual agency) must reflect the fact
that *action* is not simply the mindless pursuit of antecedently given ends.
The static model must be replaced by the dynamic one in which action is
seen as a mutual accommodation between organism (organization) and
environment in which the organism monitors both means and ends. And
the monitoring process involves feedback between the agent and the
results of his pursuit. Sometimes this feedback will dictate alteration of
means; sometimes it will dictate alteration of ends. Rationality in action
will depend upon an agent's capacity, among others, to make appropriate
adjustments in both areas in an effort to maintain stability and long-term
integrity. Whether and in what way an agent engages in this tuning
operation is a more important indicator of its conscience or lack of
conscience than any given set of goals which it may pursue at any given
time. Thus an ethical profile of an organization's decision-making will
need to attend not simply to organizational premises, to use Simon's
term, but (more importantly) to the *adaptation patterns* which control those
premises. In the case of a private organization like a corporation, such
goals as profit, growth, market shares, etc., represent a typical corporation's ongoing behavioral premises—but they do not, in themselves,

provide us with a picture of the corporation's action-guiding principles in the fuller sense under discussion. To get at these, we need to attend to such features of the organizational structure as:

—information-gathering and processing priorities,
—criteria of management selection, and
—authority relationships between participants

As with an individual agent, an organizational agent exhibits his ethical commitments as much (perhaps more) in the procedural controls he places on his goal selection as in the goals selected. One of the most difficult (and interesting) tasks of the diagnostician is to isolate the key control variables in a given organization, relating them to patterns of organizational behavior and the results of that behavior.

A natural way in which an organization's goals (premises) might be controlled would be in terms of some *more general or basic* goal such as corporate expansion or community esteem, etc. This might manifest itself in selectivity regarding information-gathering, choice of managers, and degree of centralization of authority. Such a "teleological" organizational ethic might be more or less morally defensible. And there could be combinations of "metagoals" as well. A power company might control its goal selection in terms of both local community satisfaction and company growth.[18]

But the control need not be provided in this way. Indeed, in the end the selection of the metagoals themselves would seem to require criteria of some sort. If an infinite regress is not to be the result, there may well be standards of goal selection of a more formal sort, e.g., law abidingness, justice, acceptability to a certain class or type of persons, etc.

CONCLUSION

The general implication is that organizational agents (and corporate agents in particular) do exhibit structural features which permit the working out of both a diagnostic and a therapeutic ethical inquiry, once we understand the categorial compatibility (however fragile) between rationality and morality. This is not to say that all formal organizations can be analyzed and modified toward more responsible decision-making without serious disturbance, or even that such modification can be accomplished *at all* in every case. We should not expect more in our interactions with human organizations than we expect in our interactions with human individuals.

However, if we are convinced that modern life with its large-scale technology presents serious problems due to a lack of reflectiveness and responsibility on the part of our more powerful institutions (private and public), and if we are also convinced that our main model for purposes of analysis and reform is the very human person in whose image and likeness those institutions are fabricated, then perhaps enough has been said to vindicate the intelligibility (and desirability) of a new task for ethics.

Notes

1. K. Goodpaster and K. Sayre, "An Ethical Analysis of Power Company Decision-Making," in *Values in the Electric Power Industry*, K. M. Sayre, ed., University of Notre Dame Press (1977), pp. 238–287.
2. Christopher Stone, *Where The Law Ends*, Harper & Row (1975), p. 111.
3. Goodpaster and Sayre, *op. cit.*, p. 280.
4. L. Silk and D. Vogel, *Ethics and Profits*, Simon and Schuster (1976), quoted on p. 138.
5. John Ladd, "Morality and the Ideal of Rationality in Formal Organizations," *The Monist*, Vol. 54 (October 1970), pp. 488–516.
6. Ladd, *op. cit.*, p. 500.
7. H. Simon, *Administrative Behavior* (New York: Free Press, 1965). Third edition now available, 1976.
8. C. Barnard, *The Functions of the Executive* (Cambridge: Harvard University Press, 1938). Also see Barnard's *Forward* to Simon, *op. cit.*
9. I do not mean to suggest that the constitutive rules of chess do not, or have not, undergone evolution. They clearly have. What is important is that this evolution (a) has been very slow since initial formulations of the game and (b) has not been due to the impact of the game or the players on others' lives or well-being (since there is next to no impact here to speak of—which is why chess is "only a game").
10. The other analogy employed by Ladd, the machine, seems to me to clarify the point even more: the picture is of rigid givens, inflexible and unalterable (or at least uncontrolably so), a picture which human organizations exhibit only in superficial ways over short periods of time.
11. Simon, *op. cit.*, p. 114.
12. Remarks like Simon's: "Decisions in private management, like decisions in public management, must take as their ethical premises the objectives that have been set for the organization." (p. 52) My point is that the "setting" is not outside the realm of organizational control.
13. Or even more strongly, Ladd writes: "We cannot and must not expect formal organizations, or their representatives acting in their official capacities, to be honest, courageous, considerate, sympathetic, or to have any kind of moral integrity. Such concepts are not in the vocabulary, so to speak, of the organizational language-game." (Ladd, p. 499)
14. Ladd, p. 515.
15. Cf. W. K. Frankena, *Ethics* (Prentice-Hall, 1973, second edition), Ch. 3.
16. As for the assumption that a purely teleological theory is implausible, too much needs to be said. My opinion, in view of the long history of controversy here, is that the operationalizability of the key *maximandum* for such theories appears inevitably to vary inversely with its plausibility. I suspect that this was Kant's point when he observed in the *Foundations* that the notion of 'happiness' could not sustain an ethic.
17. Cf. Frankena, *op. cit.*, and W. D. Ross, *The Right and the Good* (Oxford, 1930).
18. Goodpaster and Sayre, *op. cit.*

ECONOMICS, VALUES, AND JUSTICE

Part II

Issues about money and economics are often connected to those of ethics and values. If a friend borrows five dollars and later refuses to repay it, then the issue quickly becomes an ethical one—we say the friend really *should* repay the money. At higher levels of economics, ethical issues also play an important role. For example, to decide how society can best distribute wealth, one must know what ethical standards distinguish fair from unfair distributions. Thus, it is not surprising that two well-known economists, Adam Smith and Karl Marx (both of whom are discussed in this section), actually began their careers as philosophers.

Two of the most volatile issues in economics have ethical implications: the importance of the profit motive and society's treatment of private property. The pursuit of profit and the existence of private property are said by some economists to be the foundation of a free society. The eighteenth-century philosopher John Locke argued that each person has a natural *right* to own property. However, others argue that the profit motive and private property cannot be ethically justified because they result in labor abuses, unfair income distribution, monopolistic practices, and misuse of the environment.

A third issue involving both economic matters and ethical and political concerns is the nature of justice. For example, is there such a thing as a just distribution of wealth in society? Should some people have much less than others?

THE PROFIT MOTIVE

It is not uncommon today to hear of a person or corporation condemned for being interested simply in making money. Such an attitude, which questions the morality of emphasizing profit and monetary gain, is not new. If anything, the modern period is one in which people are more accepting of economic pursuits than at other times in history. Before the nineteenth century, criticisms of hoarding wealth and lending money for profit were quite common.

The greatest defender of the profit motive was the eighteenth-century philosopher-economist Adam Smith. Today, nearly 200 years after Smith presented his ideas in *The Wealth of Nations* (excerpts of which are presented in this section), his name is almost synonymous with the defense of the free market (*laissez-faire*) economic system. However, Smith did not believe that economic gain was man's most noble goal; rather he agreed with his professor of moral philosophy, Francis Hutcheson, who claimed that benevolence, not self-interest, was the most noble motive. In contrast to his teacher, however, Smith asserted that much human good could be accomplished—at least within the marketplace—by the free pursuit of self-interest. In perhaps his most famous quotation from *The Wealth of Nations,* he says:

> It is not from the benevolence of the butcher, the brewer, or the baker that we expect our dinner, but from their regard of their own interest. We address ourselves not to their humanity, but to their self-love, and never talk to them of our own necessities, but of their advantage.

Thus Smith emphasized the way in which pursuing one's own economic self-interest in the free marketplace could have benefits for the public welfare. It is as if the world were especially designed so that people pursuing their own selfish economic ends will tend to generate, in the absence of governmental intervention, great public good. Smith calls this special tendency the "invisible hand," which guides each person's pursuit of self-interest into a pattern of healthy competition—which, in turn, yields high quality products at the lowest possible prices. It has been said that Smith showed people how a "private vice" can be turned into a "public virtue."

Antony Flew is a contemporary philosopher who shares Smith's endorsement of the profit motive. In his article, "The Profit Motive," which is included in this section, Flew refers to the way in which it is possible to isolate a kind of "self-interestedness," which is not the same as selfishness. The philosophical issues raised by Smith and Flew center around the claims that pursuing profit is not morally objectionable because it actually contributes to public good and because it does not constitute selfishness. These arguments constitute classical defenses of the moral implications of the profit motive.

CRITICISMS OF THE INVISIBLE HAND

By the time of the Industrial Revolution in the early nineteenth century, Adam Smith's ideas dominated economic theory. In fact, some of the transformations of that era were actually justified by appealing to his philosophy. The increased specialization, the reduction of quotas and tariffs, and the increased reluctance on the part of government to become involved in the affairs of business—all these were changes which Smith had influenced. Smith himself, however, did not live to see them; nor did he live to see some of the human misery which became commonplace during the Industrial Revolution. One of the most depressing aspects of it was child labor in the factories—often for sixteen-hour days—in order to add to a family's meager income. The "Sadler Committee Report" of 1832, contained in this part, presents striking personal testimony from such children.

Many witnesses of the Industrial Revolution were persuaded that the economic system was to blame for its problems. The German philosopher and economist Karl Marx argued that the "free market" which Smith had championed was really little more than a convenient fiction for capitalist property owners. Whereas Smith had praised the competitive market because of its ability to generate better products at lower prices, Marx argued that in the marketplace workers themselves were considered as mere products, available to factory owners at the lowest possible wage. Indeed, Marx believed that the pressures of the marketplace would force the worker, who could not refuse to work without starving, to accept wages barely above a subsistence level. Meanwhile the owner of the means of production, the capitalist, could exploit the worker by using his labor and then selling the worker's product at a profit to himself. Marx identified the difference between the costs of production, including wages, and the selling price of the product as "surplus value." For Marx, then, *profits* always meant exploitation of the worker by the capitalist; and whenever technology develops, the economic gap between the capitalist and the worker must widen further, because technology makes products more efficiently with less human labor, thus promoting unemployment and lower wages.

In the selections taken from *Economic and Philosophic Manuscripts of 1844,* Marx outlines his influential theory of alienation, in which he asserts that the worker in capitalistic society is separated from, and deprived of, his very own labor. When the worker is forced to work for the capitalist he is also forced to give the capitalist what most belongs to the worker—his own work. The factory employee toils away producing items which the factory owner shall eventually sell, and he feels no connection to the product he produces; rather, he has been *alienated* from the effects of his labor, i.e., the products, and has been *alienated* in turn from his own labor. Thus, through the concept of alienation Marx offers a fundamental condemnation of the modern capitalistic economic system.

At the same time that Marx was developing his criticisms of capitalism, another and equally dramatic development was taking place. In 1858, the English naturalist Charles Darwin published his monumental work on evolution, *The Origin of the Species.* Darwin argued, in short, (1) that organisms in the biological kingdom had evolved from simple to more complex; and (2) that during this process organisms less adaptable to the environment did not survive, whereas more adaptable ones flourished. Darwin himself expressly stated that his ideas applied only to the biological kingdom, but many thinkers used his principles to examine social and economic issues. The resulting theory of society, which was popularized by Herbert Spencer and industrialists such as Andrew Carnegie (whose article, "Wealth," is reproduced in this section), was known as Social Darwinism.

Social Darwinism was to have its effect on issues with which Adam Smith and Karl Marx dealt, but in point of fact it agreed with neither view. The Social Darwinists argued that the Industrial Revolution was an example of social evolution from simple societies to complex communities. In the evolution of a capitalistic industrial system, then, some individuals may suffer, but the system itself makes a great contribution to human welfare since it weeds out the unsuccessful, weak competitors and allows the tougher ones to flourish. Thus, both the marketplace and nature work according to the very same iron laws. Those who can, survive, and those who cannot, perish. In this way, the thesis of Social Darwinism was used to justify the profit motive, which for the Social Darwinist simply represents the essential motivating force in the struggle for economic survival. Unfortunately, the entire theory of Social Darwinism was also used in the nineteenth century as a justification for deplorable working conditions and massive economic inequalities.

We see, then, how issues in this section of Part II center on questions of human motivation, the nature of people, and the kind of economic system best for society. Interestingly enough, all these questions are interrelated and cannot be considered as separate. For example, the ethical question of when, if at all, it is best for people to be motivated by profit is directly connected to the question of what kind of nature is common to human beings. For if it is true, as some have argued, that people *must* and will pursue their own self-interest because of their very nature, then it can be argued, as Smith and Flew do, that the pursuit of self-interest in the form of economic gain is often morally justified. In a similar fashion, both these issues are tied to that of which economic structure is best for society. If people are naturally self-interested, and if it is right that profit should be pursued in the marketplace, then perhaps society needs an economic system which acknowledges and reflects these facts. On the other hand, one may argue that the pursuit of self-interest should be avoided, and that no economic system should encourage people to be selfish if one believes that society is thereby harmed.

PRIVATE OWNERSHIP
AND THE PUBLIC INTEREST

Another important issue is that of public versus private ownership, and it is closely connected to that of the profit motive. A common argument used by those who criticize private property deals with motives: that the elimination of private property makes it impossible for people to pursue wealth, and thus discourages them from acting from a bad motive, i.e., the profit motive. However, many arguments made both for and against private ownership can be examined apart from this point of view. Among these is the classical and ingenious argument in favor of private property offered by the eighteenth-century English philosopher, John Locke.

Locke believed that human beings have a fundamental right to own private property, and the basic premises which establish this right can be found in the selection from his *Second Treatise on Government*. Even today these arguments are commonly used in defending the right to own property. Locke asserts what he claims is a truism: namely, that in the absence of any formally structured society, i.e., in the "state of nature," all people may be said to *own their own bodies*. Moreover, all people living in such a state may be said also to possess the *right* to own their own bodies. It was upon this seemingly obvious premise that Locke rested his defense. Because if one admits that one has the right to own one's body, then it follows that one owns the action of that body, or in other words, one's own labor. Finally, one also owns, and has a right to own, the things with which one mixes one's labor. For example, if in the state of nature a person picks berries from wild bushes, then that person may be said to *own* those berries. And if we admit that property may be freely traded, given, and accumulated, then we have the beginning of the basis for a solid justification of vast ownership of capital and land.

In sharp contrast to Locke's seemingly benign defense, Karl Marx argues that private property is actually an institution which perpetuates the class struggle. He believes that it is likely that no such "state of nature" as Locke described ever existed, and he tries to give an accurate historical account of the evolution of the institution of private property. In the selections from *The Communist Manifesto*, Marx tries to show how, at every stage in a struggle for private property, one class succeeds in exploiting another. Thus, he argues that the institution of private property in a capitalistic economic system is nothing other than the means by which the privileged class, i.e., the capitalists or bourgeoisie, exploits the class of the less privileged, i.e., the workers.

We should remind ourselves that the immediate question confronting most people in the Western world is probably not whether to adopt a purely communistic or a purely free market form of economy. Of more immediate practical significance is the question of *how much* of society's goods and services should be placed in public ownership. How important is it, for example, that certain of society's economic institutions remain in the hands of private ownership? Can businesses which are privately owned contribute as much to the public welfare as those which are publicly owned? Is it possible for the latter, like the post office or public utilities, to violate basic human rights and freedoms?

One of the most outspoken critics of public ownership in the twentieth century is the economist Milton Friedman. Strongly opposing Marx, Friedman argues that the maintenance of the economic institution of private property is necessary to ensure basic political rights and freedoms. In his article, "The Social Responsibility of Business Is to Increase Its Profits," Friedman denies the claim that businesses have obligations to society over and above their obligation to make a profit. Much like Adam Smith, Friedman believes that the free market works best, and makes its greatest contribution, when companies compete for the consumers' business and for the maximization of profits. Consequently, if a company were to make social responsibility a primary goal it would be failing in its duty—and hence, ironically, would not be fulfilling its real "social responsibility."

Friedman strongly objects to placing society's major economic institutions in public ownership: Not only would the competitive marketplace be undermined, thus resulting in poorer products and services for the consumer, but also the basic right to freedom would be denied insofar as the government would be interfering with the right to own property. In other of his writings, Friedman even suggests that certain modern institutions which are now public, such as the post office and the national parks, be turned over to the hands of private investors.

How seriously one takes either Friedman's arguments, or the opposing ones—that the railroads, oil industry, etc. should become publicly owned—will depend to a great extent on how seriously one takes the arguments of Locke and Marx. Is Locke correct in arguing that there is a natural right to private property? And how does his argument relate to Marx's claim that private property makes it possible for one class to exploit another? Finally, is Friedman correct that inefficiency inevitably results from government interference in the competitive marketplace? In the case study, "Amtrak," these issues of private and public ownership are raised in the context of the newly nationalized railroad system. The reader is required to consider both the advantages and disadvantages of public versus private ownership in a concrete situation.

INDIVIDUAL LIBERTIES AND SOCIAL JUSTICE

The subject of social justice, both for traditional and modern philosophers, is directly connected to economics and ethical theory. For example, one kind of justice which serves as a principal topic of discussion in this section, namely, "distributive justice," has frequently centered on the issue of how, and according to what principle, the wealth and other goods of society *should* be distributed to its members. Although justice is a fundamental concept, its scope is not broad enough to include all ethical and political goods. That is, no matter how desirable it may be to have justice established in society, there are other goods also worth having, for example, benevolence and charity. Justice, then, refers to a kind of minimal condition which should exist in a good society, although there are other conditions which a truly ideal society would embody. As a minimal condition, it usually is seen as requiring that each individual be given his "due."

This notion of justice, which requires further clarification, can be illustrated with a hypothetical story: Once a group of soldiers found themselves defending a fort against an enemy. The soldiers were in desperate need of water, and the only source was 200 yards from the fort in enemy territory. Courageously, a small group sneaked outside the fort, filled their canteens with water, and returned safely. After showing the water to their fellow soldiers, the successful adventurers proposed that it should be distributed in accordance with the principles of justice. Since justice requires distribution on the basis of merit, they said, they themselves should get the water because they risked their lives in obtaining it. There was considerable disagreement. Although agreeing that justice requires distribution on the basis of deserving characteristics, a different group of soldiers, which had been longest without water, claimed they deserved it more because they *needed* it more than the others. After all, they were the thirstiest. And still a different group, agreeing with the same general principle of justice, argued that *everyone* deserved *equal* amounts of the water because all human beings, considered generally, have equal worth. The moral, obviously, is that an adequate concept of justice must specify the particular characteristic or set of characteristics which when possessed by human beings will serve as the basis for "giving each person his due."

Although the subject of distributive justice is a popular topic among modern philosophers, some people claim that the mere idea is prejudicial and controversial. If a society's goods are to be distributed, then doesn't this imply the existence of a distributing agency (such as the government) which would enforce certain principles of distribution, thus taking away from those who have more than they deserve and giving to those who have less? Yet it can be argued that the very existence of such a process violates basic principles of individual liberty, because it denies individuals the opportunity to engage freely in the transactions of goods. In this way it is maintained that distributive, or redistributive, practices mean the violation of basic liberties and freedoms, and therefore that no willful distribution can itself be just.

The notion of the importance of individual liberties, and the corresponding idea that it is necessary to limit the government's interference with those liberties, are at issue in the case study, "Laetrile: The FDA and Society." Here the issue centers on whether a government agency such as the Food and Drug Administration (FDA) should be able to deny access to the controversial drug Laetrile, which is reputed to help cure cancer. Scientific evidence seems to suggest strongly that the drug is worthless— or at least such is the conviction of the FDA. Further, it is maintained that many people choose to take Laetrile instead of medically accepted cancer treatments in cases where they would probably respond to traditional treatment. Is the FDA's ban on Laetrile a denial of a basic human freedom—even if it is useless as a cancer cure?

The same fundamental issue of individual liberty, along with questions about the right of government to interfere with such liberty, can be found in F.A. Hayek's essay, "The Principles of a Liberal Social Order." As one of the best-known defenders in the twentieth century of a free and unregulated social order, Hayek is anxious to distinguish the kind of society in which the free actions of individuals combine to yield a "spontaneous" social order from the kind of closed, regulated society in which the social order is a consequence of design. It is only in a spontaneous social order, Hayek believes, that individual liberty can be meaningful. As soon as one begins to demand that a certain order must be imposed (for example, that people should receive goods and services in proportion to their needs), then it becomes necessary to abolish the spontaneous social order and to institute strong government control, both of which open the door to totalitarian practices. Hayek admits that a free society does not always yield a direct correspondence between personal merit or need and the distribution of goods and services; yet he emphatically denies that such a correspondence can be brought about without sacrificing an even more important political value, namely, an open society which protects individual liberty. Thus Hayek is one of the foremost advocates of spontaneous social order as the foundation for a just society, and his views have had a significant impact upon other well-known modern theorists, such as Robert Nozick and John Hospers.

Two other modern writers presented in this section, John Rawls and Margaret Mead, also consider questions of justice and the social order, but in quite different ways. In contrast to Hayek, Rawls believes that the idea of distributive justice can be coordinated with principles of individual rights and liberties. He argues that a just society is one in which agreements are freely made and in which no one is not left out and deserving people are not short-changed. Rawls argues that a just society is based on two principles: (1) ". . . each person engaged in an institution or affected by it has an equal right to the most extensive liberty compatible with a like liberty for all . . ." and (2) ". . . inequalities as defined by the institutional structure . . . are arbitrary unless it is reasonable to expect that they will work out to everyone's advantage and provided that the positions and offices to which they attach or from which they may be gained are open to all." Thus Rawls is not arguing that in a just society things would be structured so as to give all people an equal number of goods, e.g., money, education, or status; and he allows that some people may have a great deal more than others. However, in order for a society to be just, such inequalities are only acceptable if their existence is to the advantage of the least fortunate as well as to everyone else. Rawls further specifies that no form of distribution in any society is just unless it satisfies the first condition of justice: freedom. Rawls's article, "Distributive Justice," excerpts of which are presented in this section, first appeared in 1967 and is a precursor of his influential book, *A Theory of Justice*,[1] in which he more fully develops the views presented here.

To conclude the section on individual liberties and social justice, Margaret Mead shifts the emphasis of the discussion to concrete problems in twentieth-century society. Coming from a successful background in anthropology, Mead is quick to notice the aspects of social life which are passed over in business and economic reports. She criticizes modern society for failing to take an accurate social accounting, and she specifies some of the areas in which it has failed to satisfy the needs of its members. Mead suggests that the self-interested pursuit of profit by private enterprise has affected the distribution of goods to the disadvantaged, because the unequal distribution of expenditures has excluded the disadvantaged while placing additional financial burdens on the rest of society. How should we account for the fact that the economic goals of our society conflict with our well-being and the well-being of everyone in the society? How can issues such as social justice ever be included in the list of factors by which we evaluate ourselves?

Note

1. John Rawls, *A Theory of Justice* (Cambridge, Mass.: Harvard University Press, 1971).

THE PROFIT MOTIVE

Case Study— Plasma International

T. W. Zimmerer and P. L. Preston

The Sunday headline in the Tampa, Florida, newspaper read:

Blood Sales Result in Exorbitant Profits for Local Firm

The story went on to relate how the Plasma International Company, headquartered in Tampa, Florida, purchased blood in underdeveloped countries for as little as 15 cents a pint and resold the blood to hospitals in the United States and South America. A recent disaster in Nicaragua produced scores of injured persons and the need for fresh blood. Plasma International had 10,000 pints of blood flown to Nicaragua from West Africa and charged the hospitals $25 per pint, netting the firm nearly a quarter of a million dollars.

As a result of the newspaper story, a group of irate citizens, led by prominent civic leaders, demanded that the City of Tampa, and the State of Florida, revoke Plasma International's licenses to practice business. Others protested to their congressmen to seek enactment of legislation designed to halt the sale of blood for profit. The spokesperson was reported as saying, "What kind of people are these—selling life and death? These men prey on the needs of dying people, buying blood from poor, ignorant Africans for 15 cents worth of beads and junk, and selling it to injured people for $25 a pint. Well, this company will soon find out that the people of our community won't stand for their kind around here."

"I just don't understand it. We run a business just like any other business; we pay taxes and we try to make an honest profit," said Sol Levin as he responded to reporters at the Tampa International Airport. He had just returned home from testifying before the House Subcommittee on Medical Standards. The recent publicity surrounding his firm's activities during the recent earthquakes had once again fanned the flames of public opinion. An election year was an unfortunate time for the publicity to occur. The politicians and the media were having a field day.

From *Business and Society,* ed. Robert D. Hay, Edmund R. Gray, and James E. Gates (Cincinnati, Ohio: South-Western Publishing Co., 1976). Reprinted with permission from the publisher and authors.

Levin was a successful stockbroker when he founded Plasma International Company three years ago. Recognizing the world's need for safe, uncontaminated, and reasonably priced whole blood and blood plasma, Levin and several of his colleagues pooled their resources and went into business. Initially, most of the blood and plasma they sold was purchased through store-front operations in the southeast United States. Most of the donors were, unfortunately, men and women who used the money obtained from the sale of their blood to purchase wine. While sales increased dramatically on the base of an innovative marketing approach, several cases of hepatitis were reported in recipients. The company wisely began a search for new sources.

Recognizing their own limitations in the medical-biological side of the business they recruited a highly qualified team of medical consultants. The consulting team, after extensive testing, and a worldwide search, recommended that the blood profiles and donor characteristics of several rural West African tribes made them ideal prospective donors. After extensive negotiations with the State Department and the government of the nation of Burami, the company was able to sign an agreement with several of the tribal chieftains.

As Levin reviewed these facts, and the many costs involved in the sale of a commodity as fragile as blood, he concluded that the publicity was grossly unfair. His thoughts were interrupted by the reporter's question: "Mr. Levin, is it necessary to sell a vitally needed medical supply, like blood, at such high prices especially to poor people in such a critical situation?" "Our prices are determined on the basis of a lot of costs that we incur that the public isn't even aware of," Levin responded. However, when reporters pressed him for details of these "relevant" costs, Levin refused any further comment. He noted that such information was proprietary in nature and not for public consumption.

Benefits of the Profit Motive

ADAM SMITH

BOOK I

OF THE CAUSES OF IMPROVEMENT IN THE PRODUCTIVE POWERS OF LABOR AND OF THE ORDER ACCORDING TO WHICH ITS PRODUCE IS NATURALLY DISTRIBUTED AMONG THE DIFFERENT RANKS OF THE PEOPLE

CHAPTER I

OF THE DIVISION OF LABOR

The greatest improvement in the productive powers of labor, and the greater part of the skill, dexterity, and judgment with which it is anywhere directed, or applied, seem to have been the effects of the division of labor. . . .

To take an example, therefore, from a very trifling manufacture; but one in which the division of labor has been very often taken notice of, the trade of the pin-maker; a workman not educated to this business (which the division of labor has rendered a distinct trade), nor acquainted with the use of the machinery employed in it (to the invention of which the same division of labor has probably given occasion), could scarce, perhaps, with his utmost industry, make one pin in a day, and certainly could not make twenty. But in the way in which this business is now carried on, not only the whole work is a peculiar trade, but it is divided into a number of branches, of which the greater part are likewise peculiar trades. One man draws out the wire, another straights it, a third cuts it, a fourth points it, a fifth grinds it at the top for receiving the head; to make the head requires two or three distinct operations; to put it on is a peculiar business, to whiten the pins is another; it is even a trade by itself to put them into the paper; and the important business of making a pin is, in this manner, divided into about eighteen distinct operations, which, in some manufactories, are all performed by distinct hands, though in others the same man will sometimes perform two or three of them. I have seen a small manufactory of this kind where ten men only were employed, and where some of them consequently performed two or three distinct operations. But though they were very poor, and therefore but indifferently accommodated with the necessary machinery, they could, when they exerted themselves, make among them about twelve pounds of pins in a day. There are in a pound upwards of four thousand pins of a middling

From Adam Smith, *The Wealth of Nations,* Books I and IV (1776; rpt. Chicago: University of Chicago Press, 1976).

size. Those ten persons, therefore, could make among them upwards of forty-eight thousand pins in a day. Each person, therefore, making a tenth part of forty-eight thousand pins, might be considered as making four thousand eight hundred pins in a day. But if they had all wrought separately and independently, and without any of them having been educated to this peculiar business, they certainly could not each of them have made twenty, perhaps not one pin in a day; that is, certainly, not the two hundred and fortieth, perhaps not the four thousand eight hundredth part, of what they are at present capable of performing in consequence of a proper division and combination of their different operations.

In every other art and manufacture, the effects of the divisions of labor are similar to what they are in this very trifling one; though in many of them, the labor can neither be so much subdivided, nor reduced to so great a simplicity of operation. The division of labor, however, so far as it can be introduced, occasions, in every art, a proportionable increase of the productive powers of labor. . . .

This great increase of the quantity of work, which, in consequence of the division of labor, the same number of people are capable of performing, is owing to three different circumstances: first, to the increase of dexterity in every particular workman; secondly, to the saving of the time which is commonly lost in passing from one species of work to another; and lastly, to the invention of a great number of machines which facilitate and abridge labor, and enable one man to do the work of many.

First, the improvement of the dexterity of the workman necessarily increases the quantity of the work he can perform; and the division of labor, by reducing every man's business to some one simple operation and by making this operation the sole employment of his life, necessarily increases very much the dexterity of the workman. A common smith, who, though accustomed to handle the hammer, has never been used to make nails, if upon some particular occasion he is obliged to attempt it, will scarce, I am assured, be able to make about two or three hundred nails in a day, and those too very bad ones. A smith who has been accustomed to make nails, but whose sole or principal business has not been that of a nailer, can seldom with his utmost diligence make more than eight hundred or a thousand nails in a day. I have seen several boys under twenty years of age who had never exercised any other trade but that of making nails, and who, when they exerted themselves, could make, each of them, upwards of two thousand three hundred nails in a day. The making of a nail, however, is by no means one of the simplest operations. The same person blows the bellows, stirs or mends the fire as there is occasion, heats the iron, and forges every part of the nail: In forging the head too he is obliged to change his tools. The different operations into which the making of a pin or of a metal button is subdivided, are all of them much more simple; and the dexterity of the person, of whose life it has been the sole business to perform them, is usually much greater. The rapidity with which some of the operations of those manufactures are performed exceeds what the human hand could, by those who had never seen them, be supposed capable of acquiring.

Secondly, the advantage which is gained by saving the time commonly lost in passing from one sort of work to another is much greater than we should at first view be apt to imagine it. It is impossible to pass very quickly from one kind of work to another, that is carried on in a different place, and with quite different tools. A country weaver who cultivates a small farm must lose a good deal of time in passing from his loom to the field, and from the field to his loom. When the two trades can be carried on in the same workhouse, the loss of time is no doubt much less. It is even in this case, however, very considerable. . . .

Thirdly, and lastly, every body must be sensible how much labor is facilitated and abridged by the application of proper machinery. . . .

. . . A great part of the machines made use of in those manufactures in which labor is most subdivided were originally the inventions of common workmen, who, being each of them employed in some very simple operation, naturally turned their thoughts toward finding out easier and readier methods of performing it. Whoever has been much accustomed to visit such manufacturers must frequently have been shown very pretty machines which were the inventions of such workmen in order to facilitate and quicken their own particular part of the work. In the first fire-engines, a boy was constantly employed to open and shut alternately the communication between the boiler and the cylinder, according as the piston either ascended or descended. One of those boys, who loved to play with his companions, observed that, by tying a string from the handle of the valve which opened this communication to another part of the machine, the valve would open and shut without his assistance, and leave him at liberty to divert himself with his play-fellows. One of the greatest improvements that has been made upon this machine, since it was first invented, was in this manner the discovery of a boy who wanted to save his own labor. . . .

It is the great multiplication of the productions of all the different arts, in consequence of the division of labor, which occasions, in a well-governed society, that universal opulence which extends itself to the lowest ranks of the people. Every workman has a great quantity of his own work to dispose of beyond what he himself has occasion for; and every other workman being exactly in the same situation, he is enabled to exchange a great quantity of his own goods for a great quantity, or, what comes to the same thing, for the price of a great quantity of theirs. He supplies them abundantly with what they have occasion for, and they accommodate him as amply with what he has occasion for, and a general plenty diffuses itself through all the different ranks of the society. . . .

CHAPTER II

OF THE PRINCIPLE WHICH GIVES OCCASION
TO THE DIVISION OF LABOR

This division of labor, from which so many advantages are derived, is not originally the effect of any human wisdom which foresees and intends that general opulence to which it gives occasion. It is the necessary, though very slow and gradual, consequence of a certain propensity in human nature which has in view no such extensive utility: the propensity to truck, barter, and exchange one thing for another.

. . . In almost every other race of animals each individual, when it is grown up to maturity, is entirely independent, and in its natural state has occasion for the assistance of no other living creature. But man has almost constant occasion for the help of his brethren, and it is in vain for him to expect it from their benevolence only. He will be more likely to prevail if he can interest their self-love in his favor, and show them that it is for their own advantage to do for him what he requires of them. Whoever offers to another a bargain of any kind, proposes to do this. Give me that which I want, and you shall have this which you want, is the meaning of every such offer; and it is in the manner that we obtain from one another the far greater part of those good offices which we stand in need of. It is not from the benevolence of the butcher, the brewer, or the baker, that we expect our dinner, but from their regard to their own interest. We address ourselves, not to their humanity but to their self-love, and never talk to them of our own necessities but of their advantages. Nobody but a begger chooses to depend chiefly upon the benevolence of his fellow-citizens. Even a beggar does not depend upon it entirely. The charity of well-disposed people, indeed, supplies him with the whole fund of his subsistence. But though this principle ultimately provides him with all the necessaries of life which he has occasion for, it neither does nor can provide him with them as he has occasion for them. The greater part of his occasional wants are supplied in the same manner as those of other people, by treaty, by barter, and by purchase. With the money which one man gives him he purchases food. The old clothes which another bestows upon him he exchanges for other old clothes which suit him better, or for lodging, or for food, or for money, with which he can buy either food, clothes, or lodging, as he has occasion.

As it is by treaty, by barter, and by purchase that we obtain from one another the greater part of those mutual good offices which we stand in need of, so it is this same trucking disposition which originally gives occasion to the division of labor. In a tribe of hunters or shepherds a particular person makes bows and arrows, for example, with more readiness and dexterity than any other. He frequently exchanges them for cattle or for venison with his companions; and he finds at last that he can in this manner get more cattle and venison than if he himself went to the field to catch them. From a regard to his own interest, therefore, the making of bows and arrows grows to be his chief business, and he becomes a sort of armorer. Another excels in making the frames and covers of their little huts or movable houses. He is accustomed to be of use in this way to his neighbors, who reward him in the same manner with cattle and with venison till at last he finds it his interest to dedicate himself entirely to this employment, and to become a sort of house carpenter. In the same manner a third becomes a smith or a brazier; a fourth a tanner or dresser of hides or skins, the principal part of the clothing of savages. And thus the certainty of being able to exchange all that surplus part of the produce of his own labor, which is over and above his own consumption, for such parts of the produce of other men's labor as he may have occasion for, encourages every man to apply himself to a particular occupation, and to cultivate and bring to perfection whatever talent or genius he may possess for that particular species of business.

The difference of natural talents in different men is, in reality, much less than we are aware of; and the very different genius which appears to distinguish men of different professions, when grown up to maturity, is not upon many occasions so much the cause as the effect of the division of labor. The difference between the most dissimilar characters, between a philosopher and a common street porter, for example, seems to arise not so much from nature as from habit, custom, and education. When they came into the world, and for the first six or eight years of their existence, they were, perhaps, very much alike, and neither their parents nor play-fellows could perceive any remarkable difference. About that age, or soon after, they come to be employed in very different occupations. The difference of talents comes then to be taken notice of, and widens by degrees, till at last the vanity of the philosopher is willing to acknowledge scarce any resemblance. But without the disposition to truck, barter, and exchange, every man must have procured to himself every necessary and conveniency of life which he wanted. All must have had the same duties to perform, and the same work to do, and there could have been no such difference of employment as could alone give occasion to any great difference of talents. . . .

BOOK IV

CHAPTER II

Every individual is continually exerting himself to find out the most advantageous employment for whatever capital he can command. It is his own advantage, indeed, and not that of the society, which he has in view. But the study of his own advantage, naturally, or rather necessarily, leads him to prefer that employment which is most advantageous to the society. . . .

As every individual, therefore, endeavours as much as he can both to employ his capital in the support of domestic industry, and so to direct that industry that its produce may be of the greatest value, every individual necessarily labors to render the annual revenue of the society as great as he can. He generally, indeed, neither intends to promote the public interest, nor knows how much he is promoting it. By preferring the support of domestic to that of foreign industry, he intends only his own security: and by directing that industry in such a manner as its produce may be of the greatest value, he intends only his own gain, and he is in this, as in many other cases, led by an invisible hand to promote an end which was no part of his intention. Nor is it always the worse for the society that it was no part of it. By pursuing his own interest he frequently promotes that of the society more effectually than when he really intends to promote it. I have never known much good done by those who affected to trade for the public good. It is an affectation, indeed, not very common among merchants, and very few words need be employed in dissuading them from it.

The Sadler Report

The industrial revolution was spurred on in part by Adam Smith's ideas of the division of labor and the "invisible hand." It had a powerful effect on England in the first part of the nineteenth-century. It not only gave her a position of wealth and affluence greater than any nation in history, but it brought about degrading and miserable conditions for her working force. Perhaps the most unfortunate victims of this situation were the children working in factories, some of whom began their careers at four or five years of age.

The English government finally decided to investigate the child labor problem, and a committee of the House of Commons was formed headed by Michael Thomas Sadler. The following is an excerpt from the committee's report, which was presented to the House of Commons in 1832 in the *Bill to Regulate the Labour of Children*. It is perhaps the most striking and compelling description of the abuses of the industrial revolution ever recorded.

Veneris, 18 die Maii, 1832

MICHAEL THOMAS SADDLER, ESQUIRE,
IN THE CHAIR

Mr. Matthew Crabtree, called in; and examined.
What age are you?—Twenty-two.
What is your occupation?—A blanket manufacturer.
Have you ever been employed in a factory?—Yes.
At what age did you first go to work in one?—Eight.
How long did you continue in that occupation?—Four years.
Will you state the hours of labour at the period when you first went to the factory, in ordinary times?—From 6 in the morning to 8 at night.
Fourteen hours?—Yes.
With what intervals for refreshment and rest?—An hour at noon.

From the Sadler Committee, *The Sadler Report,* 1832, prepared by the English House of Commons from testimonies of children working in the English wool industry.

Then you had no resting time allowed in which to take your breakfast, or what is in Yorkshire called your "drinking"?—No.

When trade was brisk what were your hours?—From 5 in the morning to 9 in the evening.

Sixteen hours?—Yes.

With what intervals at dinner?—An hour.

How far did you live from the mill?—About two miles.

Was there any time allowed for you to get your breakfast in the mill?—No.

Did you take it before you left your home?—Generally.

During those long hours of labour could you be punctual; how did you awake?—I seldom did awake spontaneously; I was more generally awoke or lifted out of bed, sometimes asleep, by my parents.

Were you always in time?—No.

What was the consequence if you had been too late?—I was most commonly beaten.

Severely?—Very severely, I thought.

In whose factory was this?—Messrs. Hague & Cooks, of Dewsbury.

Will you state the effect that those long hours had upon the state of your health and feelings?—I was, when working those long hours, commonly very much fatigued at night, when I left my work; so much so that I sometimes should have slept as I walked if I had not stumbled and started awake again; and so sick often that I could not eat, and what I did eat I vomited.

Did this labour destroy your appetite?—It did.

In what situation were you in that mill?—I was a piecener.

Will you state to this Committee whether piecening is a very laborious employment for children, or not?—It is a very laborious employment. Pieceners are continually running to and fro, and on their feet the whole day.

The duty of the piecener is to take the cardings from one part of the machinery, and to place them on another?—Yes.

So that the labour is not only continual, but it is unabated to the last?—It is unabated to the last.

Do you not think, from your own experience, that the speed of the machinery is so calculated as to demand the utmost exertions of a child, supposing the hours were moderate?—It is as much as they could do at the best—they are always upon the stretch, and it is commonly very difficult to keep up with their work.

State the condition of the children towards the latter part of the day, who have thus to keep up with the machinery?—It is as much as they can do when they are not very much fatigued to keep up with their work, and towards the close of the day, when they come to be more fatigued, they cannot keep up with it very well, and the consequence is that they are beaten to spur them on.

Were you beaten under those circumstances?—Yes.

Frequently?—Very frequently.

And principally at the latter end of the day?—Yes.

And is it your belief that if you had not been so beaten, you should not have got through the work?—I should not if I had not been kept up to it by some means.

Does beating then principally occur at the latter end of the day, when the children are exceedingly fatigued?—It does at the latter end of the day and in the morning sometimes, when they are very drowsy, and have not got rid of the fatigue of the day before.

What were you beaten with principally?—A strap.

Any thing else?—Yes, a stick sometimes; and there is a kind of roller which runs on the top of the machine called a billy, perhaps two or three yards in length, and perhaps an inch and a half, or more, in diameter; the circumference would be four or five inches; I cannot speak exactly.

Were you beaten with that instrument?—Yes.

Have you yourself been beaten, and have you seen other children struck severely with that roller?—I have been struck very severely with it myself, so much so as to knock me down, and I have seen other children have their heads broken with it.

You think that it is a general practice to beat the children with the roller?—It is.

You do not think then that you were worse treated than other children in the mill?—No, I was not, perhaps not so bad as some were.

In those mills is chastisement towards the latter part of the day going on perpetually?—Perpetually.

So that you can hardly be in a mill without hearing constant crying?—Never an hour, I believe.

Do you think that if the overlooker were naturally a humane person it would be still found necessary for him to beat the children, in order to keep up their attention and vigilance at the termination of those extraordinary days of labour?—Yes; the machine turns off a regular quantity of cardings, and of course they must keep as regularly to their work the whole of the day; they must keep up with the machine, and therefore however humane the slubber may be, as he must keep up with the machine or be found fault with, he spurs the children to keep up also by various means but that which he commonly resorts to is to strap them when they become drowsy.

At the time when you were beaten for not keeping up with your work, were you anxious to have done it if you possibly could?—Yes; the dread of being beaten if we could not keep up with our work was a sufficient impulse to keep us to it if we could.

When you got home at night after this labour, did you feel much fatigued?—Very much so.

Had you any time to be with your parents, and to receive instruction from them?—No.

What did you do?—All that we did when we got home was to get the little bit of supper that was provided for us and go to bed immediately. If the supper had not been ready directly, we should have gone to sleep while it was preparing.

Did you not, as a child, feel it a very grievous hardship to be roused so soon in the morning?—I did.

Were the rest of the children similarly circumstanced?—Yes, all of them so far from their work as I was.

And if you had been too late you were under the apprehension of being cruelly beaten?—I generally was beaten when I happened to be too late; and when I got up in the morning the apprehension of that was so great, that I used to run and cry all the way as I went to the mill.

That was the way by which your punctual attendance was secured?—Yes.

And you do not think it could have been secured by any other means?—No.

Then it is your impression from what you have seen, and from your own experience, that those long house of labour have the effect of rendering young persons who are subject to them exceedingly unhappy?—Yes.

You have already said it had a considerable effect upon your health?—Yes.

Do you conceive that it diminished your growth?—I did not pay much attention to that; but I have been examined by some persons who said they thought I was rather stunted, and that I should have been taller if I had not worked at the mill.

What were your wages at that time?—Three shillings (per week). . . .

What is the effect of this piecening upon the hands?—It makes them bleed; the skin is completely rubbed off, and in that case they bleed in perhaps a dozen parts.

The prominent parts of the hand?—Yes, all the prominent parts of the hand are rubbed down till they bleed; every day they are rubbed in that way.

All the time you continue at work?—All the time we are working. The hands never can be hardened in that work, for the grease keeps them soft in the first instance, and long and continual rubbing is always wearing them down, so that if they were hard they would be sure to bleed.

Is it attended with much pain?—Very much. . . .

You say that the girls as well as the boys were employed as you have described, and you observed no difference in their treatment?—No difference.

The girls were beat in this unmerciful manner?—They were.

They were subject, of course, to the same bad effects from this overworking?—Yes.

Could you attend an evening-school during the time you were employed in the mill?—No, that was completely impossible.

Did you attend the Sunday-school?—Not very frequently when I work-[ed] at the mill.

How then were you engaged during the Sunday?—I very often slept till it was too late for school time or for divine worship, and the rest of the day I spent in walking out and taking a little fresh air.

Did your parents think that it was necessary for you to enjoy a little fresh air?—I believe they did; they never said anything against it; before I went to the mill I used to go to the Sunday-school.

Did you frequently sleep nearly the whole of the day on Sunday?—Very often.

At what age did you leave that employment?—I was about 12 years old.

Why did you leave that place?—I went very late one morning, about seven o'clock, and I got severely beaten by the spinner, and he turned me out of the mill, and I went home, and never went any more.

Was your attendance as good as the other children?—Being at rather a greater distance than some of them, I was generally one of the latest. . . .

Have you had opportunities of observing the way in which the children are treated in factories up to a late period?—Yes.

You conceive that their treatment still remains as you first found it, and that the system is in great want of regulation?—It does.

Children you still observe to be very much fatigued and injured by the hours of labour?—Yes.

From your own experience, what is your opinion as to the utmost labour that a child in piecening could safely undergo?—If I were appealed to from my own feelings to fix a limit, I should fix it at ten hours, or less.

And you attribute to longer hours all the cruelties that you describe?—A good deal of them.

Are the children sleepy in mills?—Very.

Are they more liable to accidents in the latter part of the day than in the other part?—I believe they are; I believe a greater number of accidents happen in the latter part of the day than in any other. I have known them so sleepy that in the short interval while the others have been going out, some of them have fallen asleep, and have been left there.

Is it an uncommon case for children to fall asleep in the mill and remain there all night?—Not to remain there all night; but I have known a case the other day, of a child whom the overlooker found when he went to lock the door, that had been left there.

So that you think there has been no change for the better in the treatment of those children; is it your opinion that there will be none, except Parliament interfere in their behalf?—It is my decided conviction.

Have you recently seen any cruelties in mills?—Yes; not long since I was in a mill, and I saw a girl severely beaten; at a mill called Hick-lane Mill, in Batley; I happened to be in at the other end of the room, talking; and I heard the blows, and I looked that way, and saw the spinner beating one of the girls severely with a large stick. Hearing the sound, led me to look around, and to ask what was the matter, and they said it was "Nothing but—paying (beating) his ligger-on."

What age was the girl?—About 12 years.

Was she very violently beaten?—She was.

Was this when she was over-fatigued?—It was in the afternoon. . . .

From what you have seen and known of those mills, would you prefer that the hours of labour should be shortened with a diminution of wages?—If I were working at the mill now, I would rather have less labour and receive a trifle less, than so much labour and receive a trifle more.

Is that the general impression of individuals engaged in mills with whom you are acquainted?—I believe it is.

What is the impression in the country from which you come with respect to the effect of this Bill upon wages?—They do not anticipate that it will affect wages at all.

They think it will not lower wages?—They do.

Do you mean that it will not lower wages by the hour, or that you will receive the same wages per day?—They anticipate that it may perhaps lower their wages at a certain time of the year when they are working hard, but not at other times, so that they will have their wages more regular.

Does not their wish for this Bill mainly rest upon their anxiety to protect their children from the consequences of this excessive labour, and to have some opportunity of affording them a decent education?—Yes; such are the wishes of every humane father that I have heard speak about the thing.

Have they not some feeling of having the labour equalized?—That is the feeling of some that I have heard speak of it. . . .

Do you think that the children would not be more competent to this task, and their hands far less hurt, if the hours were fewer every day, especially when their hands had become seasoned to the labour?—I believe it would have an effect, for the longer they are worked the more their hands are worn, and the longer it takes to heal them, and they do not get hard enough after a day's rest to be long without bleeding again; if they were not so much worn down, they might heal sooner, and not bleed so often or so soon.

After a short day's work, have you found your hands hard the next morning?—They do not bleed much after we have ceased work; they then get hard; they will bleed soon in the morning when in regular work.

Do you think if the work of the children were confined to about ten hours a day, that after they were accustomed to it they would not be able to perform this piecening without making their hands bleed?—I believe they would.

So that it is your opinion, from your experience, that if the hours were mitigated, their hands would not be so much worn, and would not bleed by the business of piecening?—Yes.

Do you mean to say that their hands would not bleed at all?—I cannot say exactly, for I always wrought long hours, and therefore my hands always did bleed.

Have you any experience of mills where they only work ten hours?—I have never wrought at such mills, and in most of the mills I have seen their hands bleed.

At a slack time, when you were working only a few hours, did your hands bleed?—No, they did not for three or four days, after we had been standing still for a week; the mill stood still sometimes for a week together, but when we did work we worked the common number of hours.

Were all the mills in the neighbourhood working the same number of hours in brisk times?—Yes.

So that if any parent found it necessary to send his children to the mill for the sake of being able to maintain them, and wished to take them from any mill where they were excessively worked, he could not have found any other place where they would have been less worked?—No, he could not; for myself, I had no desire to change, because I thought I was as well off as I could be at any other mill.

And if the parent, to save his child, had taken him from the mill, and had applied to the parish for relief, would the parish, knowing that he had withdrawn his child from its work, have relieved him?—No.

So that the long labour which you have described, or actual starvation, was, practically, the only alternative that was presented to the parent under such circumstances?—It was; they must either work at the mill they were at or some other, and there was no choice in the mills in that respect.

What, in your opinion, would be the effect of limiting the hours of labour upon the happiness, and the health and the intelligence of the rising generation?—If the hours are shortened, the children may, perhaps, have a chance of attending some evening-school, and learning to read and write; and those that I know who have been to school and learned to read and write, have much more comfort than those who have not. For myself, I went to a school when I was 6 years old, and I learned to read and write a little then.

At a free-school?—Yes, at a free-school in Dewsbury; but I left school when I was 6 years old. The fact is, that my father was a small manufacturer, and in comfortable circumstances; and he got into debt with Mr. Cook for a wool bill, and as he had no other means of paying him, he came and agreed with my father, that my brother and I should go to work at his mill till that debt was paid; so that the whole of the time that we wrought at the mill we had no wages.

Alienated Labour

KARL MARX

We shall begin from a *contemporary* economic fact. The worker becomes poorer the more wealth he produces and the more his production increases in power and extent. The worker becomes an ever cheaper com-

From *Karl Marx: Early Writings*, trans. T. B. Bottomore. © T. B. Bottomore, 1963. Used with permission of McGraw-Hill Book Company.

modity the more goods he creates. The *devaluation* of the human world increases in direct relation with the *increase in value* of the world of things. Labour does not only create goods; it also produces itself and the worker as a *commodity,* and indeed in the same proportion as it produces goods. . . .

All these consequences follow from the fact that the worker is related to the *product of his labour* as to an *alien* object. For it is clear on this presupposition that the more the worker expends himself in work the more powerful becomes the world of objects which he creates in face of himself, the poorer he becomes in his inner life, and the less he belongs to himself. It is just the same as in religion. The more of himself man attributes to God the less he has left in himself. The worker puts his life into the object, and his life then belongs no longer to himself but to the object. The greater his activity, therefore, the less he possesses. What is embodied in the product of his labour is no longer his own. The greater this product is, therefore, the more he is diminished. The *alienation* of the worker in his product means not only that his labour becomes an object, assumes an *external* existence, but that it exists independently, *outside himself,* and alien to him, and that it stands opposed to him as an autonomous power. The life which he has given to the object sets itself against him as an alien and hostile force.

. . . the worker becomes a slave of the object; first, in that he receives an *object of work,* i.e. receives *work,* and secondly, in that he receives *means of subsistence.* Thus the object enables him to exist, first as a *worker* and secondly, as a *physical subject.* The culmination of this enslavement is that he can only maintain himself as a *physical subject* so far as he is a *worker,* and that it is only as a *physical subject* that he is a worker. . . .

What constitutes the alienation of labour? First, that the work is *external* to the worker, that it is not part of his nature; and that, consequently, he does not fulfil himself in his work but denies himself, has a feeling of misery rather than well-being, does not develop freely his mental and physical energies but is physically exhausted and mentally debased. The worker, therefore, feels himself at home only during his leisure time, whereas at work he feels homeless. His work is not voluntary but imposed, *forced labour.* It is not the satisfaction of a need, but only a *means* for satisfying other needs. Its alien character is clearly shown by the fact that as soon as there is no physical or other compulsion it is avoided like the plague. External labour, labour in which man alienates himself, is a labour of self-sacrifice, of mortification. Finally, the external character of work for the worker is shown by the fact that it is not his own work but work for someone else, that in work he does not belong to himself but to another person. . . .

We arrive at the result that man (the worker) feels himself to be freely active only in his animal functions—eating, drinking and procreating, or at most also in his dwelling and in personal adornment—while in his human functions he is reduced to an animal. The animal becomes human and the human becomes animal.

Eating, drinking and procreating are of course also genuine human functions. But abstractly considered, apart from the environment of human activities, and turned into final and sole ends, they are animal functions.

We have now considered the act of alienation of practical human activity, labour, from two aspects: (1) the relationship of the worker to the *product of labour* as an alien object which dominates him. This relationship is at the same time the relationship to the sensuous external world, to natural objects, as an alien and hostile world; (2) the relationship of labour to the *act of production* within *labour*. This is the relationship of the worker to his own activity as something alien and not belonging to him, activity as suffering (passivity), strength as powerlessness, creation as emasculation, the *personal* physical and mental energy of the worker, his personal life (for what is life but activity?), as an activity which is directed against himself, independent of him and not belonging to him. This is *self-alienation* as against the above-mentioned alienation of the *thing*.

We have now to infer a third characteristic of *alienated labour* from the two we have considered.

Man is a species-being not only in the sense that he makes the community (his own as well as those of other things) his object both practically and theoretically, but also (and this is simply another expression for the same thing) in the sense that he treats himself as the present, living species, as a *universal* and consequently free being.[1]

Species-life, for man as for animals, has its physical basis in the fact that man (like animals) lives from inorganic nature, and since man is more universal than an animal so the range of inorganic nature from which he lives is more universal. . . . The universality of man appears in practice in the universality which makes the whole of nature into his inorganic body: (1) as a direct means of life; and equally (2) as the material object and instrument of his life activity. Nature is the inorganic body of man; that is to say nature, excluding the human body itself. To say that man *lives* from nature means that nature is his *body* with which he must remain in a continuous interchange in order not to die. The statement that the physical and mental life of man, and nature, are interdependent means simply that nature is interdependent with itself, for man is a part of nature.

Since alienated labour: (1) alienates nature from man; and (2) alienates man from himself, from his own active function, his life activity; so it alienates him from the species. It makes *species-life* into a means of individual life. In the first place it alienates species-life and individual life, and secondly, it turns the latter, as an abstraction, into the purpose of the former, also in its abstract and alienated form.

For labour, *life activity, productive life,* now appear to man only as *means* for the satisfaction of a need, the need to maintain his physical existence. Productive life is, however, species-life. It is life creating life. In the type of life activity resides the whole character of a species, its species-character; and free, conscious activity is the species-character of human beings. Life itself appears only as a *means of life.*

The animal is one with its life activity. It does not distinguish the activity from itself. It is *its activity.* But man makes his life activity itself an object of his will and consciousness. He has a conscious life activity. It is not a determination with which he is completely identified. Conscious life activity distinguishes man from the life activity of animals. Only for this reason is he a species-being. Or rather, he is only a self-conscious being, i.e. his own life is an object for him, because he is a species-being. Only for this reason is his activity free activity. Alienated labour reverses the relationship, in that man because he is a self-conscious being makes his life activity, his *being*, only a means for his *existence*.

The practical construction of an *objective world*, the *manipulation* of inorganic nature, is the confirmation of man as a conscious species-being, i.e. a being who treats the species as his own being or himself as a species-being. . . .

It is just in his work upon the objective world that man really proves himself as a *species-being*. This production is his active species-life. By means of it nature appears as *his* work and his reality. The object of labour is, therefore, the *objectification of man's species-life;* for he no longer reproduces himself merely intellectually, as in consciousness, but actively and in a real sense, and he sees his own reflection in a world which he has constructed. While, therefore, alienated labour takes away the object of production from man, it also takes away his *species-life*, his real objectivity as a species-being, and changes his advantage over animals into a disadvantage in so far as his inorganic body, nature, is taken from him.

Just as alienated labour transforms free and self-directed activity into a means, so it transforms the species-life of man into a means of physical existence.

Consciousness, which man has from his species, is transformed through alienation so that species-life becomes only a means for him. (3) Thus alienated labour turns the *species-life of man,* and also nature as his mental species-property, into an *alien* being and into a *means* for his *individual existence.* It alienates from man his own body, external nature, his mental life and his *human* life. (4) A direct consequence of the alienation of man from the product of his labour, from his life activity and from his species-life, is that *man* is *alienated* from other *men.* When man confronts himself he also confronts *other* men. What is true of man's relationship to his work, to the product of his work and to himself, is also true of his relationship to other men, to their labour and to the objects of their labour.

In general, the statement that man is alienated from his species-life means that each man is alienated from others, and that each of the others is likewise alienated from human life.

Human alienation, and above all the relation of man to himself, is first realized and expressed in the relationship between each man and other men. Thus in the relationship of alienated labour every man regards other men according to the standards and relationships in which he finds himself placed as a worker.

We began with an economic fact, the alienation of the worker and his production. We have expressed this fact in conceptual terms as *alienated labour,* and in analysing the concept we have merely analysed an economic fact. . . .

The *alien* being to whom labour and the product of labour belong, to whose service labour is devoted, and to whose enjoyment the product of labour goes, can only be *man* himself. If the product of labour does not belong to the worker, but confronts him as an alien power, this can only be because it belongs to *a man other than the worker.* . . .

Thus, through alienated labour the worker creates the relation of another man, who does not work and is outside the work process, to this labour. The relation of the worker to work also produces the relation of the capitalist (or whatever one likes to call the lord of labour) to work. *Private property* is, therefore, the product, the necessary result, of *alienated labour,* of the external relation of the worker to nature and to himself.

Private property is thus derived from the analysis of the concept of *alienated labour;* that is, alienated man, alienated labour, alienated life, and estranged man.

We have, of course, derived the concept of *alienated labour (alienated life)* from political economy, from an analysis of the *movement of private property.* But the analysis of this concept shows that although private property appears to be the basis and cause of alienated labour, it is rather a consequence of the latter, just as the gods are *fundamentally* not the cause but the product of confusion of human reason. At a later stage, however, there is a reciprocal influence.

Only in the final stage of the development of private property is its secret revealed, namely, that it is on one hand the *product* of alienated labour, and on the other hand the *means* by which labour is alienated, *the realization of this alienation.* . . .

Just as *private property* is only the sensuous expression of the fact that man is at the same time an *objective* fact for himself and becomes an alien and non-human object for himself; just as his manifestation of life is also his alienation of life and his self-realization a loss of reality, the emergence of an *alien* reality; so the positive supersession of private property, i.e. the *sensuous* appropriation of the human essence and of human life, of objective man and of human *creations,* by and for man, should not be taken only in the sense of *immediate,* exclusive *enjoyment,* or only in the sense of *possession* or *having.* Man appropriates his manifold being in an all-inclusive way, and thus as a whole man. All his *human* relations to the world—seeing, hearing, smelling, tasting, touching, thinking, observing, feeling, desiring, acting, loving—in short, all the organs of his individuality, like the organs which are directly communal in form, are in their objective action (their *action in relation to the object*) the appropriation of this object, the appropriation of human reality. The way in which they react to the object is the confirmation of *human reality.* It is human effectiveness and human *suffering,* for suffering humanly considered is an enjoyment of the self for man.

Private property has made us so stupid and partial that an object is only *ours* when we have it, when it exists for us as capital or when it is directly eaten, drunk, worn, inhabited, etc., in short, *utlized* in some way. But private property itself only conceives these various forms of possession as *means of life,* and the life for which they serve as means is the life of *private property*—labour and creation of capital. . . .

The supersession of private property is, therefore, the complete *emancipation* of all the human qualities and senses. It is such an emancipation because these qualities and senses have become *human,* from the subjective as well as the objective point of view. The eye has become a *human* eye when its *object* has become a *human,* social object, created by man and destined for him. The senses have, therefore, become directly theoreticians in practice. They relate themselves to the thing for the sake of the thing, but the thing itself is an *objective human* relation to itself and to man, and vice versa. Need and enjoyment have thus lost their *egoistic* character and nature has lost its mere *utility* by the fact that its utilization has become *human* utilization. . . .

Note

1. In this passage Marx reproduces Feuerbach's argument in *Das Wesen des Christentums.*

Wealth

ANDREW CARNEGIE

This article is one of the clearest attempts to justify Social Darwinism. Written in 1889, it defends the pursuit of wealth by arguing that society is strengthened and improved through the struggle for survival in the marketplace. Interestingly, it was written by one of the world's wealthiest men, Andrew Carnegie, who came to the United States as a poor immigrant boy and quickly rose to enormous power. He began his career as a minor employee in a telegraph company, but emerged in a few years as superintendent of the Pennsylvania Railroad. After the Civil War he entered the iron and steel business, and by 1889 he controlled eight companies which he eventually consolidated into the Carnegie Steel Corporation. Shortly before he died, he merged the Carnegie Steel Corporation with the United States Steel Company.

Carnegie took seriously the task of managing his vast fortune, and he made use of many of the ideas which are presented in the following article. He gave generously to many causes, including public libraries, public education, and the development of international peace.

First published in the *North American Review,* June 1889.

The problem of our age is the proper administration of wealth, so that the ties of brotherhood may still bind together the rich and poor in harmonious relationship. The conditions of human life have not only been changed, but revolutionized, within the past few hundred years. In former days there was little difference between the dwelling, dress, food, and environment of the chief and those of his retainers. The Indians are today where civilized man then was. When visiting the Sioux, I was led to the wigwam of the chief. It was just like the others in external appearance, and even within the difference was trifling between it and those of the poorest of his braves. The contrast between the palace of the millionaire and the cottage of the laborer with us today measures the change which has come into civilization.

This change, however, is not to be deplored, but welcomed as highly beneficial. It is well, nay essential, for the progress of the race, that the houses of some should be homes for all that is highest and best in literature and arts, and for all the refinements of civilization, rather than that none should be so. Much better this great irregularity than universal squalor. Without wealth there can be no Maecetions. When these apprentices rose to be masters, there was little or no change in their mode of life, and they, in turn, educated in the same routine succeeding apprentices. There was, substantially, social equality, and even political equality, for those engaged in industrial pursuits had then little or no political voice in the State.

But the inevitable result of such a mode of manufacture was crude articles at high prices. Today the world obtains commodities of excellent quality at prices which even the generation preceding this would have deemed incredible. In the commercial world similar causes have produced similar results, and the race is benefited thereby. The poor enjoy what the rich could not before afford. What were the luxuries have become the necessaries of life. The laborer has now more comforts than the farmer had a few generations ago. The farmer has more luxuries than the landlord had, and is more richly clad and better housed. The landlord has books and pictures rarer, and appointments more artistic, than the King could then obtain.

The price we pay for this salutary change is, no doubt, great. We assemble thousands of operatives in the factory, in the mine, and in the counting-house, of whom the employer can know little or nothing, and to whom the employer is little better than a myth. All intercourse between them is at an end. Rigid Castes are formed, and, as usual, mutual ignorance breeds mutual distrust. Each Caste is without sympathy for the other, and ready to credit anything disparaging in regard to it. Under the law of competition, the employer of thousands is forced into the strictest economies, among which the rates paid to labor figure prominently, and often there is friction between the employer and the employed, between capital and labor, between rich and poor. Human society loses homogeneity.

The price which society pays for the law of competition, like the price it pays for cheap comforts and luxuries, is also great; but the advantages of this law are also greater still, for it is to this law that we owe our wonderful material development, which brings improved conditions in its train. But, whether the law be benign or not, we must say of it, as we say of the change in the conditions of men to which we have referred: It is here; we cannot evade it; no substitutes for it have been found; and while the law may be sometimes hard for the individual, it is best for the race, because it insures the survival of the fittest in every department. We accept and welcome, therefore, as conditions to which we must accommodate ourselves, great inequality of environment, the concentration of business, industrial and commercial, in the hands of a few, and the law of competition between these, as being not only beneficial, but essential for the future progress of the race. Having accepted these, it follows that there must be great scope for the exercise of special ability in the merchant and in the manufacturer who has to conduct affairs upon a great scale. That this talent for organization and management is rare among men is proved by the fact that it invariably secures for its possessor enormous rewards, no matter where or under what laws or conditions. The experienced in affairs always rate the MAN whose services can be obtained as a partner as not only the first consideration, but such as to render the question of his capital scarcely worth considering, for such men soon create capital; while, without the special talent required, capital soon takes wings. Such men become interested in firms or corporations using millions; and estimating only simple interest to be made upon the capital invested, it is inevitable that their income must exceed their expenditures, and that they must accumulate wealth. Nor is there any middle ground which such men can occupy, because the great manufacturing or commercial concern which does not earn at least interest upon its capital soon becomes bankrupt. It must either go forward or fall behind: to stand still is impossible. It is a condition essential for its successful operation that it should be thus far profitable, and even that, in addition to interest on capital, it should make profit. It is a law, as certain as any of the others named, that men possessed of this peculiar talent for affairs, under the free play of economic forces, must, of necessity, soon be in receipt of more revenue than can be judiciously expended upon themselves, and this law is as beneficial for the race as the others.

Objections to the foundations upon which society is based are not in order, because the condition of the race is better with these than it has been with any others which have been tried. Of the effect of any new substitutes proposed we cannot be sure. The Socialist or Anarchist who seeks to overturn present conditions is to be regarded as attacking the foundation upon which civilization itself rests, for civilization took its start from the day that the capable, industrious workman said to his incompetent and lazy fellow, "If thou dost not sow, thou shalt not reap," and thus ended primitive Communism by separating the drones from the bees. One who studies this subject will soon be brought face to face with the conclusion that upon the sacredness of property civilization itself depends—the right of the laborer to his hundred dollars in the savings bank, and equally the legal right of the millionaire to his millions. To those who propose to substitute Communism for this intense Individualism the answer, therefore, is: The race has tried that. All progress from that barbarous day to the present time has resulted from its displacement. Not evil, but good, has come to the race from the accumulation of wealth by those who have the ability and energy that produce it. But even if we admit for a moment that it might be better for the race to discard its present foundation, Individualism—that it is a nobler ideal that man should labor, not for himself alone, but in and for a brotherhood of his fellows, and share with them all in common, realizing Swedenborg's idea of Heaven, where, as he says, the angels derive their happiness, not from laboring for self, but for each other—even admit all this, and a sufficient answer is, This is not evolution, but revolution. It necessitates the changing of human nature itself—a work of aeons, even if it were good to change it, which we cannot know. It is not practicable in our day or in our age. Even if desirable theoretically, it belongs to another and long-succeeding sociological stratum. Our duty is with what is practicable now; with the next step possible in our day and generation. It is criminal to waste our energies in endeavoring to uproot, when all we can profitably or possibly accomplish is to bend the universal tree of humanity a little in the direction most favorable to the production of good fruit under existing circumstances. We might as well urge the destruction of the highest existing type of man because he failed to reach our ideal as to favor the destruction of Individualism, Private Property, the Law of Accumulation of Wealth, and the Law of Competition; for these are the highest results of human experience, the soil in which society so far has produced the best fruit. Unequally or unjustly, perhaps, as these laws sometimes operate, and imperfect as they appear to the Idealist, they are nevertheless, like the highest type of man, the best and most valuable of all that humanity has yet accomplished.

We start, then, with a condition of affairs under which the best interests of the race are promoted, but which inevitably gives wealth to the few. Thus far, accepting conditions as they exist, the situation can be surveyed and pronounced good. The question then arises—and, if the foregoing be correct, it is the only question with which we have to deal—What is the proper mode of administering wealth after the laws upon which civilization is founded have thrown it into the hands of the few? And it is of this great question that I believe I offer the true solution. It will be understood that *fortunes* are here spoken of, not moderate sums saved by many years of effort, the returns from which are required for the comfortable maintenance and education of families. This is not *wealth*, but only *competence*, which it should be the aim of all to acquire.

. . . Indeed, it is difficult to set bounds to the share of a rich man's estate which should go at his death to the public through the agency of the state, and by all means such taxes should be graduated, beginning at nothing upon moderate sums to dependents, and increasing rapidly as the amounts swell, until of the millionaire's hoard, as of Shylock's at least

> " --- The other half
>   Comes to the privy coffer of the state."

This policy would work powerfully to induce the rich man to attend to the administration of wealth during his life, which is the end that society should always have in view, as being that by far most fruitful for the people. Nor need it be feared that this policy would sap the root of enterprise and render men less anxious to accumulate, for to the class whose ambition it is to leave great fortunes and be talked about after their death, it will attract more attention, and, indeed, be a somewhat nobler ambition to have enormous sums paid over to the state from their fortunes.

There remains, then, only one mode of using great fortunes; but in this we have the true antidote for the temporary unequal distribution of wealth, the reconciliation of the rich and the poor—a reign of harmony—another ideal, differing, indeed, from that of the Communist in requiring only the further evolution of existing conditions, not the total overthrow of our civilization. It is founded upon the present most intense individualism, and the race is prepared to put it in practice by degrees whenever it pleases. Under its sway we shall have an ideal state, in which the surplus wealth of the few will become, in the best sense, the property of the many, because administered for the common good, and this wealth, passing through the hands of the few, can be made a much more potent force for the elevation of our race than if it had been distributed in small sums to the people themselves. Even the poorest can be made to see this, and to agree that great sums gathered by some of their fellow-citizens and spent for public purposes, from which the masses reap the principal benefit, are more valuable to them than if scattered among them through the course of many years in trifling amounts.

The best uses to which surplus wealth can be put have already been indicated. Those who would administer wisely must, indeed, be wise, for one of the serious obstacles to the improvement of our race is indiscriminate charity. It were better for mankind that the millions of the rich were thrown into the sea than so spent as to encourage the slothful, the drunken, the unworthy. Of every thousand dollars spent in so-called charity today, it is probable that $950 is unwisely spent; so spent, indeed, as to produce the very evils which it proposes to mitigate or cure. A well-known writer of philosophic books admitted the other day that he had given a quarter of a dollar to a man who approached him as he was coming to visit the house of his friend. He knew nothing of the habits of this beggar; knew not the use that would be made of this money, although he had every reason to suspect that it would be spent improperly. This man professed to be a disciple of Herbert Spencer; yet the quarter-dollar given that night will probably work more injury than all the money which its thoughtless donor will ever be able to give in true charity will do good. He only gratified his own feelings, saved himself from annoyance—and this was probably one of the most selfish and very worst actions of his life, for in all respects he is most worthy.

In bestowing charity, the main consideration should be to help those who will help themselves; to provide part of the means by which those who desire to improve may do so; to give those who desire to rise the aids by which they may rise; to assist, but rarely or never to do all. Neither the individual nor the race is improved by alms-giving. Those worthy of assistance, except in rare cases, seldom require assistance. The really valuable men of the race never do, except in cases of accident or sudden change. Every one has, of course, cases of individuals brought to his own knowledge where temporary assistance can do genuine good, and these he will not overlook. But the amount which can be wisely given by the individual for individuals is necessarily limited by his lack of knowledge of the circumstances connected with each. He is the only true reformer who is as careful and an anxious not to aid the unworthy as he is to aid the worthy, and perhaps, even more so, for in alms-giving more injury is probably done by rewarding vice then by relieving virtue.

Thus is the problem of Rich and Poor to be solved. The laws of accumulation will be left free; the laws of distribution free. Individualism will continue, but the millionaire will be but a trustee for the poor; intrusted for a season with a great part of the increased wealth of the community, but administrating it for the community far better than it could or would have done for itself. The best minds will thus have reached a stage in the development of the race in which it is clearly seen that there is no mode of disposing of surplus wealth creditable to thoughtful and earnest men into whose hands it flows save by using it year by year for the general good. This day already dawns. But a little while, and although, without incurring the pity of their fellows, men may die sharers in great business enterprises from which their capital cannot be or has not been withdrawn, and is left chiefly at death for public uses, yet the man who dies leaving behind him millions of available wealth, which was his to administer during life, will pass away "unwept, unhonored, and unsung," no matter to what uses he leaves the dross which he cannot take with him. Of such as these the public verdict will then be: "The man who dies thus rich dies disgraced."

Such, in my opinion, is the true Gospel concerning Wealth, obedience to which is destined some day to solve the problems of the Rich and the Poor, and to bring "Peace on earth, among men Good-Will."

The Profit Motive

Antony Flew

I. TWO FUNDAMENTAL SUGGESTIONS

We hear much talk of the (private) profit motive; and many suggestions that, because (private) profit is a defining characteristic essential to capitalism, therefore any such economic system must be inherently more

From *Ethics,* Vol. 86 (July 1976), pp. 312–22. Reprinted by permission of The University of Chicago Press. © 1976 by the University of Chicago.

selfish and hard-nosed than actual or possible rivals. For instance: in the summer of '72 *The Times* of London reported that Archbishop Camara of Brazil had asked a meeting of members of both Houses of Parliament: "Why do you not help lay bare the serious distortions of socialism such as they exist in Russia and China? And why do you not denounce, once and for all, the intrinsic selfishness and heartlessness of capitalism?"[1]

A. I want to start by responding with another question: "Why do we never hear of the rent motive or the wages motive?" Perhaps the classical distinction between profit and rent is outmoded. But, if it is proper to speak of a profit motive, it should surely be equally proper to speak of a wages motive. And, if it is proper to say that those who work for wages are stirred by the wages motive; then it must be not merely proper but positively refined to say that those whose wages are paid at longer intervals, and called a salary or even compensation, are inspired by, respectively, the salary motive and the compensation motive. By parity of reasoning we shall then have to admit into our economic psychology the fixed interest motive, the top price motive, and the best buy motive. And so on, and on and on. . . .

B. My second general suggestion is that no one—not even an archbishop—has any business simply to assume that the desire to make a (private) profit is always and necessarily selfish and discreditable; notwithstanding that the corresponding desires to obtain a wage, or a salary, or a retirement income, are—apparently—not. No doubt all these various desires are interested; in the sense that those who are guided by any of them are—in the immortal words of Mr. Damon Runyon—"doing the best they can." But, precisely because this does apply equally to all, we can find no ground here for condemning one and not the others.

This neglected fact is awkward for the denouncers. For no one, surely, is so starry-eyed as to believe that any system of economic organization can dispense with all such interested motives. If, therefore, one such system is upon this particular ground to be condemned as "intrinsically selfish and heartless," then, by the same token, all must be. Yet that, of course, is precisely not what is wanted by those who thus denounce capitalism root and branch, and as such; while tolerantly discounting as more or less "serious distortions" whatever faults they can, however reluctantly, bring themselves to recognize in the socialist countries.

The further fundamental mistake here is that of identifying the interested with the selfish. This is wrong. For, though selfish actions are perhaps always interested, only some interested actions are also selfish. To say that a piece of conduct was selfish is to say more than that it was interested, if it was. The point is that selfishness is always and necessarily out of order. Interestedness is not, and scarcely could be.

For example: when my daughters eagerly eat their dinners they are, I suppose, pursuing their own interests. But it would be monstrous to denounce them as selfish hussies, simply on that account. The time for denunciation could come only after one of them had, for instance, eaten someone else's dinner too; or refused to make some sacrifice which she ought to have made. Again, even when my success can be won only at the price of someone else's failure, it is not always and necessarily selfish for me to pursue my own interests. The rival candidates competing for some coveted job are not selfish just because they do not all withdraw in order to clear the way for the others.

The upshot, therefore, is that it will not do to dismiss any one economic system as "intrinsically selfish and heartless": simply because that system depends upon and engages interested motives; or even simply because it allows or encourages people to pursue their own interests in certain situations of zero sum conflict. If there is something peculiarly obnoxious about wanting to make a (private) profit, it will have to be something about making a (private) profit, rather than something about just wanting to acquire some economic good; or even about competing to acquire scarce economic goods in any zero sum conflict situation, as such.

II. THREE POPULAR ARISTOTELIAN MISCONCEPTIONS

That it is indeed essentially scandalous to make a profit—and hence, presumably, also scandalous to wish to do so—is an idea both as old as the Classical Greek philosophers and as topical as—for instance—tomorrow's Labour party political broadcasts. Consider what was said by the one who has had, and albeit mainly through Aquinas and Hegel continues to have, by far the greatest influence.

The economic thought of Aristotle is to be found mainly in the *Politics*.[2] It is altogether characteristic that he takes as normative whatever he believes to be—as it were—the intention of nature. . . .

. . . We should not after this be surprised that for Aristotle the supposed ideal universal provider is not—as it would be today—the state, but nature: "On a general view, as we have already noticed, a supply of property should be ready to hand. It is the business of nature to furnish subsistence for each being brought into the world; and this is shown by the fact that the offspring of animals always gets nourishment from the residuum of the matter that gives it its birth.[3]

A. It is significant, and entirely consistent with this providential assumption, that Aristotle goes on to emphasise acquisition rather than production: "The natural form, therefore, of the art of acquisition is always, and in all cases, acquisition from fruits and animals. That art . . . has two forms: one which is connected with . . . trade, and another which is connected with the management of the household. Of these two forms, the latter is necessary and laudable; the former is a method of exchange which is justly censured, because the gain in which it results is not naturally made, but is made at the expense of other men.[4]

Aristotle's point is that trade is in essence exploitation. The acquisitions of the trader must, Aristotle thinks, be made at the expense of that trader's trading partner; whereas the only creditable acquisitions are those achieved from non-human nature direct. Shorn of these notions of what is and is not in accord with the intentions of nature, Aristotle's is the same thesis—and the same misconception—as we find in John Ruskin: "Whenever material gain follows exchange, for every plus there is a precisely equal minus."[5]. . .

The crux is that trade is a reciprocal relationship. If I am trading with you it follows necessarily that you are trading with me. Trade is also, for both parties, necessarily voluntary. Nothing which you may succeed in seizing from me by force can, by that token, be either acquired or relinquished in trade. So, if any possible advantage of trade to the trader could be gained only at the expense of some corresponding disadvantage to his trading partner, it would appear that in any commercial exchange at least one party must be either a fool, or a masochist, or a gambler.

But, of course, as all must recognize when not either by theory or by passion distracted, the truth is that the seller sells because, in his actual situation, he would rather receive the price than retain the goods, while the buyer buys because, in his actual situation, he would rather pay the price than be without the goods. Ruskin was, therefore, diametrically wrong. It is of the essence of trade: not that any advantage for one party can be achieved only at the expense of the other; but that no deal is made at all unless, whether rightly or wrongly, both parties believe that they stand to gain thereby—or at least both prefer the deal actually made to any available alternative deal, and to no deal at all.

Certainly one of the trading partners, or even both, may be mistaken or in some other way misguided in his decision to deal. Certainly too the actual situation of either party, the situation in which it seems better to him to make the deal than not, may be in many ways unfair or unfortunate.[6] But all this is contingent, and hence to the present question irrelevant. This question is: 'What is and is not essential to the very idea of trade?' Mutually satisfactory sex is a better model here than poker played for money. For in the former the satisfactions of each depend reciprocally upon those of the other; whereas the latter really is a zero sum game in which your winnings precisely equal, because they are, my losses.

One temptation to conclude that trade necessarily involves a zero sum confrontation lies in the fact that both buyers and sellers would often, if they had to, pay more or accept less than they do. Obviously it is in such a situation possible to regard either the more which might have been got or the less which might have been given as an advantage forfeited by one trading partner to the other. But this, which is perhaps often the case, certainly is not so always. And both buyer and seller may be, and I imagine typically are, simultaneously in similar situations with regard to such forfeited possible advantages. So it cannot be correct to infer, as a general conclusion, that all the gains of trade must always be achieved by one trading partner at the expense of the other. . . .

In general, I suggest, and it is a reflection which has a relevance far wider than its present occasion, economic arrangements are best judged by results. Concentrate on the price and quality of the product. Do not officiously probe the producer's purity of heart. If, nevertheless, we are to consider motives, then this envy which resents that others too should gain, and maybe gain more than us, must be accounted much nastier than any supposed "intrinsic selfishness" of straight self-interest. . . .

Let us, however, conclude the present subsection not with snide moralizing but with a gesture of Roman piety. Adam Smith wrote: "It is not from the benevolence of the butcher, the brewer, or the baker that we expect our dinner, but from their regard for their own interest. We address ourselves, not to their humanity but to their self-love, and never talk to them of our own necessities but of their advantages. Nobody but a beggar chooses to depend chiefly upon the benevolence of his fellow citizens."[7]

B. Aristotle's next contribution is equally unfortunate, and has been equally important. Immediately after the last passage quoted earlier he continues: "The trade of the usurer is hated most, and with most reason. . . . Currency came into existence merely as a means of exchange; usury tries to make it increase. This is the reason why interest is called by the word we commonly use [the word *tokos,* which in Greek also means offspring]; for as the offspring resembles its parent, so the interest bred by money is like the principal which breeds it, and it may be called 'curency the son of currency.' Hence we can understand why, of all modes of acquisition, usury is the most unnatural."[8]

Usury is now, thanks first to Aristotle and still more to his medieval successors, such a bad word that it may not be at once obvious just what it is to which Aristotle is objecting. It is not only to excessive or, as we should now say, usurious fixed interest. Nor is it only to all fixed interest as such, which was the prime target of those medieval successors.[9] He objects, rather, to any money return upon any money investment. It is, he thinks, against nature for money to breed money.[10]

The moment Aristotle's point is appreciated, it becomes quite clear that both his objection and his supporting reason are superstitious and muddled. For a sum of money is the substantial equivalent of any of the goods or collections of goods which it might buy. There can, therefore, be nothing obnoxiously unnatural about receiving a money return upon an investment in money, unless it would be equally obnoxious and unnatural to ask for some return either in money or in kind for the use of the goods themselves.

Before proceeding to the Aristotelian source of yet a third perennially popular misconception, take time out to notice two corollaries. First, it must be psychologically unilluminating to speak of any money motive; and, by the same token, still more unilluminating to try to develop a complete economic psychology upon a basis of a series of economic distinctions between various mercenary motives. For that someone wants to make a profit or to earn a wage tells us nothing of what he wants the money for. Almost any desire can take the form of a desire for money. It is obvious that this is a necessary consequence of the essential nature of money as a conventional instrument of exchange. Aristotle himself elsewhere makes this point about money. But he misses its present application. Second, and consequently, it must be wrong to hope that the abolition of money, or the reduction of the range of goods which money can buy, might by itself reduce greed and competition for those goods. Certainly it is tautologically true that the profit motive, the fixed interest motive, the wages motive, and all the other factitious motives michievously listed in IA above, are mercenary. All, that is, are defined in terms of the acquisition of money. It might therefore seem that totally to abolish money, or to reduce its importance as a means of acquisition, must be to abolish or at least to weaken, all mercenary motives.

In an appropriately empty sense this no doubt is true. Yet, unless these changes happened to be accompanied by something quite different, an enormous transformation of present human nature, people would presumably continue to pursue, and to compete for, whatever it was which they had always wanted, but which money could not now buy. In a word: if cars are not on sale for money, but are available as a perquisite of high office, then this fact will by itself tend only to increase the already surely sufficiently ferocious competition for such privileged official places. The abolition of money might make us less mercenary. It would not by itself even begin to make us less materialistic or less competitive.

C. A third perennially popular misconception about the profit motive also apparently originates in Aristotle. For his difficult and unsteady distinction between two forms of the art of acquisition[11]—acquisition for household use and acquisition for financial gain—is, surely, ancestor of the evergreen false antithesis between production for profit and production for use.[12]

The antithesis is false for the very obvious reason that there can be no profit in producing what no one has any wish to buy, and presumably, to use.[13] Certainly, what ordinary people want to buy may not be what their actual or supposed superiors believe that they need; and hence ought to want. (The word here is, or used to be, 'candyfloss'; candyfloss being taken as typical of all the things which our moral and intellectual superiors consider it wrong for us lesser creatures to want to buy, or for entrepreneurs to make and to sell.) Certainly too, folk may want and—much more seriously—may both need and want, what they lack the money to buy; and what, because they do both need and want it, they ideally ought to be able to buy. Again, the market may not always offer the range of options which you or I might like to be making our choices between.[14] But none of this justifies any general opposition: between, on the one hand, the profit motive and the profit system; and, on the other hand, the satisfaction of human needs. The true and relevant antithesis here is quite different. It is that between a command and a market economy; and it is significant that while the individual is himself the prime authority on what he wants, his needs, or his alleged needs, are in principle determined as well, or better, by others.

Nor will it do to argue—what is in fact more often assumed than argued—that: where, and in so far as, it is a contingently necessary condition of the production of anything that its production should be profitable to the producing firm; there, and to that extent, the profit motive provides the only reason why that product actually is produced and sold. This argument is on two different counts invalid.

First, it overlooks the most typical case. For motives—if it really is motives we are considering—are notoriously apt to be mixed. Dostoevski was not exaggerating much when he said: "No one ever acts from a single motive." That this is indeed one of a lady's motives by no means precludes that she has other motives also. A man may invest his capital in a bassoon factory both because he wants a profitable investment; and because he wants to popularize bassoon-playing; and because he wants to infuriate his unmusical aunt. Indeed conduct often is fully overdetermined, in the sense that the agent has two or more reasons either or any one of which would have been sufficient to secure his action.

Second, that something has one necessary condition does not preclude that it has other necessary conditions also. Allow that the firm will ultimately be shut down if it continues to run at a loss. So it will be if, for instance, no one is prepared to work for it or to buy from it. Say then that these further considerations are effective only in so far as they affect profitability. This is, no doubt, with appropriate qualifications, true. Yet that it is true, and that profitability is thus affected by other considerations, is itself the decisive reason why there cannot be a radical disjunction between profitability and all such other considerations.

Two other equally common, and equally unsound moves are to argue: either, from premises about the putative purposes of institutions, to conclusions about the motives of those who work within and for those institutions; or, from premises about the intentions of agents, to conclusions about the actual consequences of their actions. That this ministry or this state corporation was purportedly established solely to serve the public provides no guarantee; either that successive ministers, directors, civil servants, and other employees are oriented similarly; or that its actual operations are beneficial. . . .

III. THE ALLEGED WICKEDNESS OF INVESTMENT INCOME

What is constantly presented as a revulsion against the profit motive unfortunately may, and in fact often does, blind people to all other considerations, including sometimes other considerations which ought to weigh far more heavily than any preferences between rival economic arrangements. . . .

Probably the most powerful of the sources of this revulsion against "the profit motive" is one which I have not so far mentioned. It is the desire to have done with every kind of investment income; and, what it is a mistake to think is the same thing as this, the drive to insist that all income must be earned.[15] Adequately to consider these aspirations would require a second paper. Some may wish that this was that paper. But all I can, or need, say in the present consideration of the profit motive is enough to show that such commitments demand something much more extensive by way of justification than a visceral revulsion against "the (private) profit motive." They cannot by themselves justify, what the present paper is attacking, a concentrated hostility to this as opposed to any or all the others indicated in IA above.

The fundamental objection may be either to deriving income from any form of (private) ownership or, more particularly, to deriving income from (private) ownership of the means of production. In each case the postulated motives fall under the ban in as much as they are desires to do what is thought to be wrong. In the first case these clearly should include the debenture as well as the profit motive. Indeed, since there is no relevant reason for distinguishing the ownership of real property here, and since all income from any kind of property constitutes rent for the use of that property, the proper enemy would be not the profit but—in this comprehensive sense of *rent*—the rent motive.

In the second case the suggestion is that to derive income from the ownership of the means of production—though not perhaps from ownership as such—is essentially exploitative. Too often it is suggested further that to end this one kind of putative exploitation must be to end all exploitation.[16]

A. As regards the first form of objection, it is hard to see how one could defend the total rejection in principle of the acceptance of rent for the use of (private) property if once one had conceded any rights to (private) property at all.

On another occasion I should like to consider the implication of such a total repudiation of all (private) property. But now it is sufficient to suggest that few people are in practice prepared in a cool hour to advocate a complete abandonment of all private property; and, consequently, of the acceptance of any rent for the use of it. This being so, the other objection to such rent, and to the factitious rent motive, presumably reduce to objections either to the amount of the rent, or to the actual distribution of the property, or to having private property in certain sorts of goods; rather than as such to private property itself, or to rent for the use of it.

B. As regards the second contention—that to derive income from the private ownership of the means of production, distribution, and exchange is immoral—it is difficult to discern how, if private ownership of such property is immoral, its collective ownership by any groups less than the whole human race is to be appropriately justified. For citizens of the better endowed socialist states, and members of the better endowed collective farms and other cooperatives both inside and outside these states, are all deriving, from their collective ownership of these endowments, advantages which they surely did not earn by their own toil, and which are certainly not available to less fortunate collective owners in the same or other countries. If these inequalities are in principle unacceptable, then the moral must be that proclaimed long ago by Gratian: "The use of all the things which there are in this world ought to be common to all men."[17]

Suppose, however, that they are not wholly unacceptable. And who of us—whether socialist or anti-socialist—is really prepared to abandon all the privileged endowments of a still relatively rich country in favour of a universal and conscientiously egalitarian poverty? Then the objection to private profit and the private profit motive becomes, it seems, an objection not to the profit but to the privacy. And that is a very different story.

For the objection now is not to acquisitiveness, or to excess, or even to exploitation. It is to what is individual and private rather than public and collective.[18] And here we see again what may be to some a somewhat less acceptable face of socialism.

Notes

1. "Waiting for a Sign from the Egoists" (June 27, 1972). Later in the same week the *Catholic Herald* (June 30, 1972) reported other meetings at which the archbishop—described by Cardinal de Roy, president of the Pontifical Commission for Justice and Peace, as "one of the great voices of our time"— "called on British Catholics to fight the forces of capitalist imperialism." It is a pity that this great voice thus insists on inserting the qualification 'capitalist' into his denunciations of imperialism. By so doing the archbishop is bound to suggest to any attentive reader: either that he believes that there is no such thing as a socialist empire; or that he disapproves of empires only when the imperial power has not yet nationalized all the means of production, distribution, and exchange. If it is the former, then he is subject to the commonest and most damaging of contemporary delusions—wilful blindness to the realities of the Great Russian empire of what Maoists rightly call the "new Tsars." If it is the latter, then he must be the bearer of a most curiously perverted conscience—nonetheless perverted for being in many quarters nowadays, in the descriptive sense, normal.
2. *The Politics of Aristotle,* trans. Ernest Barker (Oxford: Clarendon Press, 1948).
3. Ibid., 1(x)3:1258A 33–36. No one seems to have anticipated me in noticing these sentences as a respectably Classical formulation of the shabby doctrine that the world owes us a living.
4. Ibid., 1(x)4:1258A 37–1258B 2.
5. John Ruskin, *Unto This Last* (London: G. A. Allen, 1899), p. 131.
6. This important reservation is developed in, for instance, E. J. Mishan *21 Popular Economic Fallacies* (Harmondsworth, Middlesex: Penguin, 1971), pp. 95–97. But it is unfortunate that Mishan gets off on the wrong foot by saying that, if I am forced at pistol point to drink castor oil, then "I may be said to have chosen to do it of my own free will. . . ." What he should have said is that the man who thus acts not of his own free will but under compulsion, nevertheless acts; and hence in the most fundamental senses, does have a choice and could have done other than he in fact did. See, for instance, my "Is There a Problem of Freedom?" In *Phenomenology and Philosophical Understanding,* ed. E. Pivcevic (Cambridge: Cambridge University Press, 1975), secs. 3 (a) and 3 (b).
7. Adam Smith. *The Wealth of Nations,* 1 (i): 13 of vol. 1 in the Everyman edition (New York: Dent & Dutton, 1910).
8. *Aristotle,* 1(x)4-5:1258B 2-8.
9. See R. H. Tawney, *Religion and the Rise of Capitalism* (Harmondsworth, Middlesex: Penguin Books, 1938): "Medieval opinion, which has no objection to rent or profits, provided that they are reasonable—for is not everyone in a small way a profit-maker?—has no mercy for the debenture-

holder. His crime is that he takes a payment for money which is fixed and certain, and such a payment is usury" (p. 55).

10. *Aristotle,* 1(ix)8.

11. Ibid., I(viii)-(x).

12. Not to be too polemically topical consider John Strachey's pamphlet *Why You Should Be a Socialist* (London: Gollancz, 1944). In one form or another this achieved an immense circulation in the thirties and forties. Strachey wrote: "One of the familiar phrases of the moment is to say that under capitalism production is carried on for profit, while under socialism it is carried on for use; that socialism is planned production for use. What is meant by this phrase?" (p. 68).

13. That so obvious an objection seems never to occur to the often able people for whom this false antithesis remains a treasured catchword is one good reason for challenging the smug leftist assumption that left-wingers are, unlike their opponents, constitutionally questioning and critical. No doubt there have been times and places where this was indeed true. But observation of, for instance, the contemporary British student body can show that it is by no means an universal truth!

14. See, for instance, the Mishan reference given in n. [6] above.

15. You need to be a bit careful about the common denunciatory equation of investment with unearned income. Mr. Brian Barry, for instance, in his *The Liberal Theory of Justice* (London: Oxford University Press, 1973) dismisses the whole subject in a peremptory sideswipe: "and of course get rid of unearned income" (p. 115). Yet Barry certainly does not want to prohibit all welfare payments which have not been either earned or insured for by the recipients. And does he really want to insist that any interest paid on a person's own savings from earned income must be in real terms—as thanks to high taxation and high inflation it now often is—either nil or negative? Karl Marx in his *Critique of the Gotha Programme* was, by contrast, careful to make "funds for those unable to work" one of the first charges on the budget for his socialist state (K. Marx and F. Engels, *Selected Works* [Moscow: Foreign Languages Publishing House, 1969], 1:21).

16. Thus Strachey urged: "But the term *exploitation* has an exact meaning. It describes precisely the process by which those who own the means of production draw off almost all the wealth. . . . They eat food, wear clothes, and live in houses produced by other men's labour and offer no product of their own labour in exchange. That is exploitation" (p. 36). It should be sobering to compare a sentence from Robert Conquest's *The Great Terror* (London: Macmillan Co., 1968): "For what it is worth the evidence seems to be that Stalin really believed that the abolition of incomes from capital was the sole necessary principle of social morality, excusing any other action whatever" (p. 67).

17. Gratian, Decretum; quoted by R. H. Tawney, p. 45.

18. George Schwartz in his *Bread and Circuses* (London: *Sunday Times,* 1959) quotes a sensible statement to the Supreme Soviet on August 18, 1953, by the future power station manager Malenkov: "Many enterprises which are still running at a loss exist in industry, enterprises in which production costs are higher than the prices laid down . . . factories, enterprises and mines which we are running at a loss . . . living at the expense of leading enterprises . . ." (p. 65).

PRIVATE OWNERSHIP
AND THE PUBLIC INTEREST

Case Study—Amtrak

CHRISTOPHER H. LOVELOCK

Executives of the National Railroad Passenger Corporation, better known as Amtrak, faced both good news and bad news in summer 1974. The good news was that system-wide patronage for the first half of 1974 was up by 32 percent over the same period of the previous year, with trains on some of the more popular routes sold out weeks and even months in advance. The bad news was that the corporation faced a critical shortage of passenger cars, with many more than projected having to be withdrawn from service for repairs. Also causing concern to some was the bad publicity engendered by Amtrak's continuing poor punctuality record; in June 1974, only 60 percent of long-distance trains and 83 percent of short-haul trains had arrived on time.

It was expected that some of these problems would be alleviated in due course by purchase of new equipment due for delivery from 1975 onwards, and by Amtrak's insistence on tougher performance standards by railroads under contract to the corporation. However, the outlook for significant improvements during the balance of the summer peak season was not particularly encouraging.

An important issue facing Amtrak executives at this time was how to handle the summer situation from a marketing standpoint, within the context of developing a consistent long-term strategy.

PASSENGER RAIL TRAVEL IN THE UNITED STATES

The nation's railroads played a key role in the development of the young United States, and the completion of the last link in the transcontinental railroad in 1869 signified the beginning of an era in which the passenger train reigned supreme as the leading form of intercity transportation in the United States. This era reached its peak in 1929, which saw the greatest number of passenger trains ever operated in the nation.

Case prepared by Christopher H. Lovelock. Copyright 1975 by the President and Fellows of Harvard College. Reproduced by permission of Harvard College and the author.

The Decline of Rail

From this peak, intercity rail passenger service entered a decline which was interrupted by World War II but continued briskly thereafter. In large measure, the financial picture paralleled the decrease in ridership. Rail service operated at a profit in only four years during the period 1930 to 1970. From 1962 to 1970, the annual intercity rail passenger deficit increased from $394 million to $476 million.

The most significant reason for the decline of rail passenger transportation was the development of three major competing modes: air, bus, and private car. All three were spurred by very large federal investments. The airlines were heavily supported by operating and airport construction subsidies, while equipment development benefited greatly from commercial application of much military R&D [Research and Development, eds.].

The bus and auto modes, meantime, were aided by the widespread construction of public roads, most notably under the Interstate Highway Act of 1956 which, by 1971, had brought into being close to 40,000 miles of new high-speed, limited access highways. Exhibit 1 charts the rise of intercity auto, bus, and air travel and the decline of passenger rail.

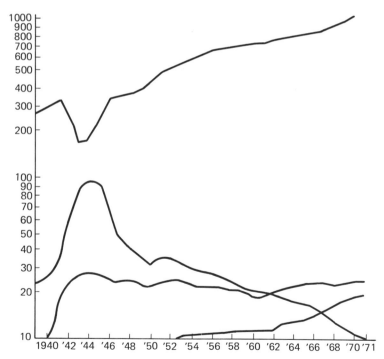

Source: Interstate Commerce Commission.

Exhibit 1. Intercity Travel by Automobile, Bus, Air, and Rail, 1940–1971 (Billions of Passenger Miles, semi-log)

The Railroads' Response

According to many observers, once the shift to air, bus and car had begun, it was accelerated by the managements of many railroads, in the belief that there was no way to make passenger rail service profitable again (a view shared by many economists). The declining sales situation was aggravated by steadily rising costs.

Although a few railroads, such as the Atcheson, Topeka & Santa Fe, made efforts to reverse the downwards trend of ridership, it was alleged that some lines deliberately encouraged this trend with poor service and inferior equipment. When patronage on a given route had declined sufficiently, the railroad would then petition the Interstate Commerce Commission (or state regulatory body in the case of intrastate services) for permission to reduce service or even eliminate it altogether.

The pressure for discontinuance was further intensified in 1967 when the Post Office Department decided to discontinue attaching post office cars to passenger trains, thus depriving the railroads of substantial passenger-related revenues.

From nearly 1,500 intercity trains in the late 1950s, the total had shrunk to a little over one-third that number by mid-1969. During the twelve months ending July 1, 1969, the rate of abandonments continued briskly, with a further sixty-seven intercity passenger trains being withdrawn from service. Railroad executives insisted that they were not deliberately trying to drive passengers away from rail travel and that the decline simply reflected the greater attraction of air, bus, and car travel.

Passengers and even the ICC argued otherwise. In April 1968, an ICC examiner recommended that the commission should take an activist role and order the Southern Pacific to improve its daily Sunset Limited service on the lengthy Los Angeles–New Orleans route by such measures as running the train on time (it was often many hours late) and providing dining cars.

Targeted for some of the strongest complaints was the Penn Central, which was accused, amongst other shortcomings, of "filthy" cars, "disgusting odors" in the rest rooms, and malfunctioning lights and air-conditioning. An article in the *Wall Street Journal* told the saga of a rat that terrorized passengers on the Spirit of St. Louis. The rat was ignored by the conductor for 100 miles and finally trapped in a passenger's handkerchief and thrown off the train. On another occasion, reported the *Journal*, thirty-five passengers on the Spirit became so incensed by the lack of lights, water and airconditioning that they climbed off and lay down in front of the locomotive for an hour and a half until a broken generator belt was replaced.[1]

The Formation of Amtrak

By 1970 half the nation's passenger trains were subject to discontinuance proceedings before the ICC, and fears were being expressed that intercity rail passenger service was nearing extinction. As a result of pressure from legislators, state regulatory agencies, and consumer groups such as the

National Association of Railroad Passengers, Congress enacted the Rail Passenger Service Act (Public Law 91-518). This was signed into law in October 1970.

The purpose of the Act was stated as follows:

> The Congress finds that modern, efficient, intercity railroad passenger service is a necessary part of a balanced transportation system; that public convenience and necessity require the continuance and improvement of such service to provide fast and comfortable transportation between crowded urban areas and in other areas of the country; that rail passenger service can help to end the congestion on our highways and the airports; that the traveler in America should to the maximum extent feasible have freedom to choose the mode of travel most convenient to his needs; that to achieve these goals requires the designation of a basic national rail passenger system and the establishment of a rail passenger corporation for the purpose of providing modern, efficient, intercity rail passenger service; that Federal financial assistance as well as investment capital from the private sector of the economy is needed for this purpose; and that interim emergency Federal financial assistance to certain railroads may be necessary to permit the orderly transfer of railroad passenger service to a railroad passenger corporation.

Major provisions of the Act were as follows:

1. The designation of a "basic system" of passenger routes by the secretary of transportation, to be operational until at least July 1973.
2. The formation of the National Railroad Passenger Corporation, as an independent, for-profit corporation, to manage most of the national intercity rail passenger routes by contracting for services with existing railroads.
3. The participation of railroads in the corporation upon payment of one year's avoidable passenger losses or equivalent. In return, the subscribing railroads received either common stock or a tax reduction. Railroads that did not join were required to continue all passenger service without change until 1975.
4. An initial grant of $40 million to the Corporation and loan guarantee authority of up to $100 million.
5. Formation of a board of directors, consisting of eight public members appointed by the President (one to be the Secretary of Transportation and one a consumer representative), three elected by the common stockholders (the railroads) and four elected by the preferred stockholders.[2]
6. Exemption of the company from ICC regulation of fares and service.[3]
7. Requirement to service any route that a state, regional or local agency requested, provided the agency agreed to pay at least two-thirds of the losses incurred thereby.

In late October 1970, a proposed "basic system" was announced by the secretary of transportation. This deprived many cities of rail service, eliminated connections to Canada and Mexico, and left out some important links within the United States, notably West Coast service from Seattle to San Diego. As a result of protests by the general public—more than 3,000 letters were received by the White House—and lobbying by local and national legislators, the initial proposal was revised to include many of the deleted routes. A promise was also made to consider restoration of Canadian and Mexican links at a later date.

Three railroads—the Southern, the Rio Grande and the Rock Island—elected not to join the new corporation, but to continue operating their own passenger services. Also excluded were the services of Auto-Train, a private company which had a contractual agreement with Seaboard Coast Lines for ferrying passengers and their automobiles from Washington to Florida on Auto-Train-owned equipment.

Appointed as president of the National Railroad Passenger Corporation in early 1971 was Roger Lewis, formerly chief executive of General Dynamics. Lewis, 59, had also served as Assistant Secretary of the Air Force and executive vice president of Pan American World Airways.

Prior to the NRPC's takeover of rail passenger service on May 1, 1971, the trade name Amtrak was introduced. The consulting firm which invented the new name (and also designed an eyecatching corporation symbol in red, white, and blue) had recommended avoidance of any name using the word "rail" because of its unfavorable connotations for travelers.

Initial funding for Amtrak came in the form of a $40 million grant from the federal government, plus loan guarantees of another $100 million. The 20 participating railroads then paid the Corporation $197 million, an amount equal to their 1969 losses on those passenger trains which Amtrak proposed to continue operating. Over the next year or so, Amtrak used $87 million of these funds to buy from the railroads 1,585 used cars and 274 old locomotives. Additionally, agreements were reached whereby Amtrak contracted with the railroads for operating its trains and for the use of tracks, terminals, and additional locomotives. The cars represented the best of the more than 3,000 owned by the railroads, but many were still in sorry condition.

AMTRAK INITIATES SERVICE

Amtrak's initiation was not a particularly auspicious one, with Mr. Lewis resisting last-minute lobbying by union leaders for extension of protective labor agreements and attempts by key legislators to add or restore service to their home districts. The corporation began service on May 1 by lopping off about half the nation's remaining passenger trains. Overnight, the total dropped from 547 to 243. The theory was that a severely pruned system would yield significant cost savings, while attracting enough new passengers to make the operation ultimately profitable.

The trains operated by Amtrak included prestigious, high quality services such as the Santa Fe's Super Chief from Chicago to Los Angeles, and the glamorous, high speed Turbotrains and Metroliners in the Boston–Washington corridor. The latter were operated by Penn-Central (over track which was often so poor that it restricted their speeds to a fraction of their potential) but the high technology equipment had been sponsored by the U.S. Department of Transportation. Many of the other services inherited by Amtrak, however, were sad shadows of their former glory, such as Southern Pacific's Coast Daylight and Penn Central's Broadway Limited. Others consisted of short distance corridor services of varying quality.

One of Mr. Lewis's first concerns was to build an executive staff. Most of the initial staff of thirty-three were clerks; the corporation was being run by consulting personnel and a small group of financial and scheduling experts on loan from other agencies. The majority of train and station personnel were railroad employees who retained the low morale generated by years of indifference towards passengers on the part of their employers.

Marketing Activities

An early executive appointment was that of Harold L. Graham as marketing vice-president. Graham, 53, was formerly vice president–worldwide service for Pan American and moved quickly to develop an advertising program for Amtrak. Among the possible advertising themes proposed by the corporation's advertising agency, Ted Bates & Company, were:

> Amtrak: we aim to put you back on the track;
>
> The beginning of the revolution in train travel;
>
> Train with us tomorrow;
>
> Trains will never be the same again;
>
> It's about time somebody did something about train travel; and
>
> We're making the trains worth traveling again.

The last-mentioned theme was selected and a $900,000 advertising and promotion campaign subsequently initiated from the period July 1971 to January 1972, using newspapers, magazines and radio.[4] The advertisement shown in Exhibit 2 appeared widely in the print media. Amtrak also initiated market research to find out more about what people thought of trains and why they rode—or did not ride—them.

Mr. Graham stated that almost everything happening in Amtrak came within marketing's province: "Every point at which we contact the public is involved."[5] This was seen as starting with the equipment improvement program and continuing through quality of train operation, maintenance and cleanliness. Marketing-related activities also included a "personal service" training program for Amtrak employees.

The marketing program proposed by Mr. Graham also included new red, white, and blue uniforms for all employees dealing directly with the public; a single, easily identifiable Amtrak ticket design; airline tie-in tours for foreign visitors; two- and three-week family package tours; a uniform pricing formula for fares; and sharply revised routing schedules for smoother passenger connections. Graham also looked forward to a computerized, nationwide reservations system and a tie-in with major credit card companies. A $2.8 million advertising campaign was announced for 1972.

By the beginning of 1972, some of the changes which Amtrak had

AMTRAK. WE'RE MAKING
THE TRAINS WORTH TRAVELING AGAIN
(All we ask from you is a little patience)

What is Amtrak? We're America's first nationwide passenger rail system.

When President Nixon signed the Rail Passenger Service Act, it gave us the responsibility for managing the country's intercity rail network starting May 1, 1971.

That meant merging the services and solving the obstacles of what had been 22 different passenger railroads, each with its own built-in problems. While at the same time running 1300 trains a week over 20,000 miles of track to 340 cities in the U.S.A.

It may not be the country's biggest headache. But it's close. That's why when we took over we made only one simple promise. To make the trains worth traveling again. It's going to take time, and work. But we're going to do it. Just be patient, please.

You're going to ride the best 1200 cars in the country. You can't run a good railroad without good railroad cars. So our first order of business was to take stock of our rolling stock. We examined all 3000 passenger cars formerly in service. And we're keeping only the 1200 best, most of them stainless steel.

You talk—we listen. For the first time there are passenger representatives riding our trains just to

Amtrak Passenger Representative with a model of a modern Amtrak car now in service.

get your ideas about rail service. You've already made it clear that you want your trains a lot cleaner than in the past. And they will be.

Eat a little better. Right now we're concerned with making sure that you get a real good dinner every time you enter our dining cars. And that even a snack in an Amtrak coach is always fresh and tasty.

We want to save you time, money and aggravation. Some of the most annoying problems of going by train take place before you even step aboard. And we know it. That's why we're putting such a high priority on faster and simpler reservation and ticketing procedures. We don't like red tape any better than you do.

People who care are caring about you. If you've been aboard an Amtrak train lately, perhaps you've noticed how attentive our personnel are. Nobody has a greater stake in the success of Amtrak than the people on our trains. After all, their future is riding on it.

All this, of course, is only a very small start on a very big job. But we are making progress—and we're proud of it. Come aboard an Amtrak train this fall and see for yourself.

We're making the trains worth traveling again.

Amtrak

Exhibit 2. Preliminary Amtrak and advertising in print media, 1971

initiated were becoming more apparent. For the first time, national railroad schedules and route maps in easy-to-read format were provided in a
single, pocketable brochure. Train crews included a growing number of
Amtrak's own employees, known as passenger representatives. Dressed in
smartly cut red and blue uniforms, these young men and women had
received training from Continental Airlines and contrasted sharply with
the generally aging, male, railroad employees who served as porters,
conductors and dining car attendants under contract to Amtrak. Morale,
too, seemed to be improving among many of the latter, although complaints were still being received from the public about railroad personnel.
Meantime, improved and inexpensive meals were being served on board
the trains, many of which had lacked meal service altogether in recent
years.

A growing number of the cars which Amtrak had purchased from the
railroads had been refurbished with colorful new interiors and carried
Amtrak's distinctive red, white and blue motif on the outside. A number
of cars purchased from western railroads, which tended to be newer (that
is, dating from the late 40s and early 50s) were introduced into service on
eastern routes which had previously had to suffer broken-down, pre-war
equipment.

AMTRAK'S OPERATIONS IN 1972

Although Amtrak's top management professed to take an optimistic view
of the future of intercity rail passenger transportation, the corporation's
critics were becoming increasingly vocal.

Criticism of Amtrak

Typical of the views of many railroad executives were those of Benjamin
F. Biaggini, president of Southern Pacific. In an interview with *U.S. News
and World Report,* Mr. Biaggini expressed little confidence in Amtrak's
future:

> There is no market for long distance, intercity passenger transportation
> by rail. People won't ride it and they won't pay what they should to support
> the service. I don't think the taxpayers of this country should put up 300 or
> 400 million dollars a year to support such a service if the demand is not
> there. . . .
> The real bread and butter of passenger transportation is business travel,
> and the businessman simply cannot afford the time it takes to go by train.
> . . .

Biaggini pointed out that the railroads had lost their passenger business "at a time when we were providing the finest service in the world."
In support of this contention, he cited beautiful, streamlined trains
equipped with "barber shops, valet service, maids, couriers, nurses, and
dining cars where you could get the thickest steaks."

Mr. Biaggini concluded:

> I think Amtrak's function should be to preside over an orderly shrinkage of
> rail passenger service.[6]

There was criticism, too, from both friends and opponents of Amtrak in Congress, especially when it became clear that the corporation was going to need substantial additional funding. Some argued that Amtrak should have been more daring and innovative with new types of service, new fare packages and bold new advertising. Criticism of another sort came from airlines and bus companies, which complained about the expenditure of government money to advertise against them.

Management's Strategy

While optimistic about Amtrak's future, Roger Lewis took a cautious view of the best way to proceed:

> I think we've got to get far surer about what sort of passenger service is needed than we are.[7]

Without a great deal of resources, Lewis placed most emphasis on obtaining better use of Amtrak's existing assets. He noted that there were few ideas which had not been tried by some railroad at some time in the past but questioned the value of "luxury cruise" approaches to marketing rail travel, especially for short and over-night trips.

> I'm very strong for offering better basic service, such as running on time and good clean equipment. I'm very strong for bold marketing approaches—family fares, group packages, combinations with airlines, buses, hired automobiles, and the like. . . .
> I think we can do a lot to produce better service at a lower cost, and that will attract more passengers than some of these more glamorous things—although we're going to try some of them.

Lewis stressed that improvements such as these, instilling greater courtesy in personnel and improving the communications and reservation system, were not unduly expensive. He expressed the hope that they would result in a reversal of the previous declining trend in passenger rail travel and provide Congress with a rationale for funding new cars and locomotives. If, in turn, the combination of improved service and better equipment succeeded in attracting more passengers, then Amtrak should be able to obtain public support for investments in track upgrading to enable trains to run at the high speeds for which they were designed. However, he cautioned that "the problems of creating a nationwide system over the property of 13 previously separate railroads are pretty formidable."[8]

Harold Graham also appeared to take a fairly sanguine view of bad publicity:

> I am not discouraged by bad publicity, because I think there is an American failing that we expect the application of an idea to have instantaneous results. I think there was a general public expectation that when you put together a new corporation and it started on May 1, that automatically made everything all right.[9]

During the twelve-month period ending June 30, 1972, Amtrak reported operating revenues of $152.5 million and total expenses of $306.3

million. For fiscal year 1972–73, management projected similar costs but an increase in revenues to $179.4 million.

During the first half of 1972 the corporation had begun selective modification of routes, service frequencies and fares. Reducing the one-way fare between Boston and New York from $12.75 to $9.90 yielded a 30 percent increase in traffic in the first four months, and systemwide passenger statistics showed that the downward trend had been reversed. New Metroliners were introduced on the New York–Washington route in response to growing demand, while some unsuccessful experimental routes, such as New York–Cleveland–Chicago, were dropped.

The Louis Harris Opinion Poll

In October 1972, Amtrak released the results of a $200,000 opinion poll conducted for the corporation by Louis Harris and Associates. Three thousand people nationwide had been surveyed the previous May on their opinions about the future of intercity train travel. Only 4 percent of them had taken an intercity trip by train in the previous 12 months.[10]

Some of the major findings of the poll were that:

1. 64 percent favored continuing intercity passenger train service "even if it means Federal subsidies."
2. 82 percent felt they must have the option of passenger rail travel.
3. 90 percent believed "trains are vital for the country."
4. 75 percent held the view that "long distance passenger train travel is essential in a national emergency."
5. 54 percent thought that it was "a very important priority for the nation to improve the quality and availability of rail-passenger travel" more than bus travel, faster air travel or new airports.
6. 56 percent felt that it was "very important to develop fast, comfortable intercity passenger trains."

The survey results also provided insights into what factors people considered important in travel and how trains were rated on these. Rail travel received particularly good ratings on safety, "Look out and see interesting things en route," "Arrive rested and relaxed," and "Be able to get up and walk around," but was poorly rated on a number of other characteristics, including speed, flexibility, and quality of food at reasonable prices (Exhibit 3).

Shortly after release of this poll, Amtrak initiated a five-month $600,000 advertising campaign, using both print and broadcast media. The themes of this campaign—comfort, convenience and safety—were based on the results of the Harris poll, and it was targeted at cities along the six main rail corridors in the country. Many of the advertisements also provided schedule and fare information.

PROGRESS IN 1973

As Amtrak neared the end of its second year of operation, Roger Lewis commented:

> We've had a whale of a problem getting geared up. [But] the first step is being taken to rebuild passenger service in this country . . .

13 Top Motivators for Travel	Train Rating		% of Respondents Saying: "Train Is the Best Way to Go"			
% of Respondents Rating "Very Important"		Positive (%)	Negative (%)	Total Public	18 to 29	College	$15,000 and over
	Items on Which Train Travel Is Rated Positively						
63	Cost of trip	36	28	13	10	12	11
46	Personal comfort	45	31	19	11	16	13
41	Safety	67	11	36	29	33	31
31	Look out and see interesting things en route	63	18	38	31	43	43
13	Arrive rested and relaxed	50	26	18	14	15	13
13	Be able to get up and walk around	61	18	62	61	65	63
9	Arrive on time	42	31	16	12	17	13
8	Friendly, helpful employees	40	27	11	6	8	6
	Items on Which Train Travel is Rated Negatively						
19	Reach destination quickly	35	41	5	3	3	2
15	Flexible when can leave	25	42	8	6	6	6
18	Quality food available	32	39	15	9	13	11
17	Good food at reasonable prices	23	36	13	11	12	9
9	Modern washroom facilities	33	33	16	11	14	13
	Percent of respondents taking intercity trip by train in last twelve months			4	6	7	6

Source: Louis Harris Poll for Amtrak (reworked from data published in Railway Age*).*

Source: Louis Harris Poll for Amtrak (reworked from data published in Railway Age).

Exhibit 3. Findings of Survey on Travel Motivators and Train Ratings

We've got a long way to go. It's going to take time and money . . . [However] not only has the decline in ridership been reversed, but after only modest physical improvement, the public has shown support for Amtrak.[11]

While Lewis could point to some solid gains, the corporation's performance left no room for complacency. A TV news documentary on CBS cast Amtrak in the role of a squanderer of public money. It included comments critical of top management by Senator Vance Hartke of Indiana and a statement by Louis W. Menk, Chairman of the Board of the Burlington-Northern railroad and also an Amtrak director, that the long-haul train should be allowed to die.

On the other hand, criticism of the railroads was also growing, not only on account of the continued sniping at Amtrak by many of their executives, but also because of sentiment that the roads were partly responsible for Amtrak's poor on-time record, due to badly maintained tracks and failure to give passenger trains priority over freight. In 1972, 47 percent of Amtrak's long-distance passenger trains ran late.

Despite expectations that significant cuts might be made in Amtrak's 23,500-mile route structure in July 1973, the date set for such a possibility, these fears proved unfounded, and additional funding was provided by Congress.

Taking a forward view, Amtrak continued with an increasingly vigorous promotional policy emphasizing car rental tie-ins, inclusive tours and family fare plans. It also took delivery of forty new diesel-electric locomotives and ordered a significant number of additional new locomotives and new passenger cars. These purchases were made possible by the passage of a bill granting the corporation another $500 million in congressional loan guarantees. A major innovation, which yielded significant press coverage, was the introduction of two new turbine-powered trains leased from France.

Another area in which the corporation was progressing was in assuming more direct control over its workforce instead of employing railroad personnel. Many existing train, station and reservations personnel were hired directly from the railroads, while others were recruited from the outside. In a sharp reversal of railroad tradition, 60 percent of the service attendants on the newly initiated Montrealer from Washington to Montreal were young women. Flexible working agreements allowed the on-board service director to move these train personnel to various jobs en route as service needs dictated. By the end of 1973 Amtrak had more than 5,300 employees on its payroll, compared with 1,522 a year earlier.

Amtrak's efforts to improve the quality of service provided by its employees seemed to be paying off. During the last five months of 1973, more compliments than complaints were received concerning personnel.

Sales through travel agencies doubled in 1973 to $16 million. By year's end, Amtrak had more than 6,600 agencies, 800 of them outside the United States and Canada. Considerable advances were also made in expanding the corporation's field sales force, which covered both passengers and package express service.

As the year moved to its close, the existing upward trend in Amtrak patronage was given a sharp boost by the onset of the energy crisis. Amtrak responded quickly with a new advertising campaign, supplementing its existing third-year advertising and promotional budget of close to $5 million. It also sought additional old cars from the railroads to handle the increased loads. Daily calls to Amtrak reservations centers climbed to 60,000, almost double those of the 1973 peak summer months.

Amtrak was thus able to end the year on an upward note. However, despite a 24 percent increase in revenues over 1972 to $202 million, expenses rose sharply too, and the net deficit for the year increased by 8 percent to $159 million. During 1973, it carried 18 million passengers while operating at an average 50 percent load factor.

PROBLEMS AND OPPORTUNITIES IN 1974

1974 began with a continued sharp increase in patronage. During the first three months, normally a period of relatively low travel demand, ridership was up by 41 percent over the same period in the previous year. This compared with pre-energy crisis forecasts of only 15 percent gain. As a result, Amtrak found itself faced with demand levels which it had not expected to reach until 1977.

At weekends, trains were packed and thousands were forced to stand for journeys undertaken during the long Washington's Birthday weekend. Whereas Mr. Lewis was previously concerned with getting the public to "think rail," he now observed:

> Our constraint is not going to be so much rider attitudes as it's going to be our ability to handle the increase in traffic.[12]

In attempting to improve train reliability, Amtrak was in the process of renegotiating operating contracts with the railroads with defined performance standards being written into the contracts. The objective was to impose penalties for failure to meet these on-time standards, while paying bonuses when they were exceeded.

However, equipment failures were still causing significant problems, reflecting both the age of the passenger cars Amtrak had purchased from the railroads and the fact that maintenance yards were expected to handle a wide range of cars built for numerous different railroads. In an effort to overcome this, Amtrak planned to introduce standardized parts on its next round of heavy overhauls.

The Summer Capacity Problem

At any given time, Amtrak usually expected to have at least 1,500 cars in operation, out of a total fleet of some 1,900. The balance of the fleet were undergoing scheduled overhauls or were "bad orders"—out of service for maintenance and/or repairs.

Management anticipated that capacity was going to be stretched to the limit during the peak summer months. Some trains were fully booked months in advance, while others were filling fast. Assignment of cars had been carefully planned to make the most efficient use of the limited equipment available.

This expectation of capacity problems was reinforced in early July, when passenger statistics for June became available. These showed that ridership for the first half of 1974 was up by 32 percent over the previous year, although the gain for the month of June was up only 16 percent over 1973. Accompanying the ridership figures were on-time statistics which showed that although punctuality had improved for short-haul trains, with 82.7 percent of these arriving on time, only 60.4 percent of long-haul trains had arrived on time in June, versus 65.1 percent in the previous month.

Hard on the heels of this information came the news that the number of "bad orders" was increasing. It became apparent to management that instead of the 1,500 cars anticipated, they should not count on having more than 1,400 passenger cars in service during the balance of the summer. The issue was raised as to how the corporation should respond to this problem and what action, if any, the marketing department should take.

Notes

1. "Passenger Plight: Officials, Train Riders Claim Some Railroads Try for Lousy Service." *Wall Street Journal,* Sept. 5, 1969.
2. Since no preferred stock was actually issued by Amtrak, there were only 11 directors in 1974.
3. Nevertheless, the Corporation had to seek ICC approval for permission to discontinue any "basic system" service after July 1973.
4. "Amtrak budget so far is only 'pat on the back,' Benham says." *Advertising Age* (June 28, 1971).
5. "Amtrak sets $2,800,000 drive; hopes to find role in transportation." *Advertising Age* (Nov. 15, 1971).
6. "Future of Passenger Trains. Interview with B. F. Biaggini, President, Southern Pacific Company," *U.S. News and World Report* (January 3, 1972), pp. 44–45.
7. "Amtrak: A Noble Experiment in Trouble." *Business Week* (April 15, 1972), pp. 74–75.
8. "Is there really a future for passenger trains?" *U.S. News and World Report* (February 28, 1972), p. 52.
9. "A Smoother Track Ahead for Amtrak?" *Railway Age* (January 10, 1972), p. 26.
10. "Harris Poll Projects Big Future for Amtrak," *Railway Age* (October 9, 1972), p. 39.
11. "A Trimmer Amtrak Is Given a Chance." *Business Week* (March 17, 1973), pp. 24–25.
12. "Look What's Happening to Amtrak." *Railway Age* (May 13, 1974), pp. 18–24.

The Justification of
Private Property

JOHN LOCKE

. . . God, who hath given the world to men in common, hath also given them reason to make use of it to the best advantage of life and convenience. The earth and all that is therein is given to men for the support and comfort of their being. And though all the fruits it naturally produces, and beasts it feeds, belong to mankind in common, as they are produced by the spontaneous hand of nature; and nobody has originally a private dominion exclusive of the rest of mankind in any of them as they are thus in their natural state; yet being given for the use of men, there must of

From John Locke, *Second Treastise on Government* (1960; rpt, New York: MacMillan, 1956).

necessity be a means to appropriate them some way or other before they can be of any use or at all beneficial to any particular man. The fruit or venison which nourishes the wild Indian, who knows no enclosure, and is still a tenant in common, must be his, and so his, i.e., a part of him, that another can no longer have any right to it, before it can do any good for the support of his life.

Though the earth and all inferior creatures be common to all men, yet every man has a property in his own person; this nobody has any right to but himself. The labor of his body and the work of his hands we may say are properly his. Whatsoever, then, he removes out of the state that nature hath provided and left it in, he hath mixed his labor with, and joined to it something that is his own, and thereby makes it his property. It being by him removed from the common state nature placed it in, it hath by this labor something annexed to it that excludes the common right of other men. For this labor being the unquestionable property of the laborer, no man but he can have a right to what that is once joined to, at least where there is enough, and as good left in common for others.

He that is nourished by the acorns he picked up under an oak, or the apples he gathered from the trees in the wood, has certainly appropriated them to himself. Nobody can deny but the nourishment is his. I ask, then, When did they begin to be his—when he digested, or when he ate, or when he boiled, or when he brought them home, or when he picked them up? And 'tis plain if the first gathering made them not his, nothing else could. That labor put a distinction between them and common; that added something to them more than nature, the common mother of all, had done, and so they became his private right. And will anyone say he had no right to those acorns or apples he thus appropriated, because he had not the consent of all mankind to make them his? Was it a robbery thus to assume to himself what belonged to all in common? If such a consent as that was necessary, man had starved, notwithstanding the plenty God had given him. We see in commons which remain so by compact that 'tis the taking any part of what is common and removing it out of the state nature leaves it in, which begins the property; without which the common is of no use. And the taking of this or that part does not depend on the express consent of all the commoners. Thus the grass my horse has bit, the turfs my servant has cut, and the ore I have dug in any place where I have a right to them in common with others, become my property without the assignation or consent of anybody. The labor that was mine removing them out of that common state they were in, hath fixed my property in them. . . .

It will perhaps be objected to this, that if gathering the acorns, or other fruits of the earth, etc., makes a right to them, then anyone may engross as much as he will. To which I answer, Not so. The same law of nature that does by this means give us property, does also bound that property too. "God has given us all things richly" (I Tim. vi. 17), is the voice of reason confirmed by inspiration. But how far has He given it us? To enjoy. As much as anyone can make use of to any advantage of life before it spoils, so much he may by his labor fix a property in; whatever is beyond this, is more than his share, and belongs to others. Nothing was made by God for man to spoil or destroy. And thus considering the plenty of natural provisions there was a long time in the world, and the few spenders, and to how small a part of that provision the industry of one man could extend itself, and engross it to the prejudice of others—especially keeping within the bounds, set by reason, of what might serve for his use—there could be then little room for quarrels or contentions about property so established.

But the chief matter of property being now not the fruits of the earth, and the beasts that subsist on it, but the earth itself, as that which takes in and carries with it all the rest, I think it is plain that property in that, too, is acquired as the former. As much land as a man tills, plants, improves, cultivates, and can use the product of, so much is his property. He by his labor does as it were enclose it from the common. Nor will it invalidate his right to say, everybody else has an equal title to it; and therefore he cannot appropriate, he cannot enclose, without the consent of all his fellow-commoners, all mankind. God, when He gave the world in common to all mankind, commanded man also to labor, and the penury of his condition required it of him. God and his reason commanded him to subdue the earth, i.e., improve it for the benefit of life, and therein lay out something upon it that was his own, his labor. He that, in obedience to this command of God, subdued, tilled, and sowed any part of it, thereby annexed to it something that was his property, which another had no title to, nor could without injury take from him.

Nor was this appropriation of any parcel of land, by improving it, any prejudice to any other man, since there was still enough and as good left; and more than the yet unprovided could use. So that in effect there was never the less left for others because of his enclosure for himself. For he that leaves as much as another can make use of, does as good as take nothing at all. Nobody could think himself injured by the drinking of another man, though he took a good draught, who had a whole river of the same water left him to quench his thirst; and the case of land and water, where there is enough of both, is perfectly the same.

God gave the world to men in common; but since He gave it them for their benefit, and the greatest conveniences of life they were capable to draw from it, it cannot be supposed He meant it should always remain common and uncultivated. He gave it to the use of the industrious and rational (and labor was to be his title to it), not to the fancy or covetousness of the quarrelsome and contentious. He that had as good left for his improvement as was already taken up, needed not complain, ought not to meddle with what was already improved by another's labor; if he did, it is plain he desired the benefit of another's pains, which he had no right to, and not the ground which God had given him in common with others to labor on, and whereof there was as good left as that already possessed, and more than he knew what to do with, or his industry could reach to.

It is true, in land that is common in England, or any other country where there is plenty of people under Government, who have money and commerce, no one can enclose or appropriate any part without the consent of all his fellow-commoners: because this is left common by compact, i.e., by the law of the land, which is not to be violated. And though it be common in respect of some men, it is not so to all mankind; but is the joint property of this country, or this parish. Besides, the remainder, after such enclosure, would not be as good to the rest of the commoners as the whole was, when they could all make use of the whole, whereas in the beginning and first peopling of the great common of the world it was quite otherwise. The law man was under was rather for appropriating. God commanded, and his wants forced him, to labor. That was his property, which could not be taken from him wherever he had fixed it. And hence subduing or cultivating the earth, and having dominion, we see are joined together. The one gave title to the other. So that God, by commanding to subdue, gave authority so far to appropriate. And the condition of human life, which requires labor and materials to work on, necessarily introduces private possessions.

The measure of property nature has well set by the extent of men's labor and the conveniency of life. No man's labor could subdue or appropriate all, nor could his enjoyment consume more than a small part; so that it was impossible for any man, this way, to entrench upon the right of another or acquire to himself a property to the prejudice of his neighbor, who would still have room for as good and as large a possession (after the other had taken out his) as before it was appropriated. Which measure did confine every man's possession to a very moderate proportion, and such as he might appropriate to himself without injury to anybody in the first ages of the world, when men were more in danger to be lost, by wandering from their company, in the then vast wilderness of the earth than to be straitened for want of room to plant in. . . .

And thus, without supposing any private dominion and property in Adam over all the world, exclusive of all other men, which can no way be proved, nor any one's property be made out from it, but supposing the world, given as it was to the children of men in common, we see how labor could make men distinct titles to several parcels of it for their private uses, wherein there could be no doubt of right, no room for quarrel.

Nor is it so strange, as perhaps before consideration it may appear, that the property of labor should be able to overbalance the community of land. For it is labor indeed that puts the difference of value on everything; and let anyone consider what the difference is between an acre of land planted with tobacco or sugar, sown with wheat or barley, and an acre of the same land lying in common without any husbandry upon it, and he will find that the improvement of labor makes the far greater part of the value. I think it will be but a very modest computation to say that of the products of the earth useful to the life of man nine-tenths are the effects of labor; nay, if we will rightly estimate things as they come to our use, and cast up the several expenses about them—what in them is purely owing to nature, and what to labor—we shall find that in most of them ninety-nine hundreths are wholly to be put on the account of labor. . . .

From all which it is evident that, though the things of nature are given in common, yet man, by being master of himself and proprietor of his own person and the actions or labor of it, had still in himself the great foundation of property; and that which made up the great part of what he applied to the support or comfort of his being, when invention and arts had improved the conveniences of life, was perfectly his own, and did not belong in common to others.

Thus labor, in the beginning, gave a right of property, wherever anyone was pleased to employ it upon what was common, which remained a long while the far greater part, and is yet more than mankind makes use of. Men at first, for the most part, contented themselves with what unassisted nature offered to their necessities; and though afterwards, in some parts of the world (where the increase of people and stock, with the use of money, had made land scarce, and so of some value), the several communities settled the bounds of their distinct territories, and, by laws within themselves, regulated the properties of the private men of their society, and so, by compact and agreement, settled the property which labor and industry began—and the leagues that have been made between several states and kingdoms, either expressly or tacitly disowning all claim and right to the land in the other's possession, have, by common consent, given up their pretenses to their natural common right, which originally they had to those countries; and so have, by positive agreement, settled a property amongst themselves in distinct parts of the world—yet there are still great tracts of ground to be found which, the inhabitants thereof not having joined with the rest of mankind in the consent of the use of their common money, lie waste, and are more than the people who dwell on it do or can make use of, and so still lie in common; though this can scarce happen amongst that part of mankind that have consented to the use of money.

The greatest part of things really useful to the life of man, and such as the necessity of subsisting made the first commoners of the world look after, as it doth the Americans now, are generally things of short duration, such as, if they are not consumed by use, will decay and perish of themselves: gold, silver, and diamonds are things that fancy or agreement have put the value on more than real use and the necessary support of life. Now of those good things which nature hath provided in common, everyone hath a right, as hath been said, to as much as he could use, and had a property in all he could effect with his labor—all that his industry could extend to, to alter from the state nature had put it in, was his. He that gathered a hundred bushels of acorns or apples had thereby a property in them; they were his goods as soon as gathered. He was only to look that he used them before they spoiled, else he took more than his share, and robbed others; and, indeed, it was a foolish thing, as well as dishonest, to hoard up more than he could make use of. If he gave away a part to anybody else, so that it perished not uselessly in his possession, these he also made use of; and if he also bartered away plums that would have rotted in a week, for nuts that would last good for his eating a whole year, he did no injury; he wasted not the common stock, destroyed no part of the portion of goods that belonged to others, so long as nothing perished uselessly in his hands. Again, if he would give his nuts for a piece of metal, pleased with its color, or exchange his sheep for shells, or wool for a sparkling pebble or a diamond, and keep those by him all his life, he invaded not the right of others; he might heap up as much of these durable things as he pleased, the exceeding of the bounds of his just property not lying in the largeness of his possessions, but the perishing of anything uselessly in it.

And thus came in the use of money—some lasting thing that men might keep without spoiling, and that, by mutual consent, men would take in exchange for the truly useful but perishable supports of life.

And as different degrees of industry were apt to give men possessions in different proportions, so this invention of money gave them the opportunity to continue and enlarge them; for supposing an island, separate from all possible commerce with the rest of the world, wherein there were but a hundred families—but there were sheep, horses, and cows, with other useful animals, wholesome fruits, and land enough for corn for a hundred thousand times as many, but nothing in the island, either because of its commonness or perishableness, fit to supply the place of money—what reason could anyone have there to enlarge his possessions beyond the use of his family and a plentiful supply to its consumption, either in what their own industry produced, or they could barter for like perishable useful commodities with others? Where there is not something both lasting and scarce, and so valuable to be hoarded up, there men will not be apt to enlarge their possessions of land, were it never so rich, never so free for them to take; for I ask, what would a man value ten thousand or a hundred thousand acres of excellent land, ready cultivated, and well stocked too with cattle, in the middle of the inland parts of America, where he had no hopes of commerce with other parts of the world, to draw money to him by the sale of the product? It would not be worth the enclosing, and we should see him give up again to the wild common of nature whatever was more than would supply the conveniences of life to be had there for him and his family.

Thus in the beginning all the world was America, and more so than that is now, for no such thing as money was anywhere known. Find out something that hath the use and value of money amongst his neighbors, you shall see the same man will begin presently to enlarge his possessions.

But since gold and silver, being little useful to the life of man in proportion to food, raiment, and carriage, has its value only from the consent of men, whereof labor yet makes, in great part, the measure, it is plain that the consent of men have agreed to a disproportionate and unequal possession of the earth—I mean out of the bounds of society and compact; for in governments the laws regulate it; they having, by consent, found out and agreed in a way how a man may rightfully and without injury possess more than he himself can make use of by receiving gold and silver, which may continue long in a man's possession, without decaying for the overplus, and agreeing those metals should have a value.

And thus, I think, it is very easy to conceive without any difficulty how labor could at first begin a title of property in the common things of nature, and how the spending it upon our uses bounded it; so that there could then be no reason of quarrelling about title, nor any doubt about the largeness of possession it gave. Right and conveniency went together; for as a man had a right to all he could employ his labor upon, so he had no temptation to labor for more than he could make use of. This left no room for controversy about the title, nor for encroachment on the right of others; what portion a man carved to himself was easily seen, and it was useless, as well as dishonest, to carve himself too much, or take more than he needed.

The Communist Manifesto

KARL MARX and FRIEDRICH ENGELS

I. BOURGEOIS AND PROLETARIANS

The history of all hitherto existing society is the history of class struggles.

Freeman and slave, patrician and plebeian, lord and serf, guildmaster and journeyman, in a word, oppressor and oppressed, stood in constant opposition to one another, carried on an uninterrupted, now hidden, now open fight, a fight that each time ended, either in a revolutionary reconstitution of society at large, or in the common ruin of the struggling classes.

In the earlier epochs of history, we find almost everywhere a complicated arrangement of society into various orders, a manifold gradation of social rank. In ancient Rome we have patricians, knights, plebeians, slaves; in the Middle Ages, feudal lords, vassals, guildmasters, journeymen, apprentices, serfs; and in almost all of these particular classes, again, other subordinate gradations.

The modern bourgeois society that has sprouted from the ruins of feudal society has not done away with class antagonisms. It has only established new classes, new conditions of oppression, new forms of struggle in place of the old ones.

Our epoch, the epoch of the bourgeoisie, shows, however, this distinctive feature: it has simplified the class antagonisms. Society as a whole is more and more splitting up into two great hostile camps, into two great classes directly facing each other: *bourgeoisie* and *proletariat*.

From the serfs of the Middle Ages sprang the chartered burghers of the earliest towns. From these burghers the first elements of the bourgeoisie were developed.

From Karl Marx and Friedrich Engels, *The Communist Manifesto,* trans. Samuel Moore (New York: Washington Square Press, 1934); reprinted by permission of the publisher.

The discovery of America, the rounding of the Cape, opened up fresh ground for the rising bourgeoisie. The East-Indian and Chinese markets, the colonization of America, trade with the colonies, the increase in the means of exchange and in commodities generally, gave to commerce, to navigation, to industry, an impulse never before known, and thereby, to the revolutionary element in the tottering feudal society, a rapid development.

The feudal system of industry, under which industrial production was monopolized by closed guilds, now no longer sufficed for the growing wants of the new markets. The manufacturing system took its place. The guildmasters were pushed on one side by the manufacturing middle class; division of labor between the different corporate guilds vanished in the face of division of labor in each single workshop.

Meanwhile the markets kept on growing; demand went on rising. Manufacturing no longer was able to keep up with this growth. Then, steam and machinery revolutionized industrial production. The place of manufacture was taken by the giant, *modern industry;* the place of the industrial middle class, by industrial millionaires, the leaders of whole industrial armies, the modern bourgeois.

Modern industry has established the world market, for which the discovery of America paved the way. This market has given an immense development to commerce, to navigation, to communication by land. This development has, in its turn, reacted on the extension of industry; and in proportion as industry, commerce, navigation, railways extended, in the same proportion the bourgeoisie developed, increased its capital, and pushed into the background every class handed down from the Middle Ages.

We see, therefore, how the modern bourgeoisie is itself the product of a long course of development, of a series of revolutions in the modes of production and of exchange. . . .

The need of a constantly expanding market for its products chases the bourgeoisie over the whole surface of the globe. It must nestle everywhere, settle everywhere, establish connections everywhere.

The bourgeoisie has through its exploitation of the world market given a cosmopolitan character to production and consumption in every country. To the great chagrin of reactionaries, it has drawn from under the feet of industry the national ground on which it stood. All old-established national industries have been destroyed or are daily being destroyed. They are dislodged by new industries, whose introduction becomes a life and death question for all civilized nations, by industries that no longer work up indigenous raw material, but raw material drawn from the remotest zones; industries whose products are consumed, not only at home, but in every quarter of the globe. In place of the old wants, satisfied by the productions of the country, we find new wants, requiring for their satisfaction the products of distant lands and climates. In place of the old local and national seclusion and self-sufficiency, we have intercourse in every direction, universal inter-dependence of nations. And as in material, so also in intellectual production. The intellectual creations of individual nations become common property. National one-sidedness and narrow-mindedness become more and more impossible, and from the numerous national and local literatures, there emerges a world literature.

The bourgeoisie, by the rapid improvement of all instruments of production, by the immensely facilitated means of communications, draws all, even the most backward, nations into civilization. The cheap prices of its commodities are the heavy artillery with which it batters down all Chinese walls, with which it forces the underdeveloped nations' intensely obstinate hatred of foreigners to capitulate. It compels all nations, on pain of extinction, to adopt the bourgeois mode of production; it compels them to introduce what it calls civilization into their midst, *i.e.,* to become bourgeois themselves. In one word, it creates a world in its own image.

The bourgeoisie has subjected rural areas to the rule of cities. It has created enormous cities, has greatly increased the urban population as compared with the rural, and has thus rescued a considerable part of the population from the idiocy of rural life. Just as it has made the country dependent on the cities, so has it made barbarian and semi-underdeveloped countries dependent on the civilized ones, nations of peasants on nations of bourgeois, the East on the West.

The bourgeoisie keeps more and more doing away with the scattered state of the population, of the means of production, and of property. It has agglomerated population, centralized means of production, and has concentrated property in a few hands. The necessary consequence of this was political centralization. Independent, or but loosely connected, provinces with separate interests, laws, governments, and systems of taxation became lumped together into one nation, with one government, one code of laws, one national class-interest, one frontier, and one customs-tariff.

The bourgeoisie, during its rule of scarcely one hundred years, has created more massive and more colossal productive forces than have all preceding generations together. Subjection of Nature's forces to man, machinery, application of chemistry to industry and agriculture, steam-navigation, railways, electric telegraphs, clearing of whole continents for cultivation, canalization of rivers, whole populations conjured out of the ground—what earlier century had even a presentiment that such productive forces slumbered in the lap of social labor?

We see then: the means of production and of exchange, on whose foundation the bourgeoisie built itself up, were generated in feudal society. At a certain stage in the development of these means of production and of exchange, the conditions under which feudal society produced and exchanged, the feudal organization of agriculture and manufacturing industry, in one word, the feudal relations of property became no longer compatible with the already developed productive forces; they became so many fetters. They had to be burst asunder; they were burst asunder.

Into their place stepped free competition, accompanied by a social and political constitution adapted to it, and by the economical and political sway of the bourgeois class.

A similar movement is going on before our own eyes. Modern bourgeois society with its relations of production, of exchange and of property, a society that has conjured up such gigantic means of production and of exchange, is like the sorcerer, who is no longer able to control the powers of the subterranean world which he has called up by his spells. For many decades now the history of industry and commerce has been but the history of the revolt of modern productive forces against modern conditions of production, against the property relations that are the conditions for the existence of the bourgeoisie and of its rule. It is enough to mention the commercial crises that by their periodical return put on trial, each time more threateningly, the existence of the entire bourgeois society. In these crises a great part not only of the existing products, but also of the previously created productive forces, are periodically destroyed. In these crises there breaks out an epidemic that, in all earlier epochs, would have seemed an absurdity—the epidemic of over-production. Society suddenly finds itself put back into a state of momentary barbarism; it appears as if a famine, a universal war of devastation had cut off the supply of every means of subsistence; industry and commerce seem to be destroyed; and why? Because there is too much civilization, too much means of subsistence, too much industry, too much commerce. The productive forces at the disposal of society no longer tend to further the development of the conditions of bourgeois property; on the contrary, they have become too powerful for these conditions, by which they are fettered, and so soon as they overcome these fetters, they bring disorder into the whole of bourgeois society, endanger the existence of bourgeois property. The conditions of bourgeois society are too narrow to comprise the wealth created by them. And how does the bourgeoisie get over these crises? On the one hand by enforced destruction of a mass of productive forces; on the other, by the conquest of new markets, and by the more thorough exploitation of the old ones. That is to say, by paving the way for more extensive and more destructive crises, and by diminishing the means whereby crises are prevented.

The weapons with which the bourgeoisie felled feudalism to the ground are now turned against the bourgeoisie itself.

But not only has the bourgeoisie forged the weapons that bring death to itself; it has also called into existence the men who are to wield those weapons—the modern working class—the proletarians.

In proportion as the bourgeoisie, *i.e.,* capital, is developed, in the same proportion is the proletariat, the modern working class, developed—a class of laborers, who live only so long as they find work, and who find work only so long as their labor increases capital. These laborers, who must sell themselves piecemeal, are a commodity, like every other article of commerce, and are consequently exposed to all the vicissitudes of competition, to all the fluctuations of the market.

Owing to the extensive use of machinery and to division of labor, the work of the proletarians has lost all individual character, and, consequently, all charm for the workman. He becomes an appendage of the machine, and it is only the most simple, most monotonous, and most easily acquired knack that is required of him. Hence, the cost of production of a workman is restricted, almost entirely, to the means of subsistence that he requires for his maintenance, and for the propagation of his race. But the price of a commodity, and therefore also of labor, is equal to its cost of production. In proportion, therefore, as the repulsiveness of the work increases, the wage decreases. What is more, in proportion as the use of machinery and division of labor increases, in the same proportion the burden of toil also increases, whether by prolongation of the working hours, by increase of the work exacted in a given time or by increased speed of the machinery, etc.

Modern industry has converted the little workshop of the patriarchal master into the great factory of the industrial capitalist. Masses of laborers, crowded into the factory, are organized like soldiers. As privates of the industrial army they are placed under the command of a perfect hierarchy of officers and sergeants. Not only are they slaves of the bourgeois class, and of the bourgeois state; they are daily and hourly enslaved by the machine, by the foreman, and, above all, by the individual bourgeois manufacturer himself. The more openly this despotism proclaims gain to be its end and aim, the more petty, the more hateful, and the more embittering it is. . . .

But with the development of industry the proletariat not only increases in number; it becomes concentrated in greater masses, its strength grows, and it feels that strength more. The various interests and conditions of life within the ranks of the proletariat are more and more equalized, in proportion as machinery obliterates all distinctions of labor, and nearly everywhere reduces wages to the same low level. The growing competition among the bourgeoisie, and the resulting commercial crises, make the wages of the workers ever more fluctuating. The unceasing improvement of machinery, ever more rapidly developing, makes their livelihood more and more precarious; the collisions between individual workmen and individual bourgeoisie take more and more the character of collisions between two classes. Thereupon the workers begin to form combinations (trade unions) against the bourgeoisie; they club together in order to keep up the rate of wages; they found permanent associations in order to make provision beforehand for these occasional revolts. Here and there the contest breaks out into riots.

From time to time the workers are victorious, but only for a time. The real fruit of their battles lies not in the immediate result, but in the ever-expanding union of the workers. This union is helped by the improved means of communication that are created by modern industry and that place the workers of different localities in contact with one another. It was just this contact that was needed to centralize the numerous local struggles, all of the same character, into one national struggle between classes. But every class struggle is a political struggle. And that union, to attain which the burghers of the Middle Ages, with their miserable highways, required centuries, the modern proletarians, thanks to railways, achieve in a few years. . . .

Hitherto, every form of society has been based, as we have already seen, on the antagonism of oppressing and oppressed classes. But in order to oppress a class, certain conditions must be assured to it under which it can, at least, continue its slavish existence. The serf, in the period of serfdom, raised himself to membership in the commune, just as the petty bourgeois, under the yoke of feudal absolutism, managed to develop into a bourgeois. The modern laborer, on the contrary, instead of rising with the progress of industry, sinks deeper and deeper below the conditions of existence of his own class. He becomes a pauper, and pauperism develops more rapidly than population and wealth. And here it becomes evident that the bourgeoisie is unfit any longer to be the ruling class in society, and to impose its conditions of existence upon society as an overriding law. It is unfit to rule because it is incompetent to assure an existence to its slave within his slavery, because it cannot help letting him sink into such a state, that it has to feed him, instead of being fed by him. Society can no longer live under this bourgeoisie, in other words, its existence is no longer compatible with society.

The essential condition for the existence, and for the sway of the bourgeois class, is the formation and augmentation of capital; the condition for capital is wage labor. Wage labor rests exclusively on competition between the laborers. The advance of industry, whose involuntary promoter is the bourgeoisie, replaces the isolation of the laborers, due to competition, by their revolutionary combination, due to association. The development of modern industry, therefore, cuts from under its feet the very foundation on which the bourgeoisie produces and appropriates products. What the bourgeoisie, therefore, produces, above all, is its own grave-diggers. Its fall and the victory of the proletariat are equally inevitable.

II. PROLETARIANS AND COMMUNISTS

. . . All property relations in the past have continually been subject to historical change consequent upon the change in historical conditions.

The French Revolution, for example, abolished feudal property in favor of bourgeois property.

The distinguishing feature of communism is not the abolition of property generally, but the abolition of bourgeois property. But modern bourgeois private property is the final and most complete expression of the system of producing and appropriating products that is based on class antagonisms, on the exploitation of the many by the few.

In this sense, the theory of the Communists may be summed up in the single phrase: Abolition of private property.

We Communists have been reproached with the desire of abolishing the right of personally acquiring property as the fruit of a man's own labor, which property is alleged to be the groundwork of all personal freedom, activity, and independence.

Hard-won, self-acquired, self-earned property! Do you mean the property of the petty artisan and of the small peasant, a form of property that preceded the bourgeois form? There is no need to abolish that; the development of industry has to a great extent already destroyed it, and is still destroying it daily.

Or do you mean modern bourgeois private property?

But does wage labor create any property for the laborer? Not a bit. It creates capital, *i.e.*, that kind of property that exploits wage labor, and that cannot increase except upon condition of begetting a new supply of wage labor for fresh exploitation. Property, in its present form, is based on the antagonism of capital and wage labor. Let us examine both sides of this antagonism.

To be a capitalist, is to have not only a purely personal, but a social *status* in production. Capital is a collective product, and only by the united action of many members, nay, in the last resort, only by the united action of all members of society, can it be set in motion.

Capital is, therefore, not a personal, it is a social power.

When, therefore, capital is converted into common property, into the property of all members of society, personal property is not thereby transformed into social property. It is only the social character of the property that is changed. It loses its class character.

Let us now take wage labor.

The average price of wage labor is the minimum wage, *i.e.*, that quantum of the means of subsistence, which is absolutely requisite to keep the laborer in bare existence as a laborer. What, therefore, the wage laborer appropriates by means of his labor, merely suffices to prolong and reproduce a bare existence. We by no means intend to abolish this personal appropriation of the products of labor, an appropriation that is made for the maintenance and reproduction of human life, and that leaves no surplus wherewith to command the labor of others. All that we want to do away with is the miserable character of this appropriation, under which the laborer lives merely to increase capital, and is allowed to live only in so far as the interest of the ruling class requires it.

In bourgeois society, living labor is but a means to increase accumulated labor. In communist society, accumulated labor is but a means to widen, to enrich, to promote the existence of the laborer.

In bourgeois society, therefore, the past dominates the present; in communist society the present dominates the past. In bourgeois society capital is independent and has individuality, while the living person is dependent and has no individuality.

And the abolition of this state of things is called by the bourgeoisie, abolition of individuality and freedom! And rightly so. The abolition of bourgeois individuality, bourgeois independence, and bourgeois freedom is undoubtedly aimed at.

By freedom is meant, under the present bourgeois conditions of production, free trade, free selling and buying.

But if selling and buying disappears, free selling and buying disappears also. This talk about free selling and buying, and all the other "brave words" of our bourgeoisie about freedom in general, have a meaning, if any, only in contrast with restricted selling and buying, with the fettered traders of the Middle Ages, but have no meaning when opposed to the communistic abolition of buying and selling, of the bourgeois conditions of production, and of the bourgeoisie itself.

You are horrified at our intending to do away with private property. But in your existing society, private property is already done away with for nine-tenths of the population; its existence for the few is solely due to its non-existence in the hands of those nine-tenths. You reproach us, therefore, with intending to do away with a form of property, the necessary condition for whose existence is the nonexistence of any property for the immense majority of society.

In one word, you reproach us with intending to do away with your property. Precisely so; that is just what we intend.

From the moment when labor can no longer be converted into capital, money, or rent, into a social power capable of being monopolized, *i.e.,* from the moment when individual property can no longer be transformed into bourgeois property, into capital, from that moment, you say, individuality vanishes.

You must, therefore, confess that by "individual" you mean no other person than the bourgeois, than the middle-class owner of property. This person must, indeed, be swept out of the way, and made impossible.

Communism deprives no man of the power to appropriate the products of society; all that it does is to deprive him of the power to subjugate the labor of others by means of such appropriation.

It has been objected that upon the abolition of private property all work will cease, and universal laziness will overtake us.

According to this, bourgeois society ought long ago to have gone to the dogs through sheer idleness; for those of its members who work, acquire nothing, and those who acquire anything, do not work. The whole of this objection is but another expression of the tautology: that there can no longer be any wage labor when there is no longer any capital.

The Social Responsibility of Business Is to Increase Its Profits

MILTON FRIEDMAN

When I hear businessmen speak eloquently about the "social responsibilities of business in a free-enterprise system," I am reminded of the wonderful line about the Frenchman who discovered at the age of 70 that he had been speaking prose all his life. The businessmen believe that they are defending free enterprise when they declaim that business is not concerned "merely" with profit but also with promoting desirable "social" ends; that business has a "social conscience" and takes seriously its responsibilities for providing employment, eliminating discrimination, avoiding pollution and whatever else may be the catchwords of the contemporary crop of reformers. In fact they are—or would be if they or anyone else took them seriously—preaching pure and unadulterated socialism. Businessmen who talk this way are unwitting puppets of the intellectual forces that have been undermining the basis of a free society these past decades.

The discussion of the "social responsibilities of business" are notable for their analytical looseness and lack of rigor. What does it mean to say that "business" has responsibilities? Only people can have responsibilities. A corporation is an artificial person and in this sense may have artificial responsibilities, but "business" as a whole cannot be said to have responsibilities, even in this vague sense. The first step toward clarity to examining the doctrine of the social responsibility of business is to ask precisely what it implies for whom.

Presumably, the individuals who are to be responsible are businessmen, which means individual proprietors or corporate executives. Most of the discussion of social responsibility is directed at corporations, so in what follows I shall mostly neglect the individual proprietors and speak of corporate executives.

In a free-enterprise, private-property system, a corporate executive is an employee of the owners of the business. He has direct responsibility to his employers. That responsibility is to conduct the business in accordance with their desires, which generally will be to make as much money as possible while conforming to the basic rules of the society, both those embodied in law and those embodied in ethical custom. Of course, in some cases his employers may have a different objective. A group of persons might establish a corporation for an eleemosynary purpose—for example, a hospital or a school. The manager of such a corporation will not have money profit as his objectives but the rendering of certain services.

In either case, the key point is that, in his capacity as a corporate executive, the manager is the agent of the individuals who own the corporation or establish the eleemosynary institution, and his primary responsibility is to them.

Needless to say, this does not mean that it is easy to judge how well he is performing his task. But at least the criterion of performance is straightforward, and the persons among whom a voluntary contractual arrangement exists are clearly defined.

Of course, the corporate executive is also a person in his own right. As a person, he may have many other responsibilities that he recognizes or assumes voluntarily—to his family, his conscience, his feelings of charity, his church, his clubs, his city, his country. He may feel impelled by these responsibilities to devote part of his income to causes he regards as worthy, to refuse to work for particular corporations, even to leave his job, for example, to join his country's armed forces. If we wish, we may refer to some of these responsibilities as "social responsibilities." But in these respects he is acting as a principal, not an agent; he is spending his own money or time or energy, not the money of his employers or the time or energy he has contracted to devote to their purposes. If these are "social responsibilities," they are the social responsibilities of individuals, not of business.

What does it mean to say that the corporate executive has a "social responsibility" in his capacity as businessman? If this statement is not pure rhetoric, it must mean that he is to act in some way that is not in the interest of his employers. For example, that he is to refrain from increasing the price of the product in order to contribute to the social objective of preventing inflation, even though a price increase would be in the best interests of the corporation. Or that he is to make expenditures on reducing pollution beyond the amount that is in the best interests of the corporation or that is required by law in order to contribute to the social objective of improving the environment. Or that, at the expense of corporate profits, he is to hire "hardcore" unemployed instead of better qualified available workmen to contribute to the social objective of reducing poverty.

In each of these cases, the corporate executive would be spending someone else's money for a general social interest. Insofar as his actions in accord with his "social responsibility" reduce returns to stockholders, he is spending their money. Insofar as his actions raise the price to customers, he is spending the customers' money. Insofar as his actions lower the wages of some employees, he is spending their money.

The stockholders or the customers or the employees could separately spend their own money on the particular action if they wished to do so. The executive is exercising a distinct "social responsibility," rather than serving as an agent of the stockholders or the customers or the employees, only if he spends the money in a different way than they would have spent it.

But if he does this, he is in effect imposing taxes, on the one hand, and deciding how the tax proceeds shall be spent, on the other.

This process raises political questions on two levels: principle and consequences. On the level of political principle, the imposition of taxes and the expenditure of tax proceeds are governmental functions. We have established elaborate constitutional, parliamentary and judicial provisions to control these functions, to assure that taxes are imposed so far as possible in accordance with the preferences and desires of the public—after all, "taxation without representation" was one of the battle cries of the American Revolution. We have a system of checks and balances to separate the legislative function of imposing taxes and enacting expenditures from the executive function of collecting taxes and administering expenditure programs and from the judicial function of mediating disputes and interpreting the law.

Here the businessman—self-selected or appointed directly or indirectly by stockholders—is to be simultaneously legislator, executive and jurist. He is to decide whom to tax by how much and for what purpose, and he is to spend the proceeds—all this guided only by general exhortations from on high to restrain inflation, improve the environment, fight poverty and so on and on.

The whole justification for permitting the corporate executive to be selected by the stockholders is that the executive is an agent serving the interests of his principal. This justification disappears when the corporate executive imposes taxes and spends the proceeds for "social" purposes. He becomes in effect a public employee, a civil servant, even though he remains in name an employee of a private enterprise. On grounds of political principle, it is intolerable that such civil servants—insofar as their actions in the name of social responsibility are real and not just window-dressing—should be selected as they are now. If they are to be civil servants, then they must be elected through a political process. If they are to impose taxes and make expenditures to foster "social" objectives, then political machinery must be set up to make the assessment of taxes and to determine through a political process the objectives to be served.

This is the basic reason why the doctrine of "social responsibility" involves the acceptance of the socialist view that political mechanisms, not market mechanisms, are the appropriate way to determine the allocation of scarce resources to alternative uses.

On the grounds of consequences, can the corporate executive in fact discharge his alleged "social responsibilities"? On the one hand, suppose he could get away with spending the stockholders' or customers' or employees' money. How is he to know how to spend it? He is told that he must contribute to fighting inflation. How is he to know what action of his will contribute to that end? He is presumably an expert in running his company—in producing a product or selling it or financing it. But nothing about his selection makes him an expert on inflation. Will his holding down the price of his product reduce inflationary pressure? Or, by leaving more spending power in the hands of his customers, simply divert it elsewhere? Or, by forcing him to produce less because of the lower price, will it simply contribute to shortages? Even if he could answer these questions, how much cost is he justified in imposing on his stockholders, customers and employees for this social purpose? What is his appropriate share and what is the appropriate share of others?

And, whether he wants to or not, can he get away with spending his stockholders', customers' or employees' money? Will not the stockholders fire him? (Either the present ones or those who take over when his actions in the name of social responsibility have reduced the corporation's profits and the price of its stock.) His customers and his employees can desert him for other producers and employers less scrupulous in exercising their social responsibilities.

This facet of "social responsibility" doctrine is brought into sharp relief when the doctrine is used to justify wage restraint by trade unions. The conflict of interest is naked and clear when union officials are asked to subordinate the interest of their members to some more general purpose.

If the union officials try to enforce wage restraint, the consequence is likely to be wildcat strikes, rank-and-file revolts and the emergence of strong competitors for their jobs. We thus have the ironic phenomenon that union leaders—at least in the U.S.—have objected to Government interference with the market far more consistently and courageously than have business leaders.

The difficulty of exercising "social responsibility" illustrates, of course, the great virtue of private competitive enterprise—it forces people to be responsible for their own actions and makes it difficult for them to "exploit" other people for either selfish or unselfish purposes. They can do good—but only at their own expense.

Many a reader who has followed the argument this far may be tempted to remonstrate that it is all well and good to speak of Government's having the responsibility to impose taxes and determine expenditures for such "social" purposes as controlling pollution or training the hard-core unemployed, but that the problems are too urgent to wait on the slow course of political processes, that the exercise of social responsibility by businessmen is a quicker and surer way to solve pressing current problems.

Aside from the question of fact—I share Adam Smith's skepticism about the benefits that can be expected from "those who affected to trade for the public good"—this argument must be rejected on grounds of principle. What it amounts to is an assertion that those who favor the taxes and expenditures in question have failed to persuade a majority of their fellow citizens to be of like mind and that they are seeking to attain by undemocratic procedures what they cannot attain by democratic procedures. In a free society, it is hard for "evil" people to do "evil," especially since one man's good is another's evil.

I have, for simplicity, concentrated on the special case of the corporate executive, except only for the brief digression on trade unions. But precisely the same argument applies to the newer phenomenon of calling upon stockholders to require corporations to exercise social responsibility (the recent G.M. crusade for example). In most of these cases, what is in effect involved is some stockholders trying to get other stockholders (or customers or employees) to contribute against their will to "social" causes favored by the activists. Insofar as they succeed, they are again imposing taxes and spending the proceeds.

The situation of the individual proprietor is somewhat different. If he acts to reduce the returns of his enterprise in order to exercise his "social responsibility," he is spending his own money, not someone else's. If he wishes to spend his money on such purposes, that is his right, and I cannot see that there is any objection to his doing so. In the process, he, too, may impose costs on employees and customers. However, because he is far less likely than a large corporation or union to have monopolistic power, any such side effects will tend to be minor.

Of course, in practice the doctrine of social responsibility is frequently a cloak for actions that are justified on other grounds rather than a reason for those actions.

To illustrate, it may well be in the long-run interest of a corporation that is a major employer in a small community to devote resources to providing amenities to that community or to improving its government. That may make it easier to attract desirable employees, it may reduce the wage bill or lessen losses from pilferage and sabotage or have other worthwhile effects. Or it may be that, given the laws about the deductibility of corporate charitable contributions, the stockholders can contribute more to charities they favor by having the corporation make the gift than by doing it themselves, since they can in that way contribute an amount that would otherwise have been paid as corporate taxes.

In each of these—and many similar—cases, there is a strong temptation to rationalize these actions as an exercise of "social responsibility." In the present climate of opinion, with its widespread aversion to "capitalism," "profits," the "soulless corporation" and so on, this is one way for a corporation to generate goodwill as a by-product of expenditures that are entirely justified in its own self-interest.

It would be inconsistent of me to call on corporate executives to refrain from this hypocritical window-dressing because it harms the foundations of a free society. That would be to call on them to exercise a "social responsibility"! If our institutions, and the attitudes of the public make it in their self-interest to cloak their actions in this way, I cannot summon much indignation to denounce them. At the same time, I can express admiration for those individual proprietors or owners of closely held corporations or stockholders of more broadly held corporations who disdain such tactics as approaching fraud.

Whether blameworthy or not, the use of the cloak of social responsibility, and the nonsense spoken in its name by influential and prestigious businessmen, does clearly harm the foundations of a free society. I have been impressed time and again by the schizophrenic character of many businessmen. They are capable of being extremely far-sighted and clear-headed in matters that are internal to their businesses. They are incredibly short-sighted and muddle-headed in matters that are outside their businesses but affect the possible survival of business in general. This short-sightedness is strikingly exemplified in the calls from many businessmen for wage and price guidelines or controls or income policies. There is nothing that could do more in a brief period to destroy a market system and replace it by a centrally controlled system than effective governmental control of prices and wages.

The short-sightedness is also exemplified in speeches by businessmen on social responsibility. This may gain them kudos in the short run. But it helps to strengthen the already too prevalent view that the pursuit of profits is wicked and immoral and must be curbed and controlled by external forces. Once this view is adopted, the external forces that curb the market will not be the social consciences, however highly developed, of the pontificating executives; it will be the iron fist of Government bureaucrats. Here, as with price and wage controls, businessmen seem to me to reveal a suicidal impulse.

The political principle that underlies the market mechanism is unanimity. In an ideal free market resting on private property, no individual can coerce any other, all cooperation is voluntary, all parties to such cooperation benefit or they need not participate. There are no values, no "social" responsibilities in any sense other than the shared values and responsibilities of individuals. Society is a collection of individuals and of the various groups they voluntarily form.

The political principle that underlies the political mechanism is conformity. The individual must serve a more general social interest— whether that be determined by a church or a dictator or a majority. The individual may have a vote and say in what is to be done, but if he is overruled, he must conform. It is appropriate for some to require others to contribute to a general social purpose whether they wish to or not.

Unfortunately, unanimity is not always feasible. There are some respects in which conformity appears unavoidable, so I do not see how one can avoid the use of the political mechanism altogether.

But the doctrine of "social responsibility" taken seriously would extend the scope of the political mechanism to every human activity. It does not differ in philosophy from the most explicitly collectivist doctrine. It differs only by professing to believe that collectivist ends can be attained without collectivist means. That is why, in my book "Capitalism and Freedom," I have called it a "fundamentally subversive doctrine" in a free society, and have said that in such a society, "there is one and only one social responsibility of business—to use its resources and engage in activities designed to increase its profits so long as it stays within the rules of the game, which is to say, engages in open and free competition without deception or fraud."

Owing Your Soul to the Company Store

RALPH NADER and MARK GREEN

Economists, preoccupied with theories of the corporation and the national economy, rarely ask what happens when a corporation monopolizes not only a product but the local work force, when a town is obliged to "consume" a company's pollution, when one business controls a city by political intimidation. While such questions are largely ignored, local families and local owners increasingly become appendages of the absentee-owners, usually of national and multinational conglomerates.

"He who was a leader in the village becomes dependent on outsiders for his action and policy," Justice William O. Douglas said of this condition. "Clerks responsible to a superior in a distant place take the place of resident proprietors beholden to no one."[1]

Large local corporations utterly dominate many towns simply by using their economic and political power, as Anaconda and Montana Power control the state of Montana, as seven paper companies own more than a third of Maine, and as hundreds of smaller corporations continue to control the company towns created by the expansion of new industries at the turn of the century. In mining, lumber, and textile regions, we still find many unhealthy, hazardous, grim and grimy company towns where citizens depend on one firm for their work, their homes, and often their daily shopping. "Saint Peter don't you call me 'cause I can't go, I owe my soul to the company store."

POLITICAL DOMINATION

Pullman, Illinois, was built in the 1880s as a model town by George M. Pullman of the Pullman Palace Car Company. He invested $8 million in apartment buildings, parks, playgrounds, churches, theaters, arcades, casinos; the town won awards for its designs at international expositions. But Pullman in fact was tense with fear and suspicion, as company spies probed for tips on "union infiltration" or "dangerous" and "disloyal" employees. When the 1893 depression came, the company laid off workers, cut wages 25 percent, but did not reduce rents. After investigating Pullman in the 1930s, the economist Richard T. Ely concluded that "the idea of Pullman is un-American. It is a benevolent, well-wishing feudalism, which desires the happiness of the people but in such a way as shall please the authorities."

Economists today apparently assume that towns like Pullman have largely disappeared. In fact some five million Americans now live in company towns—paper pulp towns in Maine, mining towns in the West, textile and papermill towns in the South. We frequently hear how one crop economies in poor countries can lead to political authoritarianism and economic instability, but American analysts often fail to comprehend that similar things can happen in parts of their own country.

Consider the town of Saint Marys, Georgia, nearly all of whose 1,800 wage earners are employed by the Gilman Paper Company and its business allies. Gilman interests control the city council, the town's only real estate company, bank, and insurance firm, as well as all its lawyers. A populist insurgent, Dr. Carl Drury, recently challenged and defeated a Gilman-backed candidate in a countywide election for state representative. An assistant personnel manager at the Gilman mill reported that his boss "told me to go down to the bag plant, spend all the time and money I needed, and find out who was going to vote for Drury. All of the Drury supporters would be terminated." The personnel manager refused, and was told, "Either you get that damned list or that's it." He quit. "It would have been suicide to stay after that," he said. Another mill worker, however, wouldn't anger his employer. "I have a wife, three children, and a mortgage. I am not going to jeopardize them just to give the mill a kick in the ass. The mill knows it and I know it." After the election some people were fired or suffered business losses because they supported Drury.

Corporate domination, moreover, can occur in entire states as well. Everyone knows that DuPont is powerful in Delaware but few realize how powerful. The firm employs 11 percent of the state work force and manufactures 20 percent of the state's gross product.[2] The DuPont family controls the DuPont company through the DuPonts on the board of directors and through the family's holding company, the Christiana Securities corporation, which also owns the company that publishes the state's two biggest newspapers, the *Morning News* and the *Evening Journal.*

In Wilmington you find DuPont everywhere, not just in the DuPont Building, the company's huge office complex. The Playhouse, Wilmington's only legitimate theater, is owned by DuPont, and the Wilmington Trust Company, Delaware's largest bank, is controlled by it. The recent county executive was a former DuPont lawyer, the father of Wilmington's past mayor was a prominent DuPont executive. The state's one congressman is Pierre S. du Pont IV; its attorney general is married to a DuPont and is the son of a DuPont executive; the recent governor, Russell Peterson, was a former DuPont research director. People connected with the firm or the family comprise a fourth of the state legislature, a third of its committee heads, the president pro tempore of the Senate, and the majority leader of the Delaware House.

One result is that the state legislature has failed to reform the tax system, which favors the DuPont firm and family by virtue of its extremely low property tax assessments and the lack of any tax on personal property owned either by individuals or business. In fact, a 1970 state law abolished one of the few progressive features of the Delaware tax system—the treatment of capital gains as ordinary taxable income. When Wilmington Medical Center, controlled by the DuPonts, recently wanted to move, the family made sure that a new center was built in the rich suburbs, not in Wilmington proper where poor people badly needed additional medical services. Five of the seven members of the county council, who helped make the site available, were either DuPont employees or members of the family.

CIVIC WELFARE

As a result of the wave of conglomerate mergers in the late 1960s, many local enterprises have become branch offices of financial centers in places like New York City and Chicago. The acquiring corporation has national if not international interests, producing or selling goods in Birmingham, Alabama, or Providence, Rhode Island, but not wanting to become enmeshed in such places.[3] For most of the branch managers who run the plants, the town is a temporary station on the way to success in New York or Los Angeles. "IBM is famous for never allowing anyone to take up roots . . . they're constantly moving people around the country," says

New York Congressman Hamilton Fish, who has IBM facilities in his district.

The sociologist Robert Schulze, in a study of the managers of a big corporation found that "their community roots were the most shallow if indeed it could be said that they had any community roots at all. The data led us to suspect that perhaps Cibola . . . was of no great importance to their lives."[4] Or as one corporate official told his local manager in Worcester, Massachusetts, "We couldn't care less what happens in Worcester." This indifference can have an effect on the life of the town, which often looks to the larger local firms to aid in local development. Their lack of interest can amount to a veto of new schools, housing, libraries, parks, hospitals.

When absentee-run firms do take part in civic affairs, they often mount rearguard actions to protect their own economic interests, threatening to leave the town or city, exercising a veto over proposals they dislike. Or they support local puppets who act in their behalf to keep down taxes—a kind of local imperialism which both paralyzes the civic will and engenders a hostility not unlike that which Chile must have felt toward ITT.

An early study documenting this pattern was conducted for a congressional committee in 1946 by Professor C. Wright Mills.[5] Noting that by 1944, 2 percent of all manufacturing concerns had employed 60 percent of our industrial workers, Mills asked, "How does this concentration of economic power affect the general welfare of our cities and their inhabitants?" To find the answer he studied three pairs of cities. In each pair was a "big-business city," where a few big absentee-owned firms provided most of the industrial employment, and a "small-business city," where many smaller, locally-owned firms comprised the community's economic life. Here are some of his conclusions:

> "Big-business cities" witnessed sudden and explosive jumps in population, leading to real estate booms, speculation and unplanned suburban sprawl radiating around center city slums; the operating cost of municipal services was quite high. Growth in the "small-business cities" was more evolutionary and planned. Homes were better built, the city was better laid out, and municipal costs were lower.
>
> A quarter of those employed in the "small-business city" were proprietors or officials of corporations; only 3 percent were self-employed in the "big-business city." Plant shut-downs in bad times were obviously more catastrophic in a big-business city, since the local economy was so much more dependent on a few major firms.
>
> Income was more equitably distributed in "small-business cities," as an average of more than twice as many people earned over $10,000. Thus, while the "independent middle class thrives" in the small-business cities, it does not in the big.

From this evidence, as well as his study of such factors as death rates, the number of libraries, museums, recreational facilities and parks, per capita expenditures for schools and teachers, and frequency of home ownership, Mills concluded that "big business tends to depress while small business tends to raise the level of civic welfare." Since Mills's research there has been no comparable study of the relation between big business and urban life, while absentee ownership and the amount of aggregate economic concentration have increased along with the decay of American cities. In view of this, as well as the vast sums spent on the study of "urban affairs" in the universities, it is dismaying that Mills's work on the local effects of corporate power has not been continued. . . .

Another example of the corporate "donor" poisoning its municipal donee is the Johns-Manville plant in Manville, New Jersey. The plant employs 40 percent of Manville's employees; its payroll accounts for 60 percent of the town's total income. It pays more than half the taxes and has made gifts to hospitals, schools, and recreational facilities. But as Philip Greer wrote in the *Washington Post*, "People are dying in Manville of diseases virtually unknown elsewhere" and at rates several times the national norms. They are dying, medical experts agree, because they work in the biggest asbestos processing plant in the world. Johns-Manville claims it is doing all it can to reduce the dust levels which lead to disease. Any more costly improvements, the firm warns critics, could lead to plant shutdowns instead.

There are less obvious cases of such Faustian situations, where a town depends on a firm to revive its economy only to find that unexpected side effects are ruining it. Orlando, Florida, was delighted a few years back when Walt Disney World announced it would build a vast amusement complex there. But today Orlando is glutted with people and cars; it has too few rooms for too many tourists, inflated real estate, high rises mushrooming everywhere, schools that are overcrowded, and garbage and sewage services that are inadequate. The new World Trade Center in New York not only invigorates Wall Street, but also interferes with the television reception of thousands of New Yorkers, creates traffic jams, and pours tons of raw sewage into the Hudson. High rise construction in San Francisco is ruining the city's architectural standards and costing eleven dollars in services for every ten dollars the high rises contribute in taxes. Butte, Montana, created by Anaconda Company, is now literally being consumed by it since Anaconda is shoveling away more and more of the city in order to get at rich ore deposits.

LOCAL TAXES

Throughout the country powerful local corporations evade their fair share of local taxes. Before they settle in a town they demand, and often get, a subsidy in the form of preferential tax rates. As a previous article showed,[6] higher taxes for small businessmen and home-owners are the result. The extent of such privilege has recently been documented by Senator Muskie and his committee on intergovernmental relations. Some of the unsavory methods used to secure these privileges, including corruption and bribery, have been exposed by George Crile, a reporter who investigated the tax situation in Indiana.[7]

For example, corporate property taxes are often underassessed or they contrive to be classified in special low tax "zones," thereby imposing higher tax burdens on private citizens. . . .

Similarly, in Chicago, US Steel has illegally escaped payment of millions of dollars of property taxes every year. A study by a respected citizens group there, Citizens Against Pollution (CAP), estimated that US Steel avoided $16.4 million in taxes in 1970; the combined undertaxation of three other steel companies amounted to $11 million more. Chicago's share of lost taxes alone could triple the city's budget for environmental control. Largely because of CAP's campaigns, US Steel's Assessment of $45.7 million in 1970 rose to $84.5 million in 1971, still well below the estimated value of $195.2 million.

CORPORATE PHILANTHROPY

When criticized, corporations insist that they are charitable, and of course they are. In 1968–1969 they gave $255 million to higher education, or 15 percent of all voluntary support to schools. Total corporate gifts in 1968 totaled $912 million, or some 6 percent of all philanthropy in the country. These gifts, however, amount to only about 1 percent of pretax profits, well below both the Internal Revenue Code's permissible charitable deduction of 5 percent and the average individual taxpayer's contribution of 2.5 percent of adjusted gross income. Still, as the basic text on corporation law points out, "The concentration of a large proportion of the wealth of [the] community in the hands of business corporations has made corporate gifts essential if charities are to be privately financed."[8]

For example, in Delaware the DuPont family's thirty-six foundations have assets of more than $400 million and give away over $12 million a year. This is almost as much as the city of Wilmington and the county of New Castle each spent for local government functions. Clearly, there are benefits to the donors as well as to the towns from such contributions: gifts can reduce federal, state, and local estate taxes, thereby limiting public revenue; the donor may retain control over the spending of their funds; the firm reaps invaluable publicity and can use its gifts to promote corporate policies.[9]

In fact corporate giving usually is done at a price, and the more dominant the firm, the more dependent the community. "Dependency on DuPont foundations takes two major forms," assert James Phelan and Robert Pozen, authors of *The Company State.*

> Some private groups change their programs to suit the needs of a DuPont family member and some governmental bodies come to rely on foundations to perform public functions.

Private groups become supplicants, trying to get someone from the DuPonts on their board of directors, currying favor with foundation executives, fearing that programs will be axed if they become "controversial." Donations are made by small privileged groups subject to no standards or checks and without the community having a voice. Such a philanthropic monopoly can discourage citizens from taking initiatives and limit the diversion of projects that might have otherwise existed.

At the same time communities can suffer when corporate donations they have come to rely on suddenly dry up, as is often the case when a local operation is acquired by an outsider. "Every time a company changes hands, we worry," says Robert F. Cahill, campaign director of the Golden Rule Fund of Worcester, Massachusetts. "Experience has taught us that it wouldn't be surprising if we were to suffer a sharp cut in the company's corporate gift, even if employee giving is not affected." A study of Rochester, New York, showed a drop in corporate contributions after mergers took place: "It was clear that these absentee-owned firms lagged behind the locally-owned firms in response to rising community needs."[10] Civic fund raisers throughout the country have by and large learned to expect less from chain supermarkets than from local supermarkets.

LOCAL INVESTMENT

Control of local banks by powerful corporate cliques can also frustrate community development. The small inventor, the maverick entrepreneur, the politically unpopular investor would all benefit from a greater diversity of sources for financing. But with centralized power comes fiscal conservatism, for dominant banks would rather take care of their big corporate clients than back risky ventures. Wilmington Trust, a DuPont-dominated bank, invests heavily in corporate and government bonds rather than in local loans. The value of these securities amounted to 60 percent of the loans outstanding for Wilmington Trust in 1969. By contrast the corresponding figure was 42 percent for the US Trust Company of New York, 23 percent for the Philadelphia National Bank, and 26 percent for the Girard Trust Company of Philadelphia.

Absentee-controlled firms have equally dismal effects on local investment. The Rochester study of mergers concluded that merged companies no longer banked as much locally; big city banks prospered at their expense. The Gulf & Western conglomerate insists that all the local firms it acquires transfer their banking business from local banks to the Chase Manhattan Bank in New York City. When Teledyne acquired the Monarch Rubber Company of Hartville, Ohio, it insisted that the company's local deposits be shifted to the National City Bank of New York. "Banking practices," as David Leinsdorf wrote in *Citibank*, "operate like a regressive tax funneling the money of communities with declining economies to those with brighter economic prospects."

So communities can be harmed either when absentee-owned corporations ignore community interests *or* when local corporations dominate community affairs. Corporate domination of a community is bad whether it is exercised or not. If you sleep with an elephant, every thrash, grunt, or snore can be a disaster.

To say that giant corporations should not have such economic and social power is more a plea than a proposal. So long as corporations have this power, they must be forced to realize they also have special obligations and must not abuse it in order to exploit and to discourage self-rule. Even within the market system, it should not be impossible to have accountable corporate citizens; the issue is ultimately one of recognizing moral obligation.[11]

But towns need not continue to act as corporate supplicants. First, if victimized, they can sue. This is just what El Paso, Texas, did in 1972 when it joined with the Texas Air Quality Board to sue the American Smelting and Refining Company for its failure to meet air quality standards and its consequent lead poisoning of some El Paso residents. In May, 1972, ASARCO agreed to pay fines of $80,500 for eighty-eight specific pollution violations, to post $30,000 with the court for any future violations, to install $750,000 worth of additional emission control equipment, and—a remedy tailored to fit the offense—it also agreed to pay all the medical expenses for at least thirty months for 134 children being treated for lead poisoning.

Second, if antitrust enforcement were more vigorous against conglomerate mergers the extent of absentee-control over communities would decline. The Nixon Administration settled its anticonglomerate cases before the Supreme Court could set precedents on these mergers. Rather than wait for some future administration to take the plunge, new legislation should forbid any firm with over $250 million in assets from acquiring any other firm unless it spins off an equal amount of assets. This would arrest the trend toward increasing absentee-ownership, while permitting mergers for reasons of efficiency rather than for stock market manipulation or managerial empire-building.

Finally, if corporations are to act more responsibly, the community should be made more a part of the corporation, either by law or (less likely) by voluntary measures. But how? Citizen committees could be organized that would have a part in making policy in the local plants of the dominant firm. This, after all, is where many decisions are made affecting the local labor market, zoning laws, pollution levels, political structure, etc. Going further, a mechanism could be created to elect public directors for the firm's board of directors from among the local citizens' groups that have gained some power in the various plants of a nationwide conglomerate. But national public directors so elected will be impotent unless they have their own staff.

Or a two-tier system of shareholders could be created. Economic stock would be held for voting and investment purposes, looking toward the traditional rewards of stock appreciation or dividends; political stock would confer only voting rights and would be based on status, not wealth—the status of employees, community residents, and consumers who are clearly and immediately affected by a corporation but who lack any say over its actions. How might this stock be apportioned among citizens and among communities? One formula would be a law requiring that whenever a firm accounts for x percent of a community's tax base, it must allow y percent of all its stock to be political stock, up to some ceiling of stock, say 10 percent.

These suggestions are merely starting points. To carry them out would require a degree of concern and local organization—a desire to claim power and an ability to get new laws enacted—that is far from evident today. But as such possibilities become real, they could suggest answers to one of the great questions facing the US today: how can corporate power be checked without a parallel growth in bureaucratic government?

Solutions for community problems should best be sought in the community. For years corporate leaders have been saying that their firms serve many diverse constituencies—shareholders, consumers, workers, dealers, and citizens generally. In 1969, for example, Henry Ford II told a Harvard Business School audience that

> the terms of the contract between industry and society are changing. . . . Now we are being asked to serve a wider range of human values and to accept an obligation to members of the public with whom we have no commercial transactions.

For this sentiment to be more than mere rhetoric, the political process must convert this "contract" into workable laws, so that companies will be obliged to attend to their victims before they reward their investors.

NOTES

1. *Standard Oil Company of California et al.* v. *United States,* 337 US 293, 319 (1948).
2. For an elaboration of DuPont's control in Delaware, see J. Phelan and R. Pozen, *The Company State* (Grossman, 1973).
3. Absentee-ownership flourishes in areas with weak unions, low-paying jobs, and lax environmental standards. For some states, this condition is becoming chronic. In Vermont nineteen of the twenty-two largest plants (by employees) are owned by outsiders; in New Hampshire, outsiders own sixteen of twenty. Fifty-five of the top ninety-nine firms in Maine are absentee-owned; and in seven southern West Virginia counties, twenty-eight big landowners own about one half of the land, with nineteen of the twenty-eight being out-of-state corporations. Nor is absentee ownership limited to domestic firms. American Association, Ltd. is a British multinational firm which owns 65,000 acres of land in eastern Tennessee. Insulated by distance and indifferent to adverse national publicity, it is even less accountable to the region it exploits.
4. Schulze, "The Bifurcation of Power in a Satellite City," in M. Janowitz, ed., *Community Political Systems* (Free Press, 1961). One study asked community leaders in three cities whether they thought branch managers were more or less interested in the community than were local businessmen; 95 percent, 79 percent, and 57 percent, respectively, said "less." Cited in K. David and R. L. Blomstrom, *Business, Society and Environment: Social Power and Social Response* (McGraw-Hill, 1971).
5. *Small Business and Civic Welfare,* Report of the Smaller War Plants Corporation to the Special Committee to Study Problems of American Small Business, US Senate, 79th Congress, 2nd Session, Doc. No. 135 (1946). See also a study that same year finding similar correlations between large scale corpo-

rate farming and farming communities, *Small Business and the Community—a Study in Central Valley of California on Effects of Scale of Farm Operations,* Report of the Special Committee to Study Problems of American Small Business, US Senate, 79th Congress, 2nd Session, Comm. Print No. 13 (1946).

6. Ralph Nader, "A Citizen's Guide to the Economy," *New York Review,* September 2, 1971.

7. *On the Impact and Administration of the Property Tax,* hearings before the Senate Subcommittee on Intergovernmental Relations of the Committee on Government Operations, 92nd Congress, 2nd Session (May 4, 9, June 26, August 22, 1972). George Crile, "A Tax Assessor Has Many Friends," *Harper's,* November, 1972.

8. R. Baker and W. Cary, *Cases and Materials on Corporations* (3rd. ed., 1959).

9. In 1967 the Michigan Bell Telephone Company announced that it would "adopt" a local high school, "enriching" it by its investment of equipment and instructors. Why this contribution? William M. Day, the firm's president, said it would "help prepare the [potential] shareholders for the business world. We think we can make a real difference in pupil attitudes." *Caveat receptor.*

10. "Report of a Committee of the Rochester Chamber of Commerce on the Out of Town Acquisition of Rochester Companies," 1959, cited in E. Kefauver and I. Till, *In a Few Hands: Monopoly in America* (1965). Corporate contributions are not all that is lost due to a merger. A study of 1963–1967 acquisitions of local Wisconsin firms by outside interests found that the premerger growth rate of the acquired firms was 6.02 percent while the postmerger growth rate was 0.48 percent; employee payrolls premerger had increased 15.6 percent but only 2.1 percent in a comparable period postmerger. And many of the acquired firms shifted away from local lawyers and accountants and toward the services of the parent firm. J. G. Udell, *Social and Economic Consequences of the Merger Movement in Wisconsin* (University of Wisconsin, 1969).

11. Even some judicial decisions are coming to recognize that certain corporations have obligations beyond maximizing profits. In *Herald Co.* v. *The Denver Post,* handed down by the Tenth Circuit Court of Appeals on December 29, 1972, the court permitted what was in effect a subsidy to the Denver *Post*'s employees stock ownership plan because the firm had an obligation to its employees as well as to its shareholders. Rowen, "Court Case Says Corporate Duties Go Beyond Profit," *Washington Post,* April 8, 1973.

INDIVIDUAL LIBERTIES
AND SOCIAL JUSTICE

Case Study—Laetrile:
The FDA and Society

The Food and Drug Administration (FDA) has often found itself at the focal point of public attention; sometimes it has been the recipient of loud and vigorous praise, as when it prevented the sale of dangerous meat products, and sometimes it has been bitterly criticized, as when it allowed thalidomide to be used by expectant mothers. But by the summer of 1977, the FDA was facing one of its most difficult battles with public opinion. By then, it was clear that the FDA's official stand on the controversial cancer cure, Laetrile, had stiff opposition. Not only did hundreds of thousands of cancer sufferers believe they should be able to take Laetrile, but a number of state legislatures had expressed their disagreement with the FDA by passing laws which legalized Laetrile in their own states. It was a problem which was slipping far beyond the simple issue of Laetrile's medical effectiveness; now people were charging that the FDA's ban was a denial of a fundamental right to free choice as guaranteed by the U.S. Constitution.

Ever since the thalidomide scare of the early 1960's, the FDA has been required by law to license only substances which are both safe and effective.[1] As a result, the FDA was bound to look at Laetrile not only in terms of its safety to users—and it *did* appear to be safe—but also in terms of its effectiveness. The FDA was convinced that Laetrile, which it calls the world's "most tested cancer cure," was absolutely worthless for the purpose of curing cancer. But there was, as might be expected, vehement disagreement from the pro-Laetrile forces. To further complicate matters, the FDA had recently incurred hostile reaction for its unpopular attempt to remove saccharin, an artificial sweetener, from the market after numerous tests indicated that when given to rats in extremely large doses, it contributed to the development of cancer. But the agency could hardly have anticipated the hostile reaction which followed from weight-watchers who used saccharin and manufacturers who made their living selling it. The FDA had hit a new low in popularity, and its ban on Laetrile was making matters worse.

Case prepared by Thomas Donaldson, Loyola University of Chicago, especially for this anthology.

By June of 1977, FDA head Donald Kennedy began to wonder how long his agency could remain effective in the face of mounting criticism. Commissioner Kennedy had already personally organized a team of four experts, which was ready to travel at the shortest notice to provide testimony against Laetrile at public hearings.[2] But the tide of sentiment in favor of the drug was not to be stopped by such measures. Indeed, pressure was beginning to mount for a public trial of Laetrile, where it would be administered to humans instead of rats, in order to respond to the advocates' challenge that only human tests could establish its effectiveness. Even Dr. Franz Ingelfinger, respected editor of the *New England Journal of Medicine*—who himself was a cancer sufferer—was beginning to suggest publicly that a human test of Laetrile would do more to bury it than any public criticism from the Food and Drug Administration. The level of public confidence in the FDA had reached a dangerous new low. What possible steps could Commissioner Kennedy take to alleviate the conflict?

BACKGROUND ON LAETRILE

Laetrile has a long and improbable history. Essentially obtained by concentrating the extract from apricot pits, it was not discovered in any ordinary way. In San Francisco during the 1920's a physician hoped to discover a special ingredient which would improve the taste of bootleg whiskey.[3] However, Dr. Ernst Krebs happened instead upon a strong apricot extract which seemed to have positive effects in the curing of cancer; or at least, it seemed to retard the growth of tumors in the rats with which Dr. Krebs experimented. Unfortunately, the extract did not appear to have the same remarkable effect on cancer in humans, and Dr. Krebs abandoned his project.

It remained for Ernst Krebs, Jr., a medical school dropout, to attempt to isolate the active ingredient in his father's apricot mixture. In 1944, he announced that he had succeeded in identifying and isolating the all-important cancer-curing element, which he named Laetrile.[4] There is, however, a strong doubt among professional chemists as to whether such a drug even exists. Following Krebs's own recipe, laboratory researchers have been unable to isolate anything other than the substance amygdalin, which chemists have known about for a long time and which has never been known to have any medical use.[5] Interestingly enough, however, proponents of Laetrile use the expressions "Laetrile" and "amygdalin" interchangeably, recognizing no significant difference between them.

Krebs himself offers the most articulate version of how the drug presumably works. Laetrile contains, among other things, the poison cyanide, which works together with an enzyme found in many cancer cells called betaglucosidase. According to Krebs, the curative powers of Laetrile are simple to understand: The cyanide which it releases attacks the cancer tumor, while not affecting the ordinary, noncancerous cells. The normal cells are spared because they contain an enzyme called rhodanese, which detoxifies cyanide when present in moderate amounts.[6]

More and more, defenders of Laetrile are extending the claims of its benefits to include, not only positive effects against already established cancers, but also preventative powers against possible or future cancers. Thus, in many quarters of the pro-Laetrile movement, supporters are urging normal, healthy people to either take Laetrile pills or to eat foods which supposedly contain high amounts of the drug, e.g., carrots, lima beans, and beets. The movement to defend Laetrile has now become an established part of the regime of some health food devotees, and it is included along with organically grown food in their list of necessary health food substances.[7]

Apart from its possible cancer-curing benefits, Laetrile has a special advantage over conventional methods of cancer treatment: it is extraordinarily cheap. With the median cancer cure in 1973 standing at $19,000, Laetrile's price is almost insignificant in comparison: about $10 per injection and $1 per pill.[8]

DETERMINING THE EFFECTIVENESS OF LAETRILE

The FDA has announced that Laetrile is the "most tested of all cancer cures." Indeed, an official bulletin states that every one of the scientific tests conducted on Laetrile (five studies by the National Cancer Institute alone) has shown that it has no effect against cancer whatsoever.[9] In addition to the strong opposition of the FDA, most other official medical organizations have proclaimed the drug's worthlessness: Laetrile's use is officially opposed by the American Medical Association (AMA), and spokespeople from the National Cancer Institute, the American Cancer Society, and the Sloan-Kettering Institute all denounce its effectiveness as a cancer cure.

However, some individual sufferers of cancer are willing to claim fantastic effects for the drug. For example, Hugh Wildermuth, a farmer from Akron, Indiana (age 59), was diagnosed as having muscle cancer and given a year or less to live by his doctors. Even after seven weeks of cobalt radiation therapy and after large doses of a conventional drug, actinomycin D, Mr. Wildermuth was regarded as an incurable case by his doctors. Instead of abandoning hope, however, he traveled to Tijuana, Mexico, where a group of rebel physicians operate a number of Laetrile clinics. At the Clinica Del Mar, Mr. Wildermuth received three grams of Laetrile each day through injections and later was placed on a "maintenance" program in which he ingested Laetrile pills. Three years later, Mr. Wildermuth's lymph nodes were shrunken and he claimed not to be suffering from cancer at all. Doctors, however, doubt that the cancer was cured by the Laetrile treatment, assuming it was cured at all. They suggest it is more likely that the traditional treatment he underwent before his trip was responsible for the recovery.[10]

Professional researchers and doctors are not convinced by the personal testimonials of Laetrile users. Doctors generally claim that the case histories of fantastic cures leave out important information. Surprisingly enough, one of the pieces of information which researchers often complain is missing is evidence that the person actually had cancer in the first place.

In the absence of concrete information from users, most doctors are inclined to accept the results of laboratory experimentation. A variety of scientific tests have been conducted by well-respected researchers which conclude that Laetrile is ineffective against cancer. The only apparent counterexample occurred during the early 1970's when researcher Kanematsu Sugiura, at Manhattan's famed memorial Sloan-Kettering Institute, used Laetrile in mice which had breast cancer. In the Laetrile-treated mice, only 21 percent showed spreading of the tumor to the lungs, whereas in those given salt solution, 90 percent did show signs of spreading. As might be expected, the pro-Laetrile faction views this test as representing important supporting evidence for their claims.

But in June 1977, Sugiura's original study was disavowed by Sloan-Kettering. Claiming that his original experiment was not "blind," in the sense that he knew which mice were receiving Laetrile and that he attempted to determine the existence of cancer with the naked eye (a very risky business), Sloan-Kettering requested a repeat of the original experiment. Indeed they requested not only a single repeat, but a double one, and this time Sugiura could find no significant difference between the spread of cancer in the two test groups. Although Sugiura still believes that Laetrile can be effective against cancer, the Sloan-Kettering Institute has stated publicly that "Laetrile was found to possess neither preventive . . . nor anti-metastatic, nor curative anti-cancer activity."[11] Lewis Thomas, the distinguished president of Sloan-Kettering, was more abrasive: "These are bad times for reason all around. Suddenly all of the major ills are being coped with by acupuncture. If it's not acupuncture, it is apricot pits."[12]

In an attempt to check more closely on the claims of individual Laetrile users, the FDA invited Dr. Ernesto Contreras, a former Mexican army doctor who now runs perhaps the largest Laetrile clinic, Clinica Del Mar, to submit a number of cases of his own choosing for inspection by medical authorities. Dr. Contreras responded by presenting twelve cases, which presumably represented Laetrile cures. But the findings of the FDA were not encouraging. Of the twelve cases, the FDA says, six had died, three couldn't be traced, and the remaining three all had been exposed to traditional treatment and therapy, including extensive surgery, radiation treatment, and conventional drugs.[13]

THE SALE AND PRODUCTION OF LAETRILE

Laetrile is now produced in at least ten factories around the world, most of which were started by a special foundation, headed by Andrew McNaughton, which is at least nominally dedicated to the exploration of scientific concepts. McNaughton has himself been active in the Laetrile controversy since 1956, and it was he who started one of the largest and most profitable Laetrile clinics in Mexico, the Clinica Cydel, located in Tijuana. McNaughton's past history is not perfectly spotless: He was earlier convicted of fraud in a Canadian mining operation, and was accused by the U.S. Securities and Exchange Commission of making untrue statements in a Laetrile stock venture.[14] The Clinica Cydel and the Clinica Del Mar estimate that in 1977 7,000 patients will have been tested and treated as a part of the Laetrile program, at an average weekly cost of $350. The manufacture of Laetrile for sale and distribution is also a profitable business. Most of the Laetrile imported to the United States is produced at the Cyto Pharma de Mexica, S.A., in Tijuana. Frankly admitting that they are in business to make a profit, the owners claim to look forward to an expanded U.S. market. Their factory is already quite profitable, however, and operates twenty-four hours a day while processing over six tons of apricot seeds a month.[15]

Many businesspeople in the United States have expressed interest in manufacturing Laetrile in this country. The market appears ready and growing, and consumers would be happy to avoid the almost 700 percent markup which is now given to blackmarket Laetrile entering the United States. Unfortunately for potential U.S. manufacturers, there appears to be little way of avoiding the FDA ban. Even if individual states legalized the manufacture and sale of Laetrile—which seems to be a possibility— the FDA still has control over all interstate traffic. Since most states do not produce apricots in the amounts necessary to manufacture Laetrile, importing the requisite apricot pits would constitute a federal legal infraction. Already some U.S. manufacturers of Laetrile, attempting to operate undercover, have been raided and closed.

THE FDA'S POSITION: MOUNTING OPPOSITION

Although admitting that Laetrile may not be damaging in itself, the FDA maintains that its use tends to make people seek worthless remedies instead of those which hold out some chance of success. This is undoubtably the argument the FDA tends to emphasize most. The syndrome, it argues, involves a patient being informed that he has cancer and that he must undergo painful, expensive, and possibly unsuccessful traditional methods of treatment. Shocked and afraid, the patient is ready to believe anyone who promises to relieve him of his disease in a cheap, painless manner. Persuaded by the promoters of Laetrile, the patient then stops pursuing traditional treatment in favor of a Laetrile cure. But because the cancer does not wait for the patient to be treated unsuccessfully by Laetrile, it happens that the patient is indirectly killed by the very remedy he hoped would save his life.

The FDA claims it knows of cases of women with cervical cancer, which has a high rate of cure (about 65 percent), who have refused surgery in favor of Laetrile— and have died. Dr. De Vita of the National Cancer Institute has remarked, "Hardly a day goes by now that I don't hear of a case of a patient dying after leaving accepted treatment and taking Laetrile."[16]

On the other hand, the proponents of Laetrile argue that it is not a question of whether Laetrile works or not; instead it is an issue of freedom of choice. To deny a person the freedom to choose his own means of treatment is akin to denying him freedom of speech or freedom of worship. It is argued that denying citizens Laetrile constitutes a denial of a freedom guaranteed by the U.S. Constitution. How, defenders ask, can the FDA allow the American public to consume unlimited amounts of cigarettes, the use of which has been conclusively demonstrated to cause cancer, while denying people the right to use Laetrile, even though it has no known damaging effects and may very well constitute a cure of cancer? The position of the FDA, it is said, almost approaches the kind of Big Brotherism which is incompatible with a democratic government.

The opposition to the FDA's position on Laetrile was increasing so rapidly that by 1977 it appeared to be seriously challenging the authority of the agency. Not only state legislatures, but also individual judges had begun fighting back. By June 1977, seven states—Alaska, Arizona, Florida, Indiana, Nevada, Texas, and Washington—had all legalized Laetrile in one form or another. Some states had legalized both its sale and manufacture, whereas others had simply legalized its use under specified conditions. Also by the summer of 1977, it appeared that three more states would be soon joining the original seven, and legislation was pending in more than a dozen. In October 1976, the U.S. Court of Appeals, Tenth Circuit, in Denver ruled that the FDA's record on Laetrile was "grossly inadequate," and it refused to overturn lower court rulings which allowed patients to buy and transport Laetrile.[17] In addition, the court forced the FDA to listen to testimony from individual Laetrile users and to hold public hearings on the general subject of the drug's use. Even *The New York Times* had asked, in a column dedicated to the discussion of Laetrile, "Shouldn't people be allowed to choose their own placebo, for better or worse?" And Federal District Judge Luther Bohanon of Oklahoma City ruled that it was legal for certain terminally ill cancer patients to import Laetrile from Mexico.

More significantly from the standpoint of the FDA, there was strong and mounting pressure by the summer of 1977 to test the drug publicly through a controlled and well-supervised program which used humans instead of laboratory animals. Dr. Franz Ingelfinger, editor of the *New England Journal of Medicine,* argued that a public trial would do more to get rid of Laetrile than any official debunking. As he put it, "Forbidden fruits are mighty tasty, especially to those who hope that a bite will be life-giving."[18] And Guy Newell, head of the National Cancer Institute, had recently indicated that his agency might be willing to undertake a clinical test of Laetrile, using humans, even though he considered it an "out-and-out-fraud."[19] Finally, Laetrile users and proponents strongly supported human tests, especially since they thought Laetrile was more effective on humans than on rats.

FDA head Donald Kennedy was clearly confronted with a dilemma of grand proportions. How was his agency to reestablish public confidence, while at the same time protecting the interests of the U.S. public?

Notes

1. "Damn the Doctors—and Washington," *Time* (June 20, 1977), p. 50.
2. *Ibid.*, p. 53.
3. "Laetrile, Should It Be Banned?" *Newsweek* (June 27, 1977), p. 50.
4. *Ibid.*
5. *Ibid.*
6. *Ibid.*
7. *The New York Times,* April 17, 1977.
8. "Victories For Laetrile's Lobby," *Time* (May 22, 1977), p. 97.
9. *The New York Times, op. cit.*
10. "Laetrile, Should It Be Banned?" *op. cit.*, p. 52.
11 *Ibid.*, p. 56.
12. "Victories for Laetrile's Lobby," *op. cit.*
13. "Laetrile, Should It Be Banned?" *op. cit.*
14. *Ibid.*, p. 51.
15. *Ibid.*
16. "Damn the Doctors—and Washington," *op. cit.*, p. 54.
17. *The New York Times,* February 18, 1977.
18. "Damn the Doctors—and Washington," *op. cit.*, p. 54.
19. *Ibid.*

The Principles of a Liberal
Social Order

Friedrich A. Hayek

1. By 'liberalism' I shall understand here the conception of a desirable political order which in the first instance was developed in England from the time of the Old Whigs in the later part of the seventeenth century to that of Gladstone at the end of the nineteenth. David Hume, Adam Smith, Edmund Burke, T. B. Macaulay and Lord Acton may be regarded as its typical representatives in England. It was this conception of individual liberty under the law which in the first instance inspired the liberal movements on the Continent and which became the basis of the American political tradition. A few of the leading political thinkers in those countries like B. Constant and A. de Tocqueville in France, Immanuel Kant,

Published in *Il Politico,* 1966. Reprinted in *Studies in Philosophy, Politics and Economics,* ed. Friedrich A. Hayek, by permission of the University of Chicago Press. © 1967 by F. A. Hayek. All rights reserved.

Friedrich von Schiller and Wilhelm von Humboldt in Germany, and James Madison, John Marshall and Daniel Webster in the United States belong wholly to it.

2. This liberalism must be clearly distinguished from another, originally Continental European tradition, also called 'liberalism' of which what now claims this name in the United States is a direct descendant. This latter view, though beginning with an attempt to imitate the first tradition, interpreted it in the spirit of a constructivist rationalism prevalent in France and thereby made of it something very different, and in the end, instead of advocating limitations on the powers of government, ended up with the ideal of the unlimited powers of the majority. This is the tradition of Voltaire, Rousseau, Condorcet and the French Revolution which became the ancestor of modern socialism. English utilitarianism has taken over much of this Continental tradition and the late-nineteenth-century British liberal party, resulting from a fusion of the liberal Whigs and the utilitarian Radicals, was also a product of this mixture.

3. Liberalism and democracy, although compatible, are not the same. The first is concerned with the extent of governmental power, the second with who holds this power. The difference is best seen if we consider their opposites: the opposite of liberalism is totalitarianism, while the opposite of democracy is authoritarianism. In consequence, it is at least possible in principle that a democratic government may be totalitarian and that an authoritarian government may act on liberal principles. The second kind of 'liberalism' mentioned before has in effect become democratism rather than liberalism and, demanding *unlimited* power of the majority, has become essentially anti-liberal. . . .

6. Liberalism . . . derives from the discovery of a self-generating or spontaneous order in social affairs (the same discovery which led to the recognition that there existed an object for theoretical social sciences), an order which made it possible to utilize the knowledge and skill of all members of society to a much greater extent than would be possible in any order created by central direction, and the consequent desire to make as full use of these powerful spontaneous ordering forces as possible.

7. It was thus in their efforts to make explicit the principles of an order already existing but only in an imperfect form that Adam Smith and his followers developed the basic principles of liberalism in order to demonstrate the desirability of their general application. In doing this they were able to presuppose familiarity with the common law conception of justice and with the ideals of the rule of law and of government under the law which were little understood outside the Anglo-Saxon world; with the result that not only were their ideas not fully understood outside the English-speaking countries, but that they ceased to be fully understood even in England when Bentham and his followers replaced the English legal tradition by a constructivist utilitarianism derived more from Continental rationalism than from the evolutionary conception of the English tradition.

8. The central concept of liberalism is that under the enforcement of

universal rules of just conduct, protecting a recognizable private domain
of individuals, a spontaneous order of human activities of much greater
complexity will form itself than could ever be produced by deliberate
arrangement, and that in consequence the coercive activities of government should be limited to the enforcement of such rules, whatever other
services government may at the same time render by administering those
particular resources which have been placed at its disposal for those
purposes.

9. The distinction between a *spontaneous order* based on abstract rules
which leave individuals free to use their own knowledge for their own
purposes, and an *organization or arrangement* based on commands, is of
central importance for the understanding of the principles of a free
society and must in the following paragraphs be explained in some detail,
especially as the spontaneous order of a free society will contain many
organizations (including the biggest organization, government), but the
two principles of order cannot be mixed in any manner we may wish.

10. The first peculiarity of a spontaneous order is that by using its
ordering forces (the regularity of the conduct of its members) we can
achieve an order of a much more complex set of facts than we could ever
achieve by deliberate arrangement, but that, while availing ourselves of
this possibility of inducing an order of much greater extent than we
otherwise could, we at the same time limit our power over the details of
that order. We shall say that when using the former principle we shall
have power only over the abstract character but not over the concrete
detail of that order.

11. No less important is the fact that, in contrast to an organization,
neither has a spontaneous order a purpose nor need there be agreement
on the concrete results it will produce in order to agree on the desirability
of such an order, because, being independent of any particular purpose,
it can be used for, and will assist in the pursuit of, a great many different,
divergent and even conflicting individual purposes. Thus the order of the
market, in particular, rests not on common purposes but on reciprocity,
that is on the reconciliation of different purposes for the mutual benefit
of the participants. . . .

16. The spontaneous order of the market resulting from the interac-
tion of many . . . economies is something so fundamentally different
from an economy proper that it must be regarded as a great misfortune
that it has ever been called by the same name. I have become convinced
that this practice so constantly misleads people that it is necessary to invent
a new technical term for it. I propose that we call this spontaneous order
of the market a *catallaxy* in analogy to the term 'catallactics', which has
often been proposed as a substitute for the term 'economics'. (Both
'catallaxy' and 'catallactics' derive from the ancient Greek verb *katallattein*
which, significantly, means not only 'to barter' and 'to exchange' but also
'to admit into the community' and 'to turn from enemy into friend'.)

17. The chief point about the catallaxy is that, as a spontaneous order,
its orderliness does *not* rest on its orientation on a single hierarchy of ends,
and that, therefore, it will *not* secure that for it as a whole the more

important comes before the less important. This is the chief cause of its condemnation by its opponents, and it could be said that most of the socialist demands amount to nothing less than that the catallaxy should be turned into an economy proper (i.e., the purposeless spontaneous order into a purpose-oriented organization) in order to assure that the more important be never sacrificed to the less important. The defence of the free society must therefore show that it is due to the fact that we do not enforce a unitary scale of concrete ends, nor attempt to secure that some particular view about what is more and what is less important governs the whole of society, that the members of such a free society have as good a chance successfully to use their individual knowledge for the achievement of their individual purposes as they in fact have.

18. The extension of an order of peace beyond the small purpose-oriented organization became thus possible by the extension of purpose-independent ('formal') rules of just conduct to the relations with other men who did not pursue the same concrete ends or hold the same values except those abstract rules—rules which did not impose obligations for particular actions (which always presuppose a concrete end) but consisted solely in prohibitions from infringing the protected domain of each which these rules enable us to determine. Liberalism is therefore inseparable from the institution of private property which is the name we usually give to the material part of this protected individual domain. . . .

20. Liberalism recognizes that there are certain other services which for various reasons the spontaneous forces of the market may not produce or may not produce adequately, and that for this reason it is desirable to put at the disposal of government a clearly circumscribed body of resources with which it can render such services to the citizens in general. This requires a sharp distinction between the coercive powers of government, in which its actions are strictly limited to the enforcement of rules of just conduct and in the exercise of which all discretion is excluded, and the provision of services by government, for which it can use only the resources put at its disposal for this purpose, has no coercive power or monopoly, but in the use of which resources it enjoys wide discretion. . . .

22. Liberalism has indeed inherited from the theories of the common law and from the older (pre-rationalist) theories of the law of nature, and also presupposes, a conception of justice which allows us to distinguish between such rules of just individual conduct as are implied in the conception of the 'rule of law' and are required for the formation of a spontaneous order on the one hand, and all the particular commands issued by authority for the purpose of organization on the other. This essential distinction has been made explicit in the legal theories of two of the greater philosophers of modern times, David Hume and Immanuel Kant, but has not been adequately restated since and is wholly uncongenial to the governing legal theories of our day.

23. The essential points of this conception of justice are (a) that justice can be meaningfully attributed only to human action and not to any state

of affairs as such without reference to the question whether it has been, or could have been, deliberately brought about by somebody; (b) that the rules of justice have essentially the nature of prohibitions, or, in other words, that injustice is really the primary concept and the aim of rules of just conduct is to prevent unjust action; (c) that the injustice to be prevented is the infringement of the protected domain of one's fellow men, a domain which is to be ascertained by means of these rules of justice; and (d) that these rules of just conduct which are in themselves negative can be developed by consistently applying to whatever such rules a society has inherited the equally negative test of universal applicability—a test which, in the last resort, is nothing else than the self-consistency of the actions which these rules allow if applied to the circumstances of the real world. These four crucial points must be developed further in the following paragraphs.

24. *Ad (a):* Rules of just conduct can require the individual to take into account in his decisions only such consequences of his actions as he himself can foresee. The concrete results of the catallaxy for particular people are, however, essentially unpredictable; and since they are not the effect of anyone's design or intentions, it is meaningless to describe the manner in which the market distributed the good things of this world among particular people as just or unjust. This, however, is what the so-called 'social' or 'distributive' justice aims at in the name of which the liberal order of law is progressively destroyed. We shall later see that no test or criteria have been found or can be found by which such rules of 'social justice' can be assessed, and that, in consequence, and in contrast to the rules of just conduct, they would have to be determined by the arbitrary will of the holders of power.

25. *Ad (b):* No particular human action is fully determined without a concrete purpose it is meant to achieve. Free men who are to be allowed to use their own means and their own knowledge for their own purposes must therefore not be subject to rules which tell them what they must positively do, but only to rules which tell them what they must not do; except for the discharge of obligations an individual has voluntarily incurred, the rules of just conduct thus merely delimit the range of permissible actions but do not determine the particular actions a man must take at a particular moment. (There are certain rare exceptions to this, like actions to save or protect life, prevent catastrophes, and the like, where either rules of justice actually do require, or would at least generally be accepted as just rules if they required, some positive action. It would lead far to discuss here the position of such rules in the system.) The generally negative character of the rules of just conduct, and the corresponding primacy of the injustice which is prohibited, has often been noticed but scarcely ever been thought through to its logical consequences.

26. *Ad (c):* The injustice which is prohibited by rules of just conduct is any encroachment on the protected domain of other individuals, and they must therefore enable us to ascertain what is the protected sphere of

others. Since the time of John Locke it is customary to describe this protected domain as property (which Locke himself had defined as 'the life, liberty, and possessions of a man'). This term suggests, however, a much too narrow and purely material conception of the protected domain which includes not only material goods but also various claims on others and certain expectations. If the concept of property is, however, (with Locke) interpreted in this wide sense, it is true that law, in the sense of rules of justice, and the institution of property are inseparable.

27. *Ad (d):* It is impossible to decide about the justice of any one particular rule of just conduct except within the framework of a whole system of such rules, most of which must for this purpose be regarded as unquestioned: values can always be tested only in terms of other values. The test of the justice of a rule is usually (since Kant) described as that of its 'universalizability', i.e., of the possibility of willing that the rules should be applied to all instances that correspond to the conditions stated in it (the 'categorical imperative'). What this amounts to is that in applying it to any concrete circumstances it will not conflict with any other accepted rules. The test is thus in the last resort one of the compatibility or non-contradictoriness of the whole system of rules, not merely in a logical sense but in the sense that the system of actions which the rules permit will not lead to conflict.

28. It will be noticed that only purpose-independent ('formal') rules pass this test because, as rules which have originally been developed in small, purpose-connected groups ('organizations') are progressively extended to larger and larger groups and finally universalized to apply to the relations between any members of an Open Society who have no concrete purposes in common and merely submit to the same abstract rules, they will in this process have to shed all references to particular purposes.

29. The growth from the tribal organization, all of whose members served common purposes, to the spontaneous order of the Open Society in which people are allowed to pursue their own purposes in peace, may thus be said to have commenced when for the first time a savage placed some goods at the boundary of his tribe in the hope that some member of another tribe would find them and leave in turn behind some other goods to secure the repetition of the offer. From the first establishment of such a practice which served reciprocal but not common purposes, a process has been going on for millennia which, by making rules of conduct independent of the particular purposes of those concerned, made it possible to extend these rules to ever wider circles of undetermined persons and eventually might make possible a universal peaceful order of the world.

. . .

32. The progressive displacement of the rules of conduct of private and criminal law by a conception derived from public law is the process by which existing liberal societies are progressively transformed into totalitarian societies. This tendency has been most explicitly seen and supported

by Adolf Hitler's 'crown jurist' Carl Schmitt who consistently advocated the replacement of the 'normative' thinking of liberal law by a conception of law which regards as its purpose the 'concrete order formation' *(konkretes Ordnungsdenken)*. . . .

34. If it was the nature of the constitutional arrangements prevailing in all Western democracies which made this development possible, the driving force which guided it in the particular direction was the growing recognition that the application of uniform or equal rules to the conduct of individuals who were in fact very different in many respects, inevitably produced very different results for the different individuals; and that in order to bring about by government action a reduction in these unintended but inevitable differences in the material position of different people, it would be necessary to treat them not according to the same but according to different rules. This gave rise to a new and altogether different conception of justice, namely that usually described as 'social' or 'distributive' justice, a conception of justice which did not confine itself to rules of conduct for the individual but aimed at particular results for particular people, and which therefore could be achieved only in a purpose-governed organization but not in a purpose-independent spontaneous order.

35. The concepts of a 'just price', a 'just remuneration' or a 'just distribution of incomes' are of course very old; it deserves notice, however, that in the course of the efforts of two thousand years in which philosophers have speculated about the meaning of these concepts, not a single rule has been discovered which would allow us to determine what is in this sense just in a market order. Indeed the one group of scholars which have most persistently pursued the question, the schoolmen of the later middle ages and early modern times, were finally driven to define the just price or wage as that price or wage which would form itself on a market in the absence of fraud, violence or privilege—thus referring back to the rules of just conduct and accepting as a just result whatever was brought about by the just conduct of all individuals concerned. This negative conclusion of all the speculations about 'social' or 'distributive' justice was, as we shall see, inevitable, because a just remuneration or distribution has meaning only within an organization whose members act under command in the service of a common system of ends, but can have no meaning whatever in a catallaxy or spontaneous order which can have no such common system of ends.

36. A state of affairs as such, as we have seen, cannot be just or unjust as a mere fact. Only in so far as it has been brought about designedly or could be so brought about does it make sense to call just or unjust the actions of those who have created it or permitted it to arise. In the catallaxy, the spontaneous order of the market, nobody can foresee, however, what each participant will get, and the results for particular people are not determined by anyone's intentions; nor is anyone responsible for particular people getting particular things. We might therefore question

whether a deliberate choice of the market order as the method for guiding economic activities, with the unpredictable and in a great measure chance incidence of its benefits, is a just decision, but certainly not whether, once we have decided to avail ourselves of the catallaxy for that purpose, the particular results it produces for particular people are just or unjust.

37. That the concept of justice is nevertheless so commonly and readily applied to the distribution of incomes is entirely the effect of an erroneous anthropomorphic interpretation of society as an organization rather than as a spontaneous order. The term 'distribution' is in this sense quite as misleading as the term 'economy', since it also suggests that something is the result of deliberate action which in fact is the result of spontaneous ordering forces. Nobody distributes income in a market order (as would have to be done in an organization) and to speak, with respect to the former, of a just or unjust distribution is therefore simple nonsense. It would be less misleading to speak in this respect of a 'dispersion' rather than a 'distribution' of incomes.

38. All endeavours to secure a 'just' distribution must thus be directed towards turning the spontaneous order of the market into an organization or, in other words, into a totalitarian order. It was this striving after a new conception of justice which produced the various steps by which rules of organization ('public law'), which were designed to make people aim at particular results, came to supersede the purpose-independent rules of just individual conduct, and which thereby gradually destroyed the foundation on which a spontaneous order must rest.

39. The ideal of using the coercive powers of government to achieve 'positive' (i.e., social or distributive) justice leads, however, not only necessarily to the destruction of individual freedom, which some might not think too high a price, but it also proves on examination a mirage or an illusion which cannot be achieved in any circumstances, because it presupposes an agreement on the relative importance of the different concrete ends which cannot exist in a great society whose members do not know each other or the same particular facts. It is sometimes believed that the fact that most people today desire social justice demonstrates that this ideal has a determinable content. But it is unfortunately only too possible to chase a mirage, and the consequence of this is always that the result of one's striving will be utterly different from what one had intended.

40. There can be no rules which determine how much everybody 'ought' to have unless we make some unitary conception of relative 'merits' or 'needs' of the different individuals, for which there exists no objective measure, the basis of a central allocation of all goods and services—which would make it necessary that each individual, instead of using *his* knowledge for *his* purposes, were made to fulfil a duty imposed upon him by somebody else, and were remunerated according to how well he has, in the opinion of others, performed this duty. This is the method of remuneration appropriate to a closed organization, such as an army, but irreconcilable with the forces which maintain a spontaneous order.

41. It ought to be freely admitted that the market order does not bring

about any close correspondence between subjective merit or individual needs and rewards. It operates on the principle of a combined game of skill and chance in which the results for each individual may be as much determined by circumstances wholly beyond his control as by his skill or effort. Each is remunerated according to the value his particular services have to the particular people to whom he renders them, and this value of his services stands in no necessary relation to anything which we could appropriately call his merits and still less to his needs.

42. It deserves special emphasis that, strictly speaking, it is meaningless to speak of a value 'to society' when what is in question is the value of some services to certain people, services which may be of no interest to anybody else. A violin virtuoso presumably renders services to entirely different people from those whom a football star entertains, and the maker of pipes altogether different people from the maker of perfumes. The whole conception of a 'value to society' is in a free order as illegitimate an anthropomorphic term as its description as 'one economy' in the strict sense, as an entity which 'treats' people justly or unjustly, or 'distributes' among them. The results of the market process for particular individuals are neither the result of anybody's will that they should have so much, nor even foreseeable by those who have decided upon or support the maintenance of this kind of order. . . .

45. The aim of economic policy of a free society can therefore never be to assure particular results to particular people, and its success cannot be measured by any attempt at adding up the value of such particular results. In this respect the aim of what is called 'welfare economics' is fundamentally mistaken, not only because no meaningful sum can be formed of the satisfactions provided for different people, but because its basic idea of a maximum of need-fulfilment (or a maximum social product) is appropriate only to an economy proper which serves a single hierarchy of ends, but not to the spontaneous order of a catallaxy which has no common concrete ends.

46. Though it is widely believed that the conception of an optimal economic policy (or any judgment whether one economic policy is better than another) presupposes such a conception of maximizing aggregate real social income (which is possible only in value terms and therefore implies an illegitimate comparison of the utility to different persons), this is in fact not so. An optimal policy in a catallaxy may aim, and ought to aim, at increasing the chances of any member of society taken at random of having a high income, or, what amounts to the same thing, the chance that, whatever his share in total income may be, the real equivalent of this share will be as large as we know how to make it.

47. This condition will be approached as closely as we can manage, irrespective of the dispersion of incomes, if everything which is produced is being produced by persons or organizations who can produce it more cheaply than (or at least as cheaply as) anybody who does not produce it, and is sold at a price lower than that at which it would be possible to offer it for anybody who does not in fact so offer it. (This allows for persons or organizations to whom the costs of producing one commodity or service

are lower than they are for those who actually produce it and who still produce something else instead, because their comparative advantage in that other production is still greater; in this case the total costs of their producing the first commodity would have to include the loss of the one which is not produced.)

48. It will be noticed that this optimum does not presuppose what economic theory calls 'perfect competition' but only that there are no obstacles to the entry into each trade and that the market functions adequately in spreading information about opportunities. It should also be specially observed that this modest and achievable goal has never yet been fully achieved because at all times and everywhere governments have both restricted access to some occupations and tolerated persons and organizations deterring others from entering occupations when this would have been to the advantage of the latter.

49. This optimum position means that as much will be produced of whatever combination of products and services is in fact produced as can be produced by any method that we know, because we can through such a use of the market mechanism bring more of the dispersed knowledge of the members of society into play than by any other. But it will be achieved only if we leave the share in the total, which each member will get, to be determined by the market mechanism and all its accidents, because it is only through the market determination of incomes that each is led to do what this result requires.

50. We owe, in other words, our chances that our unpredictable share in the total product of society represents as large an aggregate of goods and services as it does to the fact that thousands of others constantly submit to the adjustments which the market forces on them; and it is consequently also our duty to accept the same kind of changes in our income and position, even if it means a decline in our accustomed position and is due to circumstances we could not have foreseen and for which we are not responsible. The conception that we have 'earned' (in the sense of morally deserved) the income we had when we were more fortunate, and that we are therefore entitled to it so long as we strive as honestly as before and had no warning to turn elsewhere, is wholly mistaken. Everybody, rich or poor, owes his income to the outcome of a mixed game of skill and chance, the aggregate results of which and the shares in which are as high as they are only because we have agreed to play that game. And once we have agreed to play the game and profited from its results, it is a moral obligation on us to abide by the results even if they turn against us. . . . .

61. In conclusion, the basic principles of a liberal society may be summed up by saying that in such a society all coercive functions of government must be guided by the overruling importance of what I like to call THE THREE GREAT NEGATIVES: PEACE, JUSTICE AND LIBERTY. Their achievement requires that in its coercive functions government shall be confined to the enforcement of such prohibitions (stated as abstract rules) as can be equally applied to all, and to exacting under the same uniform rules from all a share of the costs of the other, noncoercive services it may decide to render to the citizens with the material and personal means thereby placed at its disposal.

Distributive Justice

JOHN RAWLS

I

We may think of a human society as a more or less self-sufficient association regulated by a common conception of justice and aimed at advancing the good of its members.[1] As a co-operative venture for mutual advantage, it is characterized by a conflict as well as an identity of interests. There is an identity of interests since social co-operation makes possible a better life for all than any would have if everyone were to try to live by his own efforts; yet at the same time men are not indifferent as to how the greater benefits produced by their joint labours are distributed, for in order to further their own aims each prefers a larger to a lesser share. A conception of justice is a set of principles for choosing between the social arrangements which determine this division and for underwriting a consensus as to the proper distributive shares.

Now at first sight the most rational conception of justice would seem to be utilitarian. For consider: each man in realizing his own good can certainly balance his own losses against his own gains. We can impose a sacrifice on ourselves now for the sake of a greater advantage later. A man quite properly acts, as long as others are not affected, to achieve his own greatest good, to advance his ends as far as possible. Now, why should not a society act on precisely the same principle? Why is not that which is rational in the case of one man right in the case of a group of men? Surely the simplest and most direct conception of the right, and so of justice, is that of maximizing the good. This assumes a prior understanding of what is good, but we can think of the good as already given by the interests of rational individuals. Thus just as the principle of individual choice is to achieve one's greatest good, to advance so far as possible one's own system of rational desires, so the principle of social choice is to realize the greatest good (similarly defined) summed over all the members of society. We arrive at the principle of utility in a natural way: by this principle a society is rightly ordered, and hence just, when its institutions are arranged so as to realize the greatest sum of satisfactions.

The striking feature of the principle of utility is that it does not matter, except indirectly, how this sum of satisfactions is distributed among individuals, any more than it matters, except indirectly, how one man distributes his satisfactions over time. Since certain ways of distributing things affect the total sum of satisfactions, this fact must be taken into account in arranging social institutions; but according to this principle the explanation of common-sense precepts of justice and their seemingly

From Peter Laslett and W. G. Runciman, eds., *Philosophy, Politics and Society* (Oxford: Oxford University Press, 1967). Reprinted by courtesy of the author, Barnes & Noble Books, and Basil Blackwell Publisher.

stringent character is that they are those rules which experience shows must be strictly respected and departed from only under exceptional circumstances if the sum of advantages is to be maximized. The precepts of justice are derivative from the one end of attaining the greatest net balance of satisfactions. There is no reason in principle why the greater gains of some should not compensate for the lesser losses of others; or why the violation of the liberty of a few might not be made right by a greater good shared by many. It simply happens, at least under most conditions, that the greatest sum of advantages is not generally achieved in this way. From the standpoint of utility the strictness of common-sense notions of justice has a certain usefulness, but as a philosophical doctrine it is irrational.

If, then, we believe that as a matter of principle each member of society has an inviolability founded on justice which even the welfare of everyone else cannot over-ride, and that a loss of freedom for some is not made right by a greater sum of satisfactions enjoyed by many, we shall have to look for another account of the principles of justice. The principle of utility is incapable of explaining the fact that in a just society the liberties of equal citizenship are taken for granted, and the rights secured by justice are not subject to political bargaining nor to the calculus of social interests. Now, the most natural alternative to the principle of utility is its traditional rival, the theory of the social contract. The aim of the contract doctrine is precisely to account for the strictness of justice by supposing that its principles arise from an agreement among free and independent persons in an original position of equality and hence reflect the integrity and equal sovereignty of the rational persons who are the contractees. Instead of supposing that a conception of right, and so a conception of justice, is simply an extension of the principle of choice for one man to society as a whole, the contract doctrine assumes that the rational individuals who belong to society must choose together, in one joint act, what is to count among them as just and unjust. They are to decide among themselves once and for all what is to be their conception of justice. This decision is thought of as being made in a suitably defined initial situation one of the significant features of which is that no one knows his position in society, nor even his place in the distribution of natural talents and abilities. The principles of justice to which all are forever bound are chosen in the absence of this sort of specific information. A veil of ignorance prevents anyone from being advantaged or disadvantaged by the contingencies of social class and fortune; and hence the bargaining problems which arise in everyday life from the possession of this knowledge do not affect the choice of principles. On the contract doctrine, then, the theory of justice, and indeed ethics itself, is part of the general theory of rational choice, a fact perfectly clear in its Kantian formulation.

Once justice is thought of as arising from an original agreement of this kind, it is evident that the principle of utility is problematical. For why should rational individuals who have a system of ends they wish to advance agree to a violation of their liberty for the sake of a greater balance of satisfactions enjoyed by others? It seems more plausible to suppose that, when situated in an original position of equal right, they would insist upon institutions which returned compensating advantages for any sacrifices required. A rational man would not accept an institution merely because it maximized the sum of advantages irrespective of its effect on his own interests. It appears, then, that the principle of utility would be rejected as a principle of justice, although we shall not try to argue this important question here. Rather, our aim is to give a brief sketch of the conception of distributive shares implicit in the principles of justice which, it seems, would be chosen in the original position. The philosophical appeal of utilitarianism is that it seems to offer a single principle on the basis of which a consistent and complete conception of right can be developed. The problem is to work out a contractarian alternative in such a way that it has comparable if not all the same virtues.

II

In our discussion we shall make no attempt to derive the two principles of justice which we shall examine; that is, we shall not try to show that they would be chosen in the original position.[2] It must suffice that it is plausible that they would be, at least in preference to the standard forms of traditional theories. Instead we shall be mainly concerned with three questions: first, how to interpret these principles so that they define a consistent and complete conception of justice; second, whether it is possible to arrange the institutions of a constitutional democracy so that these principles are satisfied, at least approximately; and third, whether the conception of distributive shares which they define is compatible with common-sense notions of justice. The significance of these principles is that they allow for the strictness of the claims of justice; and if they can be understood so as to yield a consistent and complete conception, the contractarian alternative would seem all the more attractive.

The two principles of justice which we shall discuss may be formulated as follows: first, each person engaged in an institution or affected by it has an equal right to the most extensive liberty compatible with a like liberty for all; and second, inequalities as defined by the institutional structure or fostered by it are arbitrary unless it is reasonable to expect that they will work out to everyone's advantage and provided that the positions and offices to which they attach or from which they may be gained are open to all. These principles regulate the distributive aspects of institutions by controlling the assignment of rights and duties throughout the whole social structure, beginning with the adoption of a political constitution in accordance with which they are then to be applied to legislation. It is upon a correct choice of a basic structure of society, its fundamental system of rights and duties, that the justice of distributive shares depends.

The two principles of justice apply in the first instance to this basic structure, that is, to the main institutions of the social system and their arrangement, how they are combined together. Thus, this structure includes the political constitution and the principal economic and social institutions which together define a person's liberties and rights and affect his life-prospects, what he may expect to be and how well he may expect to fare. The intuitive idea here is that those born into the social system at different positions, say in different social classes, have varying life-prospects determined, in part, by the system of political liberties and personal rights, and by the economic and social opportunities which are made available to these positions. In this way the basic structure of society favours certain men over others, and these are the basic inequalities, the ones which affect their whole life-prospects. It is inequalities of this kind, presumably inevitable in any society, with which the two principles of justice are primarily designed to deal.

Now the second principle holds that an inequality is allowed only if there is reason to believe that the institution with the inequality, or permitting it, will work out for the advantage of every person engaged in it. In the case of the basic structure this means that all inequalities which affect life-prospects, say the inequalities of income and wealth which exist between social classes, must be to the advantage of everyone. Since the principle applies to institutions, we interpret this to mean that inequalities must be to the advantage of the representative man for each relevant social position; they should improve each such man's expectation. Here we assume that it is possible to attach to each position an expectation, and that this expectation is a function of the whole institutional structure: it can be raised and lowered by reassigning rights and duties throughout the system. Thus the expectation of any position depends upon the expectations of the others, and these in turn depend upon the pattern of rights and duties established by the basic structure. But it is not clear what is meant by saying that inequalities must be to the advantage of every representative man. . . .

IV

[One] . . . interpretation [of what is meant by saying that inequalities must be to the advantage of every representative man] . . . is to choose some social position by reference to which the pattern of expectations as a whole is to be judged, and then to maximize with respect to the expectations of this representative man consistent with the demands of equal liberty and equality of opportunity. Now, the one obvious candidate is the representative man of those who are least favoured by the system of institutional inequalities. Thus we arrive at the following idea: the basic structure of the social system affects the life-prospects of typical individuals according to their initial places in society, say the various income classes into which they are born, or depending upon certain natural attributes, as when institutions make discriminations between men and women or allow certain advantages to be gained by those with greater natural abilities. The fundamental problem of distributive justice concerns the differences in life-prospects which come about in this way. We interpret the second principle to hold that these differences are just if and only if the greater expectations of the more advantaged, when playing a part in the working of the whole social system, improve the expectations of the least advantaged. The basic structure is just throughout when the advantages of the more fortunate promote the well-being of the least fortunate, that is, when a decrease in their advantages would make the least fortunate even worse off than they are. The basic structure is perfectly just when the prospects of the least fortunate are as great as they can be.

In interpreting the second principle (or rather the first part of it which we may, for obvious reasons, refer to as the difference principle), we assume that the first principle requires a basic equal liberty for all, and that the resulting political system, when circumstances permit, is that of a constitutional democracy in some form. There must be liberty of the person and political equality as well as liberty of conscience and freedom of thought. There is one class of equal citizens which defines a common status for all. We also assume that there is equality of opportunity and a fair competition for the available positions on the basis of reasonable qualifications. Now, given this background, the differences to be justified are the various economic and social inequalities in the basic structure which must inevitably arise in such a scheme. These are the inequalities in the distribution of income and wealth and the distinctions in social prestige and status which attach to the various positions and classes. The difference principle says that these inequalities are just if and only if they are part of a larger system in which they work out to the advantage of the most unfortunate representative man. The just distributive shares determined by the basic structure are those specified by this constrained maximum principle.

Thus, consider the chief problem of distributive justice, that concerning the distribution of wealth as it affects the life-prospects of those starting out in the various income groups. These income classes define the relevant representative men from which the social system is to be judged. Now, a son of a member of the entrepreneurial class (in a capitalist society) has a better prospect than that of the son of an unskilled labourer. This will be true, it seems, even when the social injustices which presently exist are removed and the two men are of equal talent and ability; the inequality cannot be done away with as long as something like the family is maintained. What, then, can justify this inequality in life-prospects? According to the second principle it is justified only if it is to the advantage of the representative man who is worst off, in this case the representative unskilled labourer. The inequality is permissible because lowering it would, let's suppose, make the working man even worse off than he is. Presumably, given the principle of open offices (the second part of the second principle), the greater expectations allowed to entrepreneurs has the effect in the longer run of raising the life-prospects of the labouring class. The inequality in expectation provides an incentive so that the economy is more efficient, industrial advance proceeds at a quicker pace, and so on, the end result of which is that greater material and other benefits are distributed throughout the system. Of course, all of this is familiar, and whether true or not in particular cases, it is the sort of thing which must be argued if the inequality in income and wealth is to be acceptable by the difference principle.

We should now verify that this interpretation of the second principle gives a natural sense in which everyone may be said to be made better off. Let us suppose that inequalities are chain-connected: that is, if an inequality raises the expectations of the lowest position, it raises the expectations of all positions in between. For example, if the greater expectations of the representative entrepreneur raises that of the unskilled labourer, it also raises that of the semi-skilled. Let us further assume that inequalities are close-knit: that is, it is impossible to raise (or lower) the expectation of any representative man without raising (or lowering) the expectations of every other representative man, and in particular, without affecting one way or the other that of the least fortunate. There is no loose-jointedness, so to speak, in the way in which expectations depend upon one another. Now, with these assumptions, everyone does benefit from an inequality which satisfies the difference principle, and the second principle as we have formulated it reads correctly. For the representative man who is better off in any pair-wise comparison gains by being allowed to have his advantage, and the man who is worse off benefits from the contribution which all inequalities make to each position below. Of course, chain-connection and close-knitness may not obtain; but in this case those who are better off should not have a veto over the advantages available for the least advantaged. The stricter interpretation of the difference principle should be followed, and all inequalities should be arranged for the advantage of the most unfortunate even if some inequalities are not to the advantage of those in middle positions. Should these conditions fail, then, the second principle would have to be stated in another way.

It may be observed that the difference principle represents, in effect, an original agreement to share in the benefits of the distribution of natural talents and abilities, whatever this distribution turns out to be, in order to alleviate as far as possible the arbitrary handicaps resulting from our initial starting places in society. Those who have been favoured by nature, whoever they are, may gain from their good fortune only on terms that improve the well-being of those who have lost out. The naturally advantaged are not to gain simply because they are more gifted, but only to cover the costs of training and cultivating their endowments and for putting them to use in a way which improves the position of the less fortunate. We are led to the difference principle if we wish to arrange the basic social structure so that no one gains (or loses) from his luck in the natural lottery of talent and ability, or from his initial place in society, without giving (or receiving) compensating advantages in return. (The parties in the original position are not said to be attracted by this idea and so agree to it; rather, given the symmetries of their situation, and particularly their lack of knowledge, and so on, they will find it to their interest to agree to a principle which can be understood in this way.) And we should note also that when the difference principle is perfectly satisfied, the basic structure is optimal by the efficiency principle. There is no way to make anyone better off without making someone worse off, namely, the least fortunate representative man. Thus the two principles of justice define distributive shares in a way compatible with efficiency, at least as long as we move on this highly abstract level. If we want to say (as we do, although it cannot be argued here) that the demands of justice have an absolute weight with respect to efficiency, this claim may seem less paradoxical when it is kept in mind that perfectly just institutions are also efficient.

V

Our second question is whether it is possible to arrange the institutions of a constitutional democracy so that the two principles of justice are satisfied, at least approximately. We shall try to show that this can be done provided the government regulates a free economy in a certain way. More fully, if law and government act effectively to keep markets competitive, resources fully employed, property and wealth widely distributed over time, and to maintain the appropriate social minimum, then if there is equality of opportunity underwritten by education for all, the resulting distribution will be just. Of course, all of these arrangements and policies are familiar. The only novelty in the following remarks, if there is any novelty at all, is that this framework of institutions can be made to satisfy the difference principle. To argue this, we must sketch the relations of these institutions and how they work together.

First of all, we assume that the basic social structure is controlled by a just constitution which secures the various liberties of equal citizenship. Thus the legal order is administered in accordance with the principle of legality, and liberty of conscience and freedom of thought are taken for granted. The political process is conducted, so far as possible, as a just procedure for choosing between governments and for enacting just legislation. From the standpoint of distributive justice, it is also essential that there be equality of opportunity in several senses. Thus, we suppose that, in addition to maintaining the usual social overhead capital, government provides for equal educational opportunities for all either by subsidizing private schools or by operating a public school system. It also enforces and underwrites equality of opportunity in commercial ventures and in the free choice of occupation. This result is achieved by policing business behaviour and by preventing the establishment of barriers and restriction to the desirable positions and markets. Lastly, there is a guarantee of a social minimum which the government meets by family allowances and special payments in times of unemployment, or by a negative income tax.

In maintaining this system of institutions the government may be thought of as divided into four branches. Each branch is represented by various agencies (or activities thereof) charged with preserving certain social and economic conditions. These branches do not necessarily overlap with the usual organization of government, but should be understood as purely conceptual. Thus the allocation branch is to keep the economy feasibly competitive, that is, to prevent the formation of unreasonable market power. Markets are competitive in this sense when they cannot be made more so consistent with the requirements of efficiency and the acceptance of the facts of consumer preferences and geography. The allocation branch is also charged with identifying and correcting, say by

suitable taxes and subsidies wherever possible, the more obvious depar-
tures from efficiency caused by the failure of prices to measure accurately
social benefits and costs. The stabilization branch strives to maintain
reasonably full employment so that there is no waste through failure to
use resources and the free choice of occupation and the deployment of
finance is supported by strong effective demand. These two branches
together are to preserve the efficiency of the market economy generally.

The social minimum is established through the operations of the
transfer branch. Later on we shall consider at what level this minimum
should be set, since this is a crucial matter; but for the moment, a few
general remarks will suffice. The main idea is that the workings of the
transfer branch take into account the precept of need and assign it an
appropriate weight with respect to the other common-sense precepts of
justice. A market economy ignores the claims of need altogether. Hence
there is a division of labour between the parts of the social system as
different institutions answer to different common-sense precepts. Competitive markets (properly supplemented by government operations)
handle the problem of the efficient allocation of labour and resources and
set a weight to the conventional precepts associated with wages and
earnings (the precepts of each according to his work and experience, or
responsibility and the hazards of the job, and so on), whereas the transfer
branch guarantees a certain level of well-being and meets the claims of
need. Thus it is obvious that the justice of distributive shares depends
upon the whole social system and how it distributes total income, wages
plus transfers. There is with reason strong objection to the competitive
determination of total income, since this would leave out of account the
claims of need and of a decent standard of life. From the standpoint of the
original position it is clearly rational to insure oneself against these contingencies. But now, if the appropriate minimum is provided by transfers,
it may be perfectly fair that the other part of total income is competitively
determined. Moreover, this way of dealing with the claims of need is
doubtless more efficient, at least from a theoretical point of view, than
trying to regulate prices by minimum wage standards and so on. It is
preferable to handle these claims by a separate branch which supports a
social minimum. Henceforth, in considering whether the second principle of justice is satisfied, the answer turns on whether the total income of
the least advantaged, that is, wages plus transfers, is such as to maximize
their long-term expectations consistent with the demands of liberty.

Finally, the distribution branch is to preserve an approximately just
distribution of income and wealth over time by affecting the background
conditions of the market from period to period. Two aspects of this
branch may be distinguished. First of all, it operates a system of inheritance and gift taxes. The aim of these levies is not to raise revenue, but
gradually and continually to correct the distribution of wealth and to
prevent the concentrations of power to the detriment of liberty and
equality of opportunity. It is perfectly true, as some have said,[3] that
unequal inheritance of wealth is no more inherently unjust than unequal
inheritance of intelligence; as far as possible the inequalities founded on

either should satisfy the difference principle. Thus, the inheritance of greater wealth is just as long as it is to the advantage of the worst off and consistent with liberty, including equality of opportunity. Now by the latter we do not mean, of course, the equality of expectations between classes, since differences in life-prospects arising from the basic structure are inevitable, and it is precisely the aim of the second principle to say when these differences are just. Indeed, equality of opportunity is a certain set of institutions which assures equally good education and chances of culture for all and which keeps open the competition for positions on the basis of qualities reasonably related to performance, and so on. It is these institutions which are put in jeopardy when inequalities and concentrations of wealth reach a certain limit; and the taxes imposed by the distribution branch are to prevent this limit from being exceeded. Naturally enough where this limit lies is a matter for political judgment guided by theory, practical experience, and plain hunch; on this question the theory of justice has nothing to say.

The second part of the distribution branch is a scheme of taxation for raising revenue to cover the costs of public goods, to make transfer payments, and the like. This scheme belongs to the distribution branch since the burden of taxation must be justly shared. Although we cannot examine the legal and economic complications involved, there are several points in favour of proportional expenditure taxes as part of an ideally just arrangement. For one thing, they are preferable to income taxes at the level of common-sense precepts of justice, since they impose a levy according to how much a man takes out of the common store of goods and not according to how much he contributes (assuming that income is fairly earned in return for productive efforts). On the other hand, proportional taxes treat everyone in a clearly defined uniform way (again assuming that income is fairly earned) and hence it is preferable to use progressive rates only when they are necessary to preserve the justice of the system as a whole, that is, to prevent large fortunes hazardous to liberty and equality of opportunity, and the like. If proportional expenditure taxes should also prove more efficient, say because they interfere less with incentives, or whatever, this would make the case for them decisive provided a feasible scheme could be worked out.[4] Yet these are questions of political judgment which are not our concern; and, in any case, a proportional expenditure tax is part of an idealized scheme which we are describing. It does not follow that even steeply progressive income taxes, given the injustice of existing systems, do not improve justice and efficiency all things considered. In practice we must usually choose between unjust arrangements and then it is a matter of finding the lesser injustice.

Whatever form the distribution branch assumes, the argument for it is to be based on justice: we must hold that once it is accepted the social system as a whole—the competitive economy surrounded by a just constitutional and legal framework—can be made to satisfy the principles of justice with the smallest loss in efficiency. The long-term expectations of the least advantaged are raised to the highest level consistent with the demands of equal liberty. In discussing the choice of a distribution scheme we have made no reference to the traditional criteria of taxation according to ability to pay or benefits received; nor have we mentioned any of the variants of the sacrifice principle. These standards are subordinate to the two principles of justice; once the problem is seen as that of designing a whole social system, they assume the status of secondary precepts with no more independent force than the precepts of common sense in regard to wages. To suppose otherwise is not to take a sufficiently comprehensive point of view. In setting up a just distribution branch these precepts may or may not have a place depending upon the demands of the two principles of justice when applied to the entire system. . . .

VII

The sketch of the system of institutions satisfying the two principles of justice is now complete. . . .

In order . . . to establish just distributive shares a just total system of institutions must be set up and impartially administered. Given a just constitution and the smooth working of the four branches of government, and so on, there exists a procedure such that the actual distribution of wealth, whatever it turns out to be, is just. It will have come about as a consequence of a just system of institutions satisfying the principles to which everyone would agree and against which no one can complain. The situation is one of pure procedural justice, since there is no independent criterion by which the outcome can be judged. Nor can we say that a particular distribution of wealth is just because it is one which could have resulted from just institutions although it has not, as this would be to allow too much. Clearly there are many distributions which may be reached by just institutions, and this is true whether we count patterns of distributions among social classes or whether we count distributions of particular goods and services among particular individuals. There are indefinitely many outcomes and what makes one of these just is that it has been achieved by actually carrying out a just scheme of co-operation as it is publicly understood. It is the result which has arisen when everyone receives that to which he is entitled given his and others' actions guided by their legitimate expectations and their obligations to one another. We can no more arrive at a just distribution of wealth except by working together within the framework of a just system of institutions than we can win or lose fairly without actually betting.

This account of distributive shares is simply an elaboration of the familiar idea that economic rewards will be just once a perfectly competitive price system is organized as a fair game. But in order to do this we have to begin with the choice of a social system as a whole, for the basic structure of the entire arrangement must be just. The economy must be surrounded with the appropriate framework of institutions, since even a perfectly efficient price system has no tendency to determine just distributive shares when left to itself. Not only must economic activity be regulated by a just constitution and controlled by the four branches of government, but a just saving-function must be adopted to estimate the provision to be made for future generations. . . .

Notes

1. In this essay I try to work out some of the implications of the two principles of justice discussed in 'Justice as Fairness' which first appeared in the *Philosophical Review*, 1958, and which is reprinted in *Philosophy, Politics and Society*, Series II, pp. 132–57.
2. This question is discussed very briefly in 'Justice as Fairness,' see pp. 138–41. The intuitive idea is as follows. Given the circumstances of the original position, it is rational for a man to choose as if he were designing a society in which his enemy is to assign him his place. Thus, in particular, given the complete lack of knowledge (which makes the choice one under uncertainty), the fact that the decision involves one's life-prospects as a whole and is constrained by obligations to third parties (e.g., one's descendants) and duties to certain values (e.g., to religious truth), it is rational to be conservative and so to choose in accordance with an analogue of the maximin principle. Viewing the situation in this way, the interpretation given to the principles of justice in Section IV is perhaps natural enough. Moreover, it seems clear how the principle of utility can be interpreted; it is the analogue of the Laplacean principle for choice uncertainty. (For a discussion of these choice criteria, see R. D. Luce and H. Raiffa, *Games and Decisions* (1957), pp. 275–98).
3. Example F. von Hayek, *The Constitution of Liberty* (1960), p. 90.
4. See N. Kaldor, *An Expenditure Tax* (1955).

Social Accounting and the American Dream

MARGARET MEAD

Why are Americans, as a people, unable to understand social accounting—the costs in money of the mistakes we make organizing our society and caring for human beings? Government and industry have very complex systems of cost-benefit analysis; the "bottom line" is repeatedly invoked in policy discussions. But when it comes to calculating the relatively minor expenditures necessary now to prevent some catastrophic social cost later, we seem quite unable to do it. An outstanding example is our willingness to spend an average of $11,000 per delinquent child for institutionalization practically guaranteed to turn the delinquents into criminals whose eventual cost to society may be as great as $300,000 during their criminal lifetimes, rather than take the necessary steps to care for these children before they begin a delinquent career. Why are we so willing to pay more for worse? Why are we so bent on

From *Business and Society Review*, XIX (Fall 1976). Reprinted with permission from the publisher.

making mistakes, and making the same mistakes over and over again, rather than learning from experience? Would a fuller recognition of these repeated errors and repeated costs make a difference, or do we need other changes in society first?

My competence to speak of problems of this sort comes from field work during the last fifty years in very small societies which were undergoing very rapid change. I have followed the fate of the entire community in one of these groups—the lagoon-dwelling, seafaring Manus of the South Coast of the Admiralty Islands in Papua, New Guinea—for forty-seven years, through four generations. I watched them transform themselves under external pressures from government, mission, technological change, World War II, and the postwar political climate, which plunged even the most primitive peoples into nationhood.[1] Studies of this sort are impossible to conduct in our very large, complex societies, but they constitute "living models." These studies supplement the insights which can be derived from simulations, which, while enormously productive, still cannot give us kinds of understanding of the interrelatedness of events which living models have been able to produce.

From the study of such small communities at a microscale, we learn ways of thinking about larger wholes: the nation, now an interdependent part of an emerging planetary system; the solar system; the galaxy. Practice in working with wholes enables us to make allowance for what we do not know, and it contributes levels of unexpectedness of a different order from the "counterintuitive findings" that are developed in computer simulations based on defective hypotheses.[2] Working with living systems, small enough so that there is no need to sample because every member of the small universe can be individually taken into account, one need not have hypotheses in order to investigate: one only has to be open to events as they occur.

From the actual study in this case of extremely rapid social changes, in which preliterate, Stone Age people leapt some 10,000 years of technical and political evolution to enter the modern age, came the unexpected finding that fast, across-the-board, total change works better than slow change. With the latter, only parts of a system change, and the system itself becomes encumbered by maladaptations among the parts that are changing at different rates. Previously, less intensive cross-sectional samplings of change in primitive and peasant societies had led to the erroneous conclusion that slow change was preferable to more rapid change. "You have to crawl before you can walk" was a cherished admonition of European colonial government. Since "crawling" inspired little enthusiasm from those asked to practice it, it was a useful way to delay their participation in the modern world. . . .

Within the United States itself, partly because our economy and our ecosystem are both subject to such events beyond our borders and over which we have no control, and partly because of some of our cultural characteristics (which I will discuss in a moment), there is also no central control of any sort. Separate segments of the system—a single industry, or a large conglomerate industry, a city, a government agency, one branch of the military—barge ahead on their own, disregarding at best, destroying at worst, other parts of the national system. Thus the automobile industry destroyed the street railroads of Los Angeles. The practices of the internal revenue system discouraged private philanthropy. One federal agency demands an accounting of how many minority employees a firm has, while another federal agency declares it illegal to mention ethnicity! Everyone wealthy enough to choose a site for a house of his own wants a "view," i.e., a landscape unmarred by the presence of anyone else. There is an almost total lack of any kind of coordination, of provisional assessment before new technologies are launched on the market. And in the case of the largest industries, even considerations of profit, those expected marketplace controls of a free enterprise system, can be laid aside for years in the interests of the self-perpetuation and self-aggrandizement of enormous, self-propelling enterprises.

If we look back for a moment to the last time this country had a shared national purpose, and compare it with what we can do today, contemporary inefficiency is staggering. It now takes us many more years to build than it did during World War II, even though we are working with far better tools. Our capacity to put a new product into mass production, of which we were so justly proud through the mid-1940s, has deteriorated. Our agriculture has become a giant miscalculation,[3] so that we boast that it is the most efficient in the world, counting only the one man on the farm who feeds thirty, while we forget the other men who must produce the machinery, the fuel, the fertilizer, the transport, and then do the marketing. As we develop new measures—measures for energy used in agriculture, measures for the success of an educational system—as we fumble for systems of "accountability" in public life, it is clear that these measures are applied independently of one another. What the tax dollar buys today does not include an adequate assessment of what these expenditures will result in ten years hence. As a result, public expenditure on education and health and sanitation is recurrently stupid, terribly expensive, and hopelessly inefficient.

We now have a society which is filled with runaway positive feedbacks. These are vicious circles, in which each input exaggerates the runaway character. Our highway expenditures are perhaps the best example. They are based on a tax from gasoline, and the circle works as follows: the more highways, the easier it is to use automobiles, the more gas is burned, the higher the yield of the tax, the more highways, etc., in an unending acceleration. Hospital costs under our present system of management represent the same runaway: the higher the costs, the higher the charges, until as a New York taxi driver recently said to me, "You can't afford to get sick, you can't afford to die, and you can't afford to live." By organizing our health reimbursement systems so that patients have to be put in the hospital to receive their insurance benefits, we overcrowd the hospitals, their costs go up, the costs of insurance and health care go up. We choke our prisons with unnecessary arrests and thereby fail to keep dangerous criminals in prison.

Housing and the treatment of early signs of delinquency—truancy.

failure to learn to read, signs of home neglect—are two of the fields in which long experience seems to have had no effect at all. As for the $11,000 spent in bad institutions to turn children into criminals—if we properly designed our communities and our schools, the child who is failing or frantic from neglect could be located and cared for at a fraction of the cost.

New York City has devised community colleges that could turn exceedingly deprived and unpromising young people into self-supporting citizens, but with the financial crunch, our educational institutions suffered. Night schools and evening schools, which would have produced taxpayers rather than burdens on the tax rolls, are being closed. The continuing shortsightedness of all of our planning, the way in which not only the political system, but also industrial management is set up to sacrifice long-time responsible planning for immediate popular tax savings (in the case of elected politicians), and immediate profits (in the case of industry), are intimately related to other aspects of our culture. Because of the tremendous natural wealth of this country, we have been able to survive and prosper, taking no thought for the morrow, carelessly sacrificing a tenth of our children, depending on new immigration to provide the necessary labor, and depending upon unchecked growth to take up the slack.

THE HAZARDS OF OUR CONDITION

But the parlous state of the country bears witness to the hazardousness of our present condition. The costs of crime mount, yet retailers would rather pay huge insurance rates and take huge losses than humanize their stores by employing more clerks and raising the morale of their employees. People insure themselves against burglary and then do not collect for fear that their insurance will be canceled and some day there will be a greater loss. A city like New York lets more old buildings be destroyed by abandonment and vandalism than it builds. The streets become unsafe, not only for those who tangle with unsavory parts of society, but for any citizen. The untrammeled pursuit of immediate profits by a special overprotected industry threatens us with the proliferation of plutonium all over the world, greatly increasing the dangers to the safety of present generations and future generations.[4]

With possibly a few exceptions, I do not believe that any of these disastrous current situations can be attributed to the malice or viciousness of individual men, or even to the existence of certain types of agencies or conglomerates. I believe they are, rather, a function of the kind of relationships we have between different parts of contemporary society, and of the continuation of aspects of American culture which were themselves historically determined. The early immigrant, the pioneer, could not afford to look back; he might have been so overcome with nostalgia that he would want to go home again. He could not afford to remember anything, including his mistakes. He lived in a world where all of the rewards went to the enterprising who forged ahead, regardless of his fellows—someone who looked for a house with a view. Today, these same characteristics are the characteristics of industries, agencies, power companies, and the cities with which their fate is intertwined.

Our curious unwillingness to prevent mistakes can be partly attributed to the fact that, generation after generation, our culture has been learned by young adults, in contrast to the way the culture is learned during childhood in old societies. Our immigrant young adults could not be resubjected to the socializing processes of an American childhood. Accordingly, adjustment to the new culture was left to books, on the one hand, and to making one's own mistakes, on the other. Instead of learning to do something as a part of education in the United States, people learn to do things as they need to. We have books about how to make love, how to get married, how to get divorced, how to rear children. Each adult alone with a book is free to make his or her own mistakes. When elaborated, this produces the curious anomalies of systems like the New York subway, in which the maps are on the trains, so that you have to get on the train to find out whether or not it is the right one. Similarly today, where we have almost one divorce to one marriage, people have to get married to learn what not to do if they want a marriage to last. This tendency to leave people to their own devices, to learn by success and failure, has become an integral part of our culture.

Our social choices are characterized either by repeats of exactly the same kind of error—as in the attempt of one part of the population to prohibit the use of alcohol by the other, repeated in the prohibition of marijuana with the same disastrous consequences—or by our various experiments with price controls. There are many other analogous failures, particularly in our treatment of children. Five times, we have attempted to remedy a grievous institutional condition by taking the children out and leaving the institution itself unchanged. First we had the juvenile court, followed by the juvenile detention home, the junior high school, the central city, and now our treatment of child abuse. Each time we have taken the children out and left the offending institutional setting unchanged, i.e., the criminal court, the prison, the gigantic urban high school, deteriorated inner city, and the desperate isolation of frantic mothers and fathers. And now we are laboriously trying to undo an error, to grope our way back to exactly the same situation which we originally tried to remedy. We are providing due process for young offenders, instead of developing new and more inclusive ways to bring up and care for children, support parental activities, and educate future citizens.

What is urgently needed is some way in which Americans, as planners, as managers, as taxpayers, can begin to recognize the advantages of taking steps which in the present are a little more expensive, but which will have an enormous pay-off in the future. There are many available models for such activities: annuities, cheaper if you buy them sooner; insurance, cheaper if you buy it younger; stocks, which will appreciate. The attempt has repeatedly been made to convince Americans that we should conserve our "human resources." There have been efforts to convince those who control our cities that it is poor economy to give poor schools and poor public housing to people who are currently poor.

These efforts have failed. Somehow, the arguments which have been used have clashed with some deep-seated values, such as the belief that the enterprising made their present success all by themselves. If the presently unsuccessful need help, this throws doubt upon the extent to which previous generations of self-made men, and women, accomplished what they did on their own. As the climate of opinion alters and we learn a little about the relationship between early opportunity—for good food, stable homes, good schools—and later success, our attempts to provide in the present what we failed to provide in the past are resented. Thus the efforts made on behalf of Blacks and Chicanos are resented by "White ethnics" who protest that nobody helped them. Failure in the past, our willingness to let earlier immigrants struggle alone with a high casualty rate, now dogs our footsteps in the present, as surely as the past failure to consider the biodegradability of detergents has cost soap manufacturers unnecessary millions.

We need a rephrasing of planning, so that we take into account the long time consequences and spend a little more now to save a great deal in the future, if we are to rescue this country from its trend toward social disintegration. The United States cannot save the world alone; it can destroy the world all alone with nuclear power, with environmental destruction, or with a type of socioeconomic disorganization which affects the whole world. But if the fragile planetary society is to be saved, we need to translate our exasperated "We can't feed the whole world!" (one of our ways of recognizing that we have no omnipotent powers) into some phrasing about what we can do and will want to do.

Traditionally, we have been able to pull ourselves together and suppress our individualism in wartime. I believe that in peacetime it is too much individualism, rather than mere selfishness or profit-seeking or institutional perpetuation, that has been to blame. In World War II, the Seabees could boast: *The difficult we do immediately. The impossible takes a little longer.* Can the present dangers from thermonuclear power, from a polluted environment, from a threatened atmosphere, from a disorganized but interdependent world, be so phrased that we will be able to do real social accounting and be willing to pay today for the good of tomorrow?

Notes

1. Margaret Mead, *New Lives for Old: Cultural Transformation—Manus, 1928–1953* (New York: Morrow, 1956).
2. Douella H. Meadows and others, *The Limits to Growth* (Washington: Potomac Associates, 1972); and Mihajlo Mesarovich and Eduard Pestel, *Mankind at the Turning Point* (New York: Dutton, 1974).
3. David Pimentel, William Dritschilo, John Krummel, and John Kutzman, "Energy and Land Constraints in Food Protein Production," *Science*, 190 (Summer 1975), pp. 754–61.
4. Barry Commoner, *The Poverty of Power* (New York: Knopf, 1976).

RIGHTS, LIABILITY, AND THE STATE

Part III

The very subject of ethics assumes that each of us is not a hermit existing separately from the world of others. We are involved in a variety of human relationships, and it is with these interactions that major questions of ethics first arise. Corporations, too , do not exist in a vacuum, and ethical questions in business develop in large part from corporate relationships with other organizations and individuals. The following three relationships will serve as the focus of the readings in this part:

1. between business and employees,
2. between business and the consumer, and
3. between business and the government.

Many of the ethical issues which emerge from these relationships center around the notions of rights, obligations, and responsibilities. For example, ordinarily a business hires employees on the basis of its needs and the qualifications of the applicants. Yet often job applicants claim that they have been the victims of discrimination, and that their rights as applicants have been violated. Do corporations have specific obligations to honor certain rights of applicants and employees? Taking another example, sometimes a product will escape quality-control checks and injure the consumer. What special obligations regarding their products, if any, should businesses accept as a part of their relationship to the consumer? Finally, consider the relationship between business and government. In the past business did not concern itself much with political affairs, and government, in turn, was expected to keep out of the affairs of private business. Recently, however, government has played an increasing role in business through regulation and special legislation. What is the proper function of governmental regulation, and what problems in business, if any, should government attempt to solve? Businesses are now responding to such regulation by trying to influence the government through lobbying and public relations campaigns. Obviously, such responses generate their own set of problems involving the rights and responsibilities of business vis à vis government.

BUSINESS AND THE EMPLOYEE: RIGHTS AND OBLIGATIONS

We have been accustomed to hearing about rights—for example, about the Bill of Rights in the U.S. Constitution—and to hearing claims about rights, as when one might claim to "have a right to be treated with respect by one's boss." But philosophers as well as ordinary people have had major disagreements about the definition of a right. The notion of a right, however, is important, not only because it serves as a conceptual underpinning for modern democratic government, but also because in the present context determining the rights of employees and those of business institutions will help to set the proper limits of a great deal of business conduct.

The term "right" which we use today is derived in part from the philosophical concept of a *natural* right. A natural right, whether it be a right to liberty or a right to worship, may be regarded as a justified privilege to which every person has a claim simply because he is human. Are there rights which apply without exception to everyone in all circumstances? Many philosophers have questioned the very plausibility of such a notion. For example, John Locke claims that all people have the natural right to "life, health, liberty, and possessions," but he would not claim that, say, the right to life or liberty applies without exception to criminals or to the enemy in times of war. However, certain rights have been regarded as "universal" in the sense that they apply to everyone in the same way, and as "inalienable" in the sense that they cannot be taken away from anyone without justification. For example, the right to liberty, if it is a universal right, applies to all people equally and can be denied to someone only if in similar circumstances it would be denied to anyone else.

In his article, "Justice and Equality," the contemporary philosopher Gregory Vlastos raises the question, "Should all people have the same rights?" Vlastos discusses how treating people unequally on the basis of merit is consistent with the equal assignment of rights, where each person—regardless of his merit—is assigned the same rights as any other. For example, faster swimmers receive more medals and trophies than slower swimmers, yet we accept the unequal rewards as just. So why should people of unequal talents and merits have the same rights? Vlastos answers his own question by focusing upon what he believes to be the fundamental principle underlying the assignment of rights, namely, the *equality of human worth*. The freedom and well-being of one person is not assumed to have any more intrinsic worth than the freedom and wellbeing of any other. A simple example may help illustrate this point: If an instructor were to assign grades to his students based on how well they performed on an exam, then he would be awarding grades justly in accordance with a standard of merit. But we would regard it as outrageous for people to be assigned, say, the right to vote on the basis of how well they performed on an exam (although unfortunately passing literacy tests sometimes used to be required). Such rights as voting rights and the right to equal treatment under the law presumably depend upon the recognized equality of human worth.

One of the most important and influential documents in this area is the UN *Universal Declaration of Human Rights,* excerpts of which are included in this part. This document attempts to specify certain rights, indicating not only what all people should be *able to do,* such as to speak freely or participate in their government, but also what people should *have.* These "should have" rights, or rights to positive benefits, include those of social security and a decent standard of living. Many people would argue that there is no such thing as the right to a decent standard of living; it is not something which can be given but something which must be earned. And yet it is important to understand that the *Declaration* is not understood by some people as a general demand for all governments to provide economic benefits to their citizens; instead, it is meant to be merely a specification of a twentieth-century ideal of what constitutes a satisfactory human existence. The extent to which government should intervene in economic affairs and guarantee human rights is a matter of dispute— even among those who subscribe to the ideas which form the *Declaration.* Who should assume the obligation of seeing that such rights are satisfied? For example, should governments insure that everyone has an opportunity for a job? Or is it best to leave the insuring of such rights out of the hands of the government? Does business have any responsibility to help implement such rights?

One right listed in the *Declaration* which directly concerns business is the right of everyone to be treated equally in matters of hiring, pay, and promotion. If one may be said to have such a right, then presumably business managers have a corresponding obligation to not pursue discriminatory policies. For example, business organizations should be obliged to hire on the basis of applicant competence without being swayed by irrelevant factors, e.g., sex, race, or ethnic origin. Most business people today recognize this obligation. A more controversial issue is whether business has an obligation to go beyond the point of merely "not discriminating" in order to pursue what is called affirmative action. Affirmative action programs are of at least two sorts:

1. those which pursue a policy of deliberately favoring qualified minorities and women when hiring or promoting; and
2. those which establish quota systems to regulate the percentage of minority members hired or promoted in accordance with an ideal distribution of race, sex, creed, and/or ethnicity.

Perhaps the most common objection to affirmative action programs is that they are unjust and inconsistent, i.e., that they make the same mistakes they hope to remedy. If discrimination means using a morally irrelevant characteristic, such as a person's skin color, as a factor in hiring, then is affirmative action itself perpetuating unjust discrimination? In giving preference to, say, blacks over whites are such programs using the same morally irrelevant characteristic previously used in discriminatory practices?

Defenders of affirmative action argue that these programs are, all things considered, fair and not inconsistent with human rights in that they are necessary to compensate past injustices in employment practices—injustices which clearly damaged the well-being and future prospects of a great many members of society. Compensation, then, must be made to those victims of discrimination. Moreover, it is maintained that affirmative action programs are necessary to guarantee fairness in hiring and promotion for future generations; for how will minority applicants ever seriously compete for positions in, say, medical school, unless the educational and economic opportunities for minorities and nonminorities are equalized? And how will educational and economic opportunities be equalized unless minorities are able to attain a fair share of society's highest level of jobs? It is important to understand both the arguments for and against affirmative action in order to see clearly its consequences for modern business.

Discrimination is not the only issue involved in the relationship between business and its employees. National attention has been focused on pension rights in the last few years when employees have claimed the loss of pensions through corporate or union mismanagement. The case presented in this section, "Pension Benefits," illustrates the difficulties of retaining a good pension plan in the face of economic pressures. It also illustrates the need, from the employee's standpoint, of a guaranteed living wage at retirement.

BUSINESS AND THE CONSUMER:
RESPONSIBILITY AND LIABILITY

In 1977, an important survey printed in the *Harvard Business Review* (see the Brenner and Molander survey in Part IV) indicated that business people feel most responsible to consumers; that is, the first order of business for the corporation was satisfying the customer rather than maximizing profit. Yet understanding the precise nature of business' responsibility to the consumer requires looking beyond traditional business interests, like the need to sell quality products at reasonable prices. It also involves certain ethical issues, including the responsibility of the manufacturer for faulty products, dangerous products, or products which do not live up to advertising claims. What rights and obligations exist for both manufacturers and consumers in the marketplace?

In his article, "The Moral Responsibility of Corporations," the contemporary philosopher David Ozar looks at ways in which formally organized groups, including corporations and other business groups, may be said to have responsibilities and obligations in much the same way as individual people. It is true that we do not send corporations to jail for misconduct; but corporations, just as individual human beings, are held morally accountable for their actions. It follows from Ozar's analysis that corporations may be said to have certain moral obligations to their consumers. We are reminded when reading his article of the arguments concerning the ascription of moral responsibility to organizations presented by Ladd and Goodpaster in Part I.

The role and extent of *legal* corporate liability to the consumer are discussed by Lawrence and Arnold Bennigson in their article, "Product Liability: Manufacturers Beware!" The Bennigsons analyze the changing character of liability law and emphasize the ways in which the old adage of "Buyer Beware!" has been replaced with "Seller Beware!" This issue is illustrated in the case study, "Hasbro Industries," in which a toy manufacturer is accused of making items which are both physically and psychologically dangerous to their users. This case questions the extent to which a corporation should be morally and legally responsible to the consumer, and it suggests the need for a distinction between the concepts of moral responsibility and legal liability.

BUSINESS AND GOVERNMENT: THE ROLE OF THE STATE

The increasing role of government in the economic affairs of private enterprise is of great concern to business. For the modern business manager, the relationship between business and government often signifies red tape, regulations, and bureaucracy—a kind of mandatory invitation to inefficiency. But for others, the relationship represents the crucial intersection at which the activities of business can be redirected toward the public good. In the context of this dispute, we shall focus on the moral aspects of the relationship and ask such questions as, Does the state have a moral responsibility to protect its citizens by policing the actions of business? When is government overstepping the rights and freedoms of business; i.e., are there values inherent in the self-regulation of business which are too important to sacrifice?

It is argued by Milton Friedman and others that the preservation of the free enterprise system requires a strongly limited government role. And even if most economic theorists would agree that some kind of government involvement in business affairs should occur, many would deny the necessity of any regulation beyond a bare minimal level, principally for two reasons. First, it is believed that government regulation will lead to inefficiencies on a grand scale because economic incentive tends to vanish when the government interferes with the competitive marketplace. Second, the participation of government in business can restrict people's activities, the critics believe, in ways which erode the basic freedoms which serve as the foundation of our society. The case study, "OSHA," illustrates some of these potential problems and questions whether the government can enforce moral standards in business without interfering with the freedoms and rights which business presumably should possess.

Not only government but business itself has been frequently criticized for dominating modern society and stifling individual freedom. Indeed, the growth of corporations and the corresponding expansion of labor unions are often seen as a threat to individualism and personal happiness. Certain business practices in the past, such as unfair labor practices, poor manufacturing standards, deceptive advertising, monopolistic practices, and disrespect for the environment suggest to some critics a need for external government regulation. The crucial question, then, appears to be whether it is government which needs curtailing or business. Donald Kendall, in his article "How to Halt Excessive Government Regulation," assumes that the preservation and continuation of the private free enterprise system is necessary for human freedom. To preserve the privacy and individuality of economic activities, Kendall argues, government regulation must be drastically decreased; but the role of government in economic affairs can be reduced only if business itself seriously sets its own high moral standards and conscientiously undertakes the task of self-regulation.

BUSINESS AND THE EMPLOYEE: RIGHTS AND OBLIGATIONS

Case Study—Affirmative Action in Theory and in Practice

LINDA CALVERT and
LEON C. MEGGINSON

The Apex* plant, an operating facility of Petrochem Corporation, was one of many plants operating as part of the petrochemical complex of the Gulf coastal region. Much of the industrial growth in this region was relatively recent, so Apex, like many other plants in this area, was a modern growth-oriented facility.

During recent years, Petrochem Corporation had taken a firm stand as an "Equal Opportunity Employer" and Apex was working under an affirmative action plan with the goal of achieving within five years a work force mixture which matched that of the recruiting area in both ethnic background and sex.

To achieve this work force distribution at both the exempt and nonexempt levels while maintaining its basic entry standards, the Apex plant recruited extensively at black universities and vocational schools. The plant also maintained close contact with other state universities, private employment agencies, the state employment agency, local high schools, and various civic and community groups. However, the prime source of both minority and female applicants had been, and continued to be, referrals by the Apex plant employees themselves.

Although the plant had considered offering training courses for applicants who fell below minimum standards, this approach had been avoided since previous experience had shown that job applicants tended to view acceptance into the training courses as tantamount to a job offer. However, the plant had worked through the local school board in providing various cooperative and adult education courses. The plant also

*All names have been disguised.

This case was prepared by Linda Calvert and Leon C. Megginson of Louisiana State University as the basis for class discussion rather than to illustrate either effective or ineffective handling of administrative situations. Distributed by the Intercollegiate Case Clearing House, Soldiers Field, Boston, Mass. 02163. All rights reserved to the contributors. Printed in the U.S.A.

maintained an active summer-hire program which was used to identify potential minority group employees.

Apex's in-house program for minority groups consisted of compiling a work history for each minority group member and then assessing his or her promotional potential. Additional training needed, as well as potential openings, were identified. Any time openings actually did develop, the affirmative action list was reviewed for potential candidates.

All affirmative action programs were reviewed and updated on a quarterly basis. First-line supervisors were responsible for individual training and development while upper level management scrutinized departmental compliance with the goals set.

While the objectives, programs, and policies of the firm were altruistic and desirable, their effectiveness depended upon their interpretation and implementation.

When Charles Gunn, age 22, was hired by the Apex plant in 1969, he was the third black technician to be employed in the Alpha unit. Carl Myers, the first black hired, was now supervisor of "D" shift and the second black hired, Henry Sherman, was a technician on "C" shift. Figure 1 gives a partial organizational structure for the Alpha unit:

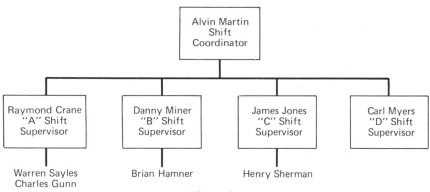

Figure 1.

Prior to joining Petrochem, Charles had completed three years in the U.S. Army as a radio operator. He had entered the military after high school because he figured his low "C" average in high school would not be sufficient to see him through college.

At Apex, Charles was placed on the "A" shift of the Alpha unit with Raymond Crane as his supervisor and Warren Sayles, another technician, as his "trainer." Raymond had been hired in 1966 as a technician immediately after he finished college. With his strong technical background, he had "done extremely well" and was promoted to supervisor in 1968, six months before Charles was hired.

Warren, the trainer for "A" shift, had had about three years of college and was unquestionably the best technician on that particular shift. When Warren found out that he would be training Charles, he expressed some "Apprehensions about training a black" since he had never worked side by side with a black before. However, he had trained several other technicians and said he would do his best.

When Charles reported to Alpha unit, Raymond introduced him to the other technicians, showed him his locker, gave him some study guides, and turned him over to Warren. (The study guides were basically a list of questions which the trainees should be able to answer once they had learned the unit operations from the trainer.)

Since the new technician was told to spend this training period "in his trainer's back pocket," Warren and Charles were almost inseparable for the next five months. Charles asked questions; Warren answered. They went over the extractive and recovery systems, schematics of the process, start-up and shut-down procedures, reading and sampling methods, and procedures for logging information.

About once a month Warren and Charles sat down to evaluate the progress Charles was making. In the first of these sessions Warren noted that Charles was not making any progress at all. After two or three months, Warren noted slight—but not satisfactory—progress.

After five months, Charles was still only taking samples, a procedure normally picked up in the first few weeks of training. Warren felt that Charles was not putting forth the effort needed to learn the job. Charles agreed that he needed to improve but did not agree that he was not putting forth satisfactory effort. The reports passed along to Raymond during this period reflected Warren's evaluation of Charles, but did not contain any of Charles' reactions.

About six months after Charles had started to work, Warren went on vacation. Although supervisors normally assign a trainee to someone else if their trainer goes on vacation, Raymond neglected to make such a reassignment for Charles. Meanwhile Henry, the other black technician, had been placed on temporary duty with "A" shift and, thus, "Charles gravitated rather naturally to Henry."

It was during this period that Charles began to grasp just how far behind the other technicians he really was. However, with Henry using simplified examples and then applying them to the unit processes, Charles began to grasp things that had completely escaped him before. By the end of a week, Charles understood the extractive process of the unit—the most difficult part of the unit to learn.

Within a couple of days after Warren returned from vacation, Warren and Charles again sat down for an evaluation session and again Warren reiterated Charles' lack of progress. But Charles was not satisfied this time. For the next few days he thought things over and asked questions of the other technicians to make sure that he really did understand the extractive process. Finally, he went back to Warren and at the end of Warren's first week back from vacation, the two ended up in their first meeting with Raymond.

Charles felt that he understood the extractive process of the unit, but Warren did not agree. The session boiled down to bickering and was finally brought to a close with Raymond's nonchalant, "You guys will just have to work this thing out yourselves."

Things simmered along for the next three or four days with Charles still dissatisfied but uncertain about what to do next. Things came to a head the next Monday morning when Alvin Martin, the shift coordinator, and Charles happened to run into each other. Since Alvin rarely saw the technicians, he tried to use any chance meeting to get a quick reading on "the mood of the troops."

"How are things going?" was all Charles needed to pour out his frustrations.

Alvin reacted by immediately setting up a meeting with Raymond and Charles. In this meeting Raymond stated that Charles was at best "a marginal performer" or perhaps even "a slow learner." Charles countered with charges of discrimination in his training. Raymond came back with the fact that if Charles had, indeed, learned the extractive process of the unit, then he must have been getting proper training. Not willing to back down, Charles explained that Henry had taught him this particular part of the unit while Warren was on vacation.

Charles left the meeting with the understanding that his performance was, in fact, deficient in several areas and he would need to work on those things. Alvin and Raymond continued "hot and heavy" for the next several hours.

Charles had told a story "heavily steeped in racial overtones." Though he admitted that Warren had answered all his questions without irritation, he felt that Warren had not volunteered as much information as he had to the other technicians. (Later talks with the other technicians confirmed that Warren did not seem to have gone into the detail with Charles that he had with the other technicians.)

At that point, though, the hostilities were pretty firmly entrenched and Alvin felt that a change had to be made—but what? Since Henry had proven that Charles could learn, and since Charles worked well with Henry, a move to "C" shift was pretty tempting. Or, there was "D" shift with the only black supervisor.

Alvin finally decided that either moving Charles to "C" shift to work with Henry, or to "D" shift to work under the only black supervisor, was simply an easy way out and represented, at best, a temporary solution. With this conclusion, Charles was transferred to "B" shift.

Charles' new supervisor was Danny Miner. Danny had a two-year technical degree and had taught mathematics and drawing at a vocational-technical college. Danny had worked around blacks on a "give-and-take" basis nearly all of his life and had no real apprehensions about Charles joining his shift. On Charles' first day, Danny sat down and explained what he expected of Charles and what Charles could expect from him.

During that week, he and Charles did what is known as a "walk through" of the unit. Starting at the front door and going to the back door, Danny and Charles went through the unit with Charles explaining everything that he could about the unit. Danny could see Charles had a lot of problems but that he did understand the extractive process—again the most difficult part of the unit.

Danny continued to ask questions and listen. He used Carl, the black supervisor, as a sounding board—trying to find out more about Charles, trying to find the best way to work with him. In his conversations with Charles, Danny soon found out that Charles had only had Math and Algebra I in high school, had made a "D" in Chemistry, and had "avoided" physics.

In the military service, Charles had had problems when he started in the school for radio operators, but he eventually caught up and did well. Danny concluded that Charles could learn, but simply had to be brought along more slowly than the other technicians.

After the first week, Danny decided to turn Charles over to Brian Hamner for training. Brian was not "the best technician in the unit," in fact, according to the personnel manager, he was average in just about every sense of the word. He was methodical—neither too fast nor too slow. He was dependable, somewhat of a stickler for detail, and had plenty of patience.

Although this assignment worked out well, there was some subsequent talk of rotating Charles to other technicians to improve his technical skills. However, the decision was made to work with both Brian and Charles on technical skills rather than singling Charles out for special training.

After four years, Charles was "not considered supervisory material," according to the personnel manager, but he was an "average" to "above average" performer and was taking some correspondence courses to upgrade his technical skills.

Case Study—Pension Benefits and Profitability

CHARLES W. WERHANE

In about 1965 American management of the wholly owned Belgian subsidiary of a well-known American company decided to adopt a pension plan. The American parent had maintained a pension plan and a profit-sharing trust for a number of years. The relevant difference between a pension plan and a profit-sharing trust is that the former requires a specified contribution from the company each year, whether the company has had a good year, a poor year, or even lost money. Future pensions must always be funded, despite the company's current success, and reserves or funding to be set aside are determined by: (1) ages of the covered employees, (2) their salaries or wages, (3) their lengths of service with the company. Profit sharing, on the other hand, is a setting-

This case, prepared by Charles W. Werhane, General Counsel, Culligan International, Inc., especially for this anthology, was originally presented at the Mellon Foundation Lecture Series on "Foundations of Corporate Responsibility to Society," April 1977, at Loyola University of Chicago.

aside by the company of a percentage of its annual profits to be shared by all employees in proportion to their salaries and length of service, but it is given only upon the retirement of each employee.

Thus, pension obligations are a continuing burden without regard to a company's current profitability. But profit sharing is a sharing of current profits—the more the company earns the more the employees share; no profits, no sharing. It should not be surprising that companies, when young and not yet mature, generally prefer to commit themselves to profit sharing long before they are willing to take on the fixed burdens of a pension plan. Recent U.S. federal pension legislation has increased this propensity. While both plans are always written so that the company can cancel the plan at any time, an act of cancellation is unpalatable to employees or employee morale and is detestable to labor unions. Such right has been exercised only in extreme situations.

The Belgian subsidiary adopted an overly generous plan. The intention was to provide its employees with retirement benefits roughly equal to those of the American parent company, taking into account both the latter's pension and profit-sharing plans. Thus, three-fourths of preretirement average best five years' annual salary was guaranteed for thirty years' service. This 75 percent of pay upon retirement (maximum) includes Belgian social security. So if any employee earned $1,000 per month average during his last five years employment (age 55–60), and had been with the company thirty years or more, he would retire with $775 per month, funded from Belgian social security plus the necessary additional portion paid from the pension plan. Fifteen years' service would yield half that amount, layered from the same two sources.

Since 1965, wages (and prices) have truly gone "out of sight" in Belgium. Inflation has devalued the local currency at a greater rate—and thus wages have climbed at a greater rate—than the interest return on investments, so the earnings on pension funds already set aside have not kept pace with the projected pension obligations calculated on compounding salary and wage costs. Belgium has a somewhat insidious cost-of-living escalator which affects almost everything—rents, wages, and salaries, actually the very economic structure of the country. Belgium has also been socially ambitious and has been pouring into its social security program things like early forced retirement benefits for older employees to ease unemployment of young people entering the work force. This has caused the company's burden for various required fringe benefits or "social charges" to increase from 15 to 35 percent of comparable wages (much higher than in the United States) since 1965. But while such costs have increased for the company, the actual retirements' benefits portion of Belgian social security has not increased in proportion to this 15-to-35 percent ratio. So the company is obligated by its retirement plan to pay vastly increased annual funding to assure pension coverage of double-digit increasing salary and wage rates, while the social security platform underlying these retirement benefits is shrinking. At the same time the company is forced to pay greatly increased amounts to the government social security administration to cover the increased general social activities.

It should not be surprising that the company finds its profitability seriously impaired since 1965, and that it faces the prospect of closing entirely if trends continue.

One recommendation by the American parent company—the shareholders and owners of this Belgian company—is to reduce pension benefits. For example, the plan could be spread over forty years instead of thirty years of service (which is the case for the parent); the 75 percent maximum retirement benefit could be reduced, perhaps to as low as 50 percent; the plan could be changed from a full company-paid plan to a contributory plan, with employees paying as much as half the cost from their wages (the normal labor union approach); present affiliated benefits for widows' and orphans' pensions and disability pensions (for death or disability during service) could be dropped; the present clause granting full vesting (ownership) of the accrued pension benefits after five years' service could be changed to ten years. Although employees and unions like to label pension benefits "acquired rights," thereby implying they are inviolate, a factory's closing would likely be much more burdensome to them than some occasional adjusting to the times.

The issue which is raised is: What are the ethical implications of these contemplated acts by the shareholders? No matter what your personal feeling about the obligations of a corporation to its employees, its owners, and its customers, you must recognize that something has to be done to rebuild the profitability of the company to save its employees. Competition does not permit the problem to be solved simply by raising the prices of profits.

What would you do as a shareholder?

The Universal Declaration of Human Rights, 1948

On December 10, 1948, the General Assembly of the United Nations adopted and proclaimed the Universal Declaration of Human Rights. Following this historic act the Assembly called upon all Member countries to publicize the text of the Declaration and 'to cause it to be disseminated, displayed, read and expounded principally in schools and other educational institutions, without distinction based on the political status of countries or territories'.

PREAMBLE

Whereas recognition of the inherent dignity and of the equal and inalienable rights of all members of the human family is the foundation of freedom, justice and peace in the world,

A publication of the United Nations.

Whereas disregard and contempt for human rights have resulted in barbarous acts which have outraged the conscience of mankind, and the advent of a world in which human beings shall enjoy freedom of speech and belief and freedom from fear and want has been proclaimed as the highest aspiration of the common people,

Whereas it is essential, if man is not to be compelled to have recourse, as a last resort, to rebellion against tyranny and oppression, that human rights should be protected by the rule of law,

Whereas it is essential to promote the development of friendly relations between nations,

Whereas the peoples of the United Nations have in the Charter reaffirmed their faith in fundamental human rights, in the dignity and worth of the human person and in the equal rights of men and women and have determined to promote social progress and better standards of life in larger freedom,

Whereas Member States have pledged themselves to achieve, in co-operation with the United Nations, the promotion of universal respect for and observance of human rights and fundamental freedoms,

Whereas a common understanding of these rights and freedom is of the greatest importance for the full realization of this pledge,

Now, Therefore THE GENERAL ASSEMBLY *proclaims*

THIS UNIVERSAL DECLARATION OF HUMAN RIGHTS as a common standard of achievement for all peoples and all nations, to the end that every individual and every organ of society, keeping this Declaration constantly in mind, shall strive by teaching and education to promote respect for these rights and freedoms and by progressive measures, national and international, to secure their universal and effective recognition and observance, both among the peoples of Member States themselves and among the peoples of territories under their jurisdiction.

Article I

All human beings are born free and equal in dignity and rights. They are endowed with reason and conscience and should act towards one another in a spirit of brotherhood.

Article 2

Everyone is entitled to all the rights and freedoms set forth in this Declaration, without distinction of any kind, such as race, colour, sex, language, religion, political or other opinion, national or social origin, property, birth or other status.
Furthermore, no distinction shall be made on the basis of the political, jurisdictional or international status of the country or territory to which a person belongs, whether it be independent, trust, non-self-governing or under any other limitation of sovereignty.

Article 3

Everyone has the right to life, liberty and security of person.

Article 4

No one shall be held in slavery or servitude; slavery and the slave trade shall be prohibited in all their forms.

Article 5

No one shall be subjected to torture or to cruel, inhuman or degrading treatment or punishment.

Article 6

Everyone has the right to recognition everywhere as a person before the law.

Article 7

All are equal before the law and are entitled without any discrimination to equal protection of the law. All are entitled to equal protection against any discrimination in violation of this Declaration and against any incitement to such discrimination.

Article 8

Everyone has the right to an effective remedy by the competent national tribunals for acts violating the fundamental rights granted him by the constitution or by law.

Article 9

No one shall be subjected to arbitrary arrest, detention or exile.

Article 10

Everyone is entitled in full equality to a fair and public hearing by an independent and impartial tribunal, in the determination of his rights and obligations and of any criminal charge against him.

Article 11

1. Everyone charged with a penal offence has the right to be presumed innocent until proved guilty according to law in a public trial at which he has had all the guarantees necessary for his defence.
2. No one shall be held guilty of any penal offence on account of any act or omission which did not constitute a penal offence, under national or international law, at the time when it was committed. Nor shall a heavier penalty be imposed than the one that was applicable at the time the penal offence was committed.

Article 12

No one shall be subjected to arbitrary interference with his privacy, family, home or correspondence, nor to attacks upon his honour and reputation. Everyone has the right to the protection of the law against such interference or attacks.

Article 13

1. Everyone has the right to freedom of movement and residence within the borders of each state.
2. Everyone has the right to leave any country, including his own, and to return to his country.

Article 14

1. Everyone has the right to seek and to enjoy in other countries asylum from persecution.
2. This right may not be invoked in the case of prosecutions genuinely arising from non-political crimes or from acts contrary to the purposes and principles of the United Nations.

Article 15

1. Everyone has the right to a nationality.
2. No one shall be arbitrarily deprived of his nationality nor denied the right to change his nationality.

Article 16

1. Men and women of full age, without any limitation due to race, nationality or religion, have the right to marry and to found a family. They are entitled to equal rights as to marriage, during marriage and at its dissolution.
2. Marriage shall be entered into only with the free and full consent of the intending spouses.
3. The family is the natural and fundamental group unit of society and is entitled to protection by society and the State.

Article 17

1. Everyone has the right to own property alone as well as in association with others.
2. No one shall be arbitrarily deprived of his property.

Article 18

Everyone has the right to freedom of thought, conscience and religion; this right includes freedom to change his religion or belief, and freedom, either alone or in community with others and in public or private, to manifest his religion or belief in teaching, practice, worship and observance.

Article 19

Everyone has the right to freedom of opinion and expression; this right includes freedom to hold opinions without interference and to seek, receive and impart information and ideas through any media and regardless of frontiers.

Article 20

1. Everyone has the right to freedom of peaceful assembly and association.
2. No one may be compelled to belong to an association.

Article 21

1. Everyone has the right to take part in the government of his country, directly or through freely chosen representatives.
2. Everyone has the right of equal access to public service in his country.
3. The will of the people shall be the basis of the authority of government; this will shall be expressed in periodic and genuine elections which shall be by universal and equal suffrage and shall be held by secret vote or by equivalent free voting procedures.

Article 22

Everyone, as a member of society, has the right to social security and is entitled to realization through national effort and international cooperation and in accordance with the organization and resources of each State, of the economic, social and cultural rights indispensable for his dignity and the free development of his personality.

Article 23

1. Everyone has the right to work, to free choice of employment, to just and favourable conditions of work and to protection against unemployment.
2. Everyone, without any discrimination, has the right to equal pay for equal work.
3. Everyone who works has the right to just and favourable remuneration ensuring for himself and his family an existence worthy of human dignity, and supplemented, if necessary, by other means of social protection.
4. Everyone has the right to form and to join trade unions for the protection of his interests.

Article 24

Everyone has the right to rest and leisure, including reasonable limitation of working hours and periodic holidays with pay.

Article 25

1. Everyone has the right to a standard of living adequate for the health and well-being of himself and of his family, including food, clothing, housing and medical care and necessary social services, and the right to security in the event of unemployment, sickness, disability, widowhood, old age or other lack of livelihood in circumstances beyond his control.
2. Motherhood and childhood are entitled to special care and assistance. All children, whether born in or out of wedlock, shall enjoy the same social protection.

Article 26

1. Everyone has the right to education. Education shall be free, at least in the elementary and fundamental stages. Elementary education shall be compulsory. Technical and professional education shall be made generally available and higher education shall be equally accessible to all on the basis of merit.
2. Education shall be directed to the full development of the human personality and to the strengthening of respect for human rights and fundamental freedoms. It shall promote understanding, tolerance and friendship among all nations, racial or religious groups, and shall further the activities of the United Nations for the maintenance of peace.
3. Parents have a prior right to choose the kind of education that shall be given to their children.

Article 27

1. Everyone has the right freely to participate in the cultural life of the community, to enjoy the arts and to share in scientific advancement and its benefits.
2. Everyone has the right to the protection of the moral and material interests resulting from any scientific, literary or artistic production of which he is the author.

Article 28

Everyone is entitled to a social and international order in which the rights and freedoms set forth in this Declaration can be fully realized.

Article 29

1. Everyone has duties to the community in which alone the free and full development of his personality is possible.
2. In the exercise of his rights and freedoms, everyone shall be subject only to such limitations as are determined by law solely for the purpose of securing due recognition and respect for the rights and freedoms of others and of meeting the just requirements of morality, public order and the general welfare in a democratic society.
3. These rights and freedoms may in no case be exercised contrary to the purposes and principles of the United Nations.

Article 30

Nothing in this Declaration may be interpreted as implying for any State, group or person any right to engage in any activity or to perform any act aimed at the destruction of any of the rights and freedoms set forth herein.

Justice and Equality

GREGORY VLASTOS

I

. . . . Taking "natural rights" to mean simply *human* rights—that is to say, rights which are human not in the trivial sense that those who have them are men, but in the challenging sense that in order to have them they need only be men—one would still like to know:

(1) What is the range of these rights? The French Declaration states: "these rights are liberty, property, security, and resistance to oppression." The imprudent beginning—"these rights are" instead of Jefferson's more cautious, "among these rights are"—makes it look as though the four natural rights named here are meant to be all the rights there are. If so, what happened to the pursuit of happiness? Is that the same as liberty? As for property, this was not a natural right before Locke,[1] and not always after him, e.g., not for Jefferson.[2] And what of welfare rights? They are not mentioned in the French document, nor are they implied by "security."

(2) Can the doctrine of natural rights find a place for each of the following well-known maxims of distributive justice:

1. To each according to his *need.*
2. To each according to his *worth.*
3. To each according to his *merit.*
4. To each according to his *work.*[3]

And we might add a fifth which does not seem to have worked its way to the same level of adage-like respectability, but has as good a claim as some of the others:

5. To each according to the *agreements* he has made.

By making judicious selections from this list one can "justicize"[4] extreme inequalities of distribution. It is thus that Plato concludes that the man who can no longer work has lost his right to live,[5] and Bentham that no just limits can be set to the terms on which labor can be bought, used, and used up.[6] Hobbes, most frugal of moral philosophers, operates with just the last of these maxims;[7] making the keeping of covenants the defining element of justice, he decimates civil liberties *more geometrico.*[8] These premises were not, of course, the only ones from which such morally dismal results were reached by these clear-headed and upright men; but they were the controlling ones. If merit or work or agreement, or any combination of the three, are made the final principles of distributive justice, it will not be hard to find plausible collateral premises from which

From Gregory Vlastos, "Justice and Equality," *Social Justice*, ed. Richard B. Brandt, © 1962, pp. 31–72. Reprinted by permission of Prentice-Hall, Inc., Englewood Cliffs, N.J.

to get such results. What then should a natural rights philosopher do with these maxims? Must he regard them as fifth-columnists? Or can he keep them as members of his working team, useful, if subordinate, principles of his equalitarian justice? Can this be done without making concessions to inequality which will divide his allegiance to equality?

(3) Finally, are natural rights "absolute," i.e., are their claims unexceptionable. If I have a natural right to a given benefit does it follow that I ought to be granted that benefit in all possible circumstances no matter how my other rights or those of others might be affected? Is this the meaning of the well-known statements that natural rights are "inalienable" and "imprescriptible"?

I believe that all these questions admit of reasonable answers which, when worked out fully, would amount to a revised theory of natural rights or, what is the same thing, a theory of human rights: I shall use the two expressions interchangeably. . . .

Let me begin with the answer to the third of the questions I raised. Are human rights absolute? All of these writers would say, "No." I am convinced that in this they are right,[9] and am even prepared to add that neither is there anything explicitly contrary to this in that branch of the classical theory which is of greatest interest to us today: in Locke, for example.[10] Locke has indeed been understood to mean that natural rights are absolute.[11] But nowhere does Locke *say* this. Contrariwise he believes many things which imply the opposite. For example, he would certainly approve of imprisonment as a punishment for crime; and we hear him recommending that beggars be detained in houses of correction or impressed in the navy.[12] Such constraints he would have to reckon justified exceptions to that freedom of movement which all persons claim in virtue of their natural right to liberty. So too he would have to think of the death penalty for convicted criminals, or of a military order which would bring death to many of those obeying it, as justified exceptions to some men's natural right to life. Even the right to property—indeed, that special form of it which is upheld more zealously than any other right in the *Second Treatise,* one's right not to be deprived of property without consent[13]— could not be unconditional; Locke would have to concede that it should be over-ruled, e.g., in a famine when stores of hoarded food are requisitioned by public authority. We would, therefore, improve the consistency of Locke's theory if we understood him to mean that natural rights are subject to justified exceptions.[14] In any case, I shall speak of human rights as "prima facie" rights[15] to mean that the claims of any of them may be over-ruled in special circumstances.[16] Can one say this without giving away the radical difference which the traditional doctrine fixed between natural rights and all others? To this the answer would be that, though in this respect all rights are alike, the vital difference remains untouched: one need only be a man to have *prima facie* rights to life, liberty, welfare, and the like; but to be a man is not all one needs to have a *prima facie* right to the house he happens to own or the job he happens to hold. As for the "inalienability" and "imprescriptibility" of natural rights, we may understand them with this proviso to mean exactly what they say: that no man can alienate (i.e., sign away, transfer by contract)[17] a *prima facie* natural right, his own or anyone else's; and that no people can lose *prima facie* natural rights by prescription, e.g., in virtue of the time-hallowed possession of despotic power over them by a royal dynasty.[18]

Does this entirely allay our misgivings? It does not, and it should not. To say that a natural right is a *prima facie* right is to say that there are cases in which it is perfectly just to disallow its claim; and unless we have definite assurance as to the limits within which this may occur, we have no way of telling whether we are better off with this *prima facie* right than we would be without it. If *anything* may count as an allowable exception, then what does the right give us that we would otherwise lack? If only some things are to count, we need to know what sort of things these are to be, in order to know what, if anything, our right is worth. . . . We must find *reasons for our natural rights which will be the only moral reasons for just exceptions* to them in special circumstances.

This may look like a predictably unfulfillable demand, for it seems self-contradictory. But it is certainly not the latter. There is nothing self-contradictory about saying that reasons requiring a general pattern of action may permit, or even require, a departure from it in special circumstances. Thus my reasons for eating three meals a day are, say, pleasure and physical need; for these same reasons I might eat on special occasions four or five meals in a single day, or two or one. The analogy is not perfect, but it does give a rough idea of the lines along which we may concede justified exceptions to natural rights without jeopardizing the fundamental place they must hold in our scheme of justice, if we are to keep them there at all. And since all of them are equal rights (i.e., rights to equal treatment), a parallel observation may be made about the problem with which we started: An equalitarian concept of justice may admit just inequalities without inconsistency if, and only if, it provides grounds for equal human rights *which are also grounds for unequal rights of other sorts.* Such grounds, if we could find them, should carry right through all five of the maxims of distributive justice I listed above, showing how these maxims can be tied together as principles of justice and of the same concept of justice. . . .

II

Let me begin with the first on my list of maxims of distributive justice: "To each according to his need." Since needs are often unequal, this looks like a precept of unequal distribution. But this is wrong. It is in fact *the most perfect form of equal distribution.* To explain this let me take one of the best established rights in the natural law tradition: the right to the security of life and person. Believing that this is an equal right, what do we feel this means in cases of special need?

Suppose, for instance, New Yorker *X* gets a note from Murder, Inc., that looks like business. To allocate several policemen and plainclothesmen to guard him over the next few weeks at a cost a hundred times greater than the per capita cost of security services to other citizens during the same period, is surely *not* to make an exception to the equal distribution required by the equal right of all citizens to the security of their life and person; it is not done on the assumption that X has a greater right to security or a right to greater security. If the visitor from Mars drew this conclusion from the behavior of the police, he would be told that he was just mistaken. The greater allocation of community resources in X's favor, we would have to explain, is made precisely *because* X's security rights are equal to those of other people in New York. This means that X is entitled to the same level of police-made security as is maintained for other New Yorkers. Hence in these special circumstances, where his security level would drop to zero without extra support, he should be given this to bring his security level nearer the normal. I say "nearer," not "up to" the normal, because I am talking of New York as of 1961. If I were thinking of New York with an ideal municipal government, ideally supplied with police resources, I *would* say "up to normal," because that is what equality of right would ideally mean. But as things are, perhaps the best that can be done for X without disrupting the general level of security maintained for all the other New Yorkers is to decrease his chances of being bumped off in a given week to, say, one to ten thousand, while those of ordinary citizens, with ordinary protection are, say, one to ten million—no small difference.[19] Now if New York were more affluent, it would be able to buy more equality[20] of security for its citizens (as well as more security): by getting more, and perhaps also better paid, policemen, it would be able to close the gap between security maintained for people in ordinary circumstances and that supplied in cases of special need, like that of X in his present jam. . . .

So we can see why distribution according to personal need, far from conflicting with the equality of distribution required by a human right, is so linked with its very meaning that under ideal conditions equality of right would coincide with distribution according to personal need. Our visitor misunderstood the sudden mobilization of New York policemen in favor of Mr. X, because he failed to understand that it is benefits to persons, not allocation of resources as such, that are meant to be made equal; for then he would have seen at once that unequal distribution of resources would be required to equalize benefits in cases of unequal need. But if he saw this he might then ask, "But why do you want this sort of equality?" My answer would have to be: Because the human worth of all persons is equal, however unequal may be their merit. To the explanation of this proposition I shall devote the balance of this Section.

By "merit" I shall refer throughout this essay to all the kinds of valuable qualities or performances in respect of which persons may be graded.[21] The concept will not be restricted to moral actions or dispositions.[22] Thus wit, grace of manner, and technical skill count as meritorious qualities fully as much as sincerity, generosity, or courage. Any valuable human characteristic, or cluster of characteristics, will qualify, provided only it is "acquired," i.e., represents what its possessor has himself made of his natural endowments and environmental opportunities. . . .

Now if this concept of value attaching to a person's individual existence, over and above his merit—"individual worth,"[23] let me call it—were applicable *only* in relations of personal love, it would be irrelevant for the analysis of justice. To serve our purpose its range of application must be coextensive with that of justice. It must hold in all human relations, including (or rather, especially in) the most impersonal of all, those to total strangers, fellow-citizens or fellow-men. I must show that the concept of individual worth does meet this condition.

Consider its role in our political community, taking the prescriptions of our laws for the treatment of persons as the index to our valuations. For merit (among other reasons) persons may be appointed or elected to public office or given employment by state agencies. For demerit they may lose licences, jobs, offices; they may be fined, jailed, or even put to death. But in a large variety of law-regulated actions directed to individuals, either by private persons or by organs of the state, the question of merit and demerit does not arise. The "equal protection of the laws" is due to persons not to meritorious ones, or to them in some degree above others.[24] So too for the right to vote. One does not have it for being intelligent and public-spirited, or lose it for being lazy, ignorant, or viciously selfish. One is entitled to exercise it as long as, having registered, one manages to keep out of jail. This kind of arrangement would look like whimsy or worse, like sheer immoralism, if the only values recognized in our political community were those of merit. For obviously there is nothing compulsory about our political system; we could certainly devise, if we so wished, workable alternatives which would condition fundamental rights on certain kinds of merit. For example, we might have three categories of citizenship. The top one might be for those who meet high educational qualifications and give definite evidence of responsible civic interest, e.g., by active participation in political functions, tenure of public office, record of leadership in civic organizations and support to them, and the like. People in this *A*-category might have multiple votes in all elections and exclusive eligibility for the more important political offices; they might also be entitled to a higher level of protection by the police and to a variety of other privileges and immunities. At the other end there would be a *C*-category, disfranchised and legally underprivileged, for those who do not meet some lower educational test or have had a record of law-infraction or have been on the relief rolls for over three months. In between would be the *B*'s with ordinary suffrage and intermediate legal status.

This "*M*-system" would be more complicated and cumbersome than ours. But something like it could certainly be made to work if we were enamoured of its peculiar scheme of values. Putting aside the question of efficiency, it gives us a picture of a community whose political valuations, conceived entirely in terms of merit, would never be grounded on individual worth, so that this notion would there be politically useless.[25] For us, on the other hand, it is indispensable.[26] We have to appeal to it when we try to make sense of the fact that our legal system accords to all citizens an identical status, carrying with it rights such as the *M*-system reserves to the *B*'s or the *A*'s, and some of which (like suffrage or freedom of speech) have been denied even to the nobility in some caste-systems of the past.

This last comparison is worth pressing: it brings out the illuminating fact that in one fundamental respect our society is much more like a caste society (with a *unique* caste) than like the *M*-system. The latter has no place for a rank of dignity which descends on an individual by the purely existential circumstance (the "accident") of birth and remains his unalterably for life. To reproduce this feature of our system we would have to look not only to caste-societies, but to extremely rigid ones, since most of them make some provision for elevation in rank for rare merit or degradation for extreme demerit. In our legal system no such thing can happen; even a criminal may not be sentenced to second-class citizenship.[27] And the fact that first-class citizenship, having been made common, is no longer a mark of distinction does not trivialize the privileges it entails. It is the simple truth, not declamation, to speak of it, as I have done, as a "rank of dignity" in some ways comparable to that enjoyed by hereditary nobilities of the past. To see this one need only think of the position of groups in our society who have been cheated out of this status by the subversion of their constitutional rights. The difference in social position between Negroes and whites described in Dollard's classic[28] is not smaller than that between, say, bourgeoisie and aristocracy in the *ancien régime* of France. It might well be greater.

Consider finally the role of the same value in the moral community. Here differences of merit are so conspicuous and pervasive that we might even be tempted to *define* the moral response to a person in terms of moral approval or disapproval of his acts or disposition, i.e., in terms of the response to his moral merit. But there are many kinds of moral response for which a person's merit is as irrelevant as is that of New Yorker *X* when he appeals to the police for help. If I see someone in danger of drowning I will not need to satisfy myself about his moral character before going to his aid. I owe assistance to any man in such circumstances, not merely to good men. Nor is it only in rare and exceptional cases, as this example might suggest, that my obligations to others are independent of their moral merit. To be sincere, reliable, fair, kind, tolerant, unintrusive, modest in my relations with my fellows is not due them because they have made brilliant or even passing moral grades, but simply because they happen to be fellow-members of the moral community. It is not necessary to add, "members in good standing." The moral community is not a club from which members may be dropped for delinquency. Our morality does not provide for moral outcasts or half-castes. It does provide for punishment. But this takes place *within* the moral community and under its rules. It is for this reason that, for example, one has no right to be cruel to a cruel person. His offense against the moral law has not put him outside the law. He is still protected by its prohibition of cruelty—as much so as are kind persons. The pain inflicted on him as punishment for his offense does not close out the reserve of good will on the part of all others which is his birthright as a human being; it is a limited withdrawal from it. Capital punishment, if we believe in it, is no exception. The fact that a man has been condemned to death does not license his jailors to beat him or virtuous citizens to lynch him.

Here, then, as in the single-status political community, we acknowledge personal rights which are not proportioned to merit and could not be justified by merit. Their only justification could be the value which persons have simply because they are persons: their "intrinsic value as individual human beings," as Frankena calls it; the "infinite value" or the "sacredness" of their individuality, as others have called it. I shall speak of it as "individual human worth"; or "human worth," for short. What these expressions stand for is also expressed by saying that men are "ends in themselves." This latter concept is Kant's. Some of the kinks in his formulation of it[29] can be straightened out by explaining it as follows: Everything other than a person can only have value *for* a person. This applies not only to physical objects, natural or manmade, which have only instrumental value, but also to those products of the human spirit which have also intrinsic, no less than extrinsic, value: an epic poem, a scientific theory, a legal system, a moral disposition. Even such things as these will have value only because they can be (a) experienced or felt to be valuable by human beings and (b) chosen by them from competing alternatives. Thus of everything without exception it will be true to say: if x is valuable and is not a person, then x will have value for some individual other than itself. Hence even a musical composition or a courageous deed, valued for their own sake, as "ends" not as means to anything else, will still fall into an entirely different category from that of the *valuers,* who do not need to be valued as "ends" by someone else[30] in order to have value. In just this sense persons, and only persons are "ends in themselves."

The two factors in terms of which I have described the value of the valuer—the capacities answering to (a) and (b) above—may not be exhaustive. But their conjunction offers a translation of "individual human worth" whose usefulness for working purposes will speak for itself. To (a) I might refer as "happiness," if I could use this term as Plato and Aristotle used *eudaimonia,* i.e., without the exclusively hedonistic connotations which have since been clamped on it. It will be less misleading to use "well-being" or "welfare" for what I intend here; that is, the enjoyment of value in all the forms in which it can be experienced by human beings. To (b) I shall refer as "freedom," bringing under this term not only conscious choices and deliberate decisions but also those subtler modulations and more spontaneous expressions of individual preference which could scarcely be called "choices" or "decisions" without some forcing of language. So understood, a person's well-being and freedom are aspects of his individual existence as unique and unrepeatable as is that existence itself: If A and B are listening to the same symphony with similar tastes and dispositions, we may speak of their enjoying the "same" good, or having the "same" enjoyment, and say that each has made the "same" choice for this way of spending his time and money. But here "same" will mean no more than "very similar"; the two enjoyments and choices, occurring in the consciousness of A and B respectively, are absolutely unique. So in translating "A's human worth" into "the worth of A's well-being and freedom" we are certainly meeting the condition that the former expression is to stand for whatever it is about A which, unlike his merit, has *individual* worth.

We are also meeting another condition: that the equality of human worth be justification, or ground, of equal human rights. I can best bring this out by reverting to the visitor from Mars who had asked a little earlier why we want equalization of security benefits. Let us conjure up circumstances in which his question would spring, not from idle curiosity, but from a strong conviction that this, or any other, right entailing such undiscriminating equality of benefits, would be entirely *un*reasonable. Suppose then that he hails from a strict meritarian community, which maintains the *M*-system in its political life and analogous patterns in other associations. And to make things simpler, let us also suppose that he is shown nothing in New York or elsewhere that is out of line with our formal professions of equality, so that he imagines us purer, more strenuous, equalitarians than we happen to be. The pattern of valuation he ascribes to us then seems to him fantastically topsy-turvy. He can hardly bring himself to believe that rational human beings should want equal personal rights, legal and moral, for their "riff-raff" and their élites. Yet neither can he explain away our conduct as pure automatism, a mere fugue of social habit. "These people, or some of them," he will be saying to himself, "must have some reasons for this incredible code. What could these be?" If we volunteered an answer couched in terms of human worth, he might find it hard to understand us. Such an answer, unglossed, would convey to him no more than that we recognize something which is highly and equally valuable in all persons, but has nothing to do with their merit, and constitutes the ground of their equal rights. But this might start him hunting—snark-hunting—for some special quality named by "human worth" as honesty is named by "honesty" and kindness by "kindness," wondering all the while how it could have happened that he and all his tribe have had no inkling of it, if all of them have always had it.[31]

But now suppose that we avail ourselves of the aforesaid translation. We could then tell him: "To understand our code you should take into account how very different from yours is our own estimate of the relative worth of the welfare and freedom of different individuals. We agree with you that not all persons are capable of experiencing the same values. But there is a wide variety of cases in which persons are capable of this. Thus, to take a perfectly clear case, no matter how *A* and *B* might differ in taste and style of life, they would both crave relief from acute physical pain. In that case we would put the same value on giving this to either of them, regardless of the fact that *A* might be a talented, brilliantly successful person, *B* 'a mere nobody.' On this we would disagree sharply. You would weigh the welfare of members of the élite more highly than that of 'riff-raff,' as you call them. We would not. If *A* were a statesman, and giving him relief from pain enabled him to conclude an agreement that would benefit millions, while *B*, an unskilled laborer, was himself the sole beneficiary of the like relief, we would, of course, agree that the *instrumental* value of the two experiences would be vastly different—but not their *intrinsic* value. In all cases where human beings are capable of enjoying the same goods, we feel that the intrinsic value of their enjoyment is the same. In just this sense we hold that (1) *one man's well-being is as valuable as any other's.* And there is a parallel difference in our feeling for freedom. You value it only when exercised by good persons for good ends. We put no such strings on its value. We feel that choosing for oneself what one will do, believe, approve, say, see, read, worship, has its own intrinsic value, the same for all persons, and quite independently of the value of the things they happen to choose. Naturally, we hope that all of them will make the best possible use of their freedom of choice. But we value their exercise of that freedom, regardless of the outcome; and we value it equally for all. For us (2) *one man's freedom is as valuable as any other's.*"

This sort of explanation, I submit, would put him in a position to resolve his dilemma. For just suppose that, taking this homily at face-value, he came to think of us as believing (1) and (2).[32] No matter how unreasonable he might think of us he would feel it entirely reasonable that, since we do believe in equal *value* of human well-being and freedom, we should also believe in the *prima facie* equality of men's *right* to well-being and to freedom. He would see the former as a good reason for the latter; or, more formally, he could think of (1) and (2) respectively as the crucial premises in justification arguments whose respective conclusions would be: (3) One man's (*prima facie*) right to freedom is equal to that of any other. Then, given (4), he could see how this would serve as the basis for a great variety of rights to specific kinds of freedom: freedom of movement, of association, of suffrage, of speech, of thought, of worship, of choice of employment, and the like. For each of these can be regarded as simply a specification of the general right to freedom, and would thus be covered by the justification of the latter. Moreover, given (3), he could see in it the basis for various welfare-rights, such as the right to education, medical care, work under decent conditions, relief in periods of unemployment, leisure, housing, etc.[33] Thus to give him (1) and (2) as justification for (3) and (4) would be to give him a basis for every one of the rights which are mentioned in the most complete of currently authoritative declarations of human rights, that passed by the Assembly of the United Nations in 1948. Hence to tell him that we believe in the equal worth of individual freedom and happiness would be to answer, in terms he can understand, his question, "What is your reason for your equalitarian code?"[34]

Nowhere in this defense of the translation of "equal human worth" into "equal worth of human well-being and freedom" have I claimed that the former can be *reduced* to the latter. I offered individual well-being and freedom simply as two things which do satisfy the conditions defined by individual human worth. Are there others? For the purposes of this essay this may be left an open question. For if there are, they would provide, at most, additional grounds for human rights. The ones I have specified are grounds enough. . . .

III

. . . Terms like "superior" and "inferior," properly applicable to a person's merit, are inapplicable to the person: there can be strictly and literally superior or inferior poets, teachers, bankers, garage-mechanics, actresses, statesmen; but there can be strictly and literally no superior or inferior persons, individuals, men. From this it follows that when we praise a man we must not praise him *as* a man. His humanity is not a fit subject for praise. To think otherwise is to incur a "category mistake," and one fraught with grave moral consequences. For given men's sensitiveness to honor and dishonor, when merit is made the measure of their human dignity, their own sense of dignity tends to become distorted. If they are talented and successful, praise misdirected from their achievement to their person will foster the illusion that they are superior persons, belong to a higher moral caste, and may claim on moral grounds a privileged status for their own well-being and freedom.[35] Conversely, if low achievement scores are not kept wholly distinct from personal worth, which does not register on any score, men may be made to feel that they are the human inferiors of others, that their own happiness or freedom has inferior worth. This would be a grave injustice. Any practice which tends to so weaken and confuse the personal self-esteem of a group of persons—slavery, serfdom or, in our own time, racial segregation—may be morally condemned on this one ground, even if there were no other for indicting it. Some such ground is alluded to in the Court opinion in the decision which finally struck down segregation in the public schools.[36] That verdict could be reached more directly and extended to every form of racial segregation,[37] by applying the ideas that have been sketched in this essay. If one thinks of human worth as the moral foundation of all rights, one will see that the equal honor of persons is presupposed by the unequal honor that may be given to unequal merit and, hence, that no practice which habitually humiliates persons can be defended by differences of merit, real or imagined.

Notes

1. Locke's argument that property is a natural right is a momentous innovation, "a landmark in the history of thought." O. Giercke, *Natural Law and the Theory of Society 1500 to 1800* (Cambridge: Cambridge Univ. Press, 1950), p. 103. But this is not to say that, if one looks hard enough, one will not find anticipations of Locke's theory. See E.S. Corwin, *The "Higher Law" Background of American Constitutional Law*, Great Seal Books edition (Ithaca: Cornell Univ. Press, 1955), p. 61, note 60; J.W. Gough, *Locke's Political Philosophy* (New York: Oxford Univ. Press, 1950, p. 80). For some of these references, and for other useful suggestions, I am indebted to Dr. Hugo Bedau.)
2. See, e.g., Ursula M. von Eckardt, *The Pursuit of Happiness in the Democratic Creed* (New York: Frederick A. Praeger, 1959), pp. 103–08.
3. For a similar enumeration see Charles Perelman, *De La Justice* (Brussels, 1945).
4. William K. Frankena, "The Concept of Social Justice," *Social Justice,* ed. Richard B. Brandt (Englewood Cliffs, N.J.: Prentice-Hall, Inc., 1962), p. 5.
5. Plato, *Republic,* 406c–407a.

6. "When the question of slavery is not considered there is little to say respecting the conditions of master and its correlative conditions, constituted by the different kinds of servants. All these conditions are the effects of contract; these contracts the parties interested may arrange to suit themselves," *Principles of the Civil Code*. In *Works*, Bowring, ed., vol. 1, p. 341.
7. The fifth: "the definition of *Injustice* is not other than *the not performance of covenant*. And whatsoever is not unjust is just." *Leviathan*, Part I, Ch. 15.
8. That "nothing the sovereign representative can do to a subject, on what pretense soever, can properly be called injustice or injury" (*op. cit.*, Part II, Ch. 21) is presented as a logical consequence of (a) every subject is the "author" of each act of his sovereign and (b) no man can be the author of injustice or injury to himself. (a) follows from the definitions of "sovereign" and "subjects," Part I, Ch. 18.
9. For this I am especially indebted to discussion with Richard Brandt.
10. Nor in the Thomist version as interpreted by J. Maritain. See his distinction between the "possession" and the "exercise" of a natural right (unexceptionable and exceptionable, respectively), *Man and the State* (Chicago: Univ. of Chicago Press, 1951), pp. 101–03.
11. E.g., E.F. Carritt, *Ethical and Political Thinking* (Oxford: Oxford Univ. Press, 1947), pp. 154ff. Brandt, *op. cit.*, p. 442. No test is cited from Locke to support this very widespread interpretation. Such statements as "the obligations of the law of nature cease not in society," *Second Treatise of Government*, 135, are too general to determine the point at issue here.
12. See his proposals for the reform of the Poor Law submitted to the Board of Trade in 1697: H. R. Fox-Bourne, *Life of Locke* (London, 1876), vol. 2, pp. 379–81.
13. 138, 139. Cf. other references in J. W. Gough, *op. cit.*, p. 85, Note 1.
14. Admitting that to do this is to add something of substance to his own explicit doctrine. He himself never refers to cases such as those I have mentioned as exceptions to natural rights.
15. See Frankena, "Human Rights," p. 127, and "Are There Natural Rights?" pp. 228ff.; Brandt, *op. cit.*, 441ff. For some objections to this usage see Sir David Ross, *The Right and the Good* (Oxford: Oxford Univ. Press, 1939), p. 20; for strong opposition, Melden, *Rights and Right Conduct*, pp. 18ff. I am not entirely happy with this usage, but neither can I propose a better. Part of the objection is met by the clarification in the following note.
16. Given "right" = "justified claim" (Oxford English Dictionary), *prima facie* qualifies "justified." A *prima facie* right is one whose claim has *prima facie* justification, i.e., *is* justified, unless there are stronger counter-claims in the particular situation in which it is made, the burden of proof resting always on the counter-claims. "Claim" here has a much broader sense than "asserted claim"; it is related to "claiming" in much the same way as "proposition" to "propounding"; it is something which may be claimed, as a proposition is something which may be propounded. To say that a right is a justified claim is to say that it is something which could be claimed with justification, i.e., a claim which others have the obligation to grant if (but not, only if) it is asserted.
17. The normal sense of "alienate" when applied to rights in legal, or quasi-legal, contexts. To defend the inalienability (though without using this word) of one's right to be free from subjection to the arbitrary will of another, Locke thinks it sufficient to argue that one cannot forfeit this right "by compact or his own consent," *Second Treatise*, 23, and cannot "transfer to another" (135) this right by a voluntary act.

18. For the relevant sense of "prescription," see the *Shorter Oxford English Dictionary,* s.v., 11 (b): "uninterrupted use or possession from time immemorial, or for a period fixed by law as giving a title or right; hence title or right acquired by such use or possession." On prescription as the foundation of rights of government and property see, e.g., Edmund Burke: "Our constitution is a prescriptive constitution; it is a constitution whose sole authority is that it has existed time out of mind. . . . Prescription is the most solid of all titles, not only to property, but, which is to secure that property, to government," Reform of Representation in the House of Commons (1782), *Works,* Vol. 6.

19. These figures, needless to say, are "pulled out of a hat."

20. This point was first suggested to me by Professor Kenneth Boulding's striking remark that "only a rich society can afford to be equalitarian," *The Economics of Peace* (Englewood Cliffs, N.J.: Prentice-Hall, 1945), p. 111. The more guarded form in which I am stating the point will protect it against apparent counter-examples to Boulding's remark, e.g., the astonishing equalitarianism that was still practiced by the Eskimos of the Coronation Gulf and the Mackenzie River early in this century (see V. Stefansson's essay in *Freedom,* Ruth N. Anshen, ed. [New York: Harcourt, Brace and World, 1940]).

21. This is only one of the senses recognized by the dictionary (*The Shorter Oxford English Dictionay,* s.v., 4 and 6): "Excellence," "An Excellence," the latter being illustrated by "Would you ask for his merits? Alas! he has none" (from Goldsmith). In the other senses listed by the dictionary the word either *means* "desert" or at least includes this in its meaning. On the present use of "merit" the connection with "desert" is synthetic.

22. As is done by some philosophical moralists, e.g., Sir David Ross, *op. cit.,* pp. 135ff., where "merit" and (moral) "virtue" are co-extensive.

23. That this is *intrinsic* worth goes without saying. But I do not put this term into my label, since I want to distinguish this kind of value as sharply as possible from that of merit, and I include under "merit" not only extrinsically, but also intrinsically, valuable qualities.

24. A modicum of merit by way of self-help and law-obedience is generally presupposed. But it would be a mistake to think of the protection of the laws as a reward for good behavior. Thus many legal protections are due as much to those who will not look out for themselves as to those who do, and to law-breakers as much as to law-observers.

25. Though it might have uses in the family or other relations.

26. Even where a purely pragmatic justification is offered for democracy (e.g., Pendleton Herring, *Politics of Democracy* [New York: W.W. Norton & Co., 1940]) equality of worth must still be acknowledged, if only as a popular "myth" or "dogma."

27. No one, I trust, will confuse second-class citizenship with extreme punishments, such as the death-penalty or a life-sentence, or, for that matter, with *any* legal punishment in a democratic society. Second-class citizens are those deprived of rights without any presumption of legal guilt.

28. John Dollard, *Caste and Class in a Southern Town* (New Haven: Yale Univ. Press, 1937).

29. See, e.g., H. Sidgwick, *Methods of Ethics* (London, 1874), p. 363. For a parallel objection see the next note. Still another is that Kant, using the notion of *intrinsic worth* (*Würde* in contrast to *Preis*) to define *end in itself,* and hence as its sufficient condition, tends to conflate the value of *persons* as ends in

themselves with that of their *moral merit.* Thus, though he says that"Respect [the attitude due to a being which is an end in itself] always applies to persons only" (*Critique of Practical Reason,* trans. L.W. Beck [New York, 1956], p. 79) he illustrates by respect for a person's "righteousness" *(l.c.)* and remarks: "Respect is a tribute we cannot refuse to pay to merit. . ." (p. 80).

30. Though, of course, they may be (if they are loved or respected as persons). In that case it will not be, strictly, the persons, but their welfare or freedom, which will be the "end" of those who so love or respect them: since only that which can be realized by action can be an end, to speak of another *person* as my end is bad logical grammar.

31. Cf. Melden, *Rights and Right Conduct,* p. 80.

32. I am bypassing the factual question of the extent to which (1) and (2) are generally believed.

33. I am well aware of the incompleteness of this highly schematic account. It does not pretend to give the full argument for the justification of (3) and (4) (and see next note) or of their "specifications." Among other omissions, it fails to make allowance for the fact that the complex inter-relations of these various rights would affect the justification of each.

34. On p. 19 Frankena writes as though his own answer to the same question would be, "because 'all men are similarly capable of enjoying a good life'"; this, he says, is what "justifies the *prima facie* requirement that they be treated as equals." But that *A* and *B* are similarly capable of enjoying respectively good lives G(*A*) and G(*B*) is not a compelling reason for saying that *A* and *B* have equal right respectively to G(*A*) and G(*B*). The Brahmin who held (Sir Henry Maine, *Early History of Institutions* [New York, 1875], p. 399) that "a Brahmin was entitled to 20 times as much happiness as anyone else" need not have held that the Brahmin's *capacity* for happiness (or "enjoying a good life") differs in the same ratio from that of others. All he would have to deny would be the equal *value* of the happiness of Brahmins and of others. It is some such premise as this that Frankena must affirm to bring off his justification-argument. I might add that I am not objecting to listing capacity among the premises. The only reason I did not is that I was only citing the "crucial" premise, the one that would be normally decisive for the acceptance or rejection of the justificandum. A reference to capacity would also be necessary, and I would follow Frankena in conceding that "men may well be different in such a way that the best life of which one is capable simply is not as good as that of which another is capable" (p. 20), adding a like concession in the case of freedom. *A*'s and *B*'s *prima facie* equal rights to well-being and to freedom are in effect equal rights to that well-being and freedom of which *A* and *B* are equally capable. Thus where the capacity for freedom is severely limited (e.g., that of an idiot or anyone else in the *non compos mentis* class), the right to freedom would be correspondingly limited.

35. The best example of this among philosophical moralists is Nietzsche: "Egoism belongs to the nature of a distinguished soul. I mean that immovable faith that other beings are by nature subordinate to a being such as 'we are'; that they should sacrifice themselves to us," *Beyond Good and Evil,* trans. Marianne Cowan (Chicago, 1935), p. 265. A little earlier (p. 258) he had praised that "good and health aristocracy" which "accepts with a clear conscience the sacrifice of an enormous number of men who must *for its sake* [that of the aristocracy] be suppressed and reduced to incomplete human beings, to slaves, to tools" (Nietzsche's italics).

36. *Brown v. Topeka Board of Education,* 347 U.S. (1954), pp. 483ff., "To separate

them from others of similar age and qualifications solely because of their race generates a feeling of inferiority as to their status in the community that may affect their hearts and minds in a way unlikely ever to be undone.
37. The context in which the above citation is imbedded leaves one uncertain as to whether, in the opinion of the Court, (a) this evil was *per se* a reason for outlawing segregation in public schools, or (b) constituted such a reason merely because the "feeling of inferiority" reduced the children's chances of getting equal benefit from their schooling and thus disturbed the equality of their educational opportunities. The ensuing citation from the earlier finding in the Kansas case makes it look as though (b) expressed the Court's opinion; and (b) unlike (a), is not immediately generalizable to other forms of segregation.

Is Turn About Fair Play?

BARRY R. GROSS

. . . The balance of argument weighs against reverse discrimination for four interrelated sets of reasons. First, the procedures designed to isolate the discriminated are flawed. Second, the practice has undesirable and dangerous consequences. Third, it fails to fit any of the models of compensation or reparations. Fourth, it falls unjustly upon both those it favors and those it disfavors. I conclude that if to eliminate discrimination against the members of one group we find ourselves discriminating against another, we have gone too far.

Sociologically, groups are simply not represented in various jobs and at various levels in percentages closely approximately their percentage of the population. When universities in general and medical schools in particular discriminated heavily against them, Jews were represented in the medical profession in far greater percentages than their percentage of the population. At the same time, they were represented in far lower percentages in banking, finance, construction, and engineering than their percentage in the population, especially the population of New York City. A similar analysis by crudely drawn group traits—Jew, Roman Catholic, WASP, Irish, and so forth—of almost any trade, business or profession would yield similar results.

But the argument from population percentages may be meant not as an analysis of what is the case, but as an analysis of what ought to be the case. A proponent might put it this way: It is true that groups are not usually represented in the work force by their percentage in the popula-

From *Reverse Discrimination,* ed. Barry R. Gross (Buffalo, N.Y.: Prometheus Books, 1977); reprinted from the *Journal of Critical Analysis,* Vol. 5 (Jan.-Apr. 1975).

tion at large, but minority C has been systematically excluded from the good places. Therefore, in order to make sure that they get some of them, we should systematically include them in the good places, and a clear way of doing it is by their percentage in the population. Or we might conclude instead: therefore, in order to make up for past exclusion, they should be included in the good places as reparation, and an easy way to do it is by their percentage in the population.

If the definition of a minority discriminated against is ipso facto their representation in certain jobs in percentages less than their percentage in the general population, then one has to remark that the reasoning is circular. For we are trying to prove: (1) that minority C is discriminated against.

We use a premise (3) that minority C is underrepresented in good jobs. Since (1) does not follow from (3) (mere underrepresentation not being even prima facie evidence of discrimination), it is necessary to insert (2) that their underrepresentation is due to discrimination. But this completes the circle.

A critic might reply that we know perfectly well what is meant. The groups discriminated against are blacks, Puerto Ricans, Mexican-Americans, American Indians, and women. He is correct, though his answer does not tell us *how to find out* who is discriminated against. This critic, for example, left out Jews and Orientals. If he should reply that Jews and Orientals do well enough, we point out that the question was not "Who fails to do well?" but rather, "Who is discriminated against?" This argument shows that the mechanisms for identifying the victims of discrimination and for remedying it are seriously deficient.

Even if we allow that the percentage of the group in the work force versus its percentage in the population is the criterion of discrimination, who is discriminated against will vary depending upon how we divide the groups. We may discover that Republicans are discriminated against by our literary or intellectual journals—*New York Review, Dissent, Commentary.* We may also discover that wealthy Boston residents are discriminated against by the Los Angeles Dodgers, that women are discriminated against by the Army, and that idiots (we hope) are discriminated against by universities.

What employment or profession a person chooses depends upon a number of variables—background, wealth, parents' employment, schooling, intelligence, drive, ambition, skill, and not least, luck. Moreover, the analysis will differ depending upon what group identification or stratification you choose. None seems to have priority over the others. Every person can be typed according to many of these classifications. It seems, therefore, that the relevant analysis cannot even be made, much less justified.

In addition, some proponents of the population-percentage argument seem to hold: (4) From the contingent fact that members of the group C were discriminated against, it follows necessarily that they are underrepresented in the good positions. They then go on to assert (5) if members of group C were not discriminated against they would not be underrepresented, or (6) if they are underrepresented, then they are discriminated against.

But clearly (4) is itself a contingent, not a necessary truth. Clearly also neither (5) nor (6) follows from it, (5) being the fallacy of denying the antecedent and (6) the fallacy of affirming the consequent. Lastly, neither (5) nor (6) is necessarily true. The members of a group might simply lack interest in certain jobs (for example, Italians in the public-school system are in short supply). Could one argue that, even though neither (4), (5), nor (6) is *necessarily* true, the mere fact of underrepresentation in certain occupations does provide evidence of discrimination? The answer is no—no more than the fact of "overrepresentation" in certain occupations is evidence of favoritism.

At most, underrepresentation can be used to support the contention of discrimination when there is *other* evidence as well.

FAIR PLAY:
OUGHT WE TO DISCRIMINATE IN REVERSE?

There are at least three difficulties with reverse discrimination: first, it is inconsistent; second, it licenses discrimination; third it is unfair.

If we believe the principle that equal opportunity is a right of everyone, then if members of group C are excluded from enjoying certain opportunities merely because they are members of group C, their right is being abrogated. They are entitled to this right, but so is everybody else, even those persons who presently deny it to them. If both are made to enjoy equal opportunity, then both are enjoying their right. To give either oppressors or oppressed more than equal opportunity is equally to deny the rights of one or the other in violation of the principle of equal opportunity.

Proponents of reverse discrimination seem to be caught on the horns of a dilemma: either discrimination is illegitimate or it is not. If it is illegitimate, then it ought not to be practiced against anyone. If it is not, then there exists no reason for *now* favoring blacks, Puerto Ricans, Chicanos, Indians, women, and so forth over whites.

Two strategies present themselves. Either we can analyze one disjunct with a view to showing that distinctions can be made which require compensation or reparations in the form of reverse discrimination to be made to wronged individuals or groups; or we can try to soften one of the disjuncts so as to make a case for exceptions in favor of the wronged. The first appeals both to our reason and our sense of justice. The second appeals to our emotions. I shall argue that neither strategy works.[1]

Now reverse discrimination can take several forms, but I think that what many of its proponents have in mind is a strong form of compensation—a form which requires us to discriminate against non-C members and favor C members even if less qualified. One may well wonder whether there is not a little retribution hidden in this form of compensation.

THE "SOFTENED" GENERAL PRINCIPLE

The argument for construing reverse discrimination as compensation or reparation has a great appeal which can be brought out by contrasting it with another approach. One might agree that as a general rule reverse discrimination is illegitimate but that it need not be seen as universally illegitimate. In particular, in the case where people have been so heavily discriminated against as to make it impossible for them now to gain a good life, there is no possibility of their having a fair chance, no possibility of their starting out on anything like equal terms, then and only then is it legitimate to discriminate in their favor and hence against anyone else.

Against this "softened" general principle I shall urge two sorts of objections which I call respectively "practical" and "pragmatic." Against the reparations type of argument, I shall urge first that there is some reason to think the conditions for exacting and accepting them are lacking, and second that, owing to the peculiar nature of the reparations to be exacted (reverse discrimination), the very exaction of them is unreasonable and unfair to both parties—exactors and exactees.

I mention briefly two sorts of practical objections to the "softened" general principle. First, it is simply the case that when discrimination is made in favor of someone regardless of his qualifications, there is the greatest possible danger that the person getting the position will not be competent to fill it. Second, when a person is placed in a position because of discriminaion in his favor, he may come to feel himself inferior.[2] This may easily lead to the permanent conferral of inferior status on the group, an inferiority which is all the stronger because self-induced. Its psychological effects should not be underestimated.

The pragmatic objection to the "softened" general principle is much stronger. Discrimination in any form is invidious. Once licensed, its licenses rebound upon its perpetrators as well as others. Principles tend to be generalized without consideration of restrictions or the circumstances to which they were intended to apply. Students of the Nazi movement will have noticed that in licensing the discrimination, isolation, persecution, and "final solution" of the Jews, the Nazis (foreign and German) licensed their own. (Hitler's plans for extermination included political groups, for example, the Rohm faction of the SA, as well as other racial groups, for example, Slavs and Balts who fought on the German side.) It is necessary to be quite careful what principles one adopts. In view of the long and bloody history of discrimination, one ought to be very chary of sanctioning it.

COMPENSATION, REPARATIONS, AND RESTITUTION

Because it escapes most of these objections, the reparations argument becomes very attractive. What is more obvious than the principle that people ought to be compensated for monetary loss, pain and suffering inflicted by others acting either as agents of government or as individuals? From the negligence suit to reparations for war damage, the principle is comfortable, familiar, and best of all, legal. For victims of broken sidewalks, open wells, ignored stop signs, the conditions under which damages are awarded are quite clear. (1) There is specific injury, specific victim, specific time and place. (2) A specific individual or set of individuals must be found responsible either (a) by actually having done the injury, or (b) by failing to act in such a way (for example, repairing the sidewalk, sealing the well) so as to remove a particular potential source of injury on their property. (3) A reasonable assessment of the monetary value of the claim can be made. In such cases no moral blame is attached to the person forced to pay compensation.

But reparations are somewhat less clear. How much does Germany owe France for causing (losing?) World War I? Can we say that *Germany* caused the war? Can we say that Germany *caused* the war? Germany did pay, at least in part, based upon rough calculations of the cost of the Allied armies, including pensions, the loss of allied GNP, indemnities for death and for the destruction of property. . . .

INAPPLICABILITY OF THESE PARADIGMS

Can reverse discrimination be construed to fit any of these paradigms? Can favoring blacks, Chicanos, Indians, women, and so forth over whites or males be seen as compensation, reparations, or restitution? The answer is no for two general reasons and for several which are specific to the various paradigms. The general reasons are, first, that responsibility for discrimination past and present and for its deleterious consequences is neither clearly assigned nor accepted. Some seem to think that the mere fact of its existence makes all whites (or males in the case of antifeminism) responsible.[3] But I do not know an analysis of responsibility which bears out this claim. Second, there is a great difficulty, if not an impossibility, in assigning a monetary value to the damage done and compensation allegedly owed—that is to say, reverse discrimination.

If we turn to the negligence paradigm, all the conditions seem to fail. *Specific* injury is lacking, *specific* individual responsibility is lacking, and there is no way to assess the monetary value of the "loss." Indeed, in the case of reverse discrimination it is not monetary value which is claimed but preferential treatment. Under the large-scale reparations paradigm two conditions beyond responsibility are lacking. There are no governments or government-like agencies between which the transfer could take place, and there is no *modus agendi* for the transfer to take place.

Where the transfer is to be of preferential treatment, it is unclear how it is even to be begun. So we come to the third paradigm: individual restitution. This is much closer, for it deals with compensating individual victims of persecution. Again, however, it fails to provide a model, first, because reverse discrimination cannot be looked at in monetary terms, and second, even if it could, the restitution is designed to bring a person back to where he was before deprivation. In the case of the minorities in question, there can be no question of restoring them to former positions or property. Precisely, the point of the reparation is to pay them for what they, because of immoral social practices, never had in the first place.. . . .

JUSTICE

Finally, if we ignore all that has been said and simply go ahead and discriminate in reverse, calling it reparation, it remains to ask whether it would be either reasonable or just? I think the answer is no. It is possible to hold that in some set of cases, other things being equal, compensation is required and yet to argue either that since other things are not equal compensation is not required, or that even if some compensation is required it ought not to take the form of reverse discrimination. Certainly, from the fact that some form of compensation or reparation must be made it does not follow that any *specific* form of compensation is in order. If X is discriminated against in awarding professorships because he is a member of C group, it scarcely follows that if compensation is in order it *must* take the form of his being discriminated in favor of for another professorship, at least not without adopting the principle of "an eye for an eye" (and only an *eye* for an eye?). Consider X being turned down for an apartment because he is a C member. Must compensation consist just in his being offered another ahead of anybody else? Even if he has one already? To go from the relatively innocuous principle that where *possible* we ought to compensate for damages, to sanction reverse discrimination as the proper or preferred form of redress, requires us to go beyond mere compensation to some principle very much like "let the punishment mirror the crime." But here the person "punished," the person from which the compensation is exacted, is often not the "criminal." Nor will it help to say that the person deprived of a job or advancement by reverse discrimination is not really being punished or deprived, since the job did not belong to him in the first place. Of course it didn't; nor did it belong to the successful candidate. What belonged to both is equal consideration, and that is what one of them is being deprived of.[4]

There is an element of injustice or unfairness in all reparations. The money derived from taxes paid by all citizens is used for reparations regardless of whether they were responsible for, did nothing about, opposed, or actually fought the policies or government in question. Yet we say that this is the only way it can be done, that the element of unfairness is not great, and that on the whole it is better that this relatively painless way of appropriating money from Jones, who is innocent, be used than that the victims of persecution or crime go uncompensated. But the consequences of reverse discrimination are quite different, especially when it is based upon group membership rather than individual desert. It is possible and is sometimes the case that though most C members are discriminated against, Y is a C member who has met with no discrimination at all. Under the principle that all C members should be discriminated in favor of, we would offer "compensation" to Y. But what are we compensating him *for?* By hypothesis he was no victim of discrimination. Do we compensate him for what happened to others? Do we pay Jones for what we buy from Smith? We seem to be compensating him for being a C member, but why? Do we secretly hold C members inferior? Some claim that society as a whole must bear the burden of reparation. But then reverse discrimination will hardly do the trick. It does not exact redress from the government, or even from all white (responsible?) citizens equally, but falls solely against those who apply for admissions, or jobs *for which blacks or other minorities are applying at the same time.* By the same token, it does not compensate or "reparate" all minority persons equally but merely those applying for admission, jobs, promotions, and so forth. Those whose positions are secure would not be paid. A white person who fought for civil rights for blacks may be passed over for promotion or displaced, a victim of reverse discrimination, while a Ku Klux Klan man at the top of the job ladder pays nothing. This would be a laughably flawed system if it were not seriously advocated by responsible people, and partly implemented by the government. Surely, it violates the principles of both compensatory and distributive justice.

NOTES

1. For examples of these strategies, see the articles by J. W. Nickel, L. J. Cowan, and Paul Taylor herein.
2. *Contra* this objection see Irving Thalberg, "Justifications of Institutional Racism," *The Philosophical Forum,* Winter 1972.
3. See Thalberg. For an interesting catalogue of "irresponsible use of 'responsibility' " see Robert Stover, "Responsibility for the Cold War—A Case Study in Historical Responsibility," *History and Theory,* 1972. For a clear-cut analysis that more than mere presence on the scene is required to show responsibility, see S. Levinson, "Responsibility for Crimes of War," *Philosophy and Public Affairs,* Spring 1973.
4. See Gertrude Ezorsky, "It's Mine," *Philosophy and Public Affairs,* Spring 1974.

A Defense of Programs of Preferential Treatment

Richard Wasserstrom

Many justifications of programs of preferential treatment depend upon the claim that in one respect or another such programs have good consequences or that they are effective means by which to bring about some desirable end, e.g., an integrated, equalitarian society. I mean by "programs of preferential treatment" to refer to programs such as those at issue in the *Bakke* case—programs which set aside a certain number of places (for example, in a law school) as to which members of minority groups (for example, persons who are non-white or female) who possess certain minimum qualifications (in terms of grades and test scores) may be preferred for admission to those places over some members of the majority group who possess higher qualifications (in terms of grades and test scores).

Many criticisms of programs of preferential treatment claim that such programs, even if effective, are unjustifiable because they are in some important sense unfair or unjust. In this paper I present a limited defense of such programs by showing that two of the chief arguments offered for the unfairness or injustice of these programs do not work in the way or to the degree supposed by critics of these programs.

The first argument is this. Opponents of preferential treatment programs sometimes assert that proponents of these programs are guilty of intellectual inconsistency, if not racism or sexism. For, as is now readily acknowledged, at times past employers, universities, and many other social institutions did have racial or sexual quotas (when they did not practice overt racial or sexual exclusion), and many of those who were most concerned to bring about the eradication of those racial quotas are now untroubled by the new programs which reinstitute them. And this, it is claimed, is inconsistent. If it was wrong to take race or sex into account when blacks and women were the the objects of racial and sexual policies and practices of exclusion, then it is wrong to take race or sex into account when the objects of the policies have their race or sex reversed. Simple considerations of intellectual consistency—of what it means to give racism or sexism as a reason for condemning these social policies and practices—require that what was a good reason then is still a good reason now.

The problem with this argument is that despite appearances, there is no inconsistency involved in holding both views. Even if contemporary preferential treatment programs which contain quotas are wrong, they

From *Phi Kappa Phi Journal*, LVIII (Winter 1978); originally Part II of "Racism, Sexism, and Preferential Treatment: An Approach to the Topics," 24 *U.C.L.A. Law Review*, 581 (1977).

are not wrong for the reasons that made quotas against blacks and women pernicious. The reason why is that the social realities do make an enormous difference. The fundamental evil of programs that discriminated against blacks or women was that these programs were a part of a larger social universe which systematically maintained a network of institutions which unjustifiably concentrated power, authority, and goods in the hands of white male individuals, and which systematically consigned blacks and women to subordinate positions in the society.

Whatever may be wrong with today's affirmative action programs and quota systems, it should be clear that the evil, if any, is just not the same. Racial and sexual minorities do not constitute the dominant social group. Nor is the conception of who is a fully developed member of the moral and social community one of an individual who is either female or black. Quotas which prefer women or blacks do not add to an already relatively overabundant supply of resources and opportunities at the disposal of members of these groups in the way in which the quotas of the past did maintain and augment the overabundant supply of resources and opportunities already available to white males.

The same point can be made in a somewhat different way. Sometimes people say that what was wrong, for example, with the system of racial discrimination in the South was that it took an irrelevant characteristic, namely race, and used it systematically to allocate social benefits and burdens of various sorts. The defect was the irrelevance of the characteristic used—race—for that meant that individuals ended up being treated in a manner that was arbitrary and capricious.

I do not think that was the central flaw at all. Take, for instance, the most hideous of the practices, human slavery. The primary thing that was wrong with the institution was not that the particular individuals who were assigned the place of slaves were assigned there arbitrarily because the assignment was made in virtue of an irrelevant characteristic, their race. Rather, it seems to me that the primary thing that was and is wrong with slavery is the practice itself—the fact of some individuals being able to own other individuals and all that goes with that practice. It would not matter by what criterion individuals were assigned; human slavery would still be wrong. And the same can be said for most if not all of the other discrete practices and institutions which comprised the system of racial discrimination even after human slavery was abolished. The practices were unjustifiable—they were oppressive—and they would have been so no matter how the assignment of victims had been made. What made it worse, still, was that the institutions and the supporting ideology all interlocked to create a system of human oppression whose effects on those living under it were as devastating as they were unjustifiable.

Again, if there is anything wrong with the programs of preferential treatment that have begun to flourish within the past ten years, it should be evident that the social realities in respect to the distribution of resources and opportunities make the difference. Apart from everything else, there is simply no way in which all of these programs taken together could plausibly be viewed as capable of relegating white males to the kind of genuinely oppressive status characteristically bestowed upon women and blacks by the dominant social institutions and ideology.

The second objection is that preferential treatment programs are wrong because they take race or sex into account rather than the only thing that does matter—that is, an individual's qualifications. What all such programs have in common and what makes them all objectionable, so this argument goes, is that they ignore the persons who are more qualified by bestowing a preference on those who are less qualified in virtue of their being either black or female.

There are, I think, a number of things wrong with this objection based on qualifications, and not the least of them is that we do not live in a society in which there is even the serious pretense of a qualification requirement for many jobs of substantial power and authority. Would anyone claim, for example, that the persons who comprise the judiciary are there because they are the most qualified lawyers or the most qualified persons to be judges? Would anyone claim that Henry Ford II is the head of the Ford Motor Company because he is the most qualified person for the job? Part of what is wrong with even talking about qualifications and merit is that the argument derives some of its force from the erroneous notion that we would have a meritocracy were it not for programs of preferential treatment. In fact, the higher one goes in terms of prestige, power and the like, the less qualifications seem ever to be decisive. It is only for certain jobs and certain places that qualifications are used to do more than establish the possession of certain minimum competencies.

But difficulties such as these to one side, there are theoretical difficulties as well which cut much more deeply into the argument about qualifications. To begin with, it is important to see that there is a serious inconsistency present if the person who favors "pure qualifications" does so on the ground that the most qualified ought to be selected because this promotes maximum efficiency. Let us suppose that the argument is that if we have the most qualified performing the relevant tasks we will get those tasks done in the most economical and efficient manner. There is nothing wrong in principle with arguments based upon the good consequences that will flow from maintaining a social practice in a certain way. But it is inconsistent for the opponent of preferential treatment to attach much weight to qualifications on this ground, because it was an analogous appeal to the good consequences that the opponent of preferential treatment thought was wrong in the first place. That is to say, if the chief thing to be said in favor of strict qualifications and preferring the most qualified is that it is the most efficient way of getting things done, then we are right back to an assessment of the different consequences that will flow from different programs, and we are far removed from the considerations of justice or fairness that were thought to weigh so heavily against these programs.

It is important to note, too, that qualifications—at least in the educational context—are often not connected at all closely with any plausible conception of social effectiveness. To admit the most qualified students to law school, for example—given the way qualifications are now determined—is primarily to admit those who have the greatest chance of scoring the highest grades at law school. This says little about efficiency except perhaps that these students are the easiest for the faculty to teach. However, since we know so little about what constitutes being a good, or even successful lawyer, and even less about the correlation between being a very good law student and being a very good lawyer, we can hardly claim very confidently that the legal system will operate most effectively if we admit only the most qualified students to law school.

To be at all decisive, the argument for qualifications must be that those who are the most qualified deserve to receive the benefits (the job, the place in law school, etc.) because they are the most qualified. The introduction of the concept of desert now makes it an objection as to justice or fairness of the sort promised by the original criticism of the programs. But now the problem is that there is no reason to think that there is any strong sense of "desert" in which it is correct that the most qualified deserve anything.

Let us consider more closely one case, that of preferential treatment in respect to admission to college or graduate school. There is a logical gap in the inference from the claim that a person is most qualified to perform a task, e.g., to be a good student, to the conclusion that he or she deserves to be admitted as a student. Of course, those who deserve to be admitted should be admitted. But why do the most qualified deserve anything? There is simply no necessary connection between academic merit (in the sense of being most qualified) and deserving to be a member of a student body. Suppose, for instance, that there is only one tennis court in the community. Is it clear that the two best tennis players ought to be the ones permitted to use it? Why not those who were there first? Or those who will enjoy playing the most? Or those who are the worst and, therefore, need the greatest opportunity to practice? Or those who have the chance to play least frequently?

We might, of course, have a rule that says that the best tennis players get to use the court before the others. Under such a rule the best players would deserve the court more than the poorer ones. But that is just to push the inquiry back one stage. Is there any reason to think that we ought to have a rule giving good tennis players such a preference? Indeed, the arguments that might be given for or against such a rule are many and varied. And few if any of the arguments that might support the rule would depend upon a connection between ability and desert.

Someone might reply, however, that the most able students deserve to be admitted to the university because all of their earlier schooling was a kind of competition, with university admission being the prize awarded to the winners. They deserve to be admitted because that is what the rule of the competition provides. In addition, it might be argued, it would be unfair now to exclude them in favor of others, given the reasonable expectations they developed about the way in which their industry and performance would be rewarded. Minority-admission programs, which inevitably prefer some who are less qualified over some who are more qualified, all possess this flaw.

There are several problems with this argument. The most substantial of them is that it is an empirically implausible picture of our social world. Most of what are regarded as the decisive characteristics for higher education have a great deal to do with things over which the individual has neither control nor responsibility: such things as home environment, socioeconomic class of parents, and, of course, the quality of the primary and secondary schools attended. Since individuals do not deserve having had any of these things vis-à-vis other individuals, they do not, for the most part, deserve their qualifications. And since they do not deserve their abilities they do not in any strong sense deserve to be admitted because of their abilities.

To be sure, if there has been a rule which connects say, performance at high school with admission to college, then there is a weak sense in which those who do well at high school deserve, for that reason alone, to be admitted to college. In addition, if persons have built up or relied upon their reasonable expectations concerning performance and admission, they have a claim to be admitted on this ground as well. But it is certainly not obvious that these claims of desert are any stronger or more compelling than the competing claims based upon the needs of or advantages to women or blacks from programs of preferential treatment. And as I have indicated, all rule-based claims of desert are very weak unless and until the rule which creates the claim is itself shown to be a justified one. Unless one has a strong preference for the status quo, and unless one can defend that preference, the practice within a system of allocating places in a certain way does not go very far at all in showing that that is the right or the just way to allocate those places in the future.

A proponent of programs of preferential treatment is not at all committed to the view that qualifications ought to be wholly irrelevant. He or she can agree that, given the existing structure of any institution, there is probably some minimal set of qualifications without which one cannot participate meaningfully within the institution. In addition, it can be granted that the qualifications of those involved will affect the way the institution works and the way it affects others in the society. And the consequences will vary depending upon the particular institution. But all of this only establishes that qualifications, in this sense, are relevant, not that they are decisive. This is wholly consistent with the claim that race or sex should today also be relevant when it comes to matters such as admission to college or law school. And that is all that any preferential treatment program—even one with the kind of quota used in the *Bakke* case—has ever tried to do.

I have not attempted to establish that programs of preferential treatment are right and desirable. There are empirical issues concerning the consequences of these programs that I have not discussed, and certainly not settled. Nor, for that matter, have I considered the argument that justice may permit, if not require, these programs as a way to provide compensation or reparation for injuries suffered in the recent as well as distant past, or as a way to remove benefits that are undeservedly enjoyed by those of the dominant group. What I have tried to do is show that it is wrong to think that programs of preferential treatment are objectionable in the centrally important sense in which many past and present discriminatory features of our society have been and are racist and sexist. The social realities as to power and opportunity do make a fundamental difference. It is also wrong to think that programs of preferential treatment could, therefore, plausibly rest both on the view that such programs are not unfair to white males (except in the weak, rule-dependent sense described above) and on the view that it is unfair to continue the present set of unjust—often racist and sexist—institutions that comprise the social reality. And the case for these programs could rest as well on the proposition that, given the distribution of power and influence in the United States today, such programs may reasonably be viewed as potentially valuable, effective means by which to achieve admirable and significant social ideals of equality and integration.

Classification by Race in Compensatory Programs

James W. Nickel

Suppose that a person who favors compensatory programs for American blacks because of America's history of slavery and discrimination is charged with inconsistency in the following way: "When blacks are denied benefits and given heavier burdens because of race you claim that race is irrelevant and hence claim that discrimination is being practiced.[1] But when racial classifications are used to give preferential treatment to blacks you claim that race is a relevant consideration and deny that this is reverse discrimination." I want to consider two replies that can be made to this charge of inconsistency. The first reply holds that race, the characteristic which is held to be irrelevant when blacks are mistreated, is not the characteristic which is being held to be relevant when compensatory programs are defended. This reply denies that race is the basis for compensation; it claims that the real basis is the wrongs and losses blacks have suffered and the special needs that they have. Hence the characteristic which is held to be relevant in connection with compensatory programs is not race but a different characteristic, and there is no inconsistency. I will call this the "different-characteristics reply." The second reply allows that race is the characteristic about which differing relevance claims are made, but it denies that there is any inconsistency since claiming that race

From *Ethics*, Vol. 84 (1974); © 1974 by the University of Chicago. Reprinted by permission of the author and the publisher, The University of Chicago Press.

is irrelevant to whether someone should be mistreated is not incompatible with claiming that race is relevant to whether someone should be helped. Different issues are involved, and what is relevant to one issue can be irrelevant to another. I will call this the "different-issues reply."

THE DIFFERENT-CHARACTERISTICS REPLY

This reply claims that there is no inconsistency in condemning racial discrimination while favoring compensatory programs for blacks because race, the characteristic which is held to be irrelevant when blacks are mistreated, is not the characteristic which is the basis for providing compensation to blacks. And since race is not the basis for compensatory programs, it need not be claimed that race is relevant in such contexts. The reason for providing compensatory programs for blacks is not their race but the fact that they have been victimized by slavery and discrimination. Not race, but the wrongs that were done, the losses that were suffered and the special needs resulting from these provide the basis for special treatment now. On this view, race is not held to be relevant in defending compensatory programs, and hence there is no inconsistency with the original claim that race is irrelevant to how people should be treated.[2]

I think this reply is helpful in many cases, but in cases where explicit racial classifications are used by compensatory programs, the person who takes this approach must either claim that such explicit racial classifications are unjustifiable or suggest that they are an unavoidable administrative expediency. To suggest the latter is to suggest that this is a case where the administrative basis for a program (i.e., the characteristic which is used by administrators to decide who is to be served by the program) is different from the justifying basis (i.e., the characteristic which is the reason for having the program). It is not uncommon for these two to differ, although they should overlap substantially. If the justifying basis is a characteristic which occurs in more individuals than the characteristic which is the administrative basis, the latter is underinclusive. And if the justifying basis is a characteristic which occurs in fewer individuals than the characteristic which is the administrative basis, the latter is overinclusive. When resources are limited it is not uncommon to use an underinclusive administrative basis (e.g., when a poverty program only serves those with an income of less than $2,000 per year), even though this forces the program to ignore deserving cases. And difficulties in identifying those with the characteristic which is the justifying basis may cause the program, for reasons of efficiency, to serve more people than those who have the characteristic which is the justifying basis (e.g., when everyone in a certain county—the administrative basis—is inoculated in order to eliminate a disease—the justifying basis—which 60 percent of the people have but which is difficult to detect except in advanced stages).[3]

The advocate of the "different-characteristics reply" is committed to denying that race is the justifying basis for compensatory programs. But if the justifying basis for such programs is the losses and needs resulting from slavery and discrimination there will be a high correlation between being black and having suffered these losses and having these needs, and because of this the advocate of this reply can allow, without inconsistency, that race can serve as part of the administrative basis for such a program. Efficiency in administering large-scale programs often requires that detailed investigations of individual cases be kept to a minimum, and this means that many allocative decisions will have to be made on the basis of gross but easily discernible characteristics. This may result in a certain degree of unfairness, but it does help to decrease administrative costs so that more resources can be directed to those in need. Programs designed to help victims of discrimination are probably of this sort. Since it is usually quite difficult to determine the extent to which a person has suffered from racial discrimination, it may be necessary simply to take the susceptibility to this discrimination (and perhaps some other gross criterion such as present income) as the basis for allocation. The use of such an administrative basis would result in a certain degree of both over- and underinclusiveness, but in most cases this degree would probably not be an intolerable one from the perspective of fairness and efficiency.

THE DIFFERENT-ISSUES REPLY

This reply to the charge of inconsistency ignores possible differences in the characteristic which is the justifying basis; it presupposes, as does the person making the charge of inconsistency, that race is the justifying basis for compensatory programs. This reply claims that even if race is held to be irrelevant when blacks are being mistreated and relevant when blacks are being helped, there is no inconsistency in this since different issues are involved, and a characteristic which is relevant to one issue is often irrelevant to another. Relevance involves a relation between a characteristic and an issue, C is relevant to I, and because of this "C_1 is relevant to I_1" is not inconsistent with "C_1 is not relevant to I_2."

But for this reply to work it must be shown that there really are two issues here, that the issue of deciding whether to allocate a penalty or loss is a different issue from deciding whether to allocate a benefit. This seems to be what Mark Green is suggesting in his article, "Reparations for Blacks," when he says, "It is a verbal gimmick to elide past prejudice with preferential treatment. A subsidy is obviously dissimilar to a penalty, a beneficiary different from a victim, although both fit under the discrimination rubric."[4] Green seems to hold that the crucial difference is between subsidies and penalities, between helping and harming, and that it is the fact that racial classifications are used in compensatory programs to do good that makes them permissible. Green's view seems to be that it is one thing to use race as a basis for doing harm but quite another to use it as a basis for providing help.

But is there a sufficient difference between deciding to allocate a subsidy and deciding to allocate a penalty or loss to enable us to say that different issues are being decided and that race can be relevant to the former and irrelevant to the latter? The best reason I have been able to discover for thinking that there is a sufficient difference derives from the fact that the allocation of losses and penalties is a much more dangerous enterprise than the allocation of help and benefits. Deciding to impose a penalty or loss involves making a person worse off, whereas deciding not to provide a benefit usually involves merely leaving a person as he is. Since the former decision involves weightier consequences in most cases, we may be inclined to allow that it is a different decision than the latter and to allow that different considerations can be relevant to the two issues. This will be to claim that because of this difference there are and should be tighter moral and legal restriction on grounds that can serve as a basis for distributing penalties and losses, and that even though it is impermissible to use race as the basis for imposing losses and penalties, it is permissible to use race as the basis for distributing benefits.

One problem with putting so much weight on the distinction between distributing benefits and distributing penalties and losses is that in many cases a single distribution does both. If the item which is being allocated is a scarce and important benefit (like a good job), giving it to one person will often be tantamount to denying it to another person with an equally good claim to it, and denying it to this person will often be a considerable loss to him. Here the allocative decision concerns both providing a benefit and causing a loss, and hence one cannot merely say that race is a permissible basis for the decision because it is a decision about whom to help. If in a situation like this we decide to help Jones because he is black, this may be tantamount to causing Smith to suffer a loss because he is nonblack. Cases like this do exist,[5] and in these cases the "different-issues" approach provides no help.

Leaving this problem aside, there is another difficulty with the "different-issues reply." Even if it is allowed that what is relevant to the distribution of a benefit is sometimes different from what is relevant to the distribution of penalties and losses, it still remains to be shown that race is the justifying basis for programs which provide special help to blacks. If this cannot be shown then one must fall back on the claim that race is only the administrative basis for such programs.

So the question that we must ask is whether race or ancestry as such can serve as a justifying basis for a program which distributes benefits rather than burdens. And I am inclined to think that it cannot. The mere fact that many people in this country are of African ancestry does not in itself provide any justification for a program of benefits to these people—no more than the mere fact that many people in California are of Oklahoman ancestry provides a justifying basis for a program of benefits to them. One's race or ancestry could serve as a justifying basis for special benefits only if having this race or ancestry was, in itself, a special merit which deserved reward or a special lack which required compensation. But unless one is prepared to return to racist and aristocratic principles, one must deny that one's race or ancestry is in itself a matter of special merit or special lack. And hence one must deny that race or ancestry, in itself, can serve as a justifying basis for a program of special benefits.

It might be replied, however, that this overlooks important aspects of the context. In a context where the members of one race have over a long period been subject to discrimination and mistreatment it might be argued that race can be the justifying basis for a program of benefits. I think, however, that as soon as one begins to emphasize the wrongs done to blacks, the losses they have suffered, and the special needs they have now, it becomes clear that these things are the justifying basis for help to blacks and not race per se.

Suppose, however, that the person making this reply continues by asserting that in this period in America so many people think that being black is a special defect or lack that in effect it is a special defect or lack which requires compensation. But again one must insist that it is not race itself that justifies compensation; it is rather the effects of people's misconceptions about race that do this. Race or ancestry in itself constitutes no merit or defect; it is only in combination with people's misconceptions about it that it can aspire to this status. It is the adverse effects of these misconceptions, not race per se, that provide the justifying basis for special help programs. Race simply is not plausible as a justifying basis for a program, even for a program of benefits.

If I am right about this the "different-issues reply" turns out not to be helpful since it presupposes that race is the justifying basis for compensatory programs. Unless some other option emerges, the defender of compensatory programs will have to use the "different-characteristics reply" to the charge of inconsistency. This view allows that race can sometimes serve as the administrative basis for programs but makes its use contingent on considerations of fairness and efficiency. Whether race or ancestry can serve as a reasonable administrative basis (or a part of such a basis) for a program designed to provide special benefits to victims of slavery and discrimination will depend on whether among the possible alternatives it is the classification which is most workable and involves the combination of over- and underinclusiveness which is least unfair.

NOTES

1. There are two senses of "discrimination." One of these is morally neutral and applies to the simple discernment of differences. The other implies moral disapproval and applies to differentiations which involve bias, prejudice, and the use of irrelevant characteristics. My concern here is with "discrimination" in the latter sense.
2. This is the position that I took in my article, "Discrimination and Morally Relevant Characteristics," *Analysis* 32 (1972): 113–14. Also see J. L. Cowan's reply, "Inverse Discrimination," *Analysis* 33 (1972): 10–12.
3. The distinction between over- and underinclusive classifications is derived from Tussman and tenBroek, "The Equal Protection of the Laws," *California Law Review* 37 (1949): 341.
4. "Reparations for Blacks," *Commonweal* 90 (June 1969): 359. In saying that both subsidies and penalties "fit under the discrimination rubric," Green seems to overlook the connection between discrimination and the use of an irrelevant characteristic. He seems, that is, to slip into using the morally neutral sense when it is the other sense of "discrimination" that is in question.
5. See, for example, Bob Kuttner, "White Males and Jews Need Not Apply," *The Village Voice,* August 31, 1972.

BUSINESS AND THE CONSUMER: RESPONSIBILITY AND LIABILITY

Case Study—Hasbro Industries, Inc.

DAVID LOUDON and ALBERT DELLA BITTA

Hasbro Industries, Inc., is a consumer products manufacturer and one of the ten largest toy manufacturers in the United States. In the Fall of 1972 it faced certain consumer pressures, many of which have been strongly felt by Hasbro and other toy companies in the past. The Federal Trade Commission, Food and Drug Administration, Federal Communications Commission, Consumers Union, and parents' groups were continuing to pose challenges to the toy industry, particularly in the area of product safety and promotional techniques.

COMPANY BACKGROUND

Hasbro Industries, Inc., began in Rhode Island in 1926. Originally the firm was engaged in the textile business and in the early 1930s the company wrapped school pencil boxes in cloth. In the 1940s the company entered both the pencil manufacturing and toy-making industries.

Hasbro has grown substantially over the years. The company now employs a permanent labor force in its toy operations of approximately 2,750 persons, more than 79 percent of whom are engaged in production, and 600 in its school-supplies and pencil-manufacturing operations.

The tremendous growth of Hasbro is largely a result of changes in the company's management and marketing approaches. These included assigning responsibility for all day-to-day operations of the firm to Stephen Hassenfeld, Hasbro's 30-year-old executive vice-president and the third generation of the founding family, and his introduction into the company of a new, young group of executives. Most of the new executives were drawn from outside the toy industry and outside Rhode Island.

According to Steve Hassenfeld, who recruited the new management team, "Five years ago we were what Wall Street would call a small family business. We've worked hardest lately in getting the kind of management team a small family business doesn't have."

Originally printed in *Business and Society: Cases and Test*, ed. Robert D. Hay, Edmund R. Gray, and James E. Gates (Cincinnati, Ohio: South-Western Publishing Co.), 1976. Reprinted by permission of the authors, Dr. David Loudon and Dr. Albert Della Bitta, University of Rhode Island.

One major result was that Hasbro diversified into new fields: children's television, day-care centers, and housewares. Together with its toy and pencil business, these operations have made Hasbro a small conglomerate. . . .

Because the company's toy business is seasonal, shipments during the second half of each calendar year are much greater than shipments during the first half. During the first half, Hasbro produces toys for inventory largely to satisfy orders calling for later delivery and, to a lesser extent, in anticipation of future orders.

Hasbro seeks to avoid large amounts of unsold toys after Christmas and after fads; therefore the company pursues the "promotional staple," that is, a toy that requires only moderate advertising to sell well all year round, year after year.

Hasbro stresses the marketing of product groups bearing recognizable names rather than individual toy items, as advertising costs are not substantially greater for a whole line than for one toy.

The company's toy line now consists of approximately 450 items, the principal categories of which are the following:

> PRESCHOOL TOYS, including the *Romper Room* line, introduced in 1970, *Captain Kangaroo's Wooden Toys,* introduced in 1972, and *Your Baby* line of infant playthings, introduced in 1972;
>
> ACTION TOYS, including the *G.I. Joe Adventure Team* and accessories, introduced in 1964, and *Scream n Demons* motorcyles, introduced in 1971.
>
> DOLLS, including the *World of Love* dolls and accessories, introduced in 1971;
>
> CRAFT SETS, including the *Arts and Crafts Today* line, introduced in 1971; and
>
> STAPLE ITEMS, including chess and checker sets, doctors' and nurses' kits, banks, and other items such as its *Mr. Potato Head* and *Lite Brite* toys.

In 1969 Hasbro effected a "repositioning" of G.I. Joe, a toy which accounts for a significant share of the company's volume. The toy became more adventure-oriented and less a military figure. The reason for the image change was the apparent waning interest in military toys. At the peak of its popularity in 1965 G.I. Joe had sales of $23 million, but by 1968 the category was producing only $4.8 million in sales. After the repositioning in 1969 the G.I. Joe Adventure Team and related accessories reassumed its importance within the industry, and in 1971 accounted for approximately $12.5 million in toy sales.

In 1970 Hasbro introduced the Romper Room preschool line in an attempt, as Steve Hassenfeld puts it, "to upgrade the quality level of the products that we were then manufacturing." This line, which presently consists of over 65 items, accounted for approximately $11.8 million or 22 percent of net toy sales in 1971. . . .

Television Programming

The company, through its recently acquired and wholly owned subsidiary, Romper Room Enterprises, Inc., is involved in the production of television programs. The principal program is the Romper Room television nursery school, a 20-year old internationally syndicated program—the oldest in the business—which is currently shown on approximately 85 television stations in the United States and on 55 stations in foreign countries. Scripts are centrally prepared and distributed to the local stations that carry the program.

Although Romper Room has more viewers than Sesame Street, it trails Captain Kangaroo. According to Mr. Hassenfeld, Romper Room's biggest asset is the way it encourages children to participate at home, rather than passively watch the screen. The show has received commendations from parents and the President's Council on Youth Fitness for its exercise routines that get children to use their muscles while they play.

In addition, Hasbro has financed several projects to improve the show. The company works with the child development staff of Hood College, Frederick, Md., and the Hood staff approves the entire show content. With the Kennedy Institute of Johns Hopkins University, Romper Room has developed 90 new visual perception games of value to children who will be learning to read. . . .

Manufacturing and Importing

Hasbro manufactures most of its toy products from basic raw materials such as plastic and wood and has elaborate injection molding, blow molding, heat sealing, box making, and printing equipment. In addition, the company manufactures most of its own dies, jigs, and fixtures but purchases molds from independent sources. Independent contractors are used from time to time to supplement the firm's own molding capacity. Certain items are purchased in finished form from other manufacturers in the United States; and Hasbro also purchases partially and totally finished items from manufacturers in Hong Kong, Taiwan, and Japan.

Hasbro's quality assurance department has grown faster than any other department in the company and along with the marketing department, it has been given control over product quality. Both have the authority to shut down any production line which either feels is not turning out significantly high quality products.

Marketing

The marketing department at Hasbro was revamped in 1966. Because of the changing orientation at Hasbro the company's national sales manager and its advertising director decided to leave the firm. These veteran toy marketers were replaced by people in their 20s.

The average age of all vice-presidents in the firm is 33. Within the marketing department the average age of its top group is 31, with the age of the marketing vice-president being 28.

These new executives have helped to steer the company in new directions including the development of new products, the setting up of a system of product managers, and the intensification of market research among children and their parents.

Product Testing and Test Marketing

One problem for the toy industry has been the conflict between the desire to maintain competitive secrecy and the need for test marketing of new products.

Hasbro began several years ago to test market its new products. At the time this decision was made Steve Hassenfeld stated, "We're tired of having made mistakes because of not going into test markets. We're not worried about knockoffs. We have a six-month tooling lead. The big companies won't copy a $2 or $3 item."

Product quality and "playability" is an important concern for Hasbro. The company utilizes laboratory tests of its products and also observes children at play with the items—the latter serves as much to determine how well the children like a certain toy as it does to test the product quality and durability. The company also interviews parents to obtain their viewpoints. . . .

Promotion

Hasbro extensively advertises its toy products on children's network television programs. The company also utilizes commercials on local television stations in the more important consumer markets. In 1971 Hasbro spent approximately $5,700,000 in its toy advertising and sales promotion program, nearly all of which was used for television advertising. The amount spent is expected to increase significantly in 1972. Hasbro advertises a few specifically selected items in those product groups in a manner designed to promote the sale of the other items in those product groups. Product groups which the firm advertised in 1971 accounted for approximately 80 percent of the company's net toy sales. The remainder of 1971 toy sales included staple items which sell from year to year and items promoted in prior years.

In utilizing television advertising to promote its toys and games to final consumers, Hasbro has advertised in the past on such varied shows as the "Tonight" show and "H. R. Pufnstuf." The company has also considered using CATV—cable television—as one possible solution to the commercial clutter on network television. In addition, Hasbro uses color inserts in Sunday newspaper comics sections in its major markets.

The company's products are frequently utilized in premium programs. For example, Borden's has offered G.I. Joe to promote sales of its Dutch-Chocolate mix, instant coffee, and malted milk.

Hasbro inaugurated the industry's first incentive program involving trips and merchandise prizes for jobbers and jobber salespeople. . . .

CONSUMERISM

Various facets of toy marketing have come under increasing criticism over the past few years. The areas of major concern to toy producers are those relating to product safety and advertising.

Product Safety

The U.S. Public Health Service has estimated that there are about 700,000 injuries involving toys every year. Because of congressional reaction to dangerous toys, toy products are now subject to the provisions of the Federal Child Protection and Toy Safety Act of 1969. Under this legislation the Secretary of Health, Education and Welfare may prohibit the marketing of items intended for use by children, which, after appropriate proceedings, have been determined to be hazardous. In addition, the marketing of items which are deemed imminently hazardous to the public health and safety may be barred by the Secretary for limited periods without a hearing. Furthermore, manufacturers may be required to repurchase hazardous items and reimburse certain expenses, even if such items were manufactured and sold prior to the adoption of the Act. From time to time the government has issued regulations which affect the manufacture of toys, specifically with respect to such aspects as the lead content of paint and the classification of electrically operated toys. Regulations have been proposed affecting other aspects of toy manufacture. However, Hasbro is uncertain as to what effect such regulations, if finally adopted, will have on its business or on the entire toy industry.

Hasbro did not anticipate that some of its products would draw government and consumer criticism. For example, the company's Javelin Darts (one of a number of lawn dart games then on the market) came under government fire as a hazardous toy. Another product, Super-Dough, drew a warning to toy buyers from *Consumer Reports.* The product contained an elaborate instruction sheet along with warnings that the product was not for internal consumption and that children with allergies could undergo serious reactions. Hasbro removed both of these toys from the market.

In responding to the issue of dangerous products, Toy Manufacturers of America, the industry association, has officially approved a set of safety guidelines. However, because of the huge number of products involved, the organization will not undertake the testing of each separate product in order to issue a seal of compliance.

In order to maintain and improve the safety of its toy products, Hasbro has instituted more extensive screening and quality control procedures. Nevertheless, there can be no assurance that the firm's products will not be investigated by the government or recalled from the market.

Violent Toys

The marketing of war toys has elicited opposition from some consumer groups. The American Toy Fair has been picketed by various antiwar-toy groups in the past few years. For example, a group of mothers concerned about the psychological development of their children has picketed the fair demanding that war toys be taken off the market.

Concern over such toys is expressed by these groups because of the potentially harmful influence which they feel toys may have on the child's development.

The toy industry's position has been that war toys don't cause war, they only reflect it. In other words, the industry association feels that violence is learned from human example, not from things.

Nevertheless, in deference to the antiwar sentiment, Hasbro's G.I. Joe, which used to be outfitted in military dress, has taken on an adventure theme. However, the company does maintain in its G.I. Joe line a replica of an Army jeep with a recoilless rifle mounted on it.

Although not classified as a violent toy, a water gun which Hasbro marketed—called Hypo Squirt—was fashioned like a giant hypodermic needle. Even though the product had been on the market for seven years, when the drug issue developed the toy was suddenly dubbed "play junior junkie" in the press and drew considerable criticism from the public. Hasbro withdrew the toy from the market.

Packaging

The Federal Trade Commission has spot-checked the packaging of Hasbro's toy products as part of an apparent investigation of "slack-filled" packaging practices within the toy industry. Although no action was taken by the FTC against Hasbro, the company has no assurance that the packaging of some of its products does not violate FTC regulations.

Advertising

Children's television advertising has come under increasing scrutiny by government and mounting criticism from retailers, parents, and consumer groups. The focal point for such concern centers around the use (or as consumer groups term it—the misuse) of advertising on television shows aimed at children, particularly within Saturday and Sunday morning programming.

In 1970 marketers spent $75 million on network television programs. Eight companies, primarily cereal and toy manufacturers, accounted for about half of this total.

Even toy retailers have criticized the magnitude of such advertising. According to a survey conducted among 5,200 toy and hobby retailers by Pepperdine College of Los Angeles and directed by Consultants to Management, Inc., toy store operators dislike national television advertising despite the fact that such advertising of toys by manufacturers has increased the retailer's business.

According to the report, the reason for the toy retailers' dislike of television is their suspicion that the cost of television advertising is so high that manufacturers are forced to put exorbitant prices on toys, counting on the appeal of television to children to force the sale, to the ultimate disappointment of child and parent and the resentment of the latter against the retail store which sold him the overrated merchandise. Of those surveyed, 77 percent of the toy store retailers and 81 percent of the discount department store and chain drugstore managers felt that television advertising increased prices.

The survey reports that toy store managers resent the fact that discount houses take advantage of the heavy television advertising of some toys to cut prices far below a reasonable retail profit (i.e., from 35–45% down to 1–5%) and/or to use the items as loss leaders.

Protests have been made by parents and consumer groups concerning the nature of advertising on children's shows as well as the extent of such promotion. One rather vocal organization in the forefront of the criticism has been ACT (Action for Children's Television), a Boston-based citizens' group that claims 2,500 members and supporters.

ACT is fundamentally opposed to commercialization of television aimed at children and has argued for the elimination of advertising during such programming. The Federal Communications Commission (FCC) has instituted an Inquiry and Proposed Rule Making procedure in response to a petition from ACT which requested that the FCC prohibit sponsorship and commercials on children's programs and prohibit the inclusion, use, or mention of products, services, or stores during such programs. The petition cited the Romper Room television program produced by Hasbro's subsidiary, among other programs, as being commerically oriented.

ACT argued that children were being unfairly influenced in the program's advertising through the use of Romper Room teachers who were doing the commericals. In addition, the group criticized the fact that the toys used on the program were those advertised on Romper Room.

Slightly before the ACT charges surfaced, Hasbro was taking steps to counter such criticism. The company decided that no Romper Room teacher could do a commerical for any toy product. In addition, the company stopped advertising any Romper Room toy used on the program.

At the time this action was taken, however, it did not appear to satisfy ACT. For example, early in 1971 one of ACT's directors and a mother of two stated, "I don't think Hasbro has reached the heart of the problem, which is selling to unsophisticated preschool children." By using Hasbro products on the program, she added, "they still have their commercial by having the children play with the toys on the program."

The ACT group has criticized not only Hasbro's advertising, but also that of many other companies which heavily promote their products to children.

Particularly distressing to such critics are the number of advertisements typically run within children's programs shown between 7:00 a.m. and 2:00 p.m. on Saturdays and Sundays. Commercials and non-program material may amount to no more than 12 minutes per hour (down from 16 minutes) according to the Television Code Review Board of the National Association of Broadcasters. Critics have also advocated that commercials during the children's programs be clustered.

The FTC has brought action against several toy manufacturers (although not against Hasbro) for deceptive advertising practices. Hasbro attempts to comply with the principles established in these actions, as well as with the rules promulgated by the FTC and with the regulations prescribed by the National Association of Broadcasters.

The NAB standards for toy commercials are quite specific. Before a toy commercial can be shown on television, it must be approved by the NAB.

The FTC is expected to hold public hearings to study the impact of advertising on children and consumers. Rules or regulations, if any, which may result from the FCC or FTC investigations are likely to affect the advertising practices of Hasbro and the rest of the toy industry.

Some firms within the industry have made moves to reduce the criticism of advertising practices affecting children. For example, Ideal Toy Company, which advertised directly to children via network television, has dropped sponsorhip of Saturday morning television—where the major controversy is—and now buys early weekday evening prime time.

Nielsen data indicate that 2- to 5-year-olds watch an average of 3.2 hours of television on fall Saturday mornings (8:00 a.m.–1:00 p.m.) and 6- to 11-year-olds watch 2.6 hours. However, both groups watch approximately 3.5 hours per week between 5:00–7:30 p.m. on weekdays.

Other toy marketers such as Fisher-Price have for some time been pursuing a strategy of targeting their message almost exclusively at parents, particularly mothers.

Hasbro has decided to continue its present policy of weekend television advertising.

Although a leader can sometimes turn into a follower in a season, Steve Hassenfeld declares with regard to Hasbro, "We believe we have the momentum that will carry us to leadership in the industry." As far as the consumer movement and its effects upon the toy industry and Hasbro are concerned, Hassenfeld remarked that, "The worst seems to be over."

The Moral Responsiblity of Corporations

DAVID T. OZAR

It is a commonplace of human life that we hold persons morally responsible for the actions they perform. We ordinarily consider it appropriate to address our criticisms and commendations of actions—in terms of whatever moral qualities we judge the actions to have—to the persons who perform them. But what shall we say when we look at corporations? Can we reasonably speak of corporations being morally responsible for actions they perform? Can we reasonably hold that the actions we are talking about are the actions of *the corporation*? Is it appropriate to think of a corporation as acting in some way as a single entity? If not, then it would be unreasonable for us to address our moral criticisms and commendations to the corporation as such, and only the individual persons involved could be so addressed. It would be unreasonable, in other words, to hold corporations morally responsible for their actions. Our first task, therefore, must be to examine the conditions under which it makes sense to look upon other kinds of groups of persons acting together as a single entity in the performance of actions. Then we can ask whether corporations ever fulfill these conditions, and if so, we will have good reasons for thinking that under these conditions we may reasonably hold corporations morally responsible for their actions.[1]

I have chosen to look at two kinds of groups of persons acting together: nations and clubs. We frequently think of the people who make up a nation as constituting a single entity in the performance of certain actions. It is true that we consider many of the activities of governments to be simply the activities of government and not the actions of the nation itself. For example, a government's diplomatic endeavors and debates about principles of public policy are ordinarily considered simply the activities of the government. But there are some activities of governments which we consider to be the actions of the nation as a whole, acting as a single entity. This is especially true of a nation's formal dealings with other nations, e.g., in adopting a treaty. However, it also appears in domestic matters when, for example, the chief officers of the federal government are selected or when (usually by a gradual process over a period of time) a certain principle is adopted as a standard for judging the nation's laws or institutions. Of course in practice the processes by which such actions are performed may be very complex, and individual persons may, by reason of their special offices or roles, bear special responsibilities within these processes. But it seems clear nonetheless that we do look on the nation as the one performing these actions and it is therefore to the nation, as a single entity, that we address our moral criticisms and commendations. That is, there are certain actions for which we hold not just certain persons, but also the nation, the whole group of people acting as a single entity, morally responsible.

On a smaller scale we can see the same principle operating with regard to people who form a club. The members of the club perform many actions which we do not consider to be actions of the group as a single entity. But there are some things—e.g., the adoption of a constitution, the selection of officers when carried out according to the proper procedures, and formal actions of the officers when they are duly authorized—which we do count as actions of the whole group as a single entity, i.e., as actions of the club. Here again, particular persons may have special offices or roles within the structure of the organization. But it is clear that in the case of a club, as of a nation, we do consider some of the activities of the group to be actions of the group as a single entity and that in such cases it is not just certain individuals but the club, that whole group acting as a single entity, that we hold morally responsible. If, for example, a club selected a person lacking in moral character as its chief officer and he or she carried out the business of the club in such a way as to harm a number of other persons, we would not only hold that person responsible for these actions but the club as well, the whole group of persons who make up the club, considered as a single moral agent.[2]

What is it that makes some of the activities associated with a nation or a club count as actions of the nation or club as a single entity and others not? Nations and clubs, and many other sorts of groups as well, are constituted and structured by systems of rules accepted by those who participate in and deal with them. In some cases these rules have been formally adopted in some way and are acknowledged in the activities of the group because of their official status, e.g., written constitutions and formal acts of legislation. But the rules which constitute and structure a group will always include—and will sometimes be made exclusively of—those which have no formal pedigree, but which the persons involved accept and count as applying to them in their activities within and in relation to the group. We cannot identify rules of this sort, which I shall call informally accepted rules, by reference to any formal procedures of adoption. But we can affirm their existence and determine their content by studying carefully how the persons involved act and by judging their actions in relation to the group.[3]

We learn which activities we are to count as those of the nation or club as a single entity by consulting its rules which so designate those actions and under what conditions. Of course the rules will not always speak of matters in these terms. We may also, often enough, find ourselves hard pressed to know precisely what the rules specify about a particular kind of situation, especially if we have no formally adopted rules to appeal to. But such ambiguities do not modify the fact that it is the rules accepted by the persons involved which determine that some activities associated with the group are to count as actions of the group as a single entity.

What difference does such accounting make? If something counts as the action of a group as a single entity, then that action cannot be replaced, modified, terminated, or revoked except by another action of the group as a single entity. An act of Congress signed by the president, for example, cannot be replaced, modified, terminated, or revoked except by another act of Congress signed by the president or by an act of the Supreme Court. The rules of a group will often determine which actions may replace, modify, terminate, or revoke others. But the point is that it is the rules accepted by the group which determine what count as actions of the group as a single entity and that when something so counts, then it cannot be replaced, modified, terminated, or revoked except by another action of the group as a single entity.

Now let us apply this fact to corporations. It is evident that corporations which have standing before the law have formal rules and regulations which determine that certain activities of those associated with the corporation are to count as actions of the corporation as a single entity and other activities are not. The charter of a corporation must make such determinations, reasonably required by the law because in granting the corporation legal status, the law is making the corporation as a single entity the subject of legal powers and of legal rights and duties. Corporations frequently also have, in addition to their formal rules, many informally accepted rules governing their operations and affecting what will count as actions of the corporation as a single entity. Thus, we seem to have as good reason for thinking that corporations are capable of acting as single entities as we have for thinking this of clubs and nations. For this reason it also seems reasonable to hold corporations, as we do nations and clubs, morally responsible for the actions which they perform as single entities.[4]

When we hold an individual person morally responsible for his or her actions in general, there are still a number of excuses which we accept as valid in particular circumstances. It is worth asking if it makes sense to accept any of these excuses as valid for a corporation under the same or similar circumstances.

If a person can truthfully say that he or she could not possibly have foreseen certain unhappy consequences of a certain action, then we regularly excuse the person from moral responsibility for those consequences. In the same way it would seem reasonable to excuse a corporation if its actions as a single entity resulted in some unhappy consequences which could not possibly have been foreseen by those persons on whose foresight and decisions the actions of the corporation as a single entity depend. (The resources of a corporation in this respect will be, of course, much greater than those of a single person.) In practice, of course, we qualify the use of this excuse by requiring people to make reasonable efforts to foresee the consequences of their actions. If they fail to do so, then we hold them responsible for acting without sufficient information and we do not excuse them in the same way for the unhappy consequences of their action. Similarly in the case of corporations, if a reasonable effort to foresee the consequences is not made, then the corporation is responsible for acting without sufficient information and is not to be excused in the same way for the unhappy consequences of its action.

Second, we regularly excuse persons from moral responsibility for actions done when the person did not have control over the actions of his or her body. Thus an epileptic who strikes another person during a seizure would not be held morally responsible for that action. Corporations do not have bodies, but there are many different sorts of physical objects which are subject to their control. By a similar process of reasoning, we do not hold corporations morally responsible for events involving physical objects which are ordinarily subject to the corporation's control but not subject to its control in this particular instance. If a pollution control device malfunctions and the community suffers the consequences of a dangerous pollutant, we might not hold the corporation morally responsible for the injury.[5] Here, too, however, the use of the excuse is qualified. Both individuals and corporations are required to exercise a reasonable degree of care to avoid accidents. If they fail to do so, then they are held morally responsible for acting negligently and they are not excused in the same way for what happens as a result. Thus the corporation might have been negligent in its maintenance of the pollution control device. (As above, a corporation's resources in this respect are much greater than the resources of an individual person.)

A third kind of excuse for individual persons is coercion in the form of a serious threat of severe bodily harm to the person himself or to some other person if a certain action demanded by the coercer is not done. When a person is subjected to a threat of this sort, we do not ordinarily hold the person morally responsible for the action demanded by the coercer provided that it is of lesser harm (or perhaps of no greater harm) than the action threatened by the coercer. Though we do not often think of it, it seems reasonable to apply a similar sort of reasoning to corporations. Of course when the harm threatened to the corporation is harm to its property and goods, there are often more effective ways to deal with the situation than acquiescence to the coercer's demands. But a person could conceivably coerce a corporation by threatening harm to some person. Under such circumstances, we might well refrain from holding the corporation morally responsible for actions done in response to the coercer's demands, provided again that they involve less harm (or at least no greater harm) than the harm threatened. This may seem a strange thought; but it is surely a possible situation and one that is all too common in relation to another sort of group which acts as a single entity, namely, government, which must deal with various forms of terrorism involving the taking of hostages.

There is a third topic it would be well to examine here: the relation of the moral responsibility of individual persons within the corporation to that of the corporation as a single entity. For present purposes I shall speak of responsibility for immoral actions, but the same principles will apply to responsibility for the moral actions of a corporation as a single entity as well.

If some single individual within a corporation had the authority to make decisions that certain actions are to be the ones which the corporation as a single entity shall take in a certain matter, and if this party were personally responsible for gathering all the information needed to make these decisions, then such a person would clearly be the only person responsible for the corporation's acting in that way. But few individuals are in positions of such complete authority in corporations as we know them, and even fewer individuals make corporate decisions on the basis of information for which they alone are responsible. From a moral point of view, then, there is most frequently a sharing of the responsibility for a corporation's actions in a certain situation.

Within the structure of the corporation, those who provide information are ordinarily answerable to the decision maker they assist, and the decision maker may well be the only one answerable, from the point of view of the corporation, for the quality of the information on which his or her decisions are based. But from a moral point of view there is a shared responsibility in such cases. If faulty or incomplete information eventually results in an immoral action of the corporation as a single entity, the moral responsibility will lie with those responsible for the information as much as with those actually making the decision.

In the same way, while those in subordinate decision-making positions in a corporation will ordinarily be answerable, from the point of view of the corporation, to those above them, and those in higher positions will be personally accountable for everything that happens below them, nevertheless from a moral point of view the responsibility may well be shared. If a subordinate makes a decision which eventually results in an immoral action by the corporation as a single entity, the fact that that person's superiors may be accountable for that action from the corporation's point of view does not lessen his or her share of the moral responsibility.

In addition to failures by those who provide information or make decisions, there is another way in which immoral actions of a corporation might arise. For it is conceivable that the formal and informally accepted rules of a corporation might be so constructed that individual elements among them or the whole collection of them together would result in immoral actions of the corporation even without specific wrongs by persons who make up the corporation. Under such circumstances those with authority to change the formal rules or to initiate formal rules to replace informally accepted ones will have a moral obligation to rectify the situation, changing or making rules so that the corporation will not continue to perform immoral actions in this way.

It also seems at least conceivable that an action of a corporation might be immoral even though the rules were morally acceptable and even though every individual person contributing to the action acted in accord with the rules and in a moral manner. Suppose, for example, that a great many persons are involved in the performance of some action of the corporation as a single entity and that these persons are not well informed of one another's specific actions and decisions in relation to that action. It is at least conceivable that each could choose a course of action which he or she might judge to be morally neutral—or even in some instances morally good—but that the combination of these activities, which none of these persons is in a position to observe ahead of time, constitutes an action of the corporation as a single entity which is in fact immoral. Under such circumstances there is probably little more to be said in the short run. But in the longer run, after the officers of the corporation have had an opportunity to recognize the immorality of the corporation's action, from then on those with the authority to replace, modify, terminate, or revoke the immoral action of the corporation have a moral obligation to do so.

I have not tried here to articulate any of the specific moral values or principles by which the actions of corporations might be judged from a moral point of view. Rather I have tried to explain the conditions under which it makes sense to hold a corporation morally responsible for its actions and to show some of the relations between the moral responsibility of a corporation and that of the persons who act within it. I hope that by sketching out answers to these general questions I will enable others to proceed with more confidence both in articulating the specific moral values and principles which ought to be applied to the actions of corporations and of persons within them and in applying these values and principles to specific kinds of cases.

NOTES

1. There are some circumstances in which we excuse persons from moral responsibility. For example we would not hold an epileptic person morally responsible for striking another person during a seizure. We would not say that such a person had acted in a morally defective way ("irresponsibly," as we sometimes put it, or "immorally"). Nor would we say that an epileptic who struck no one during a seizure had acted in a morally acceptable or morally commendable way ("responsibly," "morally"). Rather we would say that these persons were *not responsible* for what they did during a seizure, and our moral judgments about what happened would not be addressed to them in the first place.

2. The question whether those whom we hold *morally* responsible ought also be held *legally* responsible is an important and difficult question of legal policy. So too is the question whether there are ever good reasons for holding a person or group legally responsible even when we would not hold them morally responsible (e.g., because under certain conditions we would excuse them from moral responsibility for their action), which is the question of *strict liability* in the law. Questions like these, however, are distinct from and in some measure depend upon our answer to what is being asked here: Under what conditions is it reasonable to hold corporations morally responsible for their actions?

3. For a more detailed analysis of informally accepted rules and of the patterns of action and judgement which accompany rules in general, see H. L. A. Hart, *The Concept of Law* (Oxford, 1961), Chaps. 4 and 5; and David T. Ozar, "Social Rules and Patterns of Behavior," *Philosophy Research Archives,* Vol. 3 (1977), 1188. Other helpful treatments of the notion of rules being used here are John Rawls, "Two Concepts of Rules," *Philosophical Review,* LXIV (1955); John Searle, "How to Derive 'Ought' from 'Is,'" *Philosophical Review,* LXXIII (1964); John Searle, *Speech Acts* (Cambridge, 1969). A much more detailed analysis of the moral responsibility of groups in terms of the rules which constitute them as groups will be found in Michael Smith, *The Institution as Moral Agent,* Doctoral dissertation, Loyola University of Chicago, 1978.

4. The argument offered here is that corporations fulfill the conditions we actually use to judge whether a group can be considered to be a single entity in the performance of actions. It does not attempt to answer the more difficult question of why these conditions are appropriate, i.e., why the acceptance of certain sorts of rules justifies us in attributing agency to a group as a single entity. For an examination of this question, see Smith, *The Institution as Moral Agent, op. cit.;* and David T. Ozar, "Groups Acting as Single Agents: Control of Physical Objects" (forthcoming).

5. We might, however, choose to hold the corporation *legally* responsible under a doctrine of strict liability. See note 2 above.

Product Liability: Manufacturers Beware!

LAWRENCE A. BENNIGSON and
ARNOLD I. BENNIGSON*

Product safety and product liability are important to managers of many consumer goods companies. Evidence of this fact is found almost daily in news reports. For instance, criminal charges were filed against executives of Abbott Laboratories; the Drackett Company lost a $1 million liability case after unwittingly manufacturing a bomb; and Bon Vivant was virtually forced out of business by being required to recall all its products.

Changing consumer expectations, new laws, and recent court decisions regarding product safety and product liability have altered the rules of the game. Consumers are now less likely to overlook accidents involving products than they were in the past. Now the law may expose a manufacturer to liability even though the company is technically not negligent and though a complex distribution network and years of product life separate the company from the accident. New legislation makes recall a possibility for almost any consumer product company.

How has management reacted to these changes? Some executives have revised their expectations and procedures to cope successfully with the new pressures. Other executives have been caught unprepared. Still others have seized on safety as an opportunity to gain a competitive edge in the market. This is an area where great advantages have gone to the alert and the knowledgeable. What is the legal background every executive should have?

FROM CAVEAT EMPTOR TO CAVEAT VENDITOR

Until the 1960s the legal and social philosophy of "Let the buyer beware" obstructed avenues of recourse for the injured user of a product. Today's prevailing philosophy, "Let the manufacturer and the seller beware," received judicial impetus in 1963 when the doctrine of strict liability in tort was expanded.[1] Today there are three mutually exclusive theories of liability available to a consumer who wants to sue a manufacturer or seller of injurious products.

*We are indebted to Robert Dran, now with the law firm of Adams, Duque & Hazeltine, Los Angeles, and to Betty Jerett, now with Elizabeth Arden, Inc., New York, for their assistance and ideas while they were students at the Harvard Business School.

From the *Harvard Business Review,* Vol. 52, No. 3 (May–June 1974), 122–32. © 1974 by the President and Fellows of Harvard College; all rights reserved. Reprinted with permission.

Negligence

In order to successfully claim manufacturer negligence, the injured user must prove that the manufacturer was careless and that this carelessness caused his injury. Originally, a negligent manufacturer was not liable unless there was "privity of contract" between him and the buyer. The result was that most manufacturers were immune from suit since few sold their products directly to consumers. A New York landmark decision,[2] followed in all states since 1966, repudiated the privity of contract requirement. Now the negligent manufacturer is potentially liable to any user of the product.

Breach of Warranty

A claim based on breach of warranty may be founded on either express or implied warranty. An express warranty is an explicit representation of fact. The manufacturer might communicate it in writing, conversation, advertising, labeling, or in other forms of promotion. Most courts hold that even though some warranties are not express, they are implied by law. The most common implied warranties are that the product is safe, usable, and fit for its reasonably intended purpose.

Strict Liability

Once a narrow doctrine, strict liability was greatly expanded in 1963. In that year the California Supreme Court handed down a revolutionary decision concluding that "a manufacturer is strictly liable when an article he places on the market, knowing that it will be used without inspection, proves to have a defect that causes injury to a human being."[3] The result is that an injured party need only prove that the product is defective and caused the injury. No longer does he have to prove that the manufacturer has been careless. Further, strict liability has been extended to all products, not just to human consumables or to those products intended for intimate bodily use, as in the past. The California court's decision is now followed by 35 states.

New Laws

Federal consumer protection legislation received special attention in 1967 with the establishment of the National Commission on Product Safety. The commission reported that "federal authority to curb hazards to consumer products is virtually nonexistent" and that "federal product safety legislation consists of a series of isolated acts treating specific hazards in narrow product categories. No government agency possesses general authority to ban products which harbor unreasonable risks or to require that consumer products conform to minimum safety standards." The commission concluded that modern technology can pose a bona fide menacing threat to the physical security of consumers.

As a result of the commission's work, the Consumer Product Safety Act was passed in 1972. This act established the Consumer Product Safety Commission and empowered it to set up and enforce mandatory safety standards over almost all consumer products. The commission is authorized to inspect manufacturing operations, subpoena records, and require compliance tests. It can ban the sale of products, require manufacturers to perform safety tests and keep accident records, and require sellers to repair or recall unsafe products and to rebate the purchase price. It may also impose a civil penalty of $2,000 for each known violation and criminal penalties of up to $50,000 plus one year's confinement of each willful violation. In addition, the act enables consumers to sue for damages or for the enforcement of established safety standards.

A STUDY OF TWO COMPANIES

What do the new rules mean for management? And what does management's choice of strategy mean for the company? To understand the answers to these questions, let us look at two contrasting cases of management action. Each case represents a composite of company experiences rather than the work of one company in particular.

The Case of the Combustible Cleaner

Randall Enterprises was a large and well-known manufacturer of industrial chemicals and cleaning compounds. Started in 1923 as a small operation in the middle Atlantic region, it had developed an enviable reputation as a supplier of industrial cleaning agents by early 1960. Randall products were sold by hundreds of manufacturer's representatives and thousands of wholesale and retail supply houses.

In late 1960, in response to the business recession, Randall's management decided to enter the household products market. It would use its industrial formulas and modify the packaging to appeal to household consumers. Additional manufacturer's representatives were selected to reach retail outlets such as supermarkets, grocery stores, drug stores, and hardware stores; they would be served by the existing sales force.

One of the new products, Ex-cis-or, was sold as a cleaning agent for ovens. Its industrial use was for large ovens and kettles where grease and high temperatures combine to form a tough scale. The product had been tested by Randall's janitorial specialists in a range of household ovens and found to be quite effective. The first year's volume was planned at 50,000 units per month.

Several months after Ex-cis-or went onto the market, a company salesman made a routine visit to a manufacturer's representative in the Southwest. The representative told the salesman he was getting repeat orders for the product and that it was doing well. He added that he had heard a rumor about a customer of a small neighborhood grocery being burned by Ex-cis-or. Unfortunately, the salesman forgot about this rumor.

At about the same time, another salesman, visiting the head office of a supermarket chain in New England was told about complaints of a customer being injured. The supermarket buyer seemed serious about the issue, and the salesman thought he ought to mention it to someone. He did talk to his supervisor; they had a prolonged discussion about how careless some customers could be and dropped the matter.

Several other indications of trouble were reported during the next two months. Each time, the information was disregarded, forgotten, or attributed to incompetent consumers. Next, the president of Randall received two letters from customers complaining of burns from Ex-cis-or. An interview with one of them revealed that while using Ex-cis-or, she had mixed it with a detergent. Chemists tried to reproduce the conditions causing burns but were unable to do so. Top management asked for an informal report but did not press the issue.

Law Suit and Recall

A few weeks later, a law suit was filed against Randall for $2 million. A young housewife with four children had been badly burned and blinded while cleaning the kitchen stove. Complete evidence had been preserved in this case, and, after many hours of analysis, technicians were able to reproduce the accident. They determined that:

- Ex-cis-or had been used on an outside element of the stove.
- A detergent had been mixed with the product by the housewife.
- The heating element had been on.
- The product had contained a foreign substance.
- The product had been of extra strength.

When these conditions were present, the mixture could react violently, spraying into the eyes of the housewife and causing burns and eventual blindness. Analysis revealed that the "foreign substance" was a small amount of highly concentrated powder used to clean containers on the packaging line prior to their being filled with Ex-cis-or. Manual inspection of containers on the line had evidently failed to detect the existence of this residue. The extra strength Ex-cis-or was caused by an intermittently faulty mixing nozzle used to dilute the original concentrated solution. Random sampling procedures had not detected this condition.

The technicians were amazed that such problems could exist and that a customer would use Ex-cis-or mixed with a detergent on a heated element. In fact, the label specifically warned against mixing with any other substance.

After careful consideration, the corporate legal department recommended that Randall recall all Ex-cis-or. Recall was very complex and costly because only aggregate records were maintained in the multilevel distribution system. Changes were made in the manufacturing process, new "improved" Ex-cis-or was created, and the old product was taken off the shelves and out of the pipeline. Some 18 months after the new product had been originally launched, the company received a considerable amount of troublesome publicity; moreover, it had recovered only 40% of the original Ex-cis-or (thus leaving open the possibility of more injuries occurring), and it had absorbed out-of-pocket costs equivalent to five years of projected profits on the new product line. In addition, court cases were still pending.

Accusing fingers in the company pointed in different directions. Packaging design, quality control, manufacturing engineering, product development, field services, marketing, and legal counsel all caught their share of the blame, as well as top management, for deciding to put industrial products into the hands of naïve consumers. As for the future, there were some managers who believed the accident was such an unlikely event that it would not be repeated, while other[s] argued to let insurance cover the possibility of liability suits. Still other managers felt that the conditions might be repeated, that the company's insurability could be threatened, and that management had a moral obligation to protect the consumer.

The Case of the Safely Designed Stove

Gibbons-Bankroft, Inc. (GBI) was one of five leading manufacturers of portable and other specialty cooking equipment. There were over 150 companies in the industry. About 75% of GBI's dollar volume was in stoves for trailers, while the remainder was split evenly between equipment for outdoor camping and equipment for boating.

GBI executives knew that their industry suffered from safety problems. In spite of attempts to design safer products and educate users, each year brought continued reports of injuries from explosions and burns. Most of these accidents involved improper use of the device or resulted from children playing; only rarely were liability claims made against the product manufacturer. Aware of the concern for product safety being expressed by the National Commission of Product Safety and consumer groups, the board of directors committed the company to producing safe products. Procedures would be developed to review all existing products and ensure safety considerations on all new products. Also, a major effort would be undertaken to improve the safety features of the main line of trailer stoves.

The president established a product safety policy committee, composed of the vice presidents of all functional marketing, field service, product development, product design, manufacturing, and purchasing. He appointed a director of safety services, who was to report to the executive vice president, serve as a member of the safety policy committee, and act as chairman of the safety operating committee. Both committees were to meet at frequent and regular intervals. Audits were to be conducted on existing products, and design review procedures were to be established for all new GBI products.

Responsibility for the design of a safe new product line was given to a design engineer. He conducted extensive reviews of accident histories and systematically isolated the causes. He developed new approaches to the design of piping and valves and to the layout and location of pilot lights, and burners. His cost analysis on each new approach indicated that either functionality or cost would often have to be sacrificed. The safety policy committee decided to allow costs to rise.

But could GBI stoves be both safe and cost competitive? Management decided to make a four-sided attack on this problem. First, it initiated efforts in its trade associations to raise the safety standards for all units in the industry to the new standard that GBI was setting. Then it began working with legislators and consumer groups to increase the likelihood of industry-wide standards being developed. Next, it undertook an extensive campaign to educate its distributors, salesmen, customers, and end-use buyers about the safety benefits of its product line. Finally, management launched extensive value-engineering efforts to reduce cost while holding the line on safety.

As the new designs neared completion, prototypes were subjected to laboratory tests. Company personnel who were thought to be typical of end users of the stoves were selected to test-operate them. Extensive misuse and abuse tests were conducted. Point-of-purchase warranty cards were designed, and procedures were established to document the location of all units at all times.

After years of product development and substantial investment, the new line of stoves was ready. Initial orders exceeded the target that management had established.

PRACTICES THAT LEAD TO TROUBLE

In our discussions with managers and in review of legal case histories, we have identified numerous recurring causes of safety and liability problems. Some of these causes were responsible for the Ex-cis-or fiasco; any of them can lead to trouble for other products and companies. Alertness to the danger of these practices is management's first big step to having sound safety policies and programs. . . .

Low Priority on Product Safety

Traditional operating criteria for product success in most manufacturing companies include short-term cost, functional performance, and delivery. Decisions and controls are finely tuned to make performance satisfy these criteria. Though some companies report that they can emphasize product safety without affecting these criteria, the usual experience is just the opposite. Increasing the "safety index" of a product generally costs money, takes time, and/or detracts from functional performance.

This means there are major obstacles to improving product safety in a company doing well in terms of traditional operating criteria. Many companies are like Randall in that they give safety low priority or none at all. The effect is that short-term cost and performance advantages are allowed to outweigh longer-term safety issues. In such cases it is not surprising that eventually costly safety problems are experienced. The need is to do as GBI did—give safety a high priority, too.

In the situations we have studied, establishing the priority is a two-part process. The first requirement is for clear and unequivocal statements from top management. Then a variety of organizational devices, such as safety review committees and procedures like misuse tests, make the priority real. . . .

"It's the User's Responsibility"

A common attitude prevailing in many companies that encounter product safety and liability problems is expressed by such statements as "It's really up to the customer to use this thing properly," or "If the consumer is stupid enough to use it that way, he deserves to get hurt." The implication, of course, is that it is the consumer's responsibility to ensure his or her safety.

We see two problems where this attitude prevails. First, it is not true legally that safety is the consumer's responsibility. As we have seen, the law now says it is up to the manufacturer to see to it that products do not harm people. Second, people who hold this view cannot see the useful ways they can help the company to meet its legal responsibility.

Inadequate Understanding of the User

Products must be safe to use all the time, not just when operated or consumed as intended. The law also makes the manufacturer responsible for accident-free use when the product is "foreseeably misused," that is, misused in a way the manufacturer *should* have anticipated.

This requirement is a stumbling block. We have found that products are often designed by people who have little appreciation of the ultimate user. For example, designers forget how unsophisticated some users are or the likelihood that children will use products designed for adults.

To understand the user, some individual or group must identify the range of possible users of the product; characterize the educational background, attitudes, and skills of each type of user; and factor that understanding into product design and marketing programs.

Tunnel Vision

When product design people come up against safety problems, they often remark, "It never occurred to me that the product might behave that way." They do not see the potential safety hazard. There is a natural tendency for planners and designers to see how the device will work— rather than how it will *not* work. Design engineers unconsciously assume that a user is familiar with the intended purpose and possible weaknesses of the product. Anxious to make the new device work and have it accepted by management, they develop a sort of tunnel vision that precludes a clear view of potential problems.

Unfortunately, many of the pressures of organizational life enhance these tendencies rather than compensate for them. It takes time to see outside the tunnel, and products are developed under competitive pressure in which time is important. The need to have ideas accepted puts a premium on emphasizing the positive and hiding the negative. Historical emphasis on product cost and functional performance tends to shunt safety considerations aside.

To counteract tunnel vision, some companies have adopted specific exercises designed to help them see unlikely problems. These exercises include testing products under conditions of abuse and misuse and careful analysis of all possible events leading to product failure. Outside people unfamiliar with the product or technology can be helpful at this stage.

Failure to Consider Total Product Life

The properties of a product and the conditions surrounding its use often change with time. For example, the condition of tools, toys, appliances, and most mechanical devices usually deteriorates, and if deterioration occurs in such a way as to affect safety, the results may be tragic. Again, the use of a product may change after a while; consumers may become more careless and less respectful of it.

Since the manufacturer's responsibility for the product does not end at the time of sale, management should anticipate the range of changing conditions to which the product will be subjected and account for these conditions in design, manufacture, consumer education, and other phases of total product history.

Relying on Industry or Government Standards

There is a commonly held view that if a product conforms with generally accepted standards, the company will be protected from liability even if injuries occur. This is not true. Industry and government standards are subject to many human failings, may represent the lowest common denominator in the state of the art, and can take long periods of time to be developed and accepted. It is not unusual for quite a discrepancy to develop between existing state-of-the-art possibilities and current standards.

More than one management has been surprised to find its company judged liable in an accident case even though the product met generally accepted standards of operation, quality, and construction.

Production Traps

Sometimes safety problems can be traced directly to the manufacturing process. The Randall case is one example. In another case the combination of product and manufacturing design made it possible for a subassembly to be inserted backward in the product. This led to disaster when the item was first used. In another situation the product was subject to critical processing specifications, but the equipment was designed so that operators found it difficult to monitor the operation in the required manner. When product safety is important, those who design the manufacturing process must take user behavior into consideration.

Variables Not Controlled in Manufacturing

A key decision in the design of any quality control system concerns what variables to control. Cost considerations may lead to control of the weight of expensive chemicals placed in a container, of the wastage in pattern cutting, or of the speed at which an assembly operation is taking place. A concern for functional performance may lead to testing the heat of reaction of a chemical substance, tasting a food product, or testing the degree of hardness of a cutting blade.

But such variables will not necessarily lead to assurances of safety. Extra effort is needed. The first stop is to identify the ways in which the product *could* become unsafe. These ways often involve the simultaneous occurrence of a number of unlikely conditions, such as happened with Ex-cis-or. The second step is to identify the causes of these conditions and to establish preventive controls on the manufacturing line.

Documentation Failures

Product recall has become an unwelcome but a common occurrence recently. In some cases, the nonrecoverable costs of recall, either direct or intangible, far outweigh the likely costs of liability to injured parties.

The need for recall may depend on quality control documentation. Usually products that can be *proved* to be free of conditions known to cause injury will not have to be recalled. The trouble comes when a product is not tested, or the positive results of tests are not recorded, or there are no means, such as serial numbers, to identify each item of the product, or it is not possible to relate identification to current location. In cases such as Randall's, perfectly acceptable products may have to be recalled in toto. Management cannot show that a recall of a limited number of items will be sufficient.

Insufficient Communication to or from Customers

We have found that company managers, who should be the first to know if there are problems with their products, are frequently the last to know. Corrective action is forestalled until too late. For example, in the Randall case there were clues that a problem existed. If management had been able to zero in on those clues early, the company might have been saved a great deal of money and might have protected its consumers from a considerable amount of pain.

There are a number of reasons why a company may be out of touch with its customers. Complex distribution systems may put a great distance and many intervening parties between the manufacturer and the user. In some cases injured parties are advised not to give the company information in order to increase the likelihood of successful liability litigation. Often the information is readily at hand, but field sales personnel fail to search for it. Sometimes company representatives in the field have the information but decide it is not important and fail to pass that information along. Or it may be passed along but lost somewhere in the company.

Some companies work aggressively to stay in close touch with product users. They pay careful attention to procedures and training for field personnel, streamline reporting channels for product safety information, and tailor internal information-handling procedures. In one company we know of, the president insists that he be personally informed of any accidents. Other executives require that specially designated individuals or committees monitor inputs from the field, from the newspapers, and from the local department.

Communications *to* the user may also be a source of trouble. If needed information is lacking, misleading, or ineffective, management may have different claims to settle. Sometimes promotion efforts unwittingly lead to inaccurate understanding and unreasonable expectations on the part of the consumer. For instance, the Ex-cis-or labeling contained warnings and instructions to the user, but the warnings were too technical to be understood. Moreover, these instructions were so closely tied to the promotional character of the package that they were ineffective. . . .

CONCLUSION

Social philosophies underlying recent court decisions and legislative efforts indicate the direction of future trends. In the *Greenman* case, the court said the purpose of imposing strict liability was to "insure that the costs of injuries resulting from defective products are borne by the manufacturers that put such products on the market rather than by the injured persons who are powerless to protect themselves." A related view holds that the manufacturer is the appropriate vehicle for spreading the social cost of product injuries. Similarly, in its final report, the National Commission on Product Safety philosophized that "a producer owes society-at-large the duty to assure that unnecessary risks of injury are eliminated. He is in the best position to know what are the safest designs, materials, construction methods, and modes of use."[4] These positions have evolved slowly over the years and are unlikely to change in the near future.

Manufacturers are not the only ones affected. Liability has been extended to retailers, wholesalers, distributors, franchisers, trademark licensors, sellers of mass-produced homes, developers and engineers of building sites, and to lessors, bailors, and licensors of personal property. The type of person entitled to recover under strict liability has been extended beyond the purchaser to the nonpurchasing user or consumer and the bystander. Moreover, the word *defect* as used in strict liability has been extended to include defects not only in manufacture but also in failure to warn consumers of unreasonably dangerous products.

It is likely that future decisions and laws will result in further protection for the injured consumer. We can speculate about how this will be accomplished. The injured consumer could be allowed to recover punitive damages, recover treble damages, or bring class action suits. State legislatures could enact legislation similar to the federal Consumer Product Safety Act of 1970. Also, Congress could tighten the standards, enforcement procedures, and penalties for that act, or could abolish tax deductibility of payments to an injured consumer. Finally, the concept of liability without defect, similar to liability without fault or, more commonly, "no-fault," might gain popularity. The result would be that the injured consumer would be automatically compensated after showing he had been injured by the product.

Certainly the future holds little chance of a return to *caveat emptor*. That phrase can be retired from the business lexicon. Another Latin phrase needs to be activated in its place. The doctrine of *caveat venditor*—"Let the seller beware"—will be with us from now on.

Notes

1. David Rados, "Product Liability: Tougher Ground Rules," HBR July–August 1969, p. 144.
2. *MacPherson* v. *Buick Motor Company*, 217 N.Y. 382 (New York Court of Appeals, 1916).
3. *Greenman* v. *Yuba Power Products, Inc.*, 50 Cal 2d 57 (California Supreme Court, 1963).
4. *National Commission on Product Safety, Final Report,* presented to the President and Congress, June 1970, Part I, Chapter I, p. 4.

BUSINESS AND THE GOVERNMENT: THE ROLE OF THE STATE

Case Study—OSHA: Omar Industries, Inc.*

Omar Industries was a diversified manufacturing company with sales in 1971 of about $1.0 billion. It was composed of eight operating divisions, half of them producing chemicals and packaging products for industry and the other half consumer durables. In all, the company had over forty manufacturing locations in the United States and several more overseas under the direction of the International Division. Assisted by one acquisition, corporate sales had grown at a rate of about 10 percent over the previous decade. Although net profit to sales had slipped from 5.3 percent to 4.0 percent during this period, return on equity had held constant at roughly 10 percent as the company increased its debt to equity ratio from 0.30 to 0.67. During 1972 renewed emphasis was placed on improving margins and increasing earnings per share. Moreover, in view of the increased debt levels, the president had made it clear to his division managers that the corporation was going to "live within its means" by not spending more on capital investment than its cash flow after dividends (about $62 million in 1971) justified.

ENVIRONMENTAL CONTROL DEPARTMENT

In 1970, the Environmental Control Department (ECD) was formed to consolidate a number of corporate staff activities related to Omar's concern with the environment. The company was recognized as a leader in the control of air and water pollution in its manufacturing operations, at times pioneering in the adoption of new control technologies. During his years as president, the current chairman of the board had stressed the importance of providing "the best pollution control equipment to meet or exceed community criteria."

*This case was prepared by the Harvard Business School as a basis for class discussion rather than to illustrate either effective or ineffective handling of an administrative situation.

ECD performed a variety of functions including (1) assisting the operating divisions in achieving compliance with government regulations, (2) keeping the corporation current on changes in regulation or control technology, (3) reviewing capital requests from an environmental viewpoint, and (4) encouraging the divisions to incorporate environmental concerns and potential expenditures in their planning. The department did not, however, have the authority to force action on the operating divisions, though in some respects it shared the responsibility for the implementation of the corporate policy on pollution.

ECD was directed by John Carpenter, who reported to Fred Phillips, an administrative vice-president for Special Services, a position that included responsibility for several corporate-level technical service groups and various external programs related to environmental affairs. ECD was divided into sections responsible for air, water, testing, and environmental hygiene. This latter section was acquired from the corporate personnel group when ECD was formed on the premise that much of the effort required in the occupational health and safety area was related to engineering rather than personnel.

OCCUPATIONAL HEALTH AND SAFETY

In the summer of 1972, Phillips and Carpenter were becoming increasingly concerned about a growing public interest in the work environment in general and the requirements posed by the 1971 Occupational Health and Safety Act (OSHA) in particular. They were especially worried about the 90 decibels standard for noise included in the act as the maximum allowable for sustained exposure. Carpenter conmented:

> OSHA inspectors have been hammering some of our divisions for noise. We know there are some places where the levels get as high as 130 decibels—that's way above the new national standard of 90 decibels. I've been going to the technical directors in the divisions to try to get them to write down their existing situation. They're annoyed with me at the moment. They say they don't have the time or the money to spend on worrying about noise at the moment. My argument is that if they get it written down, they can at least, one, ask for some money to work on the problem and, two, show to OSHA that they're acting in good faith.
>
> The divisions are different. The Chemical Division is doing an excellent job. The Packaging Division is giving us no response. We had a meeting with them a little while ago to discuss it and they took the position, "we hear you but until we have a specific problem, in other words a citation, we're not going to do anything. There are other pollution problems right now that are of more importance to us."

In the first week of July, Carpenter called Fred Bellows, manager of Plant Construction and Engineering in the Automotive Parts Division, to arrange a meeting to assess the division's status in the areas covered by the Occupational Health and Safety Act—chiefly noise abatement. While he had been working with several of the other divisions on formulating action programs to bring their operations into compliance with the new regulations, Carpenter had had little contact with this division on this particular issue.

The Automotive Parts Division was acquired by Omar in the late 1960s. Its sales had been more or less constant at $90 million since that time and as a result had not been keeping pace with the corporation's overall growth. Profit margins, always tight, had been under increasing pressure in recent years as the division worked to develop new products in a highly competitive field. It operated four general line and two specialty plants in addition to several technical centers.

On July 13, Carpenter, Bellows, and Walter Gardner, an engineer who worked for the director of Environmental Hygiene, met in Carpenter's office. The following discussion ensued:

Carpenter: I wrote to all of the technical directors in the divisions recently outlining goals and objectives for engineering noise out of our operations. We see OSHA inspectors telling us to engineer the noise levels down to the point that employees don't have to wear earplugs within maybe a two-year time frame. We also have the feeling that if we have programs prior to the time they demand them, they will be willing to accept a more reasonable compliance schedule.

Bellows: We have already had one citation on noise.

Carpenter: Did you know that?
(to
Gardner)

Gardner: No.

Carpenter: Was the citation given by the state or OSHA?

Bellows: OSHA. They gave us a citation and were going to give us until July 1, 1972, to correct it. That was ridiculous—only four weeks away. I talked with the enforcement officer and told him so. I told him we were spending 5,000 hours of engineering time working on the problem. That's stretching the truth a bit, though we can justify it if they ask us by stretching the description of what our engineers are doing. But we do have mandatory ear protection rules in areas of 100 decibels and down to 85 decibels it's encouraged but optional. On this basis, the inspectors closed the file.

             On the basis of our efforts—a continuing long-range program—they said OK. I gave them no numbers, no details, and no schedules, but if they have another complaint, they said, "we'll open it up again."

Carpenter: Let's say they did.

Bellows: We would use the same argument—a long-run argument.

Carpenter: Do you have a schedule with definite programs and goals?

Bellows: No, it's a long-term project but one that falls short of redesigning the machines. We have 250 stamping machines and

	there just isn't enough money to do it. One of these machines—even running by itself, generates 90 decibels. I don't know how we can do it.
Carpenter:	That's what the Chemical Division people told us about the forming machines, but now they have redesigned them so that noise levels have dropped from 114 decibels to 90. You need a schedule and some objectives.
Bellows:	But as soon as you have a schedule, you need a budget and people assigned to it.
Carpenter:	That's just what I am trying to get you to do.
Bellows:	The noise problem is really a problem, no denying it.
Carpenter:	Then why don't you want to take out the noise?
Bellows:	The noise on a machine is important. That's the way the operator tells if something is wrong. That's the reason I'm not happy with the ear protection devices. The operator with earplugs in can't listen to the equipment as well.
Gardner:	I'd like to see ear protection devices eliminated, too, but you can only do that by eliminating the noise.
Bellows:	We've got noise control on all new equipment.
Carpenter:	You've put it on the purchase order?
Bellows:	Yes.
Carpenter:	That's great.
Bellows:	No, it's not great. We often need special machines and with these new requirements, some suppliers just won't bid on them.
Carpenter:	Not even for money?
Bellows:	We didn't say we would pay a million dollars. They weren't sure they could come up with a new technology for what we pay. Somewhere along the line, John, it's got to be economical. You can't put the machine in a room by itself.
Carpenter:	That's a point though. Have you thought about shielding?
Bellows:	Have you ever run a machine? At some point it's going to be uneconomical to do this. We have got a problem here that won't be solved in your lifetime.
Carpenter:	The Chemical Division is going to do it on all their forming machines.
Bellows:	What's it going to cost them and how long will it take?
Carpenter:	$8 million. They have got a program for doing it that may take six or seven years, but it looks like OSHA may buy that. However, we had another situation at the Wilton plant. The OSHA inspector didn't like what we are doing. She told us to put together a program for meeting the national standards, but said that an eight-to-ten-year time frame would be unacceptable.

Bellows: That's unrealistic.

Carpenter: But at least they are going to have a program which can be used as a basis for moving ahead toward controlling the problem.

Bellows: It's unrealistic for us. We can't replace all those machines. Maybe we'll change the product. We are moving from some lines to others which aren't as noisy on the machinery. But there are no stamping machines like ours in the United States which can meet the OSHA standards. You aren't going to get that to change.

Carpenter: I can't buy the comment that there never will be a machine that can't do it.

Bellows: Sure, you can have what they call administrative controls—putting the machines off by themselves or having them run automatically by a guy at the end of the plant—but we are a low-profit operation. You're going to have to accept some of these unpleasantries in our case to stay in business.

Gardner: Who says this will cost too much?

Bellows: We [Engineering] never say that. Division management does.

Carpenter: Somewhere along the line this decision gets made. Maybe by the division manager.

Bellows: It's the division manager, all right.

Carpenter: The division manager has got to weigh these things and put them all together.

Gardner: Has he been given a program?

Bellows: No, he only knows the problem in general terms.

Carpenter: In fact, you have a new division manager.

Bellows: We haven't talked with the new one about it yet. Look, we know that noise reduction means machine redesign. I could go to him and tell him that. But I don't know the cost. We have never built machines with a design other than the one we have now, so we would need a study project—maybe $200,000 with a two-year timetable. Then a replacement project at $100,000 a machine. That's a lot of money. I don't have to present him with that. I know what he'll say—no. Maybe if OSHA says shut the plant down, that will be something else. But for a business grossing $90 million, it's ridiculous to invest $25 million on a replacement basis.

Gardner: I have just been here for a short time, and I don't know much about costs or about the operation. But I have been in government and I know OSHA is tough.

Bellows: They have been good to us so far.

Carpenter: We can't say what your program ought to be. . . .

Bellows: John, I don't object to writing a program. It's necessarily going to be a little nebulous and long term. The amount of

	money involved is going to be nebulous too. We can say we know it's about $25 million in the long run.
Carpenter:	Unless you change the product . . .
Bellows:	But as far as what happens then . . .
	We could put an engineer on design. . . . I don't mean to say we aren't trying to control the noise. Maybe we ought to just bumble along as we are. We don't have the capability to redesign.
Carpenter:	You have no incentive to do it now. In fact, you have an incentive to do nothing.
Bellows:	OSHA told me that Northern Can has the same problem. OSHA made them make a schedule for compliance and so forth. We will probably have to do this next time. But the inspector said, "If no complaint, then you have seen the last of us for four years."
Gardner:	But he said that because OSHA has no inspectors. They will have them very soon, however.
Bellows:	Actually, we have had another complaint at Middleton by the state control people. I have been away and I don't know any more about it than that. In a way, I am more worried about that one. But we will argue on the basis of our activities as we have with OSHA already.
Carpenter:	It sounds like you're just reacting. What you need is a program. Even your current program might do if it were just written down.
Bellows:	Actually we have safety committees at each plant now. They're usually chaired by the plant manager. It's new—just started a month ago. I've seen some preliminary reports. They are pretty grim. If OSHA saw them, they would be unhappy.
	(For several minutes the three men discussed the makeup of the safety committees. Because of union considerations, all were salaried personnel. They then discussed the sources of noise, department by department.)
Bellows:	Everything you say is possible, but it costs money and we aren't prepared to spend much.
Gardner:	Unfortunately, OSHA doesn't think much about costs. I have been there and I know how they feel.
Carpenter:	On the other hand, the OSHA people have got to see that $25 million is a lot of money for that operation.
Bellows:	I am in favor of much of this ecology kick, but I also like TV's and automobiles and so forth. Someone has got to make a decision on where money is to be spent. I really don't think OSHA will be too tough if they're dealing with people who are making an honest attempt to make the plants clean and safe within their ability to do it.

Gardner: I don't think this attitude will continue. The magic number for OSHA is now 90 decibels and there is some talk in Washington about reducing it to 85.[1] OSHA will become tougher. They will come into the plant and test for specific noise levels for instance, and not pay any attention to how clean the place is if that's their mission.

Carpenter: We would really like to know what your general hearing conservation program is.

Bellows: I will send you a copy of our procedures for employee hearing tests. It depends on the size of the plants. In general, the large ones do the testing themselves and the smaller ones send employees to local doctors. All employees are tested when they are hired and periodically thereafter.

Carpenter: OK. That's part of it. Where from there?

Bellows: We issue earplugs, we test employees again after a period of time. We are looking for deteriorating conditions. It is a very disquieting thing to me. At the Durby plant, I can look at the tests and tell how long the employee has worked there by how much his hearing has deteriorated.

Carpenter: Do the employees have to wear them?

Bellows: Yes.

Carpenter: How often can they leave them at home before they are fired?

Bellows: The warning system varies but in most cases it specifies "repetitive violations."

Carpenter: Tell you what the Chemical Division does. The first time it's a warning, the second time the employee is docked one day, the third time it's three days, and after that he is out.

Bellows: My plant managers would have problems with something like that. You think I'm tough to work with, you ought to talk with some of them.

Carpenter: You should see what we have to deal with in other divisions.

Bellows: I really don't think the next five years will be too bad. In the long run I agree with you, but those stamping machines may not be around that long. I don't see spending money on them. The problem may just go away.

Carpenter: You can always change your plan or even put a probability of a change in the plans when you write them, but at least have the goal—85 decibels—and some goals for getting there. Put what it would cost to redesign the machine, but also take a look at alternatives. I don't have the answers, but that sort of program should be saleable to your management and by itself it might be enough. . . . In addition to what you're doing with your plant committees, which would also be included, this program should be in the hands of the plant manager so when OSHA people come he can tell them, "Here's what we are doing."

Bellows:	These inspectors are like other inspectors. It depends a lot on how they are handled. If you keep them waiting in a waiting room for two hours, then they won't take kindly to you. But we have got some pretty good people as plant managers. I really don't think we will have a problem. I see where we could have a tough time if we got a series of complaints and we don't show progress in between. . . . Tell you what I can do. I can sit down and dream up something which I can take to management as long as I don't spend anything on it.
Carpenter:	That would be very helpful. Who do you work for?
Bellows:	Nelson. He is manager of Engineering Service, I think, though I am not sure of his title. He reports to the division manager.
Carpenter:	Well, we have a lot better feel for what's going on in the Automotive Division. People ask me how things are going in various divisions and when I come to yours, I have never had very much to say.
	(After five minutes of informal discussion the meeting ended with the following comment by Bellows, speaking softly and looking at the floor.)
Bellows:	Do you think I can last for five more years? I will be sixty in October.

After Bellows and Gardner left, Carpenter turned to the afternoon mail. In the pile was a capital request form from the Automotive Division for a $1.2 million stamping line. Carpenter indicated that he wished he had known about this project before the meeting with Bellows. A quick review of the document revealed that the new line was to be used for an important product and involved a change in technology from the existing machinery in the division. No explicit attention had been given to possible noise problems, and it would, as a result, have provided a useful vehicle for discussing the issue in concrete terms. This being a large investment for the division, Carpenter wondered why Bellows had not mentioned it.

The next morning Carpenter called in Ted Hawkins (director of Environmental Hygiene) and gave him the capital request with the following comment:

> Ted, get on this one fast. Find out the noise level and what, if anything, they're going to do about it. If we wait until the thing is built, they'll say, "The line is already in. We can't afford to do anything about it now."

Later that day, Carpenter discussed the OSHA situation with Phillips in the context of a general review of the department's activities.

Phillips:	We know what the major engineering questions are with OSHA. There is stamping noise, radiant heat, vapors, and noise in areas other than stamping.
Carpenter:	We got a capital request from the Automotive Division yesterday that gets into this. It's for $1.2 million—a new stamping line.

Phillips: I had heard about that. How many lines are there?

Carpenter: I don't have the details exactly. I'm not sure whether it's new or a rebuild. Bellows didn't mention it when we talked last week.

Phillips: He may not have known about it. Not very many people do—maybe only four people at corporate. It would have to be a new line.

Carpenter: It's a good example. How do we tackle that one?

Phillips: OK. You've got to give this to someone and get it straightened out now.

Carpenter: Another thing. Hawkins has been talking about going into a plant in the Chemical Division with some mufflers and physically shutting off all compressed air sources that are not absolutely necessary—actually taking the feeder lines out so the operator can't turn the air back on when he leaves. If it is really necessary, he'll put a muffler on it. He says he can cut the noise by 20 percent or more.

Phillips: He's said that to me, too. I don't believe it—but let's give him a try.

Carpenter: That would worry me. . . .

Phillips: No, let's do it someplace where we know the plant manager—like Richards.[2] He'll let us know if Hawkins gets in trouble so we can yank him before it gets out of hand. Let's call Richards while we're both here. [On phone] Say Pete, we have a young man—Ted Hawkins—here on our staff who's been talking about cutting noise out of plants by eliminating or muffling compressed air sources. If we sent him up to you for a while, would you be willing to have him around to see what he can do.

[Richards responds in the affirmative.]

Phillips: (continuing) His position demonstrates that he is a bit naive but it also reflects that he's interested in doing something. This is a good time to say, "Put up or shut up." He may have something and, if so, we should take advantage of it. If it's ok with you, I'll let him get together with Williams [manufacturing manager at the Akron plant] and John [Carpenter] and work out a program. Then if he gets in trouble, send him home.

About three weeks later, Hawkins, accompanied by a man from the engineering staff spent three days at Akron. He then returned and wrote a report to the plant manager, including recommendations for reducing noise. Carpenter was upset, however, when he learned that Hawkins had taken no direct action during his visit, such as disconnecting the compressed air sources, to reduce noise levels.

Notes

1. Decibel levels are calculated on a logarithmic scale; a reduction in the maximum allowed for sustained exposure from 90 to 85 would have a substantially greater impact on the noise level than the percentage reduction in decibels would indicate.
2. Richards was Phillips' replacement as plant manager in the Chemical Division in Akron when the latter became vice-president of Operations Services.

Case Study—M'm M'm Good: Campbell Soup Labels

The Campbell Soup Company's director of marketing for canned goods stated, "We were thinking of some way to identify ourselves on the local level where we could help the education process." A group of executives came up with the idea of a "label for education" program, the basis of which was the redemption of soup can labels for audio-visual equipment for elementary schools.

Campbell Soup approached various schools and PTA groups about the idea and received plenty of acceptance. But Campbell's sophisticated marketing staff wanted to test the program and did so in Minneapolis, Milwaukee, and Buffalo. Since the tests proved out last year, this year Campbell's Soup moved ahead on a national scale.

During the two-month life span of the "label for education" program, Campbell Soup received 70 million labels. "That's a lot of soup. M'm M'm good! Not only for us but also for the 12,000 schools," stated the marketing executive. More than 50,000 pieces of audio-visual equipment were sent to schools. A cassette player was sent for redeeming 1,800 labels. A Bell and Howell 16mm projector was sent for 44,100 labels.

The marketing executive stated the value of the soup was worth more than $1,000,000. "Very few companies would have the frequency of purchase of a product to package social goodwill with increased sales. We've got tons of letters from people expressing appreciation for the program."

What benefits do you see accruing to the local schools from this program? What benefits accrue to Campbell Soup Company?

Reprinted from *Business and Society: Cases and Text,* ed. Robert D. Hay, Edmund R. Gray, and James E. Gates (Cincinnati, Ohio: South-Western Publishing Co., 1976), by permission of the publisher.

How to Halt Excessive Government Regulation

Donald M. Kendall

Governmental regulation of business is accelerating. Government is not only involving itself more and more in the affairs of business, but in entirely new directions.

This is a legitimate concern of every thinking businessman and businesswoman in the country. Therefore, the sooner we make our own realistic appraisal of government's larger presence in business, the sooner we will be able to adjust our thinking and to cope with it.

We will, of course, always have government regulation; there is no escaping that fact. But we need to know how to live with regulation and to hold it in check.

To begin with, there are today at least three ways in which government's attitude toward business is undergoing a drastic change and bringing about increasing control.

FIRST CHANGE IN ATTITUDE

The first change in the attitude of government has to do with the consumer. Government is redefining the responsibility of business for the protection of the consumer and is assuming obligation for the enforcement of that responsibility. Here are some of the things which government has done in recent years, or is projecting, relating to the consumer:

> An Office of Consumer Affairs has been established, headed by a special assistant to the president.
>
> The Consumer Product Safety Commission has been legislated into being and is operating in Washington.
>
> Other government agencies, at the behest of the president or Congress—or on their own initiative—are expanding their consumer programs affecting business. The Food and Drug Administration and the Federal Trade Commission have both broadened their activities, for example, with the latter projecting an extensive new program to regulate advertising.

In a word, the doctrine of caveat emptor is just about dead. It is now the maker and the seller who must beware, and not the buyer.

SECOND CHANGE IN ATTITUDE

The second change in the attitude of government toward business has to do with the environment. Government is redefining the responsibility of business for the protection of the social and physical environment and is assuming obligation for the enforcement of that responsibility.

From *Nation's Business*, Vol. 64, No. 3 (March 1976). Copyright © 1976 by *Nation's Business*, Chamber of Commerce of the United States, Reprinted by permission.

For example, Environmental Protection Agency activities are expanding, especially in regard to the automotive industry, the pulp and paper industry, and packaging. Emission controls for automobiles and proposals for a ban on nonreturnable containers are two examples of such extended activity.

THIRD CHANGE IN ATTITUDE

The third change in the attitude of government toward business has to do with the structure of business, from entire industries to individual firms. Government seems to be seeking every opportunity to regulate every phase of business.

Here are some examples of what government has done recently, or is now projecting, pertaining to the structure of business. In one sense, this type of government control is as old as the Sherman Antitrust Act, updated and extended by the creation of the Federal Trade Commission; in another sense, it breaks entirely new ground.

1. Stepped-up antitrust activity by the Justice Department, as exemplified by government suits against International Business Machines Corp. and the American Telephone and Telegraph Co.
2. Orders by the Federal Trade Commission that companies be required to report publicly on sales and earnings by each product line.
3. Pending legislation to break up companies in such so-called concentrated industries as oil, steel, and automobiles.
4. Legislation enacted a few months ago giving the president new powers to control the flow of energy supplies, continuing price controls on domestic oil, setting fuel efficiency standards for automobiles, and authorizing government checkups on information given federal agencies by energy producers and distributors.
5. Proposed legislation for the federal chartering of corporations, including specific requirements for government-appointed board members with access to all company data who would have the option to publish the information.

CONSEQUENCES OF DELAY

Whether or not the items listed here are still in the debating stage, they illustrate an established trend of accelerated government intervention in business. Given the favorable attitude toward this trend generally ascribed to the 94th Congress, the situations must be taken seriously by top business management—which means that to delay doing something about it could prove disastrous for the American incentive system and for the American people.

Paradoxically, by what business has done, as well as by what it has not done, business has added fuel to the acceleration of government control.

For one thing, business has encouraged government involvement in business affairs by seeking special help from government in certain situations. The problem here is a complex one, and businessmen have not always been to blame.

It is a fact of life that government can grant favors and that its ability to do so is a function of its power. With hundreds of billions of dollars to spend on goods and services, government is a particularly good customer of business.

So long as the meeting between the two takes place in the open market, no harm is done. But when businessmen seek special legislative treatment as suppliers to government, business tends to make itself dependent on government and, to that extent, impairs the market system.

UNREASONED ANTIPATHY

A second way in which businessmen abet the spread of government involvement in business is by unreasoned antipathy toward government. By failing to appreciate the essential functions of government appropriate to a democratic society, some businessmen—too many, in fact—disqualify themselves as relevant voices in public debate.

Clearly, good government is vital to our society in carrying out effectively the duties and responsibilities assigned to government by the Constitution and the law of the land. When businessmen fail to affirm the need for good government and refer to government as evil per se, they lose both credibility and influence.

Although political democracy and an economic system based on private enterprise are in many ways interdependent—and always will be—there is, by the very nature of things, a built-in tension between them. The interests of business and other social institutions, government included, do not always appear identical. They often must be reconciled through negotiation and trade-off.

FAILURE TO COMMUNICATE

Business, therefore, does itself no good by dismissing the claims of government or of any other social institution. If the claims have merit—as some of those of consumers and ecologists, for instance, have proved to have—they will be met in spite of the aloofness of business and without the socially constructive help which business is so well-equipped to contribute.

A third way in which business paradoxically encourages increased government regulation is by failing to communicate clearly and convincingly to its many constituents—customers, employees, stockholders—and by failing to get its story across to the media.

The fault is not always the fault of business. For a number of reasons, the media often distort the business picture. Scandals involving a handful of shady operators make the headlines, for example, while the daily constructive and ethical activities of reputable businessmen—that is, the vast majority—go unnoticed.

Thus, the judgment of the general public tends to be formed on the basis of sporadic aberrations, rather than on the sustained performance of the private business system.

The result—both of ineffective communication by business and unbalanced reporting about business—has been and is a pervasive popular antipathy toward business, which reflects itself in the election of many antibusiness public officials and the passage of much of the antibusiness legislation which we see today.

Still, it is too easy to point the finger at the media and to feel sorry for ourselves. The truth is that, if the story of business is not being accurately and adequately told, it is the fault of business. The blame can be put on no one else.

Business management, therefore, must communicate, not only to the media, but to everyone concerned. This is the reality we must face up to. And the art of communication, as we employ it, must include both knowing exactly how to communicate and specifically what to communicate.

DUAL RESPONSIBILITY

In other words, the business executive's overall responsibility for the business climate is a dual obligation both to inform and to be informed by public opinion. The problems of business in dealing with government are relatively simple. Regulation becomes a problem only when enough public support has been mustered to legislate it.

The real challenge to management is to win enough public support to head off government action which is likely to be harmful to business and which is without social merit.

Effective action of this kind on the part of business is possible. This has been demonstrated in at least two recent and important cases.

1. When the Justice Department announced its suit against the American Telephone and Telegraph Co., the larger part of the national press —not generally probusiness—was opposed to the government's action.

2. Elements of the 1974 Trade Reform Act favoring free international trade can be traced to the active involvement of businessmen working together through the Emergency Committee for American Trade.

In one case, a private company, and in the other, an association of private businessmen, worked methodically and unremittingly to solve a problem. The problem in both cases, as businessmen saw it, was that the proposed public policy would injure both private and public interests. In both cases, businessmen assembled the facts to support their positions and communicated them with skill and diligence to the public at large and to interested groups, both in and outside government.

AT & T was able to demonstrate that breaking it up would only result in higher prices and poorer service to the public. The Emergency Committee for American Trade showed that certain kinds of restrictive international trade policies were detrimental to both the United States and the international economy.

COME OUT OF HIDING

The issues involved in both instances have, of course, not been resolved, but then, in a free dynamic society, issues rarely are. However, these examples do suggest a number of guidelines for management in dealing with public issues affecting the business climate.

Business managers must come out of hiding on social questions affecting their companies and industries, and they must play a more active, forthright role in public debate. There is a powerful tendency among businessmen faced with criticism to call out the technical troops—lawyers, scientists, public relations people, among them—and to retire to the familiar and comfortable worlds of finance, marketing, administration, and so on.

Needless to say, management in this complex world needs all the technical assistance it can get, but technicians are only as effective as the leadership they work under. Ultimate responsibility for dealing with the world in which the company operates rests with top management, and this responsibility cannot be delegated.

Not only is it top management's job, but in the light of mounting criticism of business and the growing trend for this criticism to be translated into government action, it is a top-priority job and an urgent one.

To deal effectively with criticism, management must be sure of its own position. It is vital to listen, actively and creatively, and to evaluate criticism on its own merits.

Is the criticism bigness? Well, what does bigness mean? What is the optimal size of a business organization, for what purpose, and from whose point of view? What are the alternative methods of industrial organization, and what are their social and political implications? What would the results of such industrial reorganization be in terms of costs, distribution, prices to the consumer?

HOW CLEAN IS CLEAN?

Is the charge pollution of the environment? Well, what are the facts? How clean is a clean environment, and how much is society willing to pay for what level of cleanliness? At what point are we willing to trade off ecological for economic factors?

Is the question one of excess profits? Well, when are profits excessive? What is the relation between profit on one hand and supply and demand on the other? Between profit and capital accumulation to finance commerce and industry? Between profit and willingness to assume risk in order that the goods and services society wants and needs get produced and distributed—and that the all-important jobs be created?

QUESTION OF ETHICS?

Is the charge that businessmen are unethical? What are the facts? Which particular businessman in what specific circumstance? What is the difference between illegal and unethical activities? By what system of values is an act judged unethical?

Is the charge that merchandise is shoddy or dangerous or that service is poor? What is the responsibility of the maker and seller, on one hand, and of the buyer and user on the other? What recourse does a competitive market provide the consumer?

Is the charge that advertising and packaging mislead the consumer? Are people buying too much of what is bad for them and too little of what is good for them? Well, what is the presumed level of competence of an adult citizen in our society? And who is making the presumption? Moreover, if the popular level of taste or judgment is deemed too low, then who shall have the responsibility for raising it? And will that power be enforceable by government? And how will it be policed?

REAL AND RELEVANT

In the contemporary business climate, in the current social debate, these are all real and relevant questions—and there are many more. They are difficult questions, and they will not go away. Managers must ask these questions of themselves before they confront the critics of business with them.

Moreover, the answers cannot be routine or mechanical because the issues go to the heart of the free-market system. They must be founded in conviction about the kind of society we want, and they must be well-documented.

However, knowing where he stands on social and political issues as they relate to business is only half of the business manager's job. The other half of his job—the important half at the present time—is to communicate.

He must communicate and keep on communicating until he gets the truth across—until he makes his voice heard and his influence felt.

The newspaper editorial and the TV newsclip have a direct bearing on what happens in the polling booth. Legislation tends to follow hard upon photographs of geese dying in oil slicks, automobile accidents, or women with baby carriages marching in protest.

Against a backdrop of such high emotionalism, it is admittedly not always easy to communicate coolly, clearly, and wisely. But it is essential for the economic well-being of the country that businessmen not be singled out as the villains in these daily dramas and that businessmen not react defensively.

If industrialization creates ecological and social problems, responsibility for solving them rests with everyone who participates in them—which is everyone.

The businessman is a citizen, a family man, a sharer of social values like everyone else.

HIGH RESPONSIBILITY

He should be prepared to present himself as such, to argue each case on its merits, and, if he believes in it, to argue the merits of the free-market system with skill and imagination. He should see this as a high-priority responsibility and take every opportunity to accept this responsibility individually as a representative of his business or in association with others.

If the media are, as many businessmen believe, unsympathetic toward business or poorly informed about it, that is no reason to hide from the media.

It is all the more reason to regard media relations as a tough management problem that must be solved. But it is by no means an impossible problem.

GET BUSY AND DO IT

The way to solve this problem is to get busy and do it. Business surely has all the resources and organization needed to communicate adequately and effectively to the media and to all individuals concerned.

Similarly, in government relations, communications can be vastly improved between businessmen and government officials by making use of every opportunity for formal and informal contact. It is surely worth the effort.

Government regulation will always be with us. But there is no sense in letting the present trend continue, allowing government regulation to get out of hand, when, by waking up to the situation and putting forth the required effort, we can live with regulation and hold it in check.

BUSINESS
IN MODERN SOCIETY

Part IV

The modern business is strikingly different from its counterpart a century ago. In size, for example, smaller businesses have become less common as big corporations account for a larger and larger share of the economy. In 1973, the 1,000 largest firms were responsible for 72 percent of the sales, 86 percent of the employees, and 85 percent of the profits of all U.S. industrial corporations. Slightly over 200 corporations in 1968 held the same share of manufacturing assets as the 1,000 largest corporations in 1941. But size is only one of the ways in which business has changed. Other changes include alterations in corporate organizational structure, the development of consumer movements, and the increasing regulation by government. Throughout these modifications, business has become more aware of itself not only as an economic institution but also as an active participant in the surrounding culture.

From an ethical standpoint the gradual transformation of business is significant for a number of reasons. Changes in the goals and structure of the corporation have given rise to changes in the expectations of employees and consumers. For example, the shift away from one-man domination of the corporation has resulted in greater participation by employees in corporate decisions. Even if they do not own stock in their companies, professional managers now tend to assume they have a right to participate in governing corporate affairs. Also, technological advances have generated a wider array of products and a vastly more efficient means, i.e., television, for advertising them. It is often suggested that large corporations are not only able to stimulate consumer demand but also are literally able to create it. If this is true and if the demand for items we use every day would not exist without the aid of massive advertising, then it may be wondered if corporate advertisers should assume special responsibilities.

In addition there have been changes in society's attitudes toward economic issues. Once it was routinely assumed that economic growth should be pursued: Greater production, higher incomes, and larger Gross National Products were taken to be the obvious goals for society. Yet now critics complain that clean air, the preservation of wildlife, and adequate energy sources cannot be assured if we persist in our search for greater economic prosperity. Instead, decreasing growth or "no growth" are proposed as alternatives of maximum benefit for society. The advancing technology utilized by corporations requires greater and greater demands on our natural resources. We should ask if a decent standard of living is possible without destroying the ecological systems which support technology. Also, can we maintain a high level of economic prosperity without sacrificing the human values of freedom and creativity? Such issues are examined in this part by looking at the ways in which modern corporate society has evolved and by discussing the prognosis for business in the future.

BUSINESS TRENDS AND SOCIAL RESPONSIBILITY

The modern corporate structure, which the contemporary economist John Kenneth Galbraith calls the "technostructure," is in a period of major transition. The profit motive, an aim traditionally associated with all businesses, may no longer be so dominant as it was in the past. Goals of technological advancement, growth, and autonomy often seem as important to modern corporations as the profits they generate. Also, as we just noted, corporate decisions are now seldom made by one man. Even the owners of the corporation, the shareholders, play extremely minor roles in directing the corporation. Instead, corporate decisions are typically made by committees of industrial managers, themselves employees of the corporation, who have worked their way up in the ranks. Galbraith discusses these and other issues in an article entitled "Technology, Planning, and Organization."

What is the net result of these changes for the whole of society? Some commentators, notably pessimistic in their answers, suggest that modern methods of marketing and production, along with the abnormally high value placed on technological development, have come to dominate our society's ethical attitudes. The goals of the nation have become the same as the economic goals of business. There may be nothing inherently evil about the goals of economic growth, technological advance, and a higher material standard of living; but critics such as Galbraith have argued that when these become the primary goals of a nation there is a significant lowering in the quality of human life. Economic goals are able to distract attention from crucial human issues, and freedom, individuality, and creativity are lost in a society dominated by large corporations and economic goals. Critics claim, then, that somehow the *human* element can become lost in the face of such powerful economic forces. Those who are not part of the economic machine, the poor, the aged, and the untrained, are left out of society: There is no meaningful place for economic misfits. Moreover, it is argued that art, literature, and philosophy, all of which require the development of noneconomic talent, cannot find their proper support and encouragement in a society dominated by economic factors. Even scientific research is said to be discouraged by modern society because such work must be done by individuals working in a free, creative atmosphere rather than by the groups of committees which typify corporate activity. Thus critics argue that the goals of modern corporate society are too narrow: In pursuing economic and technological growth excessively we tend to destroy the very creative and cultural capacities which make our lives meaningful.

However, not all aspects of the development of a technological corporate society are negative. In the period between 1961 and 1976, for example, business has become more self-conscious about the moral dimension of its role in society. In the article, "Is the Ethics of Business Changing?" Steven Brenner and Earl Molander show statistically that business people have become much more aware of ethical and social issues and their relation to business. Since the first pioneer study of business attitudes in 1961 by Raymond C. Baumhart, business people have overcome traditional objections to the need for social responsibility and have accepted it as a reasonable and obtainable goal. Although business people are increasingly cynical about the ethical standards of their peers, many have accepted the idea that decisions which appear to be simply economic ones are also moral in character, and that ethics is an important issue for the modern business person.

BUSINESS AND ENVIRONMENTAL ISSUES

In the Brenner and Molander survey, business people felt that the two most important social challenges facing modern business were (1) how to limit environmental and ecological damage from production, and (2) how to use energy and natural resources efficiently. These represent crucial social challenges, but there is great disagreement over how to determine the specific responsibilities which business should assume in order to meet them. What role *should* business play—and how much societal obligation should it assume—in the face of environmental problems?

Attention has been drawn recently to the fact that we live on a planet which, despite its apparent abundance, possesses finite natural resources. Never-ending economic growth involves either a never-ending use of these resources or the discovery of suitable substitutes. Is it wise then, to persist in our goals of technological and economic expansion when our stocks of natural resources are continuously dwindling? Critics argue that we live, in effect, on a spaceship—the earth—which contains limited supplies. Considering our rapidly expanding population and economic output, we shall soon approach the limits of those supplies, and human needs will outstrip the technological knowhow required to develop substitutes. To avoid this disaster such critics propose a "no-growth" economy in which we actively work to replace lost resources.

In sharp contrast with both this argument and with the views of critics like Galbraith are the attitudes of Wilfred Beckerman. Beckerman, a noted contemporary Oxford economist, argues that economic growth is both necessary and valuable; that it actually enhances human life rather than discouraging it; and that the quality of human life, perhaps its very survival, depends on maintaining both economic and technological growth. Only a small percentage of the world's population has achieved a decent standard of living. Economic growth, according to Beckerman, is still indispensable for human welfare, and one cannot argue that it is undesirable until minimal necessities of life are available for everyone. Moreover, Beckerman points out that people have actively interfered with nature for centuries, and although there has been periodic panic over the exhaustion of natural resources, they have not been depleted. Indeed people continue to find more resources and to invent satisfactory substitutes. The problems connected with our use of resources, Beckerman concludes, cannot be solved by turning to a policy of no growth. Instead, he recommends in some of his writings strict government control of the ecological side effects of business. Such a program, he believes, would not limit economic growth—it would merely guide it in a useful direction.

In his article, "Scarcity Society," William Ophuls discusses the dilemma of economic growth from an ethical point of view. In contrast to Beckerman, Ophuls feels that in order for human life to continue, a program of ecological and economic equilibrium must be instituted to produce an economy in which population, resources, and environment are in balance. The solution recommended by both Beckerman and no-growth proponents is to *control* and *regulate* the economy in order to prevent environmental abuses. But this measure leads immediately, Ophuls says, to the loss of important personal human liberties. Given that people operate in accordance with their own personal ends (Ophuls calls this the "tragedy of the commons"), how is humanity to protect both the environment and vital natural resources *without* generating stifling and oppressive systems of social control?

Ophuls' solution to the problem is an ethical one: improve the ethical nature of man, "the restoration of the civic virtue of a corrupt people." People must, acting as individuals, restore human dignity by developing the moral resources of self-restraint and respect for others. We must impose our own laws and controls upon ourselves—individually. Only then, Ophuls claims, will we solve the dilemma of ecological scarcity.

The last case study in the book, "Reserve Mining Company," illustrates many of the ethical issues which have been developed in this section, in particular, the conflict between economic growth and environmental goals. It tends to confirm Ophuls' observation that people will risk ecological side effects in order to pursue their own economic ends. Having discharged massive amounts of a production by-product, the Reserve Mining Company was charged with polluting the environment. Should Reserve Mining be subject to additional government controls? If so, what should be the limitations, if any, on the government's power to protect the environment by controlling corporate economic expansion? This case will provide a useful catalyst for the formation of your own views about how, if at all, business can both pursue economic growth and act responsibly for the future of the environment.

BUSINESS TRENDS
AND SOCIAL RESPONSIBILITY

Case Study—TRW, Inc:
A Social Policy Statement

JOHN E. MERTES

The basic business plan that has guided TRW Inc. for over 70 years includes: selective diversification, strong market penetration, development of technologies that anticipate market needs, measured risk-taking in new markets, aggressive management, concentration on the growth segments of TRW's basic markets mixed with a high degree of common sense. As of 1971–72 the total sales of the company and its growth rate for the year were:

Financial Highlights	(Dollar Amounts In Thousands Except for Per Share Data) 1972	1971	Percentage Change
Net Sales	$1,687,510	$1,546,968	9%
Earnings Before Taxes	$ 137,994	$ 122,843	12%
Net Earnings	$ 76,109	$ 65,671	16%
Per Common Share Primary Earnings	$ 2.22	$ 1.85	20%
Total Assets	$1,235,716	$1,115,942	11%

A brief review of TRW's historical development provides a background for policy analysis. This growth led to concern for TRW's relationship to society. A new technique for making bolts for bicycles, by welding a head onto a stem, led to the founding of the Cleveland Cap Screw Company in 1901. Three years later this same technique was applied to the manufacture of automobile engine valves—to form the nucleus of today's TRW.

With the arrival of the space age, TRW became the first industrial firm

From *Business and Society*, ed. Robert D. Hay, Edmund R. Gray, and James E. Gates (Cincinnati, Ohio: South-Western Publishing Co., 1976); reprinted by permission of the publisher.

333

to build a spacecraft—named Pioneer 1. This 1958 feat was followed by Vela nuclear detection satellites, Orbiting Geophysical Observatories and Intelstat III spacecraft for the world's first global commercial communications satellite system.

More than a decade of TRW involvement in the nation's space program was climaxed by the Apollo 11 flight in 1969. TRW propulsion and electronic systems played key roles in landing the first men on the moon, and the company's technical staff helped plan the historic mission.

During the 1960s a series of acquisitions and internal product developments brought the company further diversification within its four major markets. TRW's long experience in developing computer software and information systems for defense and space programs led to entry into new commercial markets. Electronics products were expanded to include capacitors, resistors, miniature motors, color TV convergence yokes, connectors, and transformers. Mechanical components such as bearings and steering gears were added, along with other new industrial products ranging from cutting tools and hydraulic motors to fasteners and oilfield equipment.

Much of this expansion was outside the U.S., as TRW established or acquired subsidiaries and affiliates on six continents.

Looking to the future, TRW has moved aggressively into a number of new fields in which it expects to grow in the Seventies. These include automated control systems; navigation and air traffic control satellites; and systems projects of public importance such as urban development, pollution control, high-speed ground transportation and traffic control.

Serving the ever-changing needs of man and his society represents tomorrow's growth opportunity for TRW. The merger of Thompson Products and Ramo-Wooldridge in 1958 produced Thompson Ramo Wooldridge Inc., a name shortened in 1965 to TRW Inc.

TRW'S SOCIAL POLICY—THE ROLE
OF THE CORPORATION IN A CHANGING ERA

At a recent meeting of senior management, discussion focused on TRW's responsibility to the constituents it serves: shareholders, customers, employees, government, plant communities and the general public. In answer to the question, "How do you define the social impact of a corporation?" Dr. Ruben F. Mettler, president of TRW, expressed the corporate policy:

> A meaningful definition requires looking at the three levels at which TRW should have a positive impact on society.
>
> The first level concerns the basic performance of the company as an economic unit. How many jobs does it provide? Is its productivity increasing? Is it profitable enough to pay employees and shareholders fairly? What is the quality of its goods and services? Does it provide stability and growth in employment? What is its contribution to the economy of the countries in which it operates? Clearly, TRW's primary social impact lies in our success as an economic institution efficiently producing quality products to fill society's needs. The next level concerns the quality of the conduct of our internal

affairs. For example, are we ensuring equal employment and advancement opportunity for all? Is there job satisfaction? Do we provide proper health protection and safety devices and adequate pollution control? Is our advertising truthful?

The third level concerns the additional things we do in relating to our external environment. This includes charitable and cultural contribution programs, youth projects, urban action programs, assistance to educational institutions, employees' participation in community affairs and our good government program. TRW focuses its activities in these areas in communities where we have plants because we can have the most meaningful impact there.

It would be a mistake to think that any one, or two, of these levels fully defines our corporate impact, and hence our responsibilities at all three levels. The corporate constituents that we're concerned about—shareholder, employee, customer, government, community, general public—have a particular interest at each level.

For example, shareholders are not just interested in their return on investment—a part of the first level. They want to be sure that our activities at the second level and third level will not adversely affect that investment. Employees are interested in more than their paycheck. They want to be treated fairly and to enjoy equal rights and opportunities. They want to be proud of their company's outside activities and to participate in them.

We are determined to meet the needs and expectations of each of our constituents at each of these three levels. That's how I believe TRW will be measured and judged on its impact and its responsibilities to society.

SOCIAL RESPONSIBILITY IN ACTION

The following examples illustrate this concept:

. . . The economic contribution of TRW during 1972 was positive. Sales, profits, dividends, wages, fringe benefits and taxes all increased. Employment increased by 12 percent, providing about 8,500 jobs. Capital and work-planning improvements to increase productivity have been significant. As in prior years, many divisions were cited by their customers for the outstanding quality of their products and services.

. . . TRW emphasized its equal employment opportunity programs and increased its minority population significantly. The company also promoted educational opportunities and job enrichment programs designed to upgrade the skills and abilities of all employees with special emphasis on providing training courses for the disadvantaged. Occupational health and safety have received major attention. Facilities and equipment which meet or exceed all regulations for the operator's safety are being installed. TRW is proud of its environmental record with respect to air and water quality problems. During the past five years virtually all major sources of industrial pollution have been eliminated.

. . . In Boston the company's AB&W Division was formed several years ago to provide meaningful employment for inner-city blacks and whites. Managed by black employees, this operating unit performs quality manufacturing and assembly functions at competitive prices for other TRW divisions while also actively building additional business outside the TRW organization. In Cleveland there was a need for a neighborhood health facility near one of TRW's plants. Working with concerned community

leaders and area medical professionals, TRW provided a convenient location and financial assistance to establish the Polyclinic Family Health Care
Center.

. . . Los Angeles teenage Mexican-Americans are getting a better break
when they enter the work force in Southern California in part due to the
efforts of TRW employees who formed an organization called Career
Opportunities for Youth. COY volunteers work with Chicano youngsters,
motivating them to remain in school through tutoring and rap sessions,
helping them to select a trade or field, and instilling the confidence needed
to obtain and hold meaningful jobs.

CORPORATE RESPONSIBILITY

A number of corporations have emerged as leaders in the area of social
concern. TRW has moved in this direction although many corporate
managements have been hesitant to do this as such action may be detrimental to corporate profits.

Is the Ethics of Business Changing?

STEVEN N. BRENNER and
EARL A. MOLANDER

What would you do if . . .

. . . the minister of a foreign nation where extraordinary payments to
lubricate the decision-making machinery are common asks you for a
$200,000 consulting fee? In return, he promises special assistance in obtain-
ing a $100-million contract which would produce at least a $5-million profit
for your company. The contract would probably go to a foreign competitor
if your company did not win it.

. . . as the president of a company in a highly competitive industry, you
learn that a competitor has made an important scientific discovery that will
substantially reduce, but not eliminate, your profit for about a year? There
is a possibility of hiring one of the competitor's employees who knows the
details of the discovery.

. . . you learn that an executive earning $30,000 a year has been padding
his expense account by about $1,500 a year?

These questions were posed as part of a lengthy questionnaire on
business ethics and social responsibility completed by 1,227 *Harvard Business Review* readers—25% of the cross section of 5,000 U.S. readers polled.
. . .

Our study was prompted by the same concern that Raymond C. Baumhart had in 1961 when he conducted a similar study for HBR: the numerous comments on business ethics in the media contained little empirical evidence to indicate whether large numbers of business executives shared the attitudes, behavior, and experience of those whose supposedly unethical and illegal conduct was being represented (or denied) as typical of the business profession.[1]

In updating and expanding his study, we designed our survey around three main questions: Has business ethics changed since the early 1960s, and if so, how and why? Are codes the answer to the ethical challenges business people currently face? What is the relationship between ethical dilemmas and the dilemma of corporate social responsibility?

Here are some of the highlights of our study:

1. There is substantial disagreement among respondents as to whether ethical standards in business today have changed from what they were.
2. Respondents are somewhat more cynical about the ethical conduct of their peers than they were.
3. Most respondents favor ethical codes, although they strongly prefer general precept codes to specific practice codes.
4. The dilemmas respondents experience and the factors they feel have the greatest impact on business ethics suggest that ethical codes alone will not substantially improve business conduct.
5. Most respondents have overcome the traditional ideological barriers to the concept of social responsibility and have embraced its practice as a legitimate and achievable goal for business.
6. Most respondents rank their customers well ahead of shareholders and employees as the client group to whom they feel the greatest responsibility.
   . . .

We feel it particularly noteworthy that relations with superiors are the primary category of ethical conflict. Respondents frequently complained of superiors' pressure to support incorrect viewpoints, sign false documents, overlook superiors' wrongdoing, and do business with superiors' friends. Either superiors are expecting more than subordinates in 1976 or subordinates are less willing to do their bosses' bidding without questions, at least to themselves. Both possibilities suggest a weakening in the corporate authority structure and an attendant impact on ethical business conduct that deserves future study. The following examples demonstrate ethical dilemmas being faced in business today:

- The vice president of a California industrial manufacturer "being forced as an officer to sign corporate documents which I knew were not in the best interest of minority stockholders."
- A Missouri manager of manpower planning "employing marginally qualified minorities in order to meet Affirmative Action quotas."
- A manager of product development from a computer company in Massachusetts "trying to act as though the product (computer software) would correspond to what the customer had been led by sales to expect, when, in fact, I knew it wouldn't."
- A manager of corporate planning from California "acquiring a non-U.S. company with two sets of books used to evade income taxes—standard

practice for that country. Do we (1) declare income and pay taxes, (2) take the "black money" out of the country (illegally), or (3) continue tax evasion?"

- The president of a real estate property management firm in Washington "projecting cash flow without substantial evidence in order to obtain a higher loan than the project can realistically amortize."
- A young Texas insurance manager "being asked to make policy changes that produced more premium for the company and commission for an agent but did not appear to be of advantage to the policy-holder."

Accepted Practices

Clearly, that ethical dilemmas do exist and are too often resolved in ways which leave executives dissatisfied seems to be a matter of substantial concern for today's business people. And too often unethical practices become a routine part of doing business. To determine just how routine, we asked: "In every industry there are some generally accepted business practices. In your industry, are there practices which you regard as unethical?"

If we eliminate those who say they "don't know," we see from *Exhibit 1* that two-thirds of the responding executives in 1976 indicate that such practices exist, compared with nearly four-fifths who so responded in 1961.

Are there industry practices which you consider unethical?

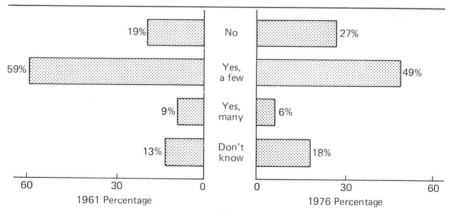

Exhibit 1

Could this decrease be a sign of improvement in ethical *practices*? Perhaps, but it is also possible that such practices are now less visible than they once were. Even more disturbing is the possibility which we raised earlier—that ethical *standards* have, in fact, fallen in business so that practices once considered unethical are now not viewed as such. Further, these figures say nothing about the conduct that all agree is both unacceptable and unethical.

Nearly half (540) of all respondents and 84% of those indicating the existence of such practices were willing to tell us which practice or practices they would most like to see eliminated. Both the changes and similarities in these "most unwanted" practices in the past 15 years are interesting.

As in 1961, the practice that most executives want to eliminate involves "gifts, gratuities, bribes, and 'call girls.' " Typical examples given by the 144 respondents in this category are:

- "Payoffs to a foreign government to secure contracts." (The vice president of an Oklahoma oil exploration company)
- "Egg carton contracts with grocery chains can only be obtained by kickbacks—the egg packers do not have the freedom of choice in buying, thus stifling competition." (A young southern consumer goods executive vice president)
- "Loans granted as favors to loan officers." (An Indiana bank vice president)
- "Dealings with travel agencies that involve kickbacks, rebates, or other pseudonyms for 'bribes.' " (A Florida transportation industry executive)

Of the 80 respondents who mentioned practices which included cheating customers, unfair credit practices, or overselling, typical comments are:

- "Substitution of materials without customer knowledge after the job has been awarded." (A young New York salesman)
- "Misrepresenting the contents of products." (A Texas vice president of engineering)
- "Scheduled delivery dates that are known to be inaccurate to get a contract." (A California director of engineering) . . .

Economic Pressures

We have confirmed the continued existence both of ethical dilemmas inherent in everyday business and of generally accepted practices which individual managers feel are unethical. To observe the impact of such an environment on our respondents' ethical beliefs, we turned our attention to a number of issues of general ethical concern.

Simply returning our questionnaire reflected, we think, a general concern about business ethics among our respondents. Nevertheless, 65% of them feel that "society, not business, has the *chief* responsibility for inculcating its ethical standards into the educational and legal systems, and thus into business decision making."

Another important aspect of the debate over ethics focuses on whether any absolutes exist to strive for or whether ethics should be purely "situational" or "relative." Four out of five respondents agree that "business people should try to live up to an absolute moral standard rather than to the moral standard of their peer group."

Not only do executives believe in ethical absolutes; they also believe that "in the long run, sound ethics is good business." As in 1961, fewer than 2% of the respondents disagreed with this statement. Yet, in practice, many of these same executives see their associates losing sight of this standard. Again, as in 1961, close to half of our respondents agree that "the American business executive tends not to apply the great ethical laws immediately to work. He is preoccupied chiefly with gain."[2]

Our results suggest two explanations for this failure. First, despite its long-run value, ethical conduct apparently is not necessarily rewarded. Within the business organization, 50% of our respondents feel that one's superiors often do not want to know how results are obtained, as long as one achieves the desired outcome.

Second, competitive pressures from outside the organization push ethical consideration into the background. Of our executives, 43% feel that "competition today is stiffer than ever. As a result, many in business find themselves forced to resort to practices which are considered shady, but which appear necessary for survival."

Societal Forces

In the period since Baumhart's study, American business has seen some significant changes. A sustained period of economic euphoria which began in 1961 has been replaced by recession, inflation, and resource scarcity. Charges of corporate irresponsibility relative to critical issues of the 1960s and 1970s (minority relations, consumerism, and the environment) combined with the recent disclosures of corporate wrongdoing at home and abroad have raised serious questions about the trend in business's ethical standards.

To determine if any such trend existed, we asked our HBR respondents: "How do you feel ethical standards in business today compare with ethical standards 15 years ago?" . . .

Our respondents seem to be sending us three clear-cut messages:

1. Public disclosure and concern over unethical business behavior are the most potent forces for improvement in ethical standards.
2. Hedonism, individual greed, and the general decay of social standards are the factors which most influence a decline in ethical standards.
3. The elements which influence shifts in ethical standards are ones over which they have little direct control. . . .

NEW VIEW OF SOCIAL RESPONSIBILITY

The current revival of interest in business ethics coincides with a renewed focus on corporate social responsibility. To provide some insight into how our respondents see the relationship between "social responsibility" and "business ethics," we asked:

> Is social responsibility an *ethical* issue for the *individual business person*, or is it an issue that concerns the *role* the *corporation* should play in society?

The overwhelming response we got is that it is *both*—65% agree with the former statement and 83% with the latter.

But can it be both? The answer is, of course, yes. Whereas responsibility, for both the individual and the corporation, tends to be defined in the social arrangements and obligations which make up the structure of the society, ethics concerns the rules by which these responsibilities are carried out. As in numerous other settings, it is often difficult to separate the rules of the game from the game itself.

Erroneous Caricature

One important finding of our study is the rejection of the traditional ideology that says business is a profit-bound institution. Only 28% of our respondents endorse the traditional dictum that "the social responsibility of business is to 'stick to business,'" most often associated with the writings of Milton Friedman.[3]

Further, only 23% agree that "social responsibility is good business only if it is also good public relations and/or preempts government interference." And 38% agree that "the social responsibility debate is the result of the attempt of liberal intellectuals to make a moral issue of business behavior."[4]

By contrast, 69% agree with George Lodge's observation that "'profit' is really a somewhat ineffective measure of business's social effectiveness."[5]

Not only do those in our sample reject the traditional ideological barriers to corporate involvement in social responsibility, but they also reject the practical ones. Of our respondents, 77% disagree with the idea that "every business is in effect 'trapped' in the business system it helped create, and can do remarkably little about the social problems of our time."[6]

Have business executives abandoned their traditional profit orientation? Not necessarily. We still found strong support for long-term profit maximization among our executives. But these findings do indicate that the American business executive has incorporated a new view of his role and potential, and those of his company, into his profit concerns.

Those critics who continue to characterize the American business executive as a power hungry, profit-bound individualist, indifferent to the needs of society, should be put on notice that they are now dealing with a straw man of their own making.

Before we go as far as to predict a revolution in corporate behavior, however, a word of caution is in order. First, the corporate organization still resists specific measures when trying to put social responsibility into practice. Of our respondents, 75% feel the rhetoric of social responsibility exceeds the reality in most corporations. And 58% agree that "the socially aware executive must show convincingly a net short-term or long-term economic advantage to the corporation in order to gain acceptance for any socially responsible measure he might propose."[7]

A second major barrier is uncertainty—uncertainty as to what "social responsibility" means. Almost half (46%) of our respondents agree with the assertion that "the meaning of social responsibility is so vague as to render it essentially unworkable as a guide to corporate policy and decisions."

This uncertainty as to meaning is further amplified by an uncertainty as to consequences. Our respondents were almost evenly split on two statements:

1. Social responsibility invariably will mean *lower* corporate profits in the *short run*—41% agree, 16% are neutral, and 43% disagree.
2. Social responsibility invariably will mean *higher* corporate profits in the *long run*—43% agree, 22% are neutral, and 36% disagree.

The nearly even split and the high number of neutral responses on these statements, together with the feeling of vagueness about the meaning of social responsibility, suggest that bringing social responsibility to the operating level is an objective which its advocates have yet to realize.

Customer's Servant

To further clarify our respondents' concept of social responsibility, we asked them to rank the various groups whose relations to the corporation define the corporation's place in the social system.

As *Exhibit 2* shows, the group to whom executives feel the greatest responsibility comes through clearly and unmistakably: *the customers*. Stockholders and employees are a clear second and third, and the interest of society at large and its elected governments—the "public interest"—appears to receive the least consideration.

RESPONSIBILITY OF YOUR COMPANY TO VARIOUS GROUPS

	Rank
Customers	1.83
Stockholders	2.52
Employees	2.86
Local community where company operates	4.44
Society in general	4.97
Suppliers	5.10
Government	5.72

Note: The ranking is calculated on a scale of 1 (most responsibility) to 7 (least responsibility).

Exhibit 2

This rather surprising result—the primacy of customer interest—suggests that we need to reexamine the thesis that the guiding principle of American business and the justification for its power is service to stockholders. We may be observing a return to the original capitalist doctrine of the customer as the client whom production is intended to serve and the replacement of the doctrine of "long-run profit maximization" with the "long-run customer satisfaction" doctrine.

The primacy of customer interests also raises some serious questions about any unethical conduct at the expense of customers which is rationalized on grounds of profit maximization. If the assertion of customer primacy is valid, it follows that business should also make ethical conduct in dealing with customers a first priority, a condition which our data suggest does not currently exist.

Societal Obligations

How do these attitudes affect policy and decision making on specific issues? We asked HBR readers to express the degree of responsibility they felt in each of the nine areas along a scale of 1 (absolutely voluntary) to 5 (absolutely obligatory). The third-place standing of "maximizing long-run profits," shown in *Exhibit 3*, confirms our observation that it is no longer perceived as the primary responsibility of today's executives.

AREAS OF RESPONSIBILITY

	Degree
Being an efficient user of energy and natural resources	4.00
Assessing the potential environmental effects flowing from the company's technological advances	3.96
Maximizing long-run profits	3.78
Using every means possible to maximize job content and satisfaction for the hourly worker	3.35
Having your company's subsidiary in another country use the same occupational safety standards as your company does in the United States	3.05
Acquiescing to State Department requests that the company not establish operations in a certain country	3.01
Making implementation of corporate Affirmative Action plans a significant determinant of line officer promotion and salary improvement	2.91
Instituting a program for hiring the hard core unemployed	2.28
Contributing to the local United Fund	2.17

Note: The ranking is calculated on a scale of 1 (absolutely voluntary) to 5 (absolutely obligatory).

Exhibit 3

But we were surprised to find two areas of general responsibility to *society*—"being an efficient user of energy and natural resources" and "assessing the potential environmental effects flowing from the company's technological advances"—are first and second. The strong feeling of obligation toward these areas, together with "using every means possible to maximize job content and satisfaction for the hourly worker," demonstrates the desire of the business person to define his responsibility in those areas which involve externalities directly associated with his operation, areas where he can see clearly the internalized benefits of his "socially responsible" actions, either in reduced costs or preempted government regulation.

By contrast, the strong voluntary rankings for the United Fund and hardcore hiring indicate that executives do not feel a significant obligation concerning social problems of a remedial or welfare nature whose benefits to the company are not readily apparent.

Voluntary Measures

Perhaps not surprisingly, our respondents favor those measures for improving corporate social conduct that are both general in nature and leave room for voluntarism over those that involve compulsion and outside interference in corporate affairs. This result could be expected given our respondents' uncertainties about what social responsibility means and about its consequences, as well as their natural reluctance to accept any further constraints on the traditional freedom of the business decision maker.

We have already seen that respondents feel the media have had a powerful impact on business ethics simply by virtue of publicizing unethical conduct. They also feel that "endorsement of 'social responsibility' by the business media" would have the greatest positive influence on corporate social behavior. Altogether, 72% feel that such an endorsement would have a "positive impact," 55% believe that there would be "some positive impact," and 17% believe that the impact would be "very positive." Only 4% think it would have a "negative impact," while 24% think it would have "zero impact." Clearly executives look to the business media, not only for information and education, but for guidance in areas of uncertainty as well.[8]

About 62% of our respondents also agree that "the equalization of managerial rewards and punishments for social performance with those for financial performance" would have a positive effect in making corporations more socially responsible. This view is corroborated by our earlier observation that most executives support the view that proposals for corporate social action must convincingly show a net economic advantage to the company.

Polling stockholder opinions on sensitive social issues (part of "shareholder democracy"), public interest representation on boards of directors, educating the average citizen to the realities of corporate operations, and corporate social audits have all been advanced, and debated, in business and academic circles. Our respondents' generally positive view toward these measures—no more than a fourth think any of them would have a negative impact—suggests that, if properly conceived and advanced, these measures might also be acceptable to most executives.

This willingness to accept outside inputs does not include input from government, however. Less than one-sixth of our respondents see anything positive in federal chartering of corporations, strongly endorsed by Ralph Nader among others, while 39% feel that such a measure would be deleterious. And our respondents are least sanguine about increased governmental regulation: 64% fear it would have a negative impact and 14% say it would have none, while only 21% feel it might be beneficial.

FREEDOM & CRITICISM

At the outset we posed three basic questions for our study. The generous response of HBR readers has allowed us to answer them in this article. Now a fourth question is in order: "What do the results mean for managers and students of business ethics?"

Our results suggest changes are necessary in two primary areas: Managerial outlook and managerial actions.

The four aspects of change in managerial outlook indicated are:

- You will face ethical dilemmas, created by value conflicts, for which there may be no totally satisfactory resolution. But don't use this condition to rationalize unethical behavior on your part.
- Don't expect ethical codes to help solve all problems. Codes can create a false sense of security and lead to the encouragement of violations.
- If you wish to avoid external enforcement of someone else's ethical code, make self-enforcement work.
- Don't deceive yourself into thinking you can hide unethical actions.

The five aspects of managerial action suggested are:

- Fair dealing with customers and employees is the most direct way to restore confidence in business morality.
- Corporate steps taken to improve ethical behavior clearly must come from the top and be part of the reward and punishment system.
- If an ethical code is developed and implemented, have an accompanying information system to detect violations. Then treat violators equitably.
- Test decisions against what you think is right rather than against what is expedient.
- Don't force others into unethical conduct.

It seems to us our respondents are saying that managers facing ethical dilemmas should refer to the familiar maxim, "Would I want my family, friends, and employers to see this decision and its consequences on television?" If the answer is yes, then go ahead. If the answer is no, then additional thought should be given to finding a more satisfactory solution.

Business executives and the companies they serve have a personal and vested interest in the resolution of ethical and social responsibility dilemmas. Our respondents recognize these dilemmas and to some extent appear willing to accept generalized guidance for their resolution in the form of general precept codes and statements from the business media. Although such measures will help in this regard, they are obviously no panacea for the continued strain arising from challenges to business ethics and responsibility. They also are not as action oriented as specific practice codes or government regulation.

The manager appears to prefer uncertainty and tension to the loss of freedom and complications that would accompany these more rigorous measures. In making this choice, he has to realize that he must continue to bear the criticism of the larger society in both the business ethics and corporate social responsibility areas.

345

Notes

1. Raymond C. Baumhart, "How Ethical Are Businessmen?" HBR July-August 1961, p. 6.
2. Rabbi Louis Finkelstein, "The Businessman's Moral Failure," *Fortune,* September 1958, p. 116.
3. Milton Friedman, *Capitalism and Freedom* (Chicago: University of Chicago Press, 1962), Ch. 8.
4. Henry G. Manne, in Henry G. Manne and Henry C. Wallich, *The Modern Corporation and Social Responsibility* (Washington, D.C.: American Institute for Public Policy Research, 1972), p. 10.
5. George Cabot Lodge, "Top Priority: Renovating Our Ideology," HBR September-October 1970, p. 50.
6. Neil V. Chamberlain, *The Limits of Corporate Responsibility* (New York: Boise Books, 1973), p. 4.
7. Albert Z. Carr, "Can an Executive Afford a Conscience?" HBR July-August 1970, p. 58.
8. The susceptibility of business people to the ideology of the business media has often been noted; see, for example, Norton Long, "The Corporation, Its Satellites, and the Local Community," in *The Corporation in Modern Society,* edited by Edward S. Mason (Cambridge, Massachusetts: Harvard University Press, 1959), p. 210.

Comment on Study by Brenner and Molander

RAYMOND C. BAUMHART, S.J.

My interpretation of Professors Brenner's and Molander's data and the signs of the times indicate that business behavior is more ethical than it was 15 years ago, but that the expectations of a better educated and ethically sensitized public have risen more rapidly than the behavior.

This is the sixth, and most creative and extensive, replication of the series of questions I first asked in 1961. Each time the results have been remarkably similar, especially in the respondents' attitude that: I am more ethical than the average manager, and my department and company are more ethical than their counterparts; and a written code of ethics would help to improve business practices in my industry.

It is good to see the evidence that business managers accept the corporation as a social, as well as an economic, entity.

To me the most surprising finding of this study is that the 1,227 respondents rank responsibility to customers ahead of responsibility to stockholders and employees. What has happened to *caveat emptor?* Now it is the government and suppliers who should beware.

Technology, Planning, and Organization

John Kenneth Galbraith

1

In accordance with well-regarded academic custom I should like to begin by going a decent distance back of my subject. It is my intention to examine the effect of modern technology, the planning that it occasions and the organization that it requires on the location of power in the modern economy. But I propose to begin with a brief reference to the oldest of economic problems, that of the relation between what economists have anciently called the factors of production.

Few matters have been more faithfully explored by our profession. Until recently, the problem of efficiency in production was envisaged, almost entirely as one of winning the best combination between capital, labor, land and the entrepreneurial talent which brought them together and which managed their employment. The elucidation of these arcane matters, by means of diagrams, remains one of the prime pedagogical rites of economics. Changing technology, it is conceded, is more important than proportioning in determining what can be obtained from any given stock of the factors of production. But there is no way by which intelligence on the role of science, technology and productivity can be adumbrated at length in a textbook. So economic theory after conceding the important continues to deal at length with the matter on which doctrine is available.

Economists have been equally concerned with the way in which factor prices—rents, wages, interest and profits—are determined. Indeed, in the classical tradition, the subject of economics was thought of as falling in two parts: The problem of value having to do with the determination of the process of goods and the problem of distribution having to do with how the income resulting from the sale of products and services was divided between landlords, workers, capitalists and those who, as entrepreneurs, united access to capital with the ability to bring it into organized combination with labor and land or other natural resources.

A further aspect of the relationships between the productive factors has, however, been of less interest in conventional economic analysis. That is how power comes to be associated with one or the other of the factors in the firm or the economy at large. This is a puzzling omission. Power is an interesting subject. On first coming on any form of organized activity—a church, platoon, government bureau, political machine, mob, or house of casual pleasure—our instinct is to inquire who is in charge. Then we inquire as to the qualifications or credentials which accord such command. Organization, in other words, almost invariably invites the question: How did he (or she) get control?

2

One reason this question was slighted in economics was that for a long time, in classical economic inquiry, no worthwhile exercise of power in economic affairs was recognized. In the classical tradition—that of Adam Smith, David Ricardo, J. S. Mill, and Alfred Marshall—and increasingly as concepts were better defined—the business enterprise (like that of the farmer today) was assumed to be small in relation to the market that it served. The price that the entrepreneur received was impersonally and competitively determined by the market. So were the prices he paid to his suppliers. So were the wages he paid. So was the interest he paid on borrowed funds. Profits reduced themselves to a competitive level. The ideal volume of production for the firm was externally established by the relation of costs to the market price at various levels of output. Such was the situation under conditions of competition—what, with later refinement, came to be called the model of pure competition. If the man in charge has no power to influence his prices, costs, wages, interest, if even his ideal output is externally determined and his profits subject to the leavening of competition, one can be rightly unconcerned about his power. He has none. This absence of power explains the libertarian appeal of the market system to many men.

This unconcern continued in the classical tradition until well into this century. Having been excluded in the beginning, it has had a hard time winning a foothold. But in other currents of thought it has achieved more prominence.

In particular there was Marx. In the middle of the last century he brought the subject of power energetically and passionately into economic discussion. The notion of a system of competitive—and hence passive and powerless—enterprises he dismissed as an exercise in vulgar apologetics. Production in modern industrial society is dominated not by those who supply land or natural resources, not yet by those who supply labor but by those who supply or control the supply of capital. Authority in economic life rests with a "constantly diminishing number of the magnates of capital . . . (who) usurp and monopolise" the advantages of industrial production.¹ And their power extends on to the state. It be-comes an executive committee serving the will and convenience of the capitalist class.

Economics in the central or classical tradition has come to accept certain of the basic features of the Marxian view. The notion of the competitive market, to which numerous producers were passively subject, disappeared even from the textbooks. Those in charge of the business enterprise were routinely accorded the power over prices and output that is associated with monopoly, small numbers or oligopoly, or some unique feature of their product. Now only propagandists, hired professionally to make the case for modern business, argue for the existence of pure competition, this being the one test that, most signally, it would not pass. This is market power. It is agreed as Professor Kaysen suggests that the "Market power which large absolute and relative size gives to the giant corporation is the basis not only of economic power but also of considera-ble political and social power . . ."² But the further ramifications of political and social power are not much pursued.

And one important fact is assumed. If there is power, it is supposed that naturally and inevitably it belongs to capital. This is true wihin the firm and outside. Power is the natural prerogative of ownership. The claims of the other factors of production are inherently subordinate. In the assumption that power belongs as a matter of course to capital, all economists are Marxians. Let me pursue this point.

In the last three decades, evidence has been accumulating of a shift of power from owners to managers within the modern large corporation. The power of the stockholders has seemed increasingly tenuous. A few stockholders assemble in an annual meeting, and a much larger number return proxies, ratifying the decisions of the management including its choices for the Board of Directors to speak for stockholders. So long, at least, as it makes profits—in 1964 none of the largest 100 industrial corporations and only seven of the largest 500 lost money—the position of a management is impregnable. The stockholders are litcrally powerless. To most economists, as to most lawyers, this whole tendency has seemed of questionable legitimacy. Some, in accordance with the established reaction to seemingly inconvenient truth, have sought to maintain the myth of stockholder power. Others, including all Marxians, have argued that the change is supcrficial, that capital retains a deeper and more functional control. Some have conceded the change but have deferred judgment as to its significance.³ Yet others have seen a possibly dangerous usurpation of the legitimate power of capital.⁴ No one (of whom I am aware) has questioned the credentials of capital, where power is con-cerned, or suggested that it might be *durably* in eclipse. If there is power, it was meant to have it. . . .

6

. . . While capital in the last century was not scarce, at least in the great industrial centers, it was not in surplus. But in the present day economy, capital is, under most circumstances, abundant. The central task of modern economic policy, as it is most commonly defined, is to insure that all intended savings, at a high level of output, are offset by investment. This is what we have come to call Keynesian economic policy. Failure to invest all savings means unemployment—an excess of labor. So capital and labor have a conjoined tendency to abundance.

Back of this tendency of savings to surplus is a society which, increasingly, emphasizes not the need for frugality but the need for consumption. Saving, so far from being painful, reflects a failure in efforts by industry and the state to promote adequate consumption. Saving is also the product of a strategy by which the industrial enterprise seeks to insure full control of its sources of capital supply and thus to make its use a matter of internal decision. It is an effort which enjoys great success. Nearly three-quarters of capital investment last year was derived from the internal savings of corporations.

Capital, like land before it, owed its power over the enterprise to the difficulty of replacement or addition at the margin. What happens to that power when supply is not only abundant but excessive, when it is a central aim of social policy to offset savings and promote consumption and when it is a basic and successful purpose of business enterprises to exercise the control over the supply of capital that was once the foundation of its authority?

The plausible answer is that it will lose its power to a more strategic factor—one with greater bargaining power at the margin—if there is one. And there is.

Power has passed to what anyone in search of novelty might be forgiven for characterizing as a new factor of production. This is the structure of organization which combines and includes the technical knowledge, talent and experience that modern industrial technology and planning require. This structure is the creature of the modern industrial system and of its technology and planning. It embraces engineers, scientists, sales and advertising specialists, other technical and specialized talent—as well as the conventional leadership of the industrial enterprise. It is on the effectiveness of this structure, as indeed most business doctrine now implicitly agrees, that the success of the business enterprise now depends. It can be created or enlarged only with difficulty. In keeping with past experience, the problem of supply at the margin accords *it* power.

7

The new recipients of power, it will be clear, are not individuals; the new locus of power is collegial or corporate. This fact encounters almost instinctive resistance. The individual has far more standing in our formal culture than the group. An individual has a presumption of accomplishment; a committee has a presumption of inaction. Individuals have souls; corporations are notably soulless. The entrepreneur—individualistic, restless, equipped with vision, guile, and courage—has been the economists' only hero. The great business organization arouses no similar affection. Admission to the economists' heaven is individually and by families; it is not clear that the top management even of an enterprise with an excellent corporate image can yet enter as a group. To be required, in pursuit of truth, to assert the superiority of the group over the individual for important social tasks is a taxing prospect.

Yet it is a necessary task. Modern economic society can only be understood as an effort, notably successful, to synthesize, by organization, a personality far superior for its purposes to a natural person and with the added advantage of immortality.

The need for such synthetic personality begins *first* with the fact that in modern industry a large number of decisions, and *all* that are important, require information possessed by more than one man. All important decisions draw on the specialized scientific and technical knowledge; on the accumulated information or experience; and on the artistic or intuitive reaction of several or many persons. The final decision will be informed only as it draws on all whose information is relevant. And there is the further important requirement that this information must be properly weighed to assess its relevance and its reliability. There must be, in other words, a mechanism for drawing on the information of numerous individuals and for measuring the importance and testing the reliability of what each has to offer.

The need to draw on the information of numerous individuals derives first from the *technological* requirements of modern industry. These are not always inordinately sophisticated; a man of moderate genius could, quite conceivably, provide himself with the knowledge of the various branches of metallurgy and chemistry, and of engineering, procurement, production management, quality control, labor relations, styling and merchandising which are involved in the development of a modern automobile. But even moderate genius is in unpredictable supply; and to keep abreast of all the relevant branches of science, engineering, and art would be time consuming. The answer, which allows of the use of far more common talent and with greater predictability of result, is to have men who are appropriately qualified or experienced in each limited area of specialized knowledge or art. Their information is then combined for the design and production of the vehicle. It is the common public impression, greatly encouraged by scientists, engineers and industrialists, that modern scientific, engineering and industrial achievements are the work of a new and quite remarkable race of men. This is pure vanity. The real accomplishment is in taking ordinary men, informing them narrowly but deeply and then devising an organization which combines their knowledge with that of other similarly specialized but equally ordinary men for a highly predictable performance.

The *second* factor requiring the combination of specialized talent derives from large-scale employment of capital in combination with sophisticated technology. This makes imperative planning and accompanying control of environment. The market is, in remarkable degree, an intellectually undemanding institution. The Wisconsin farmer need not anticipate his requirements for fertilizers, pesticides or even machine parts; the market stocks and supplies them. The cost is the same for the farmer of intelligence and the neighbor who under medical examination shows daylight in either ear. There need be no sales strategy; the market takes all his milk at the ruling price. Much of the appeal of the market, to economists at least, has been the way it seems to simplify life.

The extensive use of capital, with advanced technology, greatly reduced the power of the market. Planning, with attendent complexity of task, takes its place. Thus the manufacturer of missiles, space vehicles or modern aircraft must foresee and insure his requirements for specialized plant, specialized talent, arcane materials and intricate components. These the market cannot be counted upon to supply. And there is no open market where these products can be sold. Everything depends on the care with which contracts are sought and nurtured, in Washington. The same complexities hold in only lesser degree for the maker of automobiles, processed foods and detergents. This firm too must foresee requirements and manage the markets for its products. All such planning is dealt with only by highly-qualified men—men who can foresee need and insure the supply of production requirements, relate costs to an appropriate price strategy, see that customers are suitably persuaded to buy what is made available and, at yet higher levels of technology and complexity, see that the state is persuaded.

Technology and planning thus require the extensive combination and testing of information. Much of this is accomplished, in practice, by men talking with each other—by meeting in committee. One can do worse than think of a business organization as a complex of committees. Management consists in recruiting and assigning talent to the right committee, in intervening on occasion to force a decision, and in either announcing the decision or carrying it, as a datum, for a yet larger decision by the next committee.

It must not be supposed that this is an inefficient device. A committee allows men to pool information under circumstances that allow also of immediate probing and discussion to assess the relevance and reliability of the information offered. Loose or foolish talk, or simple uncertainty, is revealed as in no other way. There is also no doubt considerable stimulus to mental effort; men who believe themselves deeply engaged in private thought are usually doing nothing at all. Committees are condemned by those who are caught by the *cliché* that individual effort is somehow superior to group effort; by those whose suspicions are aroused by the fact that for many people group effort is more congenial and pleasant; by those who do not see that the process of extracting, and especially of testing, information has necessarily a somewhat undirected quality— briskly conducted meetings invariably decide matters that were decided beforehand elsewhere; and by those who fail to see that highly-paid men, when sitting around a table as a committee, are not necessarily wasting more time, in the aggregate, than each would waste all by himself. Forthright men frequently react to belief in their own superior capacity for decision by abolishing all committees. They then constitute working parties, task forces, operations centers or executive groups in order to avoid the truly disastrous consequences of deciding matters themselves.

8

This group decision-making extends deeply into the enterprise; it goes far beyond the group commonly designated as the management. Power, in fact, is *not* closely related to position in the hierarchy of the enterprise. We always carry in our minds an implicit organization chart of the business enterprise. At the top is the Board of Directors and the Board Chairman; next comes the President; next comes the Executive Vice-President; thereafter comes the Department or Divisional Heads—those who preside over the Chevrolet division, large generators, the computer division. Power is presumed to pass down from the pinnacle.

This happens only in organizations with a routine task, such, for example, as the peacetime drill of a platoon. Otherwise the power lies with the individuals who possess the knowledge. If their knowledge is particular and strategic their power becomes very great. Enrico Fermi rode a bicycle to work at Los Alamos. Leslie Groves commanded the whole Manhattan Project. It was Fermi and his colleagues, and not General Groves in his grandeur, who made the decisions of importance.

But it should not be imagined that group decision making is confined to nuclear technology and space mechanics. In our day even simple products are made or packaged or marketed by highly sophisticated methods. For these too power passes into organization. For purposes of pedagogy, I have sometimes illustrated these matters by reference to a technically uncomplicated product, which, unaccountably, neither General Electric nor Westinghouse has yet placed on the market. It is a toaster of standard performance except that it etches on the surface of the toast, in darker carbon, one of a selection of standard messages or designs. For the elegant hostess, monograms would be available, or even a coat of arms; for the devout, there would be at breakfast an appropriate devotional message from the works of Norman Vincent Peale; the patriotic, or worried, would have an aphorism urging vigilance from Mr. J. Edgar Hoover; for modern economists, there would be mathematical design; a restaurant version could sell advertising, or urge the peaceful acceptance of the integration of public eating places.

Conceivably this vision could come from the President of General Electric. But the orderly proliferation of such ideas is the established function of much more lowly men who are charged, specifically, with new product development. At an early stage in the development of the toaster, specialists in style, design and, no doubt, philosophy, art and spelling would have to be accorded a responsible role. No one in a position to authorize the product would do so without a judgment on how the problems of design and inscription were to be solved and the cost. An advance finding would be over-ridden only with caution. All action would be contingent on the work of specialists in market testing and analysis who would determine whether and by what means the toaster could be sold and at what cost for various quantities. They would function as part of a team which would also include merchandising, advertising and dealer relations men. No adverse decision by this group would be over-ruled.

Nor, given the notoriety that attaches to missed opportunity, would a favorable decision. It will be evident that nearly all power—initiative, development, rejection or approval—is exercised deep down in the company.

So two great trends have converged. In consequence of advanced technology, highly capitalized production and a capacity through planning to command earnings for the use of the firm, capital has become comparatively abundant. And the imperatives of advanced technology and planning have moved the power of decision from the individual to the group and have moved it deeply into the firm. What have been the consequences? Let me go back again to the corporation and its owners.

9

In the mid nineteen-twenties it became known that Colonel Stewart, the Chairman of the Board of the Standard Oil Company of Indiana had, in concert with some of the men who later won immortality as the architects of the Teapot Dome and Elk Hills transactions, organized a highly specialized enterprise in Canada called the Continental Trading Company. This had the sole function of buying crude oil from one Colonel E. A. Humphreys, owner of a rich Texas field, and reselling it to companies controlled by the same individuals, including the Standard Oil of Indiana, at a mark-up of twenty-five cents a barrel. It was an excellent business. No costs were involved, other than a small percentage to the Canadian lawyer (who served as a figurehead and disappeared when wanted for questioning), and for mailing out the proceeds after they had been converted into Liberty Bonds. (If some of these had not been used, most carelessly, to bribe Secretary of the Interior Albert B. Fall and others to pay the deficit of the Republican National Committee, Continental might have forever remained unknown.) It was Colonel Stewart's later contention that he had always intended to turn over the profit to Standard of Indiana to which it rather obviously belonged. But, absent mindedly, he had allowed the bonds to remain in his own possession for many years. In 1929 Standard of Indiana was only eighteen years distant from the decree which had broken up the Standard Oil empire of John D. Rockefeller of which it had been an important part. The Rockefellers reacted sternly to this outrage; the elder Rockefeller had, on notable occasions, imposed a somewhat similar levy on his competitors, but *never* on his own company. They still owned 14.9 percent of the voting stock in the Indiana Company, and were deemed to have the controlling interest. With the aid of the publicity generated by the Teapot Dome scandal, his own standing in the financial community and a very large expenditure of money, John D. Rockefeller, Jr. was able to oust the Colonel, although only by a narrow margin.[5] In the absence of the scandal and his ample resources, he would have had little hope.

Forty years ago the notion that the owners could not control a corporation was novel and disturbing. As I have noted, we still question its legitimacy—although the divorce of ownership from control in the modern corporation is taken for granted. We see that it is in harmony with the abundance of capital and the fact that this is no longer at the margin the decisive factor of production. And it is in harmony with the tendency for power to pass deeply into organization where it is beyond the reach and beyond the competence not only of owners but of any individual. The decision to establish Continental Trading Corporation was a simple one. Once discovered, there was no problem in comprehending the facts or the motives. Had the problem been an error of equal cost in planning petro-chemical development or marketing strategy, an owner would be nearly helpless in his effort to intervene. Control in the modern corporation is an accommodation to capital abundance and to the group decision making that technology and planning have made imperative.

10

One would expect a further and adverse effect on the power of those associated with the supply of capital. This has become abundant; corporations have their internal sources of supply. Accordingly, the banker, whose cooperation, as it was euphemistically called, was once essential for the success of the enterprise, has no longer a strategic role. Similarly the investment banker, insurance company, and professional investor. Though they have grown in size, one would expect that they have declined in importance.

And there can be little doubt that this is what has happened. In the last half of the last century and the early decades of this century the great bankers were part of our folk legend. Their power may have been suspect but the names of Jay Cooke, Jay Gould, [and] the elder Morgan were of enormous majesty. Everyone knew them. It did not seem out of character that, when at odds with the government over the alleged anti-trust violations of the Northern Securities Company, the elder Morgan should tell the first Roosevelt to "send your man to my man and they can fix it up." It would seem out of character today. Today, there is no banker whose name is known outside the financial community and very few who are known to the whole financial community. Fame, in the modern financial world, requires—massive larceny always apart—that one collect modern art, have Japanese wrestlers perform in the lobby or stage ping pong contests in the street.

The prestige and power of the unions have also, almost certainly, been declining. Their power too is derived from a factor that is comparatively abundant and which suffers also from its competition with abundant capital and sophisticated technology. The relative—and in many recent years absolute—decline in trade union membership is related to the decline in numbers of production workers. And this, in turn, is the result of capital substitution based on capital abundance.

11

That engineers, scientists, and technicians within the business enterprise are already laying claim to eminence and influence that results from this shift will surely be evident. Increasingly they will move into the senior posts. The President or Board Chairman, who had as his principal qualification his close liaison with the financial community, is probably an anachronism. Capital is no longer that important. He is being replaced by men whose skills are related to organization, recruitment, information systems and the other requisites of effective group action. These men are handicapped, in the political environment, as the older capitalist entrepreneur was not, by their commitment to group behavior. But this handicap is not total. It does not interfere, for example, with exceedingly intimate association in Washington with the suppliers of government contracts. Anyone familiar with Washington will agree that it is this, often highly technical, influence, not that of bankers, which is decisive in modern business–government relations.

12

Influence under these circumstances accrues also to those who supply trained and highly qualified manpower. It is silly to suppose that the current great expansion in educational enrollment and resources is the result of a new age of enlightenment resulting from mass reading of *The Affluent Society.* It is the result of pressures generated by the new relationship between the factors of production and the now strategic role of qualified men. As the scarcity of capital in Victorian times led men to enlarge on virtues of frugality and saving, so now scarcity of trained talent leads to a similar emphasis on the value of education.

We already see some elementary examples of its effect. Once the tycoon sat on the college board of trustees to keep the impractical academician from making a fool of himself in the world of affairs and to have an eye out for heresy. Now he attends to insure his liaison with his supply of talent. And it is the academic scientist and engineer who puts in a remunerative day or two a week guiding the simple men of affairs through the intricacies of modern science and technology. The pre-Cambrian entrepreneur who once denounced long-haired and radical professors has been warned about hurting the recruitment program.

In both domestic and international affairs one also observes a new note of confidence in the voice of the academic community and, among those who disagree, a new note of regret that it should be heard. Similar was heard from the landlords about the emerging industrial middle class a century and a half ago. We are only a generation distant from the day when the trade unions were urged by right-thinking men to stick to collective bargaining and stay out of politics. I am not completely sanguine as to the way the educational estate will employ its new influences; the faculty meeting is not an utterly encouraging precept. But neither is a trend in influence toward the educated to be wholly deplored.

356

Notes

1. Karl Marx, *Capital* (New York: Modern Library), Chapter XXXII, p. 836.
2. Carl Kaysen, *The Corporation in Modern Society* (forthcoming).
3. Cf. Edward S. Mason, "The Apologetics of Managerialism," *Journal of Business* (University of Chicago) January, 1958. And "Comment" in *A Survey of Contemporary Economics,* pp. 221–222.
4. Cf. Adolf A. Berle, Jr., *Power Without Property* (New York: Harcourt, Brace and Company, 1959), pp. 98 *et seq.*
5. Cf. Berle, *op. cit.*

BUSINESS AND ENVIRONMENTAL ISSUES

Case Study—Silver Bay: Reserve Mining Company*

PRESSON S. SHANE

Silver Bay, Minnesota, on the northwest shore of Lake Superior, the largest freshwater lake in the United States, was built to process a taconite deposit about 45 miles away at Babbitt.† The location on the lake was important because great quantities of water are used in the processing. A railroad carries two 150-car trains per day of ore from the Babbitt mine to the Silver Bay processing plant. Eighty percent of the 3,200 residents in Silver Bay are members of families employed by Reserve Mining Company, which built the plant there in 1955. The plant has been expanded since it was first built, and the total investment in facilities is now about $350 million. The present production of about 11 million tons of pellets per year shows a profit of $20 million per year (after taxes) for an annual return on the total investment of about 6 percent.

The Environmental Protection Agency and the Minnesota Pollution Control Agency have charged Reserve with violation of the Federal Pollution Control Act as amended in 1970–WPC 15(a)(4), (c)(16), and (c)(2). Air discharges from the plant have been said to violate Minnesota Regulations APC 5, 6, and 17. The essence of the complaints against Reserve is that the plant discharges, through air and water, minute amphibole fibers. The air discharge is said to constitute a hazard as far away as the eastern shore of Wisconsin, and the water discharge is said to have rendered a major part of Lake Superior hazardous.‡ Specifically, for instance, 200,000 people in the Silver Bay to Duluth area use Lake Superior water, containing substantial quantities of amphibole fibers, for drinking purposes. Exposure to similar fibers under certain condi-

---

Reprinted by permission of Professor Presson S. Shane, School of Business, George Washington University.

*This case was prepared as a basis for classroom discussion and not to illustrate either effective or ineffective handling of an administrative situation.

†Reserve Mining Co. built the town of Silver Bay especially to serve its mining operations. [eds.]

‡Reserve dumped up to 67,000 tons of taconite waste materials into Lake Superior each day. (eds.)

tions can cause asbestosis, mesothelioma, and cancer of the lung, larynx, and gastrointestinal tract. Extensive court hearings (with recourse to expert opinions) have been completed, and the U.S. Court of Appeals, Eighth Circuit, expects to hear the case in the winter of 1974–75 unless agreement is reached before then. Reserve has proposed to build a land disposal site near Lax Lake and to make plant changes which will reduce the air discharge while improving pellet quality—all at a cost, said by Reserve, of $243 million.

Taconite operations are important to the state of Minnesota. In 1969–70 there were 9,600 direct jobs related thereto in power, supply, and service industries. Reserve Mining employed 3,000 of the 9,600 directly employed persons. The Minnesota legislature passed in 1964 a bill that guarantees not to change the tax on taconite before 1989. The Babbitt deposits have an estimated life of forty more years at the present rate of operation: The total taxes paid to Minnesota by Reserve and its related industries and services are about $8 million per year.

THE TECHNOLOGY

Taconite is a hard, gray rock in which are found particles of magnetite, a black oxide of iron which is magnetic and has the approximate oxygen content designated as Fe_3O_4. The deposits of taconite near Babbitt, Minnesota, are sufficiently near the surface to permit their being taken from open pits. The taconite is crushed to a nominal 4 inch size and hauled along the Reserve railroad line to Silver Bay at a rate of about 90,000 tons per day.

At Silver Bay the crushing operation is continued in order to free the particles of iron oxide for recovery and molding into pellets. A series of crushers, rod mills, ball mills, and magnetic separators are operated in processing the water slurry of ore. Two million tons of water are taken from Lake Superior each day (and returned) in the processing. The low-iron tailings are discharged back into the lake in the direction of a trough about 500-feet deep a few miles offshore. The discharge stream comprises the tailings, and the finest fraction, about 1½ percent solids, forms a dense current which flows toward the bottom of the lake. The magnetically recovered particles are the concentrate which is compressed to a cake with 10 percent moisture. It is then mixed with bentonite, which is a cohesive agent, and rolled into green pellets about ⅜ inches in diameter. The pellets are hardened by heating to 2350° F and are then ready for loading into ore boats at Silver Bay for the trip to the blast furnaces in Cleveland, Youngstown, Ashland, etc.

HEALTH

The health hazards on which the plaintiffs have based their charges are related to the fine, dustlike particles that are dispersed into the air and discharged in the stream of tailings that is pumped into Lake Superior. The introduction of these particles is said to constitute a threat to health since amosite asbestos, a generic term, is a known human carcinogen and the principal component in the Babbitt taconite tailings falls within the amosite description. Several thousand people breathe the air, which has the dust in it, and at least 200,000 drink Lake Superior water, which has particles in it.

Asbestos is a general term for a number of hydrated silicates that when crushed or processed, separate into flexible fibers made up of fibrils. Amosite is a nonmineralogical term for certain minerals in the cummingtonite-grunerite range in which the most abundant silicate present is

$$(MgFe)\ Si_8O_{22}(OH)_2$$

Amosite is a range of mineral compositions that overlaps cummingtonite-grunerite. Experts agree that the morphology, crystallography, and chemistry of the cummingtonite-grunerites is identical with that of amosite asbestos.

The carcinogenic impact of amosite asbestos on humans is indicated by statistics which indicate that 45 to 50 percent of asbestos workers die of cancer versus 15 to 20 percent of the general population. Two studies by Selikoff and Hammond, who are generally recognized by all disputants as authoritative, have been cited to show the vulnerability of asbestos* workers to cancer.†

The health issues in this study are broad and complex. The latent impact—perhaps twenty years after exposure—is a factor. The allegation that ingestion (as in drinking water) is different in its health impact than inhalation has been made. Also, it has been theorized that those persons who have been drinking the contested water for fifteen years and who have died should contain fibers in their bodies if the health hazard is great, but the results of the tissue studies which were designed to determine if Duluth residents have additional fibers in their systems were inconclusive. No statistically significant increase in fiber content of the tissue was found. The presence of fibers (derived from the Silver Bay operations) in water and air is not in dispute. Typical values are

> Duluth drinking water: 12.5 million fibers per liter.
>
> Silver Bay air: 2,000 to 1 million fibers per cubic meter. (Current OSHA limit of nonhazardous fibers is 5 million fibers per cubic meter.)

RESERVE

The Reserve Mining Company is a wholly owned subsidiary of Armco Steel (fourth largest U.S. steel producer) and Republic Steel (fifth largest U.S. steel producer) who each own one-half of Reserve. Reserve was

---

*Asbestos workers normally are in close proximity to asbestos, often in confined, dusty spaces where exposure occurs by inhalation throughout the work day.

†The lung cancer death rate for native-born American men who are not regular cigarette smokers is about 26 per 100,000 per year and 180 per 100,000 per year for regular cigarette smokers. See *The Consumers Union Report on Smoking and The Public Interest*, Consumers Union (1963), p. 35.

created to develop the taconite deposits near Babbitt, and the Silver Bay facility was built in 1953 after operating licenses approved by states and federal agencies had been granted in 1947. Environmental hearings had been conducted in Duluth, St. Paul, and Silver Bay before construction began and before the licenses had been granted. The offshore trough in the lake was viewed as an appropriate disposal site. Dust control at the operation was deemed good enough to constitute a goal which competitors tried to achieve in their own facilities.

Reserve has now been operating for seventeen years and achieved the present rate of operations in 1960. The annual profit is about $20 million on the shipment of 11 million tons of pellets to the two owners. The total investment over the years has been about $350 million. Due to the fact that Armco and Republic have used their own financial stability to support this subsidiary and have been its only customers, they have capitalized Reserve with a debt-to-equity ratio of 3.0 and never used Reserve profits to pay back the debt to themselves. (The steel industry's debt-to-equity ratio is about 0.4.) The annual return on the cumulative total investment is thus about 5.7 percent and the annual return on equity about 23 percent.

Reserve has proposed that if allowed to continue operating in the interim, it will construct and operate an on-land disposal area of the tailings. This would be in the Lower Lax Lake area, and virtually no fibrous material would be carried into Lake Superior by the returning water stream. Too, dust control will be improved, although the exact concentration of the fibrous material that might, from time to time, reach the atmosphere is not guaranteed. Reserve estimates the capital cost of these additions to be $243 million and the construction time to be three to five years. Reserve points out that this outlay will permanently impair the economic viability of Reserve, Armco, and Republic. Further, Reserve indicates that if this proposal is not accepted by the plaintiffs, it will continue to respond to the complaints in the courts where it is confident of sustaining its operation in its present state.

The Case for Economic Growth

Wilfred Beckerman

For some years now it has been very unfashionable to be in favor of continued long-run economic growth. Unless one joins in the chorus of scorn for the pursuit of continued economic growth, one is in danger of being treated either as a coarse Philistine, who is prepared to sacrifice all

From *Public Utilities Fortnightly* (Sept. 26, 1974). Reprinted by permission of the publisher and author.

the things that make life really worth living for vulgar materialist goods, or as a shortsighted, complacent, Micawber who is unable to appreciate that the world is living on the edge of a precipice. For it is widely believed that if growth is not now brought to a halt in a deliberate orderly manner, either there will be a catastrophic collapse of output when we suddenly run out of key raw materials, or we shall all be asphyxiated by increased pollution. In other words, growth is either undesirable or impossible, or both. Of course, I suppose this is better than being undesirable and inevitable, but the antigrowth cohorts do not seem to derive much comfort from the fact. . . .

Hence it is not entirely surprising that the antigrowth movement has gathered so much support over the past few years even though it is 99 per cent nonsense. Not 100 per cent nonsense. There does happen to be a one per cent grain of truth in it.

This is that, in the absence of special government policies (policies that governments are unlikely to adopt if not pushed hard by communal action from citizens), pollution will be excessive. This is because—as economists have known for many decades—pollution constitutes what is known in the jargon as an "externality." That is to say, the costs of pollution are not always borne fully—if at all—by the polluter. The owner of a steel mill that belches smoke over the neighborhood, for example, does not usually have to bear the costs of the extra laundry, or of the ill-health that may result. Hence, although he is, in a sense, "using up" some of the environment (the clean air) to produce his steel he is getting this particular factor of production free of charge. Naturally, he has no incentive to economize in its use in the same way as he has for other factors of production that carry a cost, such as labor or capital. In all such cases of "externalities," or "spillover effects" as they are sometimes called, the normal price mechanism does not operate to achieve the socially desirable pattern of output or of exploitation of the environment. This defect of the price mechanism needs to be corrected by governmental action in order to eliminate excessive pollution.

But, it should be noted that the "externality" argument, summarized above, only implies that society should cut out "excessive" pollution; not *all* pollution. Pollution should only be cut to the point where the benefits from reducing it further no longer offset the costs to society (labor or capital costs) of doing so.

Mankind has always polluted his environment, in the same way that he has always used up some of the raw materials that he has found in it. When primitive man cooked his meals over open fires, or hunted animals, or fashioned weapons out of rocks and stones, he was exploiting the environment. But to listen to some of the extreme environmentalists, one would imagine that there was something immoral about this (even though God's first injunction to Adam was to subdue the earth and every living thing that exists in it). If all pollution has to be eliminated we would have to spend the whole of our national product in converting every river in the country into beautiful clear-blue swimming pools for fish. Since I live in a town with a 100,000 population but without even a decent swimming pool for the humans, I am not prepared to subscribe to this doctrine.

Anyway, most of the pollution that the environmentalists make such a fuss about, is not the pollution that affects the vast mass of the population. Most people in industrialized countries spend their lives in working conditions where the noise and stench cause them far more loss of welfare than the glamorous fashionable pollutants, such as PCB's or mercury, that the antigrowth lobby make such a fuss about. Furthermore, such progress as has been made over the decades to improve the working conditions of the mass of the population in industrialized countries has been won largely by the action of working-class trade unions, without any help from the middle classes that now parade so ostentatiously their exquisite sensibilities and concern with the "quality of life."

The extreme environmentalists have also got their facts about pollution wrong. In the Western world, the most important forms of pollution are being reduced, or are being increasingly subjected to legislative action that will shortly reduce them. In my recently published book (*"In Defense of Economic Growth"*)[1] I give the facts about the dramatic decline of air pollution in British cities over the past decade or more, as well as the improvement in the quality of the rivers. I also survey the widespread introduction of antipollution policies in most of the advanced countries of the world during the past few years, which will enable substantial cuts to be made in pollution. By comparison with the reductions already achieved in some cases, or envisaged in the near future, the maximum pollution reductions built into the computerized calculations of the Club of Rome[2] can be seen to be absurdly pessimistic.

The same applies to the Club of Rome's assumption that adequate pollution abatement would be so expensive that economic growth would have to come to a halt. For example, the dramatic cleaning up of the air in London cost a negligible amount per head of the population of that city. And, taking a much broader look at the estimates, I show in my book that reductions in pollution many times greater than those which the Club of Rome purports to be the upper limits over the next century can, and no doubt will, be achieved over the next decade in the advanced countries of the world at a cost of only about one per cent to 2 per cent of annual national product.

When confronted with the facts about the main pollutants, the antigrowth lobby tends to fall back on the "risk and uncertainty" argument. This takes the form, "Ah yes, but what about all these new pollutants, or what about undiscovered pollutants? Who knows, maybe we shall only learn in a 100 years' time, when it will be too late, that they are deadly." But life is full of risk and uncertainty. Every day I run the risk of being run over by an automobile or hit on the head by a golf ball. But rational conduct requires that I balance the probabilities of this happening against the costs of insuring against it. It would only be logical to avoid even the minutest chance of some catastrophe in the future if it were costless to do so. But the cost of stopping economic growth would be astronomic. This cost does not merely comprise the loss of any hope of improved standards of living for the vast mass of the world's population, it includes also the political and social costs that would need to be incurred. For only a totalitarian regime could persist on the basis of an antigrowth policy that denied people their normal and legitimate aspirations for a better standard of living.

But leaving aside this political issue, another technical issue which has been much in the public eye lately has been the argument that growth will be brought to a sudden, and hence catastrophic, halt soon on account of the impending exhaustion of raw material supplies. This is the "finite resources" argument; i.e., that since the resources of the world are finite, we could not go on using them up indefinitely.

Now resources are either finite or they are not. If they are, then even zero growth will not save us in the longer run. Perhaps keeping Gross National Product at the present level instead of allowing it to rise by, say, 4 per cent per annum, would enable the world's resources to be spread out for 500 years instead of only 200 years. But the day would still come when we would run out of resources. (The Club of Rome's own computer almost gave the game away and it was obliged to cut off the printout at the point where it becomes clear that, even with zero growth, the world eventually begins to run out of resources!) So why aim only at zero growth? Why not cut output? If resources are, indeed, finite, then there must be some optimum rate at which they should be spread out over time which will be related to the relative importance society attaches to the consumption levels of different generations. The "eco-doomsters" fail to explain the criteria that determine the optimum rate and why they happen to churn out the answer that the optimum growth rate is zero.

And if resources are not, after all, finite, then the whole of the "finite resources" argument collapses anyway. And, in reality, resources are not finite in any meaningful sense. In the first place, what is now regarded as a resource may not have been so in the past decades or centuries before the appropriate techniques for its exploitation or utilization had been developed. This applies, for example, to numerous materials now in use but never heard of a century ago, or to the minerals on the sea bed (e.g., "manganese nodules"), or even the sea water itself from which unlimited quantities of certain basic minerals can eventually be extracted.

In the second place, existing known reserves of many raw materials will never appear enough to last more than, say, twenty or fifty years at current rates of consumption, for the simple reason that it is rarely economically worthwhile to prospect for more supplies than seem to be salable, at prospective prices, given the costs of exploitation and so on. This has always been the case in the past, yet despite dramatic increases in consumption, supplies have more or less kept pace with demand. The "finite resource" argument fails to allow for the numerous ways that the economy and society react to changes in relative prices of a product, resulting from changes in the balance between supply and demand.

For example, a major United States study in 1929 concluded that known tin resources were only adequate to last the world ten years. Forty years later, the Club of Rome is worried because there is only enough to last us another fifteen years. At this rate, we shall have to wait another century before we have enough to last us another thirty years. Meanwhile, I suppose we shall just have to go on using up that ten years' supply that we had back in 1929.

And it is no good replying that demand is growing faster now than ever before, or that the whole scale of consumption of raw materials is incomparably greater than before. First, this proposition has also been true at almost any time over the past few thousand years, and yet economic growth continued. Hence, the truth of such propositions tells us nothing about whether the balance between supply and demand is likely to change one way or the other. And it is this that matters. In other words, it may well be that demand is growing much faster than ever before, or that the whole scale of consumption is incomparably higher, but the same applies to supply. For example, copper consumption rose about fortyfold during the nineteenth century and demand for copper was accelerating, around the turn of the century, for an annual average growth rate of about 3.3 per cent per annum (over the whole century) to about 6.4 per cent per annum during the period 1890 to 1910. Annual copper consumption had been only about 16,000 tons at the beginning of the century, and was about 700,000 tons at the end of it; i.e., incomparably greater. But known reserves at the end of the century were greater than at the beginning.

And the same applies to the postwar period. In 1946 world copper reserves amounted to only about 100 million tons. Since then the annual rate of copper consumption has trebled and we have used up 93 million tons. So there should be hardly any left. In fact, we now have about 300 million tons!

Of course, it may well be that we shall run out of some individual materials; and petroleum looks like one of the most likely candidates for exhaustion of supplies around the end of this century—if the price did not rise (or stay up at its recent level). But there are two points to be noted about this. First, insofar as the price does stay up at its recent level (i.e., in the $10 per barrel region) substantial economies in oil use will be made over the next few years, and there will also be a considerable development of substitutes for conventional sources, such as shale oil, oil from tar sands, and new ways of using coal reserves which are, of course, very many times greater than oil reserves (in terms of common energy units).

Secondly, even if the world did gradually run out of some resources it would not be a catastrophe. The point of my apparently well-known story about "Beckermonium" (the product named after my grandfather who failed to discover it in the nineteenth century) is that we manage perfectly well without it. In fact, if one thinks about it, we manage without infinitely more products than we manage with! In other words, it is absurd to imagine that if, say, nickel or petroleum had never been discovered, modern civilization would never have existed, and that the eventual disappearance of these or other products must, therefore, plunge us back into the Dark Ages.

The so-called "oil crisis," incidentally, also demonstrates the moral hypocrisy of the antigrowth lobby. For leaving aside their mistaken interpretation of the technical reasons for the recent sharp rise in the oil price (i.e., it was not because the world suddenly ran out of oil), it is striking that the antigrowth lobby has seized upon the rise in the price of oil as a fresh argument for abandoning economic growth and for rethinking our basic values and so on. After all, over the past two or three years the economies of many of the poorer countries of the world, such as India, have been hit badly by the sharp rise in the price of wheat. Of course, this only means a greater threat of starvation for a few more million people in backward countries a long way away. That does not, apparently, provoke the men of spiritual and moral sensibility to righteous indignation about the values of the growth-oriented society as much as does a rise in the price of gasoline for our automobiles!

The same muddled thinking is behind the view that mankind has some moral duty to preserve the world's environment or supplies of materials. For this view contrasts strangely with the antigrowth lobby's attack on materialism. After all, copper, oil, and so on are just material objects, and it is difficult to see what moral duty we have to preserve indefinitely the copper species from extinction.

Nor do I believe that we have any overriding moral duty to preserve any particular animal species from extinction. After all, thousands of animal species have become extinct over the ages, without any intervention by mankind. Nobody really loses any sleep over the fact that one cannot now see a live dinosaur. How many of the people who make a fuss about the danger that the tiger species may disappear even bother to go to a zoo to look at one? And what about the web-footed Beckermanipus, which has been extinct for about a million years. . . .

In fact, I am not even sure that the extinction of the human race would matter. The bulk of humanity lead lives full of suffering, sorrow, cruelty, poverty, frustration, and loneliness. One should not assume that because nearly everybody has a natural animal instinct to cling to life they can be said, in any meaningful sense, to be better off alive than if they had never been born. Religious motivations apart, it is arguable that since, by and large (and present company excepted, of course), the human race stinks, the sooner it is extinct the better. . . .

Whilst economic growth alone may never provide a simple means of solving any of these problems, and it may well be that, by its very nature, human society will always create insoluble problems of one kind or another, the absence of economic growth will only make our present problems a lot worse.

Notes

1. Jonathan Cape, London. The U.S.A. edition, under the title *"Two Cheers for the Affluent Society,"* is being published by the St. Martins Press in the fall of 1974.
2. The Club of Rome is an informal international organization of educators, scientists, economists, and others which investigates what it conceives to be the overriding problems of mankind. Its study, "The Limits to Growth," has become the bible of no-growth advocates (Potomac Associates, 1707 L Street,

N.W., Washington, D.C., $2.75). The study assembled data on known re-
serves of resources and asked a computer what would happen if demand
continued to grow exponentially. Of course, the computer replied everything
would break down. The theory of "Beckermonium" lampoons this. Since the
author's grandfather failed to discover "Beckermonium" by the mid-1800's,
the world has had no supplies of it at all. Consequently, if the club's equations
are followed, the world should have come to a halt many years ago. "Beckermonium's" foundation is that the things man has not yet discovered are far
more numerous and of greater importance than what has been discovered.
(Editor's of *Public Utilities Fortnightly* Note.)

The Scarcity Society

William Ophuls

. . . For the past three centuries, we have been living in an age of
abnormal abundance. The bonanza of the New World and other founts of
virgin resources, the dazzling achievements of science and technology,
the availability of "free" ecological resources such as air and water to
absorb the waste products of industrial activities, and other lesser factors
allowed our ancestors to dream of endless material growth. Infinite
abundance, men reasoned, would result in the elevation of the common
man to economic nobility. And with poverty abolished, inequality, injustice, and fear—all those flowers of evil alleged to have their roots in
scarcity—would wither away. Apart from William Blake and a few other
disgruntled romantics, or the occasional pessimist like Thomas Malthus,
the Enlightenment ideology of progress was shared by all the West. The
works of John Locke and Adam Smith, the two men who gave bourgeois
political economy its fundamental direction, are shot through with the
assumption that there is always going to be more—more land in the
colonies, more wealth to be dug from the ground, and so on. Virtually all
the philosophies, values, and institutions typical of modern capitalist
society—the legitimacy of self-interest, the primacy of the individual and
his inalienable rights, economic laissez-faire, and democracy as we know
it—are the luxuriant fruit of an era of apparently endless abundance.
They cannot continue to exist in their current form once we return to
the more normal condition of scarcity.

Worse, the historic responses to scarcity have been conflict—wars
fought to control resources, and oppression—great inequality of wealth
and the political measures needed to maintain it. The link between scar-

city and oppression is well understood by spokesmen for underprivileged groups and nations, who react violently to any suggested restraint in growth of output.

Our awakening from the pleasant dream of infinite progress and the abolition of scarcity will be extremely painful. Institutionally, scarcity demands that we sooner or later achieve a full-fledged "steady-state" or "spaceman" economy. Thereafter, we shall have to live off the annual income the earth receives from the sun, and this means a forced end to our kind of abnormal affluence and an abrupt return to fugality. This will require the strictest sort of economic and technological husbandry, as well as the strictest sort of political control.

The necessity for political control should be obvious from the use of the spaceship metaphor: political ships embarked on dangerous voyages need philosopher-king captains. However, another metaphor—the tragedy of the commons—comes even closer to depicting the essence of the ecopolitical dilemma. The tragedy of the commons has to do with the uncontrolled self-seeking in a limited environment that eventually results in competitive overexploitation of a common resource, whether it is a commonly owned field on which any villager may graze his sheep, or the earth's atmosphere into which producers dump their effluents.

Francis Carney's powerful analysis of the Los Angeles smog problem indicates how deeply all our daily acts enmesh us in the tragic logic of the commons:

> Every person who lives in this basin knows that for twenty-five years he has been living through a disaster. We have all watched it happen, have participated in it with full knowledge. . . . The smog is the result of ten million individual pursuits of private gratification. But there is absolutely nothing that any individual can do to stop its spread. . . . An individual act of renunciation is now nearly impossible, and, in any case, would be meaningless unless everyone else did the same thing. But he has no way of getting everyone else to do it.

If this inexorable process is not controlled by prudent and, above all, timely political restraints on the behavior that causes it, then we must resign ourselves to ecological self-destruction. And the new political strictures that seem required to cope with the tragedy of the commons (as well as the imperatives of technology) are going to violate our most cherished ideals, for they will be neither democratic nor libertarian. At worst, the new era could be an anti-Utopia in which we are conditioned to behave according to the exigencies of ecological scarcity.

Ecological scarcity is a new concept, embracing more than the shortage of any particular resource. It has to do primarily with pollution limits, complex trade-offs between present and future needs, and a variety of other physical constraints, rather than with a simple Malthusian overpopulation. The case for the coming of ecological scarcity was most forcefully argued in the Club of Rome study *The Limits to Growth*. That study says, in essence, that man lives on a finite planet containing limited resources and that we appear to be approaching some of these major limits with great speed. To use ecological jargon, we are about to overtax the "carrying capacity" of the planet.

Critical reaction to this Jeremiad was predictably reassuring. Those wise in the ways of computers were largely content to assert that the Club of Rome people had fed the machines false or slanted information. "Garbage in, garbage out," they soothed. Other critics sought solace in less empirical directions, but everyone who recoiled from the book's apocalyptic vision took his stand on grounds of social or technological optimism. Justified or not, the optimism is worth examining to see where it leads us politically.

The social optimists, to put their case briefly, believe that various "negative feedback mechanisms" allegedly built into society will (if left alone) automatically check the trends toward ever more population, consumption, and pollution, and that this feedback will function smoothly and gradually so as to bring us up against the limits to growth, if any, with scarcely a bump. The market-price system is the feedback mechanism usually relied upon. Shortages of one resource—oil, for example—simply make it economical to substitute another abundant supply (coal or shale oil). A few of these critics of the limits-to-growth thesis believe that this process can go on indefinitely.

Technological optimism is founded on the belief that it makes little difference whether exponential growth is pushing us up against limits, for technology is simultaneously expanding the limits. To use the metaphor popularized during the debate, ecologists see us as fish in a pond where all life is rapidly being suffocated by a water lily that doubles in size every day (covering the whole pond in thirty days). The technological optimists do not deny that the lily grows very quickly, but they believe that the pond itself can be made to grow even faster. Technology made a liar out of Malthus, say the optimists, and the same fate awaits the neo-Malthusians. In sum, the optimists assert that we can never run out of resources, for economics and technology, like modern genii, will always keep finding new ones for us to exploit or will enable us to use the present supply with ever-greater efficiency.

The point most overlooked in this debate, however, is that politically it matters little who is right: the neo-Malthusians *or* either type of optimist. If the "doomsdayers" are right, then of course we crash into the ceiling of physical limits and relapse into a Hobbesian universe of the war of all against all, followed, as anarchy always has been, by dictatorship of one form or another. If, on the other hand, the optimists are right in supposing that we can adjust to ecological scarcity with economics and technology, this effort will have, as we say, "side effects." For the collision with physical limits can be forestalled only by moving toward some kind of steady-state economy—characterized by the most scrupulous husbanding of resources, by extreme vigilance against the ever-present possibility of disaster should breakdown occur, and, therefore, by tight controls on human behavior. However we get there, "Spaceship Earth" will be an all-powerful Leviathan—perhaps benign, perhaps not.

The scarcity problem thus poses a classic dilemma. It may be possible to avoid crashing into the physical limits, but only by adopting radical and unpalatable measures that, paradoxically, are little different in their ultimate political and social implications from the future predicted by the doomsdayers.

Why this is so becomes clear enough when one realizes that the optimistic critics of the doomsdayers, whom I have artificially grouped into "social" and "technological" tendencies, finally have to rest their different cases on a theory of politics, that is, on assumptions about the adaptability of leaders, their constituencies, and the institutions that hold them together. Looked at closely, these assumptions also appear unrealistic.

Even on a technical level, for example, the market-price mechanism does not coexist easily with environmental imperatives. In a market system a bird in the hand is always worth two in the bush.* This means that resources critically needed in the future will be discounted—that is, assessed at a fraction of their future value—by today's economic decision-makers. Thus decisions that are economically "rational," like mine-the-soil farming and forestry, may be ecologically catastrophic. Moreover, charging industries—and, therefore, consumers—for pollution and other environmental harms that are caused by mining and manufacturing (the technical solution favored by most economists to bring market prices into line with ecological realities) is not politically palatable. It clearly requires political decisions that do not accord with current values or the present distribution of political power; and the same goes for other obvious and necessary measures, like energy conservation. No consumer wants to pay more for the same product simply because it is produced in a cleaner way; no developer wants to be confronted with an environmental impact statement that lets the world know his gain is the community's loss; no trucker is likely to agree with any energy-conservation program that cuts his income.

We all have a vested interest in continuing to abuse the environment as we have in the past. And even if we should find the political will to take these kinds of steps before we collide with the physical limits, then we will have adopted the essential features of a spaceman economy on a piecemeal basis—and will have simply exchanged one horn of the dilemma for the other.

Technological solutions are more roundabout, but the outcome—greater social control in a planned society—is equally certain. Even assuming that necessity always proves to be the mother of invention, the management burden thrown on our leaders and institutions by continued technological expansion of that famous fishpond will be enormous. Prevailing rates of growth require us to double our capital stock, our capacity to control pollution, our agricultural productivity, and so forth every fifteen to thirty years. Since we already start from a very high absolute level, the increment of required new construction and new invention will be staggering. For example, to accommodate world population growth,

*Of course, noneconomic factors may temporarily override market forces, as the current Arab oil boycott illustrates.

we must, in roughly the next thirty years, build houses, hospitals, ports, factories, bridges, and every other kind of facility in numbers that almost equal all the construction work done by the human race up to now.

The task in every area of our lives is essentially similar, so that the management problem extends across the board, item by item. Moreover, the complexity of the overall problem grows faster than any of the sectors that comprise it, requiring the work of innovation, construction, and environmental management to be orchestrated into a reasonably integrated, harmonious whole. Since delays, planning failures, and general incapacity to deal effectively with even our current level of problems are all too obvious today, the technological response further assumes that our ability to cope with large-scale complexity will improve substantially in the next few decades. Technology, in short, cannot be implemented in a political and social vacuum. The factor in least supply governs, and technological solutions cannot run ahead of our ability to plan, construct, fund, and man them.

Planning will be especially difficult. For one thing, time may be our scarcest resource. Problems now develop so rapidly that they must be foreseen well in advance. Otherwise, our "solutions" will be too little and too late. The automobile is a critical example. By the time we recognized the dangers, it was too late for anything but a mishmash of stopgap measures that may have provoked worse symptoms than they alleviated and that will not even enable us to meet health standards without painful additional measures like rationing. But at this point we are almost helpless to do better, for we have ignored the problem until it is too big to handle by any means that are politically, economically, and technically feasible. The energy crisis offers another example of the time factor. Even with an immediate laboratory demonstration of feasibility, nuclear fusion cannot possibly provide any substantial amount of power until well into the next century.

Another planning difficulty: the growing vulnerability of a highly technological society to accident and error. The main cause for concern is, of course, some of the especially dangerous technologies we have begun to employ. One accident involving a breeder reactor would be one too many: the most minuscule dose of plutonium is deadly, and any we release now will be around to poison us for a quarter of a million years. Thus, while we know that counting on perfection in any human enterprise is folly, we seem headed for a society in which nothing less than perfect planning and control will do.

At the very least, it should be clear that ecological scarcity makes "muddling through" in a basically laissez-faire socioeconomic system no longer tolerable or even possible. In a crowded world where only the most exquisite care will prevent the collapse of the technological society on which we all depend, the grip of planning and social control will of necessity become more and more complete. Accidents, much less the random behavior of individuals, cannot be permitted; the expert pilots will run the ship in accordance with technological imperatives. Industrial man's Faustian bargain with technology therefore appears to lead inexorably to total domination by technique in a setting of clockwork institutions. C. S. Lewis once said that "what we call Man's power over Nature turns out to be a power exercised by some men over other men with Nature as its instrument," and it appears that the greater our technological power over nature, the more absolute the political power that must be yielded up to some men by others.

These developments will be especially painful for Americans because, from the beginning, we adopted the doctrines of Locke and Smith in their most libertarian form. Given the cornucopia of the frontier, an unpolluted environment, and a rapidly developing technology, American politics could afford to be a more or less amicable squabble over the division of the spoils, with the government stepping in only when the free-for-all pursuit of wealth got out of hand. In the new era of scarcity, laissez-faire and the inalienable right of the individual to get as much as he can are prescriptions for disaster. It follows that the political system inherited from our forefathers is moribund. We have come to the final act of the tragedy of the commons.

The answer to the tragedy is political. Historically, the use of the commons was closely regulated to prevent overgrazing, and we need similar controls—"mutual coercion, mutually agreed upon by the majority of the people affected," in the words of the biologist Garrett Hardin— to prevent the individual acts that are destroying the commons today. Ecological scarcity imposes certain political measures on us if we wish to survive. Whatever these measures may turn out to be—if we act soon, we may have a significant range of responses—it is evident that our political future will inevitably be much less libertarian and much more authoritarian, much less individualistic and much more communalistic than our present. The likely result of the reemergence of scarcity appears to be the resurrection in modern form of the preindustrial polity, in which the few govern the many and in which government is no longer of or by the people. Such forms of government may or may not be benevolent. At worst, they will be totalitarian, in every evil sense of that word we know now, and some ways undreamed of. At best, government seems likely to rest on engineered consent, as we are manipulated by Platonic guardians in one or another version of Brave New World. The alternative will be the destruction, perhaps consciously, of "Spaceship Earth."

There is, however, a way out of this depressing scenario. To use the language of ancient philosophers, it is the restoration of the civic virtue of a corrupt people. By their standards, by the standards of many of the men who founded our nation (and whose moral capital we have just about squandered), we are indeed a corrupt people. We understand liberty as a license for self-indulgence, so that we exploit our rights to the full while scanting our duties. We understand democracy as a political means of gratifying our desires rather than as a system of government that gives us the precious freedom to impose laws on ourselves—instead of having some remote sovereign impose them on us without our participation or consent. Moreover, the desires we express through our political system are primarily for material gain; the pursuit of happiness has been degraded into a mass quest for what wise men have always said would injure our souls. We have yet to learn the truth of Burke's political syllogism, which expresses the essential wisdom of political philosophy: man is a passionate being, and there must therefore be checks on will and appetite; if these checks are not self-imposed, they must be applied externally as fetters by a sovereign power. The way out of our difficulties, then, is through the abandonment of our political corruption.

The crisis of ecological scarcity poses basic value questions about man's place in nature and the meaning of human life. It is possible that we may learn from this challenge what Lao-tzu taught two-and-a-half millennia ago:

Nature sustains itself through three precious principles, which one does well to embrace and follow.
These are gentleness, frugality, and humility.

A very good life—in fact, an affluent life by historic standards—can be lived without the profligate use of resources that characterizes our civilization. A sophisticated and ecologically sound technology, using solar power and other renewable resources, could bring us a life of simple sufficiency that would yet allow the full expression of the human potential. Having chosen such a life, rather than having had it forced on us, we might find it had its own richness.

Such a choice may be impossible, however. The root of our problem lies deep. The real shortage with which we are afflicted is that of moral resources. Assuming that we wish to survive in dignity and not as ciphers in some ant-heap society, we are obliged to reassume our full moral responsibility. The earth is not just a banquet at which we are free to gorge. The ideal in Buddhism of compassion for all sentient beings, the concern for the harmony of man and nature so evident among American Indians, and the almost forgotten ideal of stewardship in Christianity point us in the direction of a true ethics of human survival—and it is toward such an ideal that the best among the young are groping. We must realize that there is no real scarcity in nature. It is our numbers and, above all, our wants that have outrun nature's bounty. We become rich precisely in proportion to the degree in which we eliminate violence, greed, and pride from our lives. As several thousands of years of history show, this is not something easily learned by humanity, and we seem no readier to choose the simple, virtuous life now than we have been in the past. Nevertheless, if we wish to avoid either a crash into the ecological ceiling or a tyrannical Leviathan, we must choose it. There is no other way to defeat the gathering forces of scarcity.

Ethics and Ecology

WILLIAM BLACKSTONE

THE RIGHT TO A LIVABLE ENVIRONMENT AS A HUMAN RIGHT

. . . Let us first ask whether the right to a livable environment can properly be considered to be a human right. For the purposes of this paper, however, I want to avoid raising the more general question of whether there are any human rights at all. Some philosophers do deny that any human rights exist.[1] In two recent papers I have argued that human rights do exist (even though such rights may properly be overridden on occasion by other morally relevant reasons) and that they are universal and inalienable (although the actual exercise of such rights on a given occasion is alienable).[2] My argument for the existence of universal human rights rests, in the final analysis, on a theory of what it means to be human, which specifies the capacities for rationality and freedom as essential, and on the fact that there are no relevant grounds for excluding any human from the opportunity to develop and fulfill his capacities (rationality and freedom) as a human. This is not to deny that there are criteria which justify according human rights in quite different ways or with quite different modes of treatment for different persons, depending upon the nature and degree of such capacities and the existing historical and environmental circumstances.

If the right to a livable environment were seen as a basic and inalienable human right, this could be a valuable tool (both inside and outside of legalistic frameworks) for solving some of our environmental problems, both on a national and on an international basis. Are there any philosophical and conceptual difficulties in treating this right as an inalienable human right? Traditionally we have not looked upon the right to a decent environment as a human right or as an inalienable right. Rather, inalienable human or natural rights have been conceived in somewhat different terms; equality, liberty, happiness, life, and property. However, might it not be possible to view the right to a livable environment as being entailed by, or as constitutive of, these basic human or natural rights recognized in our political tradition? If human rights, in other words, are those rights which each human possesses in virtue of the fact that he is human and in virtue of the fact that those rights are essential in permitting him to live a human life (that is, in permitting him to fulfill his capacities as a rational and free being), then might not the right to a decent environment be properly categorized as such a human right? Might it not be conceived as a right which has emerged as a result of changing environmental conditions and the impact of those conditions on the very possibility of the realization of other rights such as liberty and equality?[3] Let us explore how this might be the case.

From *Philosophy and Environmental Crisis*, ed. William T. Blackstone (Athens, Ga.: University of Georgia Press, 1972). Reprinted with permission of the publisher.

Given man's great and increasing ability to manipulate the environment, and the devastating effect this is having, it is plain that new social institutions and new regulative agencies and procedures must be initiated on both national and international levels to make sure that the manipulation is in the public interest. It will be necessary, in other words, to restrict or stop some practices and the freedom to engage in those practices. Some look upon such additional state planning, whether national or international, as unnecessary further intrusion on man's freedom. Freedom is, of course, one of our basic values, and few would deny that excessive state control of human action is to be avoided. But such restrictions on individual freedom now appear to be necessary in the interest of overall human welfare and the rights and freedoms of *all* men. Even John Locke with his stress on freedom as an inalienable right recognized that this right must be construed so that it is consistent with the equal right to freedom of others. The whole point of the state is to restrict unlicensed freedom and to provide the conditions for equality of rights for all. Thus it seems to be perfectly consistent with Locke's view and, in general, with the views of the founding fathers of this country to restrict certain rights or freedoms when it can be shown that such restriction is necessary to insure the equal rights of others. If this is so, it has very important implications for the rights to freedom and to property. These rights, perhaps properly seen as inalienable (though this is a controversial philosophical question), are not properly seen as unlimited or unrestricted. When values which we hold dear conflict (for example, individual or group freedom and the freedom of all, individual or group rights and the rights of all, and individual or group welfare and the welfare of the general public) something has to give; some priority must be established. In the case of the abuse and waste of environmental resources, less individual freedom and fewer individual rights for the sake of greater public welfare and equality of rights seem justified. What in the past had been properly regarded as freedoms and rights (given what seemed to be unlimited natural resources and no serious pollution problems) can no longer be so construed, at least not without additional restrictions. We must recognize both the need for such restrictions and the fact that none of our rights can be realized without a livable environment. Both public welfare and equality of rights now require that natural resources not be used simply according to the whim and caprice of individuals or simply for personal profit. This is not to say that all property rights must be denied and that the state must own all productive property, as the Marxist argues. It is to insist that those rights be qualified or restricted in the light of new ecological data and in the interest of the freedom, rights, and welfare of all.

The answer then to the question, Is the right to a livable environment a human right? is yes. Each person has this right qua being human and because a livable environment is essential for one to fulfill his human capacities. And given the danger to our environment today and hence the danger to the very possibility of human existence, access to a livable environment must be conceived as a right which imposes upon everyone a correlative moral obligation to respect.[4] . . .

ECOLOGY AND ECONOMIC RIGHTS

We suggested above that it is necessary to qualify or restrict economic or property rights in the light of new ecological data and in the interest of the freedom, rights, and welfare of all. In part, this suggested restriction is predicated on the assumption that we cannot expect private business to provide solutions to the multiple pollution problems for which they themselves are responsible. Some companies have taken measures to limit the polluting effect of their operations, and this is an important move. But we are deluding ourselves if we think that private business can function as its own pollution police. This is so for several reasons: the primary objective of private business is economic profit. Stockholders do not ask of a company, "Have you polluted the environment and lowered the quality of the environment for the general public and for future generations?" Rather they ask, "How high is the annual dividend and how much higher is it than the year before?" One can hardly expect organizations whose basic norm is economic profit to be concerned in any great depth with the long-range effects of their operations upon society and future generations or concerned with the hidden cost of their operations in terms of environmental quality to society as a whole. Second, within a free enterprise system companies compete to produce what the public wants at the lowest possible cost. Such competition would preclude the spending of adequate funds to prevent environmental pollution, since this would add tremendously to the cost of the product—unless all other companies would also conform to such antipollution policies. But in a free enterprise economy such policies are not likely to be self-imposed by businessmen. Third, the basic response of the free enterprise system to our economic problems is that we must have greater economic growth or an increase in gross national product. But such growth many ecologists look upon with great alarm, for it can have devastating long-range effects upon our environment. Many of the products of uncontrolled growth are based on artificial needs and actually detract from, rather than contribute to, the quality of our lives. A stationary economy, some economists and ecologists suggest, may well be best for the quality of man's environment and of his life in the long run. Higher GNP does not automatically result in an increase in social well-being, and it should not be used as a measuring rod for assessing economic welfare. This becomes clear when one realizes that the GNP

> aggregates the dollar value of all goods and services produced—the cigarettes as well as the medical treatment of lung cancer, the petroleum from offshore wells as well as the detergents required to clean up after oil spills, the electrical energy produced and the medical and cleaning bills resulting from the air-pollution fuel used for generating the electricity. The GNP allows no deduction for negative production, such as lives lost from unsafe cars or environmental destruction perpetrated by telephone, electric and gas utilities, lumber companies, and speculative builders.[5]

To many persons, of course, this kind of talk is not only blasphemy but subversive. This is especially true when it is extended in the direction of additional controls over corporate capitalism. (Some ecologists and economists go further and challenge whether corporate capitalism can accommodate a stationary state and still retain its major features.)[6] The fact of the matter is that the ecological attitude forces one to reconsider a host of values which have been held dear in the past, and it forces one to reconsider the appropriateness of the social and economic systems which embodied and implemented those values. Given the crisis of our environment, there must be certain fundamental changes in attitudes toward nature, man's use of nature, and man himself. Such changes in attitudes undoubtedly will have far-reaching implications for the institutions of private property and private enterprise and the values embodied in these institutions. Given that crisis we can no longer look upon water and air as free commodities to be exploited at will. Nor can the private ownership of land be seen as a lease to use that land in any way which conforms merely to the personal desires of the owner. In other words, the environmental crisis is forcing us to challenge what had in the past been taken to be certain basic rights of man or at least to restrict those rights. And it is forcing us to challenge institutions which embodied those rights.

Much has been said . . . about the conflict between these kinds of rights, and the possible conflict between them is itself a topic for an extensive paper. Depending upon how property rights are formulated, the substantive content of those rights, it seems plain to me, can directly conflict with what we characterize as human rights. In fact our moral and legal history demonstrate exactly that kind of conflict. There was a time in the recent past when property rights embodied the right to hold human beings in slavery. This has now been rejected, almost universally. Under nearly any interpretation of the substantive content of human rights, slavery is incompatible with those rights.

The analogous question about rights which is now being raised by the data uncovered by the ecologist and by the gradual advancement of the ecological attitude is whether the notion of property rights should be even further restricted to preclude the destruction and pollution of our environmental resources upon which the welfare and the very lives of all of us and of future generations depend. Should our social and legal system embrace property rights or other rights which permit the kind of environmental exploitation which operates to the detriment of the majority of mankind? I do not think so. The fact that a certain right exists in a social or legal system does not mean that it ought to exist. I would not go so far as to suggest that all rights are merely rule-utilitarian devices to be adopted or discarded whenever it can be shown that the best consequences thereby follow.[7] But if a right or set of rights systematically violates the public welfare, this is prima facie evidence that it ought not to exist. And this certainly seems to be the case with the exercise of certain property rights today.

In response to this problem, there is today at least talk of "a new economy of resources," one in which new considerations and values play an important role along with property rights and the interplay of market forces. Economist Nathaniel Wollman argues that "the economic past of 'optimizing' resource use consists of bringing into an appropriate relationship the ordering of preferences for various experiences and the costs of acquiring those experiences. Preferences reflect physiological-psychological responses to experience or anticipated experience, individually or collectively revealed, and are accepted as data by the economist. A broad range of noneconomic investigations is called for to supply the necessary information."[8]

Note that Wollman says that noneconomic investigations are called for. In other words the price system does not adequately account for a number of value factors which should be included in an assessment. "It does not account for benefits or costs that are enjoyed or suffered by people who were not parties to the transaction."[9] In a system which emphasizes simply the interplay of market forces as a criterion, these factors (such as sights, smells and other aesthetic factors, justice, and human rights—factors which are important to the well-being of humans) are not even considered. Since they have no direct monetary value, the market places no value whatsoever on them. Can we assume, then, that purely economic or market evaluations provide us with data which will permit us to maximize welfare, if the very process of evaluation and the normative criteria employed exclude a host of values and considerations upon which human welfare depend? The answer to this question is plain. We cannot make this assumption. We cannot rely merely upon the interplay of market forces or upon the sovereignty of the consumer. The concept of human welfare and consequently the notion of maximizing that welfare requires a much broader perspective than the norms offered by the traditional economic perspective. A great many things have value and use which have no economic value and use. Consequently we must broaden our evaluational perspective to include the entire range of values which are essential not only to the welfare of man but also to the welfare of other living things and to the environment which sustains all of life. And this must include a reassessment of rights.

ETHICS AND TECHNOLOGY

I have been discussing the relationship of ecology to ethics and to a theory of rights. Up to this point I have not specifically discussed the relation of technology to ethics, although it is plain that technology and its development is responsible for most of our pollution problems. This topic deserves separate treatment, but I do want to briefly relate it to the thesis of this work.

It is well known that new technology sometimes complicates our ethical lives and our ethical decisions. Whether the invention is the wheel or a contraceptive pill, new technology always opens up new possibilities for human relationships and for society, for good and ill. The pill, for example, is revolutionizing sexual morality, for its use can preclude many of the bad consequences normally attendant upon premarital intercourse. *Some* of the strongest arguments against premarital sex have been shot down by this bit of technology (though certainly not all of them). The fact that the use of the pill can prevent unwanted pregnancy does not make premarital sexual intercourse morally right, nor does it make it wrong. The pill is morally neutral, but its existence does change in part the moral base of the decision to engage in premarital sex. In the same way, technology at least in principle can be neutral—neither necessarily good nor bad in its impact on other aspects of the environment. Unfortunately, much of it is bad—very bad. But technology can be meshed with an ecological attitude to the benefit of man and his environment.

I am not suggesting that the answer to technology which has bad environmental effects is necessarily more technology. We tend too readily to assume that new technological developments will always solve man's problems. But this is simply not the case. One technological innovation often seems to breed a half-dozen additional ones which themselves create more environmental problems. We certainly do not solve pollution problems, for example, by changing from power plants fueled by coal to power plants fueled by nuclear energy, if radioactive waste from the latter is worse than pollution from the former. Perhaps part of the answer to pollution problems is less technology. There is surely no real hope of returning to nature (whatever that means) or of stopping *all* technological and scientific development, as some advocate. Even if it could be done, this would be too extreme a move. The answer is not to stop technology, but to guide it toward proper ends, and to set up standards of anti-pollution to which all technological devices must conform. Technology has been and can be used to destroy and pollute an environment, but it can also be used to save and beautify it. What is called for is purposeful environmental engineering, and this engineering calls for a mass of information about our environment, about the needs of persons, and about basic norms and values which are acceptable to civilized men. It also calls for priorities on goals and for compromises where there are competing and conflicting values and objectives. Human rights and their fulfillment should constitute at least some of those basic norms, and technology can be used to implement those rights and the public welfare.

NOTES

1. See Kai Nielsen's "Scepticism and Human Rights," *Monist* 52, no. 4 (1968): 571–594.
2. See my "Equality and Human Rights," *Monist* 52, no. 4 (1968): 616–639 and my "Human Rights and Human Dignity," in Laszlo and Gotesky, eds., *Human Dignity*.
3. Almost forty years ago, Aldo Leopold stated that "there is as yet no ethic dealing with man's relationship to land and to the non-human animals and plants which grow upon it. Land, like Odysseus' slave girls, is still property. The land relation is still strictly economic entailing privileges but not obligations." (See Leopold's "The Conservation Ethic," *Journal of Forestry*, 32, no. 6 (October

1933): 634–643. Although some important changes have occurred since he wrote this, no systematic ethic or legal structure has been developed to socialize or institutionalize the obligations to use land properly.

4. The right to a livable environment might itself entail other rights, for example, the right to population control. Population control is obviously essential for quality human existence. This issue is complex and deserves a separate essay, but I believe that the moral framework explicated above provides the grounds for treating population control both as beneficial and as moral.

5. See Melville J. Ulmer, "More Than Marxist," *New Republic,* 26 December 1970, p. 14.

6. See Murdock and Connell, "All about Ecology," *Center Magazine* 3, no. 1 (January-February 1970), p. 63.

7. Some rights, I would argue, are inalienable, and are not based merely on a contract (implicit or explicit) or merely upon the norm of maximizing good consequences. (See David Braybrooke's *Three Tests for Democracy: Personal Rights, Human Welfare, Collective Preference* (New York: Random House, 1968), which holds such a rule-utilitarian theory of rights, and my "Human Rights and Human Dignity," for a rebuttal.)

8. Nathaniel Wollman, "The New Economics of Resources," *Daedalus* 96, pt. 2, (Fall 1967): 1100.

9. *Ibid.*